Cryptographic Security Architecture

Springer
New York
Berlin
Heidelberg
Hong Kong
London
Milan
Paris
Tokyo

Peter Gutmann

Cryptographic Security Architecture

Design and Verification

With 149 Illustrations

 Springer

Peter Gutmann
Department of Computer Science
University of Auckland
Private Bag 92019
Auckland
New Zealand
pgut001@cs.auckland.ac.nz
http://www.cs.auckland.ac.nz/~pgut001/cryptlib/

Cover illustration: During the 16th and 17th centuries the art of fortress design advanced from ad hoc methods which threw up towers and walls as needed, materials allowed, and fashion dictated, to a science based on the use of rigorous engineering principles. This type of systematic security architecture design was made famous by Sebastien le Prestre de Vauban, a portion of whose fortress of Neuf-Brisach on the French border with Switzerland is depicted on the cover.

Library of Congress Cataloging-in-Publication Data
Gutmann, Peter.
    Cryptographic Security Architecture / Peter Gutmann.
      p. cm.
    Includes bibliographical references and index.

     1. Computer security.   2. Cryptography.   I. Title.
    QA76.9.A25 G88 2002
    005.8—dc21   2002070742

ISBN 978-1-4419-2980-8   Printed on acid-free paper.

9 8 7 6 5 4 3 2 1   SPIN 10856194

Typesetting: Pages created using the author's Word files.

www.springer-ny.com

Springer-Verlag New York Berlin Heidelberg
A member of BertelsmannSpringer Science+Business Media GmbH

John Roebling had sense enough to know what he *didn't* know. So he designed the stiffness of the truss on the Brooklyn Bridge roadway to be *six times* what a normal calculation based on known static and dynamic loads would have called for. When Roebling was asked whether his proposed bridge wouldn't collapse like so many others, he said "No, because I designed it six times as strong as it needs to be, to prevent that from happening"

— *Jon Bentley, "Programming Pearls"*

Preface

Overview and Goals

This book describes various aspects of cryptographic security architecture design, with a particular emphasis on the use of rigorous security models and practices in the design. The first portion of the book presents the overall architectural basis for the design, providing a general overview of features such as the object model and inter-object communications. The objective of this portion of the work is to provide an understanding of the software architectural underpinnings on which the rest of the book is based.

Following on from this, the remainder of the book contains an analysis of security policies and kernel design that are used to support the security side of the architecture. The goal of this part of the book is to provide an awareness and understanding of various security models and policies, and how they may be applied towards the protection of cryptographic information and data. The security kernel design presented here uses a novel design that bases its security policy on a collection of filter rules enforcing a cryptographic module-specific security policy. Since the enforcement mechanism (the kernel) is completely independent of the policy database (the filter rules), it is possible to change the behaviour of the architecture by updating the policy database without having to make any changes to the kernel itself. This clear separation of policy and mechanism contrasts with current cryptographic security architecture approaches which, if they enforce controls at all, hardcode them into the implementation, making it difficult to either change the controls to meet application-specific requirements or to assess and verify them.

To provide assurance of the correctness of the implementation, this thesis presents a design and implementation process that has been selected to allow the implementation to be verified in a manner that can reassure an outsider that it does indeed function as required. In addition to producing verification evidence that is understandable to the average user, the verification process for an implementation needs to be fully automated and capable of being taken down to the level of running code, an approach that is currently impossible with traditional methods. The approach presented here makes it possible to perform verification at this level, something that had previously been classed as "beyond A1" (that is, not achievable using any known technology).

Finally, two specific issues that arise from the design presented here, namely the generation and protection of cryptovariables such as encryption and signature keys, and the application of the design to cryptographic hardware, are presented. These sections are intended to supplement the main work and provide additional information on areas that are often neglected in other works.

Organisation and Features

A cryptographic security architecture constitutes the collection of hardware and software that protects and controls the use of encryption keys and similar cryptovariables. Traditional security architectures have concentrated mostly on defining an application programming interface (API) and left the internal details up to individual implementers. This book presents a design for a portable, flexible high-security architecture based on a traditional computer security model. Behind the API it consists of a kernel implementing a reference monitor that controls access to security-relevant objects and attributes based on a configurable security policy. Layered over the kernel are various objects that abstract core functionality such as encryption and digital signature capabilities, certificate management, and secure sessions and data enveloping (email encryption). This allows them to be easily moved into cryptographic devices such as smart cards and crypto accelerators for extra performance or security. Chapter 1 introduces the software architecture and provides a general overview of features such as the object model and inter-object communications.

Since security-related functions that handle sensitive data pervade the architecture, security must be considered in every aspect of the design. Chapter 2 provides a comprehensive overview of the security features of the architecture, beginning with an analysis of requirements and an introduction to various types of security models and security kernel design, with a particular emphasis on separation kernels of the type used in the architecture. The kernel contains various security and protection mechanisms that it enforces for all objects within the architecture, as covered in the latter part of the chapter.

The kernel itself uses a novel design that bases its security policy on a collection of filter rules enforcing a cryptographic module-specific security policy. The implementation details of the kernel and its filter rules are presented in Chapter 3, which first examines similar approaches used in other systems and then presents the kernel design and implementation details of the filter rules.

Since the enforcement mechanism (the kernel) is completely independent of the policy database (the filter rules), it is possible to change the behaviour of the architecture by updating the policy database without having to make any changes to the kernel itself. This clear separation of policy and mechanism contrasts with current cryptographic security architecture approaches that, if they enforce controls at all, hardcode them into the implementation, making it difficult either to change the controls to meet application-specific requirements or to assess and verify them. The approach to enforcing security controls that is presented here is important not simply for aesthetic reasons but also because it is crucial to the verification process discussed in Chapter 5.

Once a security system has been implemented, the traditional (in fact, pretty much the only) means of verifying the correctness of the implementation has been to apply various approaches based on formal methods. This has several drawbacks, which are examined in some detail in Chapter 4. This chapter covers various problems associated not only with formal methods but with other possible alternatives as well, concluding that neither the application of formal methods nor the use of alternatives such as the CMM present a very practical means of building high-assurance security software.

Rather than taking a fixed methodology and trying to force-fit the design to fit the methodology, this book instead presents a design and implementation process that has been selected to allow the design to be verified in a manner that can reassure an outsider that it does indeed function as required, something that is practically impossible with a formally verified design. Chapter 5 presents a new approach to building a trustworthy system that combines cognitive psychology concepts and established software engineering principles. This combination allows evidence to support the assurance argument to be presented to the user in a manner that should be both palatable and comprehensible.

In addition to producing verification evidence that is understandable to the average user, the verification process for an implementation needs to be fully automated and capable of being taken down to the level of running code, an approach that is currently impossible with traditional methods. The approach presented here makes it possible to perform verification at this level, something that had previously been classed as "beyond A1" (that is, not achievable using any known technology). This level of verification can be achieved principally because the kernel design and implementation have been carefully chosen to match the functionality embodied in the verification mechanism. The behaviour of the kernel then exactly matches the functionality provided by the verification mechanism and the verification mechanism provides exactly those checks that are needed to verify the kernel. The result of this co-design process is an implementation for which a binary executable can be pulled from a running system and re-verified against the specification at any point, a feature that would be impossible with formal-methods-based verification.

The primary goal of a cryptographic security architecture is to safeguard cryptovariables such as keys and related security parameters from misuse. Sensitive data of this kind lies at the heart of any cryptographic system and must be generated by a random number generator of guaranteed quality and security. If the cryptovariable generation process is insecure then even the most sophisticated protection mechanisms in the architecture won't do any good. More precisely, the cryptovariable generation process must be subject to the same high level of assurance as the kernel itself if the architecture is to meet its overall design goal, even though it isn't directly a part of the security kernel.

Because of the importance of this process, an entire chapter is devoted to the topic of generating random number for use as cryptovariables. Chapter 6 begins with a requirements analysis and a survey of existing generators, including extensive coverage of pitfalls that must be avoided. It then describes the method used by the architecture to generate cryptovariables, and applies the same verification techniques used in the kernel to the generator. Finally, the performance of the generator on various operating systems is examined.

Although the architecture works well enough in a straightforward software-only implementation, the situation where it really shines is when it is used as the equivalent of an operating system for cryptographic hardware (rather than having to share a computer with all manner of other software, including trojan horses and similar malware). Chapter 7 presents a sample application in which the architecture is used with a general-purpose embedded system, with the security kernel acting as a mediator for access to the cryptographic functionality embedded in the device. This represents the first open-source cryptographic processor, and is capable of being built from off-the-shelf hardware controlled by the software that implements the architecture.

Because the kernel is now running in a separate physical device, it is possible for it to perform additional actions and checks that are not feasible in a general-purpose software implementation. The chapter covers some of the threats that a straightforward software implementation is exposed to, and then examines ways in which a cryptographic coprocessor based on the architecture can counter these threats. For example, it can use a trusted I/O path to request confirmation for actions such as document signing and decryption that would otherwise be vulnerable to manipulation by trojan horses running in the same environment as a pure software implementation.

Finally, the conclusion looks at what has been achieved, and examines avenues for future work.

Intended Audience

This book is intended for a range of readers interested in security architectures, cryptographic software and hardware, and verification techniques, including:

- Designers and implementers: The book discusses in some detail design issues and approaches to meeting various security requirements.

- Students and researchers: The book is intended to be both a general tutorial for study and an in-depth reference providing links to detailed background material for further research.

Acknowledgements

This book (in its original thesis form) has been a long time in coming. My thesis supervisor, Dr. Peter Fenwick, had both the patience to await its arrival and the courage to let me do my own thing, with occasional course corrections as some areas of research proved to be more fruitful than others. I hope that the finished work rewards his confidence in me.

I spent the last two years of my thesis as a visiting scientist at the IBM T.J. Watson Research Centre in Hawthorne, New York. During that time the members of the global security analysis lab (GSAL) and the smart card group provided a great deal of advice and feedback on my work, augmented by the considerable resources of the Watson research library. Leendert van Doorn, Paul Karger, Elaine and Charles Palmer, Ron Perez, Dave Safford, Doug Schales, Sean Smith, Wietse Venema, and Steve Weingart all helped contribute to the final product, and in return probably found out more about lobotomised flatworms and sheep than they ever cared to know.

Before coming to IBM, Orion Systems in Auckland, New Zealand, for many years provided me with a place to drink Mountain Dew, print out research papers, and test various implementations of the work described in this book. Paying me wages while I did this was a nice touch, and helped keep body and soul together.

Portions of this work have appeared both as refereed conference papers and in online publications. Trent Jaeger, John Kelsey, Bodo Möller, Brian Oblivion, Colin Plumb, Geoff Thorpe, Jon Tidswell, Robert Rothenburg Walking-Owl, Chris Zimman, and various anonymous conference referees have offered comments and suggestions that have improved the quality of the result. As the finished work neared completion, Charles "lint" Palmer, Trent "gcc –wall" Jaeger and Paul "lclint" Karger went through various chapters and pointed out sections where things could be clarified and improved.

Finally, I would like to thank my family for their continued support while I worked on my thesis. After its completion, the current book form was prepared under the guidance and direction of Wayne Wheeler and Wayne Yuhasz of Springer-Verlag. During the reworking process, Adam Back, Ariel Glenn, and Anton Stiglic provided feedback and suggestions for changes. The book itself was completed despite Microsoft Word, with diagrams done using Visio.

Contents

1 The Software Architecture

1.1 Introduction

Traditional security toolkits have been implemented using a "collection of functions" design in which each encryption capability is wrapped up in its own set of functions. For example there might be a "load a DES key" function, an "encrypt with DES in CBC mode" function, a "decrypt with DES in CFB mode" function, and so on [1][2]. More sophisticated toolkits hide the plethora of algorithm-specific functions under a single set of umbrella interface functions with often complex algorithm-selection criteria, in some cases requiring the setting of up to a dozen parameters to select the mode of operation [3][4][5][6]. Either approach requires that developers tightly couple the application to the underlying encryption implementation, requiring a high degree of cryptographic awareness from developers and forcing each new algorithm and application to be treated as a distinct development. In addition, there is the danger — in fact almost a certainty due to the tricky nature of cryptographic applications and the subtle problems arising from them — that the implementation will be misused by developers who aren't cryptography experts, when it could be argued that it is the task of the toolkit to protect developers from making these mistakes [7].

Alternative approaches concentrate on providing functionality for a particular type of service such as authentication, integrity, or confidentiality. Some examples of this type of design are the GSS-API [8][9][10], which is session-oriented and is used to control session-style communications with other entities (an example implementation consists of a set of GSS-API wrapper functions for Kerberos), the OSF DCE security API [11], which is based around access control lists and secure RPC, and IBM's CCA, which provides security services for the financial industry [12]. Further examples include the SESAME API [13], which is based around a Kerberos derivative with various enhancements such as X.509 certificate support, and the COE SS API [14], which provides GSS-API-like functionality using a wrapper for the Netscape SSL API and is intended to be used in the Defence Information Infrastructure (DII) Common Operating Environment (COE).

This type of design typically includes features specific to the required functionality. In the case of the session-oriented interfaces mentioned above this is the security context that contains details of a relationship between peers based on credentials established between the peers. A non-session-based variant is the IDUP-GSS-API [15], which attempts to stretch the GSS-API to cover store-and-forward use (this would typically be used for a service such as email protection). Although these high-level APIs require relatively little cryptographic awareness from developers, the fact that they operate only at a very abstract level makes it difficult to guarantee interoperability across different security services. For example, the

DCE and SESAME security APIs, which act as a programming interface to a single type of security service, work reasonably well in this role, but the GSS-API, which is a generic interface, has seen a continuing proliferation of "management functions" and "support calls" that allow the application developer to dive down into the lower layers of the code in a somewhat haphazard manner [16]. Since individual vendors can use this to extend the functionality in a vendor-specific manner, the end result is that one vendor's GSS-API implementation can be incompatible with a similar implementation from another vendor.

Both of these approaches represent an outside-in approach that begins with a particular programming interface and then bolts on whatever is required to implement the functionality in the interface. This work presents an alternative inside-out design that first builds a general crypto/security architecture and then wraps a language-independent interface around it to make particular portions of the architecture available to the user. In this case, it is important to distinguish between the architecture and the API used to interface to it. With most approaches the API *is* the architecture, whereas the approach presented in this work concentrates on the internal architecture only. Apart from the very generic APKI [17] and CISS [18][19][20][21] requirements, only CDSA [22][23] appears to provide a general architecture design, and even this is presented at a rather abstract level and defined mostly in terms of the API used to access it.

In contrast to these approaches, the design presented here begins by establishing a software architectural model that is used to encapsulate various types of functionality such as encryption and certificate management. The overall design goals for the architecture, as well as the details of each object class, are presented in this chapter. Since the entire architecture has very stringent security requirements, the object model requires an underlying security kernel capable of supporting it — one that includes a means of mediating access to objects, controlling the way this access is performed (for example, the manner in which object attributes may be manipulated), and ensuring strict isolation of objects (that is, ensuring that one object can't influence the operation of another object in an uncontrolled manner). The security aspects of the architecture are covered in the following chapters, although there is occasional reference to them earlier where this is unavoidable.

1.2 An Introduction to Software Architecture

The field of software architecture is concerned with the study of large-grained software components, their properties and relationships, and their patterns of combination. By analysing properties shared across different application areas, it's possible to identify commonalities among them that may be candidates for the application of a generic solution architecture [24][25].

A software architecture can be defined as a collection of components and a description of the interaction and constraints on interaction between these components, typically represented visually as a graph in which the components are the graph nodes and the connections that handle interactions between components are the arcs [26][27]. The connections can take a variety of forms, including procedure calls, event broadcast, pipes, and assorted message-passing mechanisms.

Software architecture descriptions provide a means for system designers to document existing, well-proven design experience and to communicate information about the behaviour of a system to people working with it, to "distil and provide a means to reuse the design knowledge gained by experienced practitioners" [28]. For example, by describing a particular architecture as a pipe-and-filter model (see Section 1.2.1), the designer is communicating the fact that the system is based on stream transformations and that the overall behaviour of the system arises from the composition of the constituent filter components. Although the actual vocabulary used can be informal, it can convey considerable semantic content to the user, removing the need to provide a lengthy and complicated description of the solution [29]. When architecting a system, the designer can rely on knowledge of how systems designed to perform similar tasks have been designed in the past. The resulting architecture is the embodiment of a set of design decisions, each one admitting one set of subsequent possibilities and discarding others in response to various constraints imposed by the problem space, so that a particular software architecture can be viewed as the architect's response to the operative constraints [30]. The architectural model created by the architect serves to document their vision for the overall software system and provides guidance to others to help them avoid violating the vision if they need to extend and modify the original architecture at a later date. The importance of architectural issues in the design process has been recognised by organisations such as the US DoD, who are starting to require contractors to address architectural considerations as part of the software acquisition process [31].

This section contains an overview of the various software architecture models employed in the cryptlib architecture.

1.2.1 The Pipe-and-Filter Model

The architectural abstraction most familiar to Unix[1] users is the pipe and filter model, in which a component reads a data stream on its input and produces a data stream on its output, typically transforming the data in some manner in the process (another analogy that has been used for this architectural model is that of a multi-phase compiler [32]). This architecture, illustrated in Figure 1.1, has the property that components don't share any state with other components, and aren't even aware of the identities of any upstream or downstream neighbours.

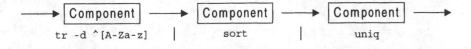

Figure 1.1. Pipe-and-filter model.

---

[1] Unix is or has been at various times a trademark of AT&T Bell Laboratories, Western Electric, Novell, Unix System Laboratories, the X/Open Consortium, the Open Group, the Trilateral Commission, and the Bavarian Illuminati.

Since all components in a pipe-and-filter model are independent, a complete system can be built through the composition of arbitrarily connected individual components, and any of them can be replaced at any time with another component that provides equivalent functionality. In the example in Figure 1.1, tr might be replaced with sed, or the sort component with a more efficient version, without affecting the functioning of the overall architecture.

The flexibility of the pipe-and-filter model has some accompanying disadvantages, however. The "pipe" part of the architecture restricts operations to batch-sequential processing, and the "filter" part restricts operations to those of a transformational nature. Finally, the generic nature of each filter component may add additional work as each one has to parse and interpret its data, leading to a loss in efficiency as well as increased implementation complexity of individual components.

1.2.2 The Object-Oriented Model

This architectural model encapsulates data and the operations performed on it inside an object abstract data type that interacts with other objects through function or method invocations or, at a slightly more abstract level, message passing. In this model, shown in Figure 1.2, each object is responsible for preserving the integrity of its internal representation, and the representation itself is hidden from outsiders.

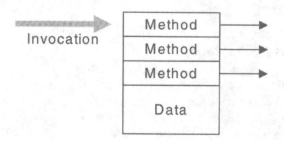

Figure 1.2. Object-oriented model.

Object-oriented systems have a variety of useful properties such as providing data abstraction (providing to the user essential details while hiding inessential ones), information hiding (hiding details that don't contribute to its essential characteristics such as its internal structure and the implementation of its methods, so that the module is used via its specification rather than its implementation), and so on. Inheritance, often associated with object-oriented models, is an organisational principle that has no direct architectural function [33] and won't be discussed here.

The most significant disadvantage of an object-oriented model is that each object must be aware of the identity of any other objects with which it wishes to interact, in contrast to the pipe-and-filter model in which each component is logically independent from every other component. The effect of this is that each object may need to keep track of a number of other objects with which it needs to communicate in order to perform its task, and a change in an object needs to be communicated to all objects that reference it.

1.2.3 The Event-Based Model

An event-based architectural model uses a form of implicit invocation in which components interact through event broadcasts that are processed as appropriate by other components, which either register an interest in a particular event or class of events, or listen in on all events and act on those which apply to the component. An example of an event-based model as employed in a graphical windowing system is shown in Figure 1.3, in which a mouse click event is forwarded to those components for which it is appropriate.

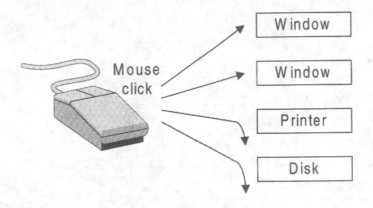

Figure 1.3. Event-based model.

The main feature of this type of architecture is that, unlike the object-oriented model, components don't need to be aware of the identities of other components that will be affected by the events. This advantage over the object-oriented model is, however, also a disadvantage since a component can never really know which other components will react to an event, and in which way they will react. An effect of this, which is seen in the most visible event-based architecture, graphical windowing systems, is the problem of multiple components reacting to the same event in different and conflicting ways under the assumption that they have exclusive rights to the event. This problem leads to the creation of complex processing rules and requirements for events and event handlers, which are often both difficult to implement and work with, and don't quite function as intended.

The problem is further exacerbated by some of the inherent shortcomings of event-based models, which include nondeterministic processing of events (a component has no idea which other components will react to an event, the manner in which they will react, or when they will have finished reacting), and data-handling issues (data too large to be passed around as part of the event notification must be held in some form of shared repository, leading to problems with resource management if multiple event handlers try to manipulate it).

1.2.4 The Layered Model

The layered architecture model is based on a hierarchy of layers, with each layer providing service to the layer above it and acting as a client to the layer below it. A typical layered system is shown in Figure 1.4. Layered systems support designs based on increasing levels of abstraction, allowing a complex problem to be broken down into a series of simple steps and attacked using top-down or bottom-up design principles. Because each layer (in theory) interacts only with the layers above and below it, changes in one layer affect at most two other layers. As with abstract data types and filters, implementations of one layer can be swapped with different implementations provided they export the same interface to the surrounding layers.

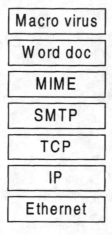

Figure 1.4. Typical seven-layer model.

Unfortunately, decomposition of a system into discrete layers isn't quite this simple, since even if a system can somehow be abstracted into logically separate layers, performance and implementation considerations often necessitate tight coupling between layers, or implementations that span several layers. The ISO reference model (ISORM) provides a good case study of all of the problems that can beset layered architectures [34].

1.2.5 The Repository Model

The repository model is composed of two different components: a central scoreboard-style data structure which represents the current state of the repository, and one or more components that interact with the scoreboard on behalf of external sources. A typical example of this type of model is a relational database.

1.2.6 The Distributed Process Model

Also known as a client-server architecture, the distributed process model employs a server process that provides services to other, client processes. Clients know the identity of the server (which is typically accessed through local or remote procedure calls), but the server usually doesn't know the identities of the clients in advance. Typical examples include database, mail, and web servers, and significant portions of Microsoft Windows (via COM and DCOM).

1.2.7 The Forwarder-Receiver Model

The forwarder-receiver model provides transparent interprocess communications (typically implemented using TCP/IP or Unix domain sockets, named pipes, or message queues) between peered software systems. The peer may be located on the same machine or on a different machine reached over a network. On the local machine, the forwarder component takes data and control information from the caller, marshals it, and forwards it to the receiver component. The receiver unmarshals it and passes it on to the remote software system, which returns results back to the caller in the same manner. This process is shown in Figure 1.5.

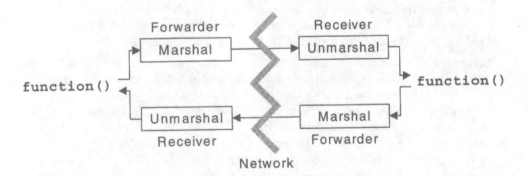

Figure 1.5. Forwarder-and-receiver model.

The forwarder-receiver model provides a means for structuring communications between components in a peer-to-peer fashion, at the expense of some loss in efficiency due to the overhead and delay of the marshalling and interprocess communication.

1.3 Architecture Design Goals

An earlier work [35] gives the design requirements for a general-purpose security service API, including algorithm, application, and cryptomodule independence, safe programming (protection against programmer mistakes), a security perimeter to prevent sensitive data from leaking out into untrusted applications, and legacy support. Most of these requirements are pure API issues and won't be covered in any more detail here. The software architecture presented here is built on the following design principles:

- Independent objects. Each object is responsible for managing its own resource requirements such as memory allocation and use of other required objects, and the interface to other objects is handled in an object-independent manner. For example a signature object would know that it is (usually) associated with a hash object, but wouldn't need to know any details of its implementation, such as function names or parameters, in order to communicate with it. In addition, each object has associated with it various security properties such as mandatory and discretionary access control lists (ACLs), most of which are controlled for the object by the architecture's security kernel, and a few object-specific properties that are controlled by the object itself.

- Intelligent objects. The architecture should know what to do with data and control information passed to objects, including the ability to hand it off to other objects where required. For example if a certificate object (which contains only certificate-related attributes but has no inherent encryption or signature capabilities) is asked to verify a signature using the key contained in the certificate, the architecture will hand the task off to the appropriate signature-checking object without the user having to be aware that this is occurring. This leads to a very natural interface in which the user knows that an object will Do The Right Thing with any data or control information sent to it without requiring it to be accessed or used in a particular manner.

- Platform-independent design. The entire architecture should be easily portable to a wide variety of hardware types and operating systems without any significant loss of functionality. A counterexample to this design requirement is CryptoAPI 2.x [36], which is so heavily tied into features of the very newest versions of Win32 that it would be almost impossible to move to other platforms. In contrast, the architecture described here was designed from the outset to be extremely portable and has been implemented on everything from 16-bit microcontrollers with no file system or I/O capabilities to supercomputers, as well as unconventional designs such as multiprocessor Tandem machines and IBM VM/ESA mainframes and AS/400 minicomputers.

- Full isolation of architecture internals from external code. The architecture internals are fully decoupled from access by external code, so that the implementation may reside in its own address space (or even physically separate hardware) without the user being aware of this. The reason for this requirement is that it very clearly defines the boundaries of the architecture's trusted computing base (TCB), allowing the architecture to be defined and analysed in terms of traditional computer security models.

- Layered design. The architecture represents a true object-based multilayer design, with each layer of functionality being built on its predecessor. The purpose of each layer is to provide certain services to the layer above it, shielding that layer from the details of how the service is actually implemented. Between each layer is an interface that allows data and control information to pass across layers in a controlled manner. In this way each layer provides a set of well-defined and understood functions that both minimise the amount of information that flows from one layer to another and make it easy to replace the implementation of one layer with a completely different one (for example, migrating a software implementation into secure hardware), because all that a new layer implementation requires is that it offer the same service interface as the one it replaces.

In addition to the layer-based separation, the architecture separates individual objects within the layer into discrete, self-contained objects that are independent of other objects both within their layer and in other layers. For example, in the lowest layer, the basic objects typically represent an instantiation of a single encryption, digital signature, key exchange, hash, or MAC algorithm. Each object can represent a software implementation, a hardware implementation, a hybrid of the two, or some other implementation.

These principles cover the software side of the architecture. Accompanying this are a set of security mechanisms, which are addressed in the next chapter.

1.4 The Object Model

The architecture implements two types of objects, container objects and action objects. A container object is an object that contains one or more items such as data, keys, certificates, security state information, and security attributes. The container types can be broken down roughly into three types: data containers (referred to as envelope or session objects), key and certificate containers (keyset objects), and security attribute containers (certificate objects). An action object is an object that is used to perform an action such as encrypting, hashing, or signing data (referred to using the generic label of encryption action object, which is very similar to the GCS-API concept of a cryptographic context [4]). In addition to these standard object types, there is also a device object type that constitutes a meta-object used to work with external encryption devices such as smart cards or Fortezza cards, that may require extra functions such as activation with a user PIN before they can be used. Once they are initialised as required, they can be used like any of the other object types whose functionality they provide. For example, an RSA action object could be created through the device object for a smart card with RSA capabilities, or a certificate object could be stored in a device object for a Fortezza card as if it were a keyset.

Each object is referenced through its handle, a small integer value unrelated to the object itself, which is used to pass control information and data to and from the object. Since each object is referred to through an abstract handle, the interface to the object is a message-based one in which messages are sent to and received from the object. cryptlib's object handles are equivalent to the "unique name" or "object number" portion of the { unique name, type, representation } tuple used in hardware-based object-oriented systems such as the Intel 432 [37] and its derivative BiiN [38], Recursiv [39], and AS/400 [40]. This provides a single systemwide-unique identifier by which all objects can be identified and that can be mapped to appropriate type and representation information by the system. Figure 1.6 illustrates a DES encryption action object and a certificate attribute container object contained inside the architecture's security perimeter and referenced through their handles. Although the external programming interface can be implemented to look like the traditional "collection of functions" one, this is simply the message-passing interface wrapped up to look like a more traditional functional interface.

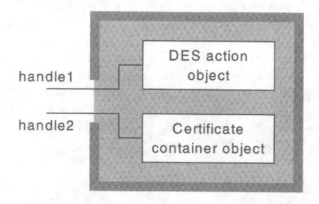

Figure 1.6. Software architecture objects.

A distinction should be made between cryptlib's message passing and the "message passing" that occurs in many object-oriented methodologies. In most widely used object-oriented environments such as C++ and Java, the term "message" is applied to describe a method invocation, which in turn is just a function call in an expensive suit. In cryptlib a message really is a message, with no direct communication or flow-of-control transfer between the source and destination except for the data contained in the message.

1.4.1 User ↔ Object Interaction

All interactions with objects, both those arising from the user and those arising from other objects, are performed indirectly via message passing. All messages sent to objects and all responses to messages are processed through a reference monitor, the cryptlib kernel, which is actually a full Orange Book-style security kernel and is discussed in more detail in the next chapter. The kernel is responsible for access control and security checking, ensuring that messages are routed to appropriate objects, and a range of object and security management functions. The message-passing mechanism connects the objects indirectly, replacing pointers and direct function calls, and is the fundamental mechanism used to implement the complete isolation of architecture internals from the outside world. Figure 1.7 shows a user application interacting with a number of objects via the cryptlib kernel.

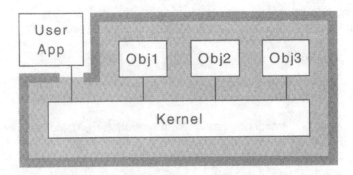

Figure 1.7. Objects accessed via the cryptlib kernel.

When the user calls a cryptlib function, the conventional function call is converted into a message by the cryptlib front-end wrapper code and passed through to the kernel. The kernel performs any necessary checking and processing and passes the message on to the object. Any returned data from the object is handled in the same manner, with the return status and optional data in the returned message being converted back into the function return data. This type of interaction with an object is shown in Figure 1.8, with a user application calling a function (for example, cryptEncrypt()), which results in the appropriate message (in this case, MESSAGE_ENCRYPT) being sent to the target object and the result being returned to the caller.

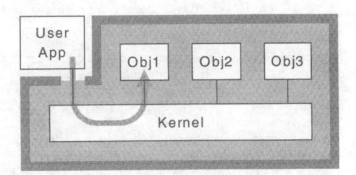

Figure 1.8. User ↔ object interaction via message passing.

Internally, objects communicate with other objects via direct (but still kernel-mediated) message passing, without the veneer of the function-based interface.

Although cryptlib is typically employed as a library linked statically or dynamically into an application, it can also be used in the forwarder-receiver model with the function-based interface acting as a forwarder that passes the messages on to the cryptlib implementation running as a separate process or even in physically separate hardware. An example of an implementation that uses cryptlib as the control firmware for embedded PC hardware is given in Chapter 7.

1.4.2 Action Objects

Action objects are a fairly straightforward implementation of the object-oriented architectural model and encapsulate the functionality of a security algorithm such as DES or RSA, with the implementation details of a software-based DES action object shown in Figure 1.9. These objects function mainly as building blocks used by the more complex object types. The implementation of each object is completely hidden from the user so that the only way the object can be accessed is by sending information to it across a carefully controlled channel.

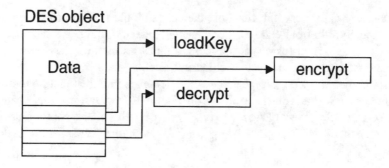

Figure 1.9. Action object internal details.

Action objects are usually attached to other objects such as data or attribute containers, although the existence of the action object is invisible to the user, who sees only the controlling container object. To the user, it appears as though they are using an envelope to encrypt data even though the work is actually being performed by the attached encryption object under the control of the envelope, or using a certificate to verify a signature even though the work is being performed by the attached public-key encryption object. The example given earlier that illustrated a certificate and encryption action object would actually be encountered in the combination shown in Figure 1.10, with the RSA public-key action object performing the encryption or signature-checking work for a controlling certificate object.

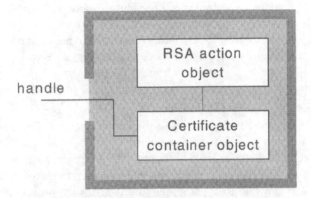

Figure 1.10. Object with dependent object.

This encryption action object can't be directly accessed by the user but can be used in the carefully controlled manner provided by the certificate object. For example, if the certificate object contains an attribute specifying that the attached public-key action object may only be used for digital signature (but not encryption) purposes then any attempt to use the object for encryption purposes would be flagged as an error. These controls are enforced directly by the kernel, as explained in later Chapters 2 and 3.

1.4.3 Data Containers

Data containers (envelope and session objects) act as a form of programmable filter object whose behaviour is modified by the control information that is pushed into it. To use an envelope, the user pushes in control information in the form of container or action objects or general attributes that control the behaviour of the container. Any data that is pushed into the envelope is then modified according to the behaviour established by the control information. For example if a digital signature action object was added to the data container as control information, then data pushed into the container would be digitally signed. If a password attribute was pushed into the container, then data pushed in would be encrypted. Data containers therefore represent the pipe-and-filter model presented in Section 1.2.1. An example of a pipe-and-filter envelope construction that might be used to implement PGP or S/MIME messaging is shown in Figure 1.11 (PGP actually compresses the data after signing rather than before, since the PGP designers felt that it was desirable to sign data directly before any additional processing had been applied [41]).

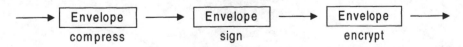

Figure 1.11. Pipe-and-filter construction using envelopes.

Session objects function in a similar manner, but the action object(s) used by the session object are usually established by exchanging information with a peered system, and the session objects can process multiple data items (for example network packets) rather than the single data item processed by envelopes — session objects are envelope objects with state. Session objects act as one-stage filters, with the filter destination being a peered system on a network. In real-world terms, envelope objects are used for functions like S/MIME and PGP, whereas session objects are used for functions such as SSL, TLS, and ssh.

This type of object can be regarded as an intelligent container that knows how to handle data provided to it based on control information that it receives. For example, if the user pushes in a password attribute followed by data, the object knows that the presence of this attribute implies a requirement to encrypt data and will therefore create an encryption action object, turn the password into the appropriate key type for the object (typically through the use of a hash action object), generate an initialisation vector, pad the data out to the cipher block size if necessary, encrypt the data, and return the encrypted result to the user. Session objects function in an almost identical manner except that the other end of the filter is located on a peered system on a network.

Data containers, although appearing relatively simple, are by far the most complex objects present in the architecture.

1.4.4 Key and Certificate Containers

Key and certificate containers (keyset objects) are simple objects that employ the repository architectural model presented in Section 1.2.5 and contain one or more public or private keys or certificates, and may contain additional information such as certificate revocation data (CRLs). To the user, they appear as an (often large) collection of encryption or certificate objects. Two typical container objects of this type are shown in Figure 1.12. Although the diagram implies the presence of huge numbers of objects, these are only instantiated when required by the user. Keyset objects are tied to whatever underlying storage mechanism is used to hold keys, typically PKCS #12 and PKCS #15 files, PGP keyrings, relational databases containing certificates and CRLs, LDAP directories, HTTP links to certificates published on web pages, and crypto tokens such as PKCS #11 devices and Fortezza cards that can act as keysets alongside their usual crypto functionality.

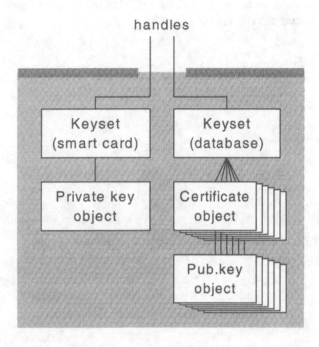

Figure 1.12. Key container objects.

1.4.5 Security Attribute Containers

Security attribute containers (certificate objects), like keyset objects, are built on the repository architectural model and contain a collection of attributes that are attached to a public/private key or to other information. For example signed data often comes with accompanying attributes such as the signing time and information concerning the signer of the data and the conditions under which the signature was generated. The most common type of security attribute container is the public-key certificate, which contains attribute information for a public (and by extension private) key. Other attribute containers are certificate chains (ordered sequences of certificates), certificate revocation lists (CRLs), certification requests, and assorted other certificate-related objects.

1.4.6 The Overall Architectural and Object Model

A representation of some of the software architectural models discussed earlier mapped onto cryptlib's architecture is shown in Figure 1.13. At the upper levels of the layered model (Section 1.2.4) are the envelopes, implementing the pipe-and-filter model (Section 1.2.1) and communicating through the distributed process model (Section 1.2.6). Below the envelopes are the action objects (one of them implemented through a smart card) that perform the processing of the data in the envelopes.

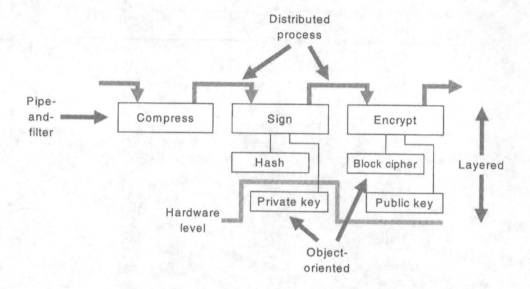

Figure 1.13. Overall software architectural model.

Not shown in this diagram are some of the other architectural models used, which include the event-based model (Section 1.2.3) used for general interobject communications, the repository model (Section 1.2.5) used for the keyset that supplied the public key that is used in the third envelope, and the forwarder-receiver model (Section 1.2.7) which is used to manage communications between cryptlib and the outside world.

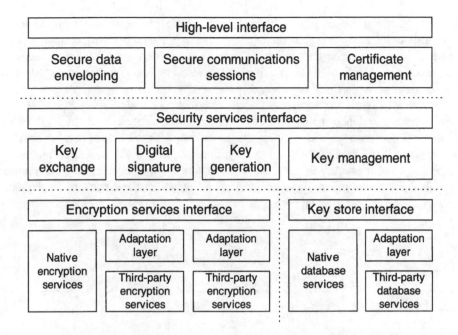

Figure 1.14. Architecture implementation.

Figure 1.13 gave an example of the architecture at a conceptual level, and the actual implementation is shown in Figure 1.14, which illustrates the layering of one level of service over one or more lower-level services.

1.5 Object Internals

Creating or instantiating a new object involves obtaining a new handle, allocating and initialising an internal data structure that stores information on the object, setting security access control lists (ACLs, covered in the next chapter), connecting the object to any underlying hardware or software if necessary (for example, establishing a session with a smart card reader or database backend), and finally returning the object's handle to the user. Although the user sees a single object type that is consistent across all computer systems and implementations, the exact (internal) representation of the object can vary considerably. In the simplest case, an object consists of a thin mapping layer that translates calls from the architecture's internal API to the API used by a hardware implementation. Since encryption action objects, which represent the lowest level in the architecture, have been designed to map directly onto the functionality provided by common hardware crypto accelerators, these can be used directly when appropriate hardware is present in the system.

If the encryption hardware consists of a crypto device with a higher level of functionality or even a general-purpose secure coprocessor rather than just a simple crypto accelerator, more of the functionality can be offloaded onto the device or secure coprocessor. For example, although a straight crypto accelerator may support functionality equivalent to basic DES and RSA operations on data blocks, a crypto device such as a PKCS #11 token would provide extended functionality including the necessary data formatting and padding operations required to perform secure and portable key exchange and signature operations. More sophisticated secure coprocessors which are effectively scaled-down PCs [42] can take on board architecture functionality at an even higher level. Figure 1.15 shows the levels at which external hardware functionality can be integrated, with the lowest level corresponding to the functionality embodied in an encryption action object and the higher levels corresponding to functionality in envelope, session, and certificate objects. This represents a very flexible use of the layered architectural model in which the hardware implementation level can move up or down the layers as performance and security requirements allow.

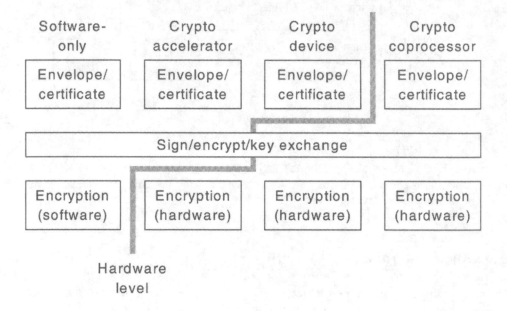

Figure 1.15. Mapping of cryptlib functionality levels to crypto/security hardware.

1.5.1 Object Internal Details

Although each type of object differs considerably in its internal design, they all share a number of common features, which will be covered here. Each object consists of three main parts:

1. State information, stored either in secure or general-purpose memory, depending on its sensitivity.

2. The object's message handler.
3. A set of function pointers for the methods used by the object.

The actual functionality of the object is implemented through the function pointers, which are initialised when the object is instantiated to refer to the appropriate methods for the object. Using an instantiation of a DES encryption action object with an underlying software implementation and an RSA encryption action object with an underlying hardware implementation, we have the encryption object structures shown in Figure 1.16.

When the two objects are created, the DES action object is plugged into the software DES implementation and the RSA action object is plugged into a hardware RSA accelerator. Although the low-level implementations are very different, both are accessed through the same methods, typically `object.loadKey()`, `object.encrypt()`, and `object.-decrypt()`. Substituting a different implementation of an encryption algorithm (or adding an entirely new algorithm) requires little more than creating the appropriate interface methods to allow an action object to be plugged into the underlying implementation. As an example of how simple this can be, when the Skipjack algorithm was declassified [43], it took only a few minutes to plug in an implementation of the algorithm. This change provided full support for Skipjack throughout the entire architecture and to all applications that employed the architecture's standard capability query mechanism, which automatically establishes the available capabilities of the architecture on startup.

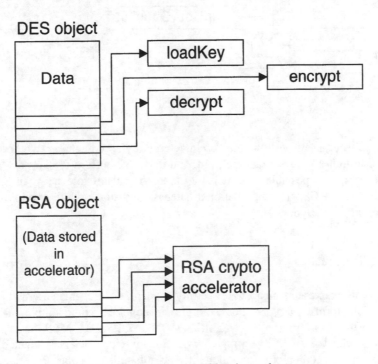

Figure 1.16. Encryption action object internal structure.

Similar implementations are used for the other cryptlib objects. Data containers (envelope and session objects) contain a general data area and a series of method pointers that are set to point to format-specific methods when the object is created. An example of two envelope objects that produce as output S/MIME and PGP messages is shown in Figure 1.17. As with the action objects presented above, changing to a new format involves substitution of different method pointers to code that implements the new format. The same mechanism is used for session objects to implement different protocols such as SSL, TLS, and ssh.

Envelope objects

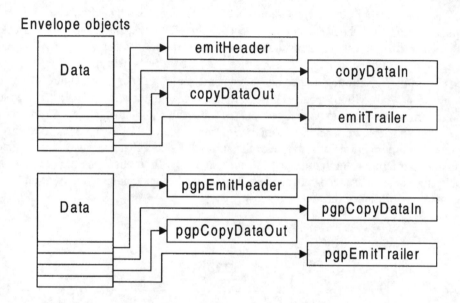

Figure 1.17. Data container object internal structure.

Keyset objects again follow this architectural style, containing method pointers to functions to initialise a keyset, and get, put, and delete keys from the keyset. By switching method pointers, it is possible to switch the underlying data store between HTTP, LDAP, PGP, PKCS #12, PKCS #15, and relational database key stores while providing an identical interface for all keyset types.

1.5.2 Data Formats

Since each object represents an abstract security concept, none of them are tied to a particular underlying data format or type. For example, an envelope could output the result of its processing in the data format used by CMS/S/MIME, PGP, PEM, MSP, or any other format required. As with the other object types, when the envelope object is created, its function pointers are set to encoding or decoding methods that handle the appropriate data formats. In addition to the variable, data-format-specific processing functions, envelope and certificate objects employ data-recognition routines that will automatically determine the format of input data (for example whether data is in CMS/S/MIME or PGP format, or whether a certificate is a certificate request, certificate, PKCS #7 certificate chain, CRL, OCSP request or response, CRMF/CMP message, or some other type of data) and set up the correct processing methods as appropriate.

1.6 Interobject Communications

Objects communicate internally via a message-passing mechanism, although this is typically hidden from the user by a more conventional functional interface. The message-passing mechanism connects the objects indirectly, replacing pointers and direct function calls, and is the fundamental mechanism used to implement the complete isolation of architecture internals from the outside world. Since the mechanism is anonymous, it reveals nothing about an object's implementation, its interface, or even its existence.

The message-passing mechanism has three parts:

1. The source object
2. The destination object
3. The message dispatcher

In order to send a message from a source to a destination, the source object needs to know the target object's handle, but the target object has no knowledge of where a message came from unless the source explicitly informs it of this. All data communicated between the two is held in the message itself. In addition to general-purpose messages, objects can also send construct and destruct messages to request the creation and destruction of an instantiation of a particular object, although in practice the destroy object message is almost never used, being replaced by a decrement reference count message that allows the kernel to manage object destruction.

In a conventional object-oriented architecture the local client will send a message to the logical server requesting a particular service. The specification of the server acts as a contract between the client and the server, with the client responsible for sending correct messages with the correct contents and the server responsible for checking each message being sent to it, ensuring that the message goes to the correct method or operation, and returning any result data to the client or returning an appropriate error code if the operation could not be performed [44]. In cryptlib's case, the cryptlib kernel acts as a proxy for the logical server, enforcing the required checks on behalf of the destination object. This means that if an object receives a message, it knows that it is of a type that is appropriate for it, that the message contents are within appropriate bounds (for example, that they contain data of a valid length or a reference to a valid object), and that the object is in a state in which processing of the message in the requested manner is an appropriate action.

To handle interobject messaging, the kernel contains a message dispatcher that maintains an internal message queue that is used to forward messages to the appropriate object or objects. Some messages are directed at a particular object (identified by the object's handle), others to an entire class of object or even to all objects. For example, if an encryption action object is instantiated from a smart card and the card is then withdrawn from the reader, the event handler for the keyset object associated with the reader may broadcast a card-withdrawal message identifying the card that was removed to all active objects, as illustrated in Figure 1.18. In practice this particular event doesn't occur because very few card reader drivers support card-removal notification even if the reader itself does. cryptlib provides a brute-force solution to this problem using a background polling thread, but many readers can't even report a card removal or change properly (one solution to this problem is examined in Section 1.10.2). Other implementations simply don't support card removal handling at all so that, for example, an MSIE SSL session that was established using smart card-based client authentication will remain active until the browser is shut down, even if the smart card has long since been removed.

The mechanism used by cryptlib is an implementation of the event-based architectural model, which is required in order to notify the encryption action object that it may need to take action based on the card withdrawal, and also to notify further objects such as envelope objects and certificates that have been created or acted upon by the encryption action object. Since the sender is completely disconnected from the receiver, it needs to broadcast the message to all objects to ensure that everything that might have an interest is notified. The message handler has been designed so that processing a message of this type has almost zero overhead compared to the complexity of tracking which message might apply to which objects, so it makes more sense to handle the notification as a broadcast rather than maintaining per-object lists of messages in which the object is interested.

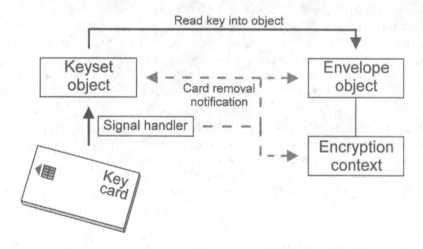

Figure 1.18. Interobject messaging example.

Each object has the ability to intelligently handle external events in a controlled manner, processing them as appropriate. Because an object controls how it handles these events, there is no need for any other object or control routine to know about the internal details or function of the object — it simply posts a notification of an event and goes about its business.

In the case of the card-withdrawal notification illustrated in Figure 1.18, the affected objects that do not choose to ignore it would typically erase any security-related information, close active OS services such as open file handles, free allocated memory, and place themselves in a signalled state in which no further use of the object is possible apart from destroying it.   Message queueing and dispatching are handled by the kernel's message dispatcher and the message handlers built into each object, which remove from the user the need to check for various special-case conditions such as smart card withdrawals. In practice, the only object that would process the message is the encryption action object. Other objects that might contain the action object (for example, an envelope or certificate object) will only notice the card withdrawal if they try to use the action object, at which point it will inform them that it has been signalled externally and is no longer usable.

Since the objects act independently, the fact that one object has changed state doesn't affect any of the other objects. This object independence is an important feature since it doesn't tie the functioning of one object to every component object it contains or uses — a smart card-based private key might only be needed to decrypt a session key at the start of a communications session, after which its presence is irrelevant. Since each object manages its own state, the fact that the encryption action object created from the key on the card has become signalled doesn't matter to the object using it after it has recovered the session key.

1.6.1 Message Routing

The kernel is also responsible for message forwarding or routing, in which a message is forwarded to the particular object for which it is appropriate. For example, if an "encrypt data" message is sent to a certificate object, the kernel knows that this type of message is inappropriate for a certificate (which is a security attribute container object) and instead forwards it on to the encryption action object attached to the certificate. This intelligent forwarding is performed entirely within the kernel, so that the end effect is one of sending the message directly to the encryption action object even though, as far as the user was concerned, it was sent to the certificate object.

This forwarding operation is extremely simple and lightweight, taking only a few instructions to perform.   Alternative methods are far more complex and require the involvement of each object in the chain of command from the logical target object to the actual target. In the simplest case, the objects themselves would be responsible for the forwarding, so that a message such as a key-size query (which is handled by an encryption action object) to a certificate would proceed as in Figure 1.19. This has the disadvantage of requiring a message to be passed through each object in turn, which has both a high overhead (compared to in-kernel forwarding) and requires that every object in the chain be available to process the message. If one of the objects is otherwise engaged, the message is stalled until the object becomes available to process it. In addition, processing the message ties up every object it passes through, greatly increasing the chances of deadlock when large numbers of objects are unavailable for further work.

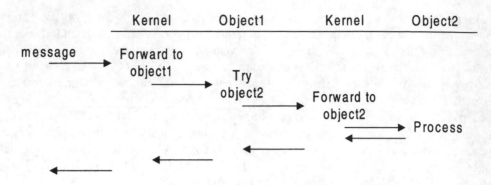

Figure 1.19. Message forwarding by objects.

A slight variation is shown in Figure 1.20, where the object doesn't forward the message itself but instead returns a "Not at this address, try here instead" status to the kernel. This method is slightly better than the previous alternative since it only ties up one object at a time, but it still has the overhead of unnecessarily passing the message through each object.

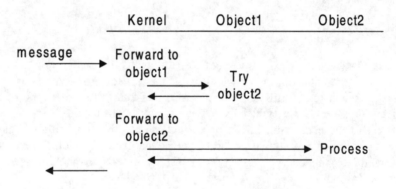

Figure 1.20. Message redirection by objects.

In contrast the in-kernel forwarding scheme shown in Figure 1.21, which is the one actually used, never ties up other objects unnecessarily and has almost zero overhead due to the use of the extremely efficient pointer-chasing algorithm used for the routing.

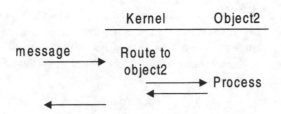

Figure 1.21. Kernel message routing.

1.6.2 Message Routing Implementation

Each message sent towards an object has an implicit target type that is used to route the message to its ultimate destination. For example, a "create signature" message has an implicit target type of "encryption action object", so if the message were sent to a certificate object, the kernel would route it towards the action object that was associated with the certificate in the manner described earlier. cryptlib's routing algorithm is shown in Figure 1.22. Although messages are almost always sent directly to their ultimate target, in the cases where they aren't this algorithm will route them towards their intended target type, either the associated object for most messages or the associated crypto device for messages targeted at devices.

```
/* Route the request through any dependent objects as required until we
   reach the required target object type */
while( object != ε && object.type != target.type )
   {
   if( target.type == OBJECT_TYPE_DEVICE )
      object = object.associated device;
   else
      object = object.associated object;
   }
```

Figure 1.22. Kernel message-routing algorithm.

Eventually the message will either reach its ultimate destination or the associated object or device handle will be empty, indicating that there is no appropriate target object present. This algorithm usually terminates immediately (the message is being sent directly to its intended target) or after a single iteration (the intended target object is directly attached to the initial target). A more formal treatment of the routing algorithm is given in Chapter 5.

Not directly shown in the pseudocode in Figure 1.22 is the fact that the algorithm also includes provisions for messages having alternate targets (in other words target.type can be multi-valued). An example of this is a "get key" message that instantiates a public- or private-key object from stored keying data, which is usually sent to a keyset object but may also be intended for a device acting as a keyset. For example, a Fortezza card usually stores an entire chain of certificates from a trusted root certificate down to that of the card owner, so a "get key" message would be used to read the certificate chain from the card as if it were a keyset object. There can never be a routing conflict for messages with alternate targets because either the main or the alternate target(s), but never more than one, can be present in any sequence of connected objects.

One potential problem that can occur when routing messages between objects is the so-called yo-yo problem, in which a message wanders up and down various object hierarchies until an appropriate target is found [45]. Since the longest object chain that can occur has a length of three (a high-level object such as a data or attribute container linked to an encryption action object linked to a device object) and because the algorithm presented above will always either route a message directly to its target or fail immediately if no target exists, the yo-yo problem can't occur.

In addition to the routable messages, there are also unroutable messages that must be sent directly to their intended targets. For example a "destroy object" message should never be routed to a target other than the one to which it is directly addressed. Other, similar messages that fall into the class of object control messages (that is, messages which are handled directly by the kernel and are never passed on to the object, an example being the increment reference count message shown in Figure 1.31) are never routed either.

1.6.3 Alternative Routing Strategies

The standard means of handling packet-switched messages is to route them individually, which has a fixed per-message overhead and may lead to blocking problems if multiple messages are being routed over a shared channel, in this case the cryptlib kernel. An alternative routing technique, wormhole routing, groups similar messages into a collection of flits, the smallest units into which messages can be decomposed, with the first flit containing routing information and the remaining flits containing data. In this way the routing overhead only applies to the header flit, and all of the other flits get a free ride in the slipstream [46][47]. By creating a virtual channel from source to destination, the routing overhead for n messages intended for the same target is reduced from n to 1. This is particularly critical in high-speed networks such as those used in multiprocessor/multicomputer systems, where switching overhead has a considerable impact on message throughput [48].

Unfortunately, such a simple solution doesn't work for the cryptlib kernel. Whereas standard packet switching is only concerned with getting a message from source to destination as quickly as possible, the cryptlib kernel must also apply extensive security checks (covered in the next chapter) to each message, and the outcome of processing one message can affect the processing of subsequent messages. Consider the effects of processing the messages shown in Figure 1.23. In this message sequence, there are several dependencies: The encryption mode must be set before the IV can be set (ECB mode has no IV, so if a mode that requires an IV isn't selected, the attempt to set an IV will fail), the mode can't be set after the key has been loaded (the kernel switches the object to the key-loaded state, which disables most further operations on it), and the object can only be used for encryption once the previous three attributes have been set.

Message	Attribute	Value
set attribute	Encryption mode	CBC
set attribute	IV	27FA170D
set attribute	Key	0F37EB2C
encrypt	—	"Secret message"

Figure 1.23. Message sequence with dependencies.

Because of these dependencies, the kernel can't arrange the messages into a sequence of flits and wormhole-route them to the destination as a single block of messages because each message affects the destination in a manner that also affects the processing of further messages. For example if a sequence of two consecutive messages { set attribute, key, *value* } were wormhole-routed to an object, the second key would overwrite the first since the kernel would only transition the object into the key-loaded state once processing of the second message had completed. In contrast in the normal routing situation the second key load would fail since the object would already be in the key-loaded state from the first key load. The use of wormhole routing would therefore void the contract between the kernel and the cryptlib objects.

If full wormhole routing isn't possible, is it possible to employ some form of partial wormhole routing, for example by caching the destination of the previous message? It turns out that, due to the design of the cryptlib object dependency hierarchy, the routes are so short (typically zero hops, more rarely a single hop) that the overhead of performing the caching is significantly higher than simply routing each message through. In addition, the complexity of the route caching code is vastly greater than the direct pointer-chasing used to perform the routing, creating the risk of misrouted messages due to implementation bugs, again voiding the contract between the kernel and cryptlib's objects. For these reasons, cryptlib individually routes each message and doesn't attempt to use techniques such as wormhole routing.

1.7 The Message Dispatcher

The message dispatcher maintains a queue of all pending messages due to be sent to target objects, which are dispatched in order of arrival. If an object isn't busy processing an existing message, a new message intended for it is immediately dispatched to it without being enqueued, which prevents the single message queue from becoming a bottleneck. For group messages (messages sent to all objects of a given type) or broadcast messages (messages sent to all objects), the message is sent to every applicable object in turn.

Recursive messages (ones that result in further messages being generated and sent to the source object) are handled by having the dispatcher enqueue messages intended for an object that is already processing a message or that has a message present in the queue and return immediately to the caller. This ensures that the new message isn't processed until the earlier message(s) for the object have been processed. If the message is for a different object, it is either processed immediately if the object isn't already processing a message or it is prepended to the queue and processed before other messages, so that messages sent by objects to associated subordinate objects are processed before messages for the objects themselves. An object won't have a new message dispatched to it until the current one has been processed. This processing order ensures that messages to the same object are processed in the order sent, and messages to different objects arising from the message to the original object are processed before the message for the original object is completed.

The dispatcher distinguishes between two message types: one-shot messages (which inform an object that an event has occurred; for example, a destroy object message), and repeatable messages (which modify an object in a certain way; for example, a message to increment an object's reference count). The main distinction between the two is that duplicate one-shot messages can be deleted whereas duplicate repeatable messages can't. Figure 1.24 shows the message processing algorithm.

```
/* Don't enqueue one-shot messages a second time */
if( message is one-shot and already present in queue )
   return;

/* Dispatch further messages to an object later */
if( message to this object is already present in queue )
   {
   insert message at existing queue position + 1;
   return;
   }

/* Insert the message for this object and dispatch all messages for this
   object */
insert message at queue start;
while( queue nonempty && message at queue start is for current object )
   {
   call the object's message handler with the message data;
   dequeue the message;
   }
```

Figure 1.24. Message-dispatching algorithm.

Since an earlier message can result in an object being destroyed, the dispatcher also checks to see whether the object still exists in an active state. If not, it dequeues all further messages without calling the object's message handler.

The operation of the dispatcher is best illustrated with an example. Assume that we have three objects A, B, and C and that something sends a message to A, which results in a message from A to B, which in turn results in B sending in a second message to A, a second message to B, and a message to C. The processing order is shown in Figure 1.25. This processing order ensures that the current object can queue a series of events for processing and guarantee execution in the order in which the events are posted.

Source	Action	Action by Kernel	Queue
User	Send message to A	Enqueue A_1 Call A's handler	A_1
A	Send message to B	Enqueue B_1 Call B's handler	B_1, A_1
B	Send message to A	Enqueue A_2	B_1, A_1, A_2
B	Send message to B	Enqueue B_2	B_1, B_2, A_1, A_2
B	Send message to C	Enqueue C Call C's handler	C, B_1, B_2, A_1, A_2
C	Processing completes	Dequeue C	B_1, B_2, A_1, A_2
B	Processing completes	Dequeue B_1 Call B's handler	B_2, A_1, A_2
B	Processing completes	Dequeue B_2	A_1, A_2
A	Processing completes	Dequeue A_1 Call A's handler	A_2
A	Processing completes	Dequeue A_2	

Figure 1.25. Complex message-queueing example.

An examination of the algorithm in Figure 1.24 will reveal that the head of the queue has the potential to become a serious hot spot since, as with stack-based CPU architectures, the top element is continually being enqueued and dequeued. In order to reduce the hot spot problem, the message dispatcher implements a stunt box [49] that allows messages targeted at objects that aren't already processing a message (which by extension means that they also don't have any messages enqueued for them) to be dispatched immediately without having to go through the no-op step of being enqueued and then immediately dequeued. Once an object is processing a message, further messages to it are enqueued as described earlier. Because of the order of the message processing, this simple shortcut is equivalent to the full queue-based algorithm without the overhead of involving the queue.

In practice, almost no messages are ever enqueued, the few that are being recursive messages, although under high-load conditions with all objects occupied in processing messages the queue could see more utilisation. In order to guard against the problems that arise in message queue implementations when the queue is filled more quickly than it can be emptied (the most publicly visible sign of which is the "This Windows application is not responding to messages" dialog), once more than a given number of messages are enqueued no further messages except control messages (those that are processed directly by the kernel, such as ones to destroy an object) are accepted. This means that one or more objects that are stalled processing a message can't poison the queue or cause deadlock problems. At worst the object handle will be unavailable for further use, with the object marked as unavailable by the kernel, but no other objects (and certainly not the kernel itself) will be affected.

1.7.1 Asynchronous versus Synchronous Message Dispatching

When processing messages, the dispatcher can handle them in one of two ways, either asynchronously, returning control to the caller immediately while processing the object in a separate thread, or synchronously, suspending the caller while the message is processed. Asynchronous message channels can require potentially unbounded capacity since the sending object isn't blocked, whereas synchronous channels are somewhat more structured since communication and synchronisation are tightly coupled so that operations in the sending object are suspended until the receiving object has finished processing the message [50]. An example of a synchronous message is shown in Figure 1.26.

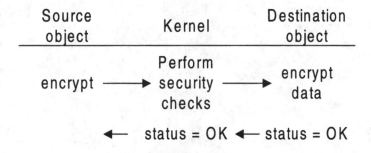

Figure 1.26. Synchronous message processing.

There are two types of messages that can be sent to an object: simple notifications and data communications that are processed immediately, and more complex, generally object-specific messages that can take some time to process, an example being "generate a key", which can take a while for many public-key algorithms. This would in theory require both synchronous and asynchronous message dispatching. However, this greatly increases the difficulty involved in verifying the kernel, so the cryptlib architecture makes each object responsible for its own handling of asynchronous processing. In practice, this means that (on systems that support it) the object has one or more threads attached to it which perform asynchronous processing. On the few remaining non-threaded systems, or if there is concern over the security implications of using multiple threads, there's no choice but to use synchronous messaging.

When a source object sends a message to a destination that may take some time to generate a result, the destination object initiates asynchronous processing and returns its status to the caller. If the asynchronous processing was initiated successfully, the kernel sets the status of the object to "busy" and enqueues any normal messages sent to it for as long as the object is in the busy state (with the aforementioned protection against excessive numbers of messages building up). Once the object leaves the busy state (either by completing the asynchronous operation or by receiving a control message from the kernel), the remaining enqueued messages are dispatched to it for processing, as shown in Figure 1.27. In this way, the kernel enforces strict serialisation of all messages sent to an object, guaranteeing a fixed order of execution even for asynchronous operations on an object. Since the objects are inherently thread-safe, the messaging mechanism is also safe when asynchronous processing is taking place.

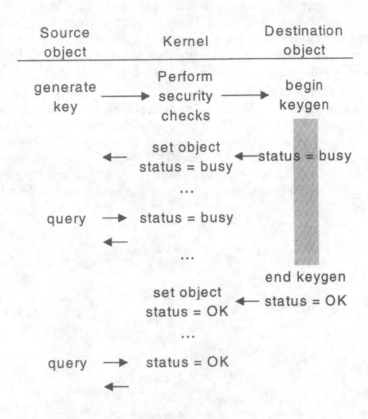

Figure 1.27. Asynchronous message processing.

1.8 Object Reuse

Since object handles are detached from the objects with which they are associated, a single object can (provided its ACLs allow this) be used by multiple processes or threads at once. This flexibility is particularly important with objects used in connection with container objects, since replicating every object pushed into a container creates both unnecessary overhead and increases the chances of compromise of sensitive information if keys and other data are copied across to each newly created object.

Instead of copying each object whenever it is reused, the architecture maintains a reference count for it and only copies it when necessary. In practice the copying is only needed for bulk data encryption action objects that employ a copy-on-write mechanism to ensure that the object isn't replicated unnecessarily. Other objects that cannot easily be replicated, or that do not need to be replicated, have their reference count incremented when they are reused and decremented when they are freed. When the object's reference count drops to zero, it is destroyed. The use of garbage collection greatly simplifies the object management process as well as eliminating security holes that arise when sensitive data is left in memory, either because the programmer forgot to add code to overwrite it after use or because the object was never cleared and freed even if zeroisation code was present [51].

The decision to use automatic handling of object cleanup was motivated by the problems inherent in alternative approaches that require explicit, programmer-controlled allocation and de-allocation of resources. These typically suffer from memory leaks (storage is allocated but never freed) and dangling pointer problems (memory is freed from one location while a second reference to it is kept active elsewhere) [52][53][54]. Since the object hierarchy maintained by the kernel is a pure tree (strictly speaking, a forest of trees), the many problems encountered with garbage collectors that work with object hierarchies that contain loops are avoided [55][56].

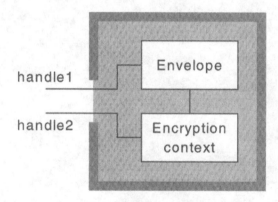

Figure 1.28. Objects with multiple references.

To see how this works, let us assume that the user creates an encryption action object and pushes it into an envelope object. This results in an action object with a reference count of 2, with one external reference (by the user) and one internal reference (by the envelope object), as shown in Figure 1.28. Typically, the user would then destroy the encryption action object while continuing to use the envelope with which it is now associated. The reference with the external access ACL would be destroyed and the reference count decremented by one, leaving the object as shown in Figure 1.29 with a reference count of 1 and an internal access ACL.

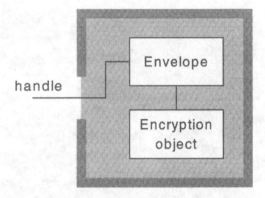

Figure 1.29. Objects with multiple references after the external reference is destroyed.

To the user, the object has indeed been destroyed since it is now accessible only to the envelope object.   When the envelope object is destroyed, the encryption action object's reference count is again decremented through a message sent from the envelope, leaving it at zero, whereupon the cryptlib kernel sends it a "destroy object" message to notify it to shut itself down. The only time objects are explicitly destroyed is through an external signal such as a smart card withdrawal or when the kernel broadcasts destroy object messages when it is closing down. At any other time, only their reference count is decremented.

The use of the reference-counting implementation allows objects to be treated in a far more flexible manner than would otherwise be the case. For example, the paradigm of pushing attributes and objects into envelopes (which could otherwise be prohibitively expensive due to the overhead of making a new copy of the object for each envelope) is rendered feasible since in general only a single copy of each object exists. Similarly, a single (heavyweight) connection to a key database can be shared across multiple threads or processes, an important factor in a number of client/server databases where a single client connection can consume a megabyte or more of memory.

Another example of how this object management technique works is provided by the case where a signing key is reused to sign two messages via envelope objects. Initially, the private-key object that is used for the signing operation is created (typically by being read from a private-key file or instantiated via a crypto token such as a smart card) and pushed into both envelopes. At this point, there are three references to it: one internal reference from each envelope and the original external reference that was created when the object was first created. This situation is shown in Figure 1.30.

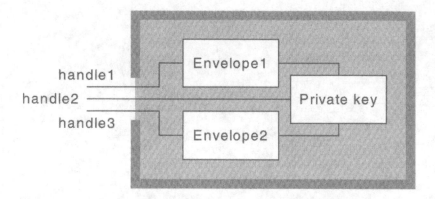

Figure 1.30. Objects with internal and external references.

The user no longer needs the reference to the private-key object and deletes the external reference to it, which decrements its reference count and has the effect that, to the user, the object disappears from view since the external reference to it has been destroyed. Since both envelopes still have references to it, the object remains active although hidden from the outside world.

The user now pushes data through the first envelope, which uses the attached private-key object to generate a signature on the data. Once the data has been signed, the user destroys the envelope, which again decrements the reference count for the attached private-key object, but still leaves it active because of the one remaining reference from the second envelope. Finally, when this envelope's job is also done and it is destroyed by the user, the private-key object's reference count drops to zero and it is destroyed along with the envelope. All of this is performed automatically by the cryptlib kernel without any explicit action required from either the user or the envelope objects.

1.8.1 Object Dependencies

Section 1.4.2 introduced the concept of dependent objects which are associated with other objects, the most common example being a public-key action object that is tied to a certificate object. Dependent objects can be established in one of two ways, the first of which involves taking an existing object and attaching it to another object. An example of where this occurs is when a public-key action object is added to an envelope, which increments the reference count since there is now one reference by the original owner of the action object and a second reference by the envelope.

The second way to establish a dependent object is by creating a completely new object and attaching it to another object. This doesn't increment the reference count since it is only referred to by the controlling object. An example of where this occurs is when a certificate object is instantiated from stored certificate data in a keyset object. This creates two independent objects, a certificate object and a public-key action object. When the two are combined by attaching the action object to the certificate, the action object's reference count isn't incremented because the only reference to it is from the certificate. In effect, the keyset object that is being used to create the action object and certificate objects is handing over its reference to the action object to the certificate object.

1.9 Object Management Message Flow

We can now combine the information presented in the previous three sections to examine the object management process in terms of interobject message flow. This is illustrated using a variation of the message sequence chart (MSC) format, a standard format for representing protocols in concurrently operating entities such as processes or hardware elements [57][58][59]. A portion of the process involved in signing a message using an envelope is shown in Figure 1.31. This diagram introduces a new object, the system object, which is used to encapsulate the state of a particular instantiation of cryptlib. The system object is the first object created by the kernel and the last object destroyed, and controls actions such as the creation of other objects, random number management, and the access privileges and rights of the currently logged-on user when cryptlib is being used as the control system for a piece of crypto hardware. The system object is the equivalent of the user object present in other message-based object-oriented architectures [60] except that its existence doesn't necessarily correspond to the presence of a logged-in user but instead represents the state of the instantiation of the system as a whole (which may or may not correspond to a logged-in user). In Figure 1.31, messages are sent to the system object to request the creation of a new object (the hash object that is used to hash the data in the envelope) and to request the application of various crypto mechanisms (typically key wrapping and unwrapping or signature creation and verification) to collections of objects, in this case the PKCS #1 signature mechanism applied using the private-key and hash objects.

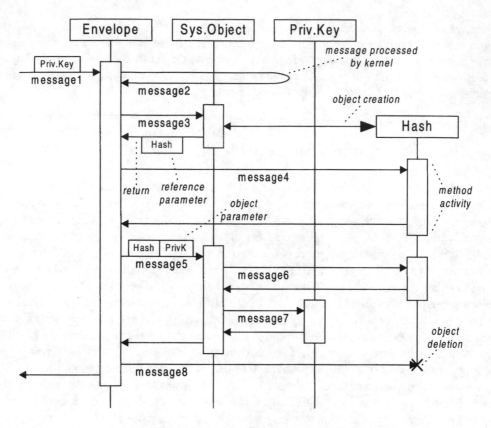

Figure 1.31. Partial data-signing message flow.

With message1, the user adds the private signature key to the envelope, which records its handle and sends it message2, an increment reference count message. This is a control message that is handled directly by the kernel, so the object itself never sees it. The envelope now sends message3 to the system object, requesting the creation of a hash object to hash its data. The system object instantiates a hash object and returns a reference to it to the envelope, which sends it message4, telling it to hash the data contained in the envelope. The private key and hash objects are now ready for signature creation, handled by the envelope sending message5 to the system object, requesting the creation of a PKCS #1 signature using the private-key and hash objects. The system object sends message6 to the hash object to read the hash value and message7 to the private-key object to generate a signature on the hash. Finally, the envelope is done with the hash object and sends it a decrement reference count message, message8, which results in its deletion by the kernel.

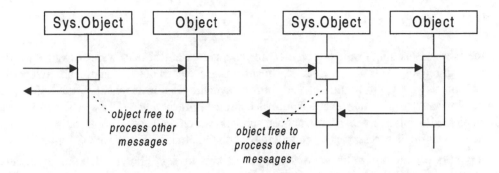

Figure 1.32. System object message processing with direct return (left) and indirect return (right).

Figure 1.31 would appear to indicate that the system object remains busy for the duration of any message processing it performs, but in fact cryptlib's fine-grained internal locking allows the system object to be unlocked while the message processing is performed, ensuring that it doesn't become a bottleneck. The standard MSC format doesn't easily allow this type of operation to be represented. An excerpt from Figure 1.31 that shows the handling of messages by the system object is shown in Figure 1.32. The system object either hands the incoming message over to the appropriate handler which returns directly to the sender (via the kernel), or in more rare cases the return value is passed through the system object on its way back to the kernel/sender. In this way, the system object can never become a bottleneck, which would be particularly troublesome if it remained busy while handling messages that took a long time to process.

The use of such fine-grained locking permeates cryptlib, avoiding the problems associated with traditional kernel locks of which the most notorious was Win16Lock, the Win16 mutex that could stop the entire system if it was acquired but never released by a process. Win16Lock was in fact renamed to Win16Mutex in Windows 95 to give it a less drastically descriptive name [61]. The effect of Win16Mutex was that most processes running on the system (both Win16 and Windows 95, which ended up calling down to 16-bit code eventually) could be stopped by Win16Mutex [62]. Since cryptlib uses very fine-grained locking and never holds a kernel lock over more than a small amount of loop-free code (that is, code that is guaranteed to terminate in a fixed, short time interval), this type of problem cannot occur.

1.10 Other Kernel Mechanisms

In order to work with the objects described thus far, the architecture requires a number of other mechanisms to handle synchronisation, background processing, and the reporting of events within the architecture to the user. These mechanisms are described below.

1.10.1 Semaphores

In the message-passing example given earlier, the source object may want to wait until the data that it requested becomes available. In general, since each object can potentially operate asynchronously, cryptlib requires some form of synchronisation mechanism that allows an object to wait for a certain event before it continues processing. The synchronisation is implemented using lightweight internal semaphores, which are used in most cases (in which no actual waiting is necessary) before falling back to the often heavyweight OS semaphores.

cryptlib provides two types of semaphores: system semaphores (that is, predefined semaphore handles corresponding to fixed resources or operations such as binding to various types of drivers, which takes place on startup) and user semaphores, which are allocated by an object as required. System semaphores have architecture-wide unique handles akin to the stdio library's predefined stdin, stdout, and stderr handles. Before performing an operation with certain types of external software or hardware such as crypto devices and key databases, cryptlib will wait on the appropriate system semaphore to ensure that the device or database has completed its initialisation.

1.10.2 Threads

The independent, asynchronous nature of the objects in the architecture means that, in the worst case, there can be dozens of threads all whirring away inside cryptlib, some of which may be blocked waiting on external events. Since this acts as a drain on system resources, can negatively affect performance (some operating systems can take some time to instantiate a new thread), and adds extra implementation detail for handling each thread, cryptlib provides an internal service thread that can be used by objects to perform basic housekeeping tasks. Each object can register service functions with this thread, which are called in a round-robin fashion, after which the thread goes to sleep for a preset time interval, behaving much like a fiber or lightweight, user-scheduled thread. This means that simple tasks such as basic status checks can be performed by a single architecture-wide thread instead of requiring one thread per object. This service thread also performs general tasks such as touching each allocated memory page that is marked as containing sensitive data whenever it runs in order to reduce the chances of the page being swapped out.

Consider an example of a smart card device object that needs to check the card status every now and then to determine whether the card has been removed from the reader. Most serial-port based readers don't provide any useful notification mechanism, but only report a "card removed" status on the next attempt to access it. Some can't even do that, requiring that the caller track the ID of the card in the reader, with the appearance of a different ID indicating a card change. This isn't terribly useful to cryptlib, which expects to be able to destroy objects that depend on the card as soon as it is removed.

In order to check for card removal, the device object registers a service function with the service thread. The registration returns a unique service ID that can be used later to deregister it. Deregistration can also occur automatically when the object that registered the service function is destroyed.

Once a service function is registered, it is called whenever the service thread runs. In the case of the device object it would query the reader to determine whether the card was still present. If the card is removed, it sends a message to the device object (running in a different thread), after which it returns, and the next service function is processed. In the meantime the device object notifies all dependent objects and destroys itself, in the process deregistering the service function. As with the message processing, since the objects involved are all thread-safe, there are no problems with synchronisation (for example, the service function being called can deregister itself without any problems).

1.10.3 Event Notification

A common method for notifying the user of events is to use one or more callback functions. These functions are registered with a program and are called when certain events occur. Typical implementations use either event-specific callbacks (so the user can register functions only for events in which they are specifically interested) or umbrella callbacks which get all events passed to them, with the user determining whether they want to act on them or not.

Callbacks have two main problems. The first of these is that they are inherently language and often OS-specific, often occurring across process boundaries and always requiring special handling to set up the appropriate stack frames, ensure that arguments are passed in a consistent manner, and so on. Language-specific alternatives to callbacks, such as Visual Basic event handlers, are even more problematic. The second problem with callbacks is that the called user code is given the full privileges of the calling code unless special steps are taken [63]. One possible workaround is to perform callbacks from a special no-privileges thread, but this means that the called code is given too few privileges rather than too many.

A better solution which avoids both the portability and security problems of callbacks is to avoid them altogether in favour of an object polling mechanism. Since all functionality is provided in terms of objects, object status checking is provided automatically by the kernel — if any object has an abnormal status associated with it (for example it might be busy performing a long-running operation such as a key generation), any attempt to use it will result in the status being returned without any action being taken.

Because of the object-based approach that is used for all security functionality, the object status mechanism works transparently across arbitrarily linked objects. For example, if the encryption object in which the key is being generated is pushed into an envelope, any attempt to use it before the key generation has completed will result in an "object busy" status being passed back up to the user. Since it is the encryption object that is busy (rather than the envelope), it is still possible to use the envelope for non-encryption functions while the key generation is occurring in the encryption object.

1.11 References

[1]   libdes, http://www.cryptsoft.com/ssleay/faq.html, 1996.

[2]   "Fortezza Cryptologic Programmers Guide", Version 1.52, National Security Agency Workstation Security Products, National Security Agency, 30 January 1996.

[3]   "BSAFE Library Reference Manual", Version 4.0, RSA Data Security, 1998.

[4]   "Generic Cryptographic Service API (GCS-API)", Open Group Preliminary Specification, June 1996.

[5]   "Microsoft CryptoAPI Application Programmers Guide", Version 1, Microsoft Corporation, 16 August 1996.

[6]   "PKCS #11 Cryptographic Token Interface Standard", Version 2.10, RSA Laboratories, December 1999.

[7]   "Lessons Learned in Implementing and Deploying Crypto Software", Peter Gutmann, *Proceedings of the 11th Usenix Security Symposium*, August 2002.

[8]   "Generic Security Service Application Programming Interface", RFC 2078 (formerly RFC 1508), John Linn, January 1997.

[9]   "Generic Interface to Security Services", John Linn, *Journal of Computer Communications*, **Vol.17**, **No.7** (July 1994), p.483.

[10] "Practical Intranet Security", Paul Ashley and Mark Vandenwauver, Kluwer Academic Publishers, 1999.

[11] "DCE Security Programming", Wei Hu, O'Reilly and Associates, July 1995.

[12] "Common Cryptographic Architecture Cryptographic Application Programming Interface", D.Johnson, G.Dolan, M.Kelly, A.Le, and S.Matyas, *IBM Systems Journal*, **Vol.30**, **No.2** (1991), p.130.

[13] "SESAME Technology Version 4", December 1995 (newer versions exist but are no longer publicly available).

[14] "Security Services Application Programming Interface (SS API) Developer's Security Guidance", Amgad Fayad and Don Faatz, MITRE Technical Report MTR 99W0000027, MITRE Corporation, March 2000.

[15] "Independent Data Unit Protection Generic Security Service Application Program Interface (IDUP-GSS-API)", RFC 2479, Carlisle Adams, December 1998.

[16] "Cryptographic APIs", Dieter Gollman, *Cryptography: Policy and Algorithms*, Springer-Verlag Lecture Notes in Computer Science, No.1029, July 1995, p.290.

[17] "Architecture for Public-key Infrastructure (APKI), Draft 3", The Open Group, 27 March 1998.

[18] "CISS: Generalised Security Libraries", Sead Muftic and Edina Hatunic, *Computers and Security*, **Vol.11**, **No.7** (November 1992), p.653.

[19] "Security Architecture for Open Distributed Systems", Sead Muftic, Ahmed Patel, Peter Sanders, and Rafael Colon, John Wiley and Sons, 1993.

[20] "Implementation of the Comprehensive Integrated Security System for computer networks", Sead Muftic, *Computer Networks and ISDN Systems*, **Vol.25**, **No.5** (1992), p.469.

[21] "Practical Intranet Security: Overview of the State of the Art and Available Technologies", Paul Ashley and Mark Vandenwauver, Kluwer Academic Publishing, 1999.

[22] "Common Data Security Architecture (CDSA) Version 2.0", The Open Group, May 1999.

[23] "A Comparison of CDSA to Cryptoki", Ruth Taylor, *Proceedings of the 22nd National Information Systems Security Conference* (formerly the National Computer Security Conference), October 1999, CDROM distribution.

[24] "Domain Models and Software Architectures", Rubén Prieto-Díaz, *ACM SIGSOFT Softare Engineering Notes*, **Vol.20, No.3** (July 1995), p.71.

[25] "Pattern-Oriented Software Architecture: A System of Patterns", Frank Buschmann, Regine Meunier, Hans Rohnert, Peter Sommerlad, and Michael Stal, John Wiley and Sons, 1996.

[26] "An Introduction to Software Architecture", David Garlan and Mary Shaw, *Advances in Software Engineering and Knowledge Engineering*, **Vol.1**, 1993.

[27] "Proceedings of the First International Workshop on Architectures for Software Systems", Seattle, Washington, April 1995.

[28] "Design Patterns : Elements of Reusable Object-Oriented Software", Erich Gamma, Richard Helm, Ralph Johnson, John Vlissides, and Grady Booch, Addison-Wesley, 1995.

[29] "Formulations and Formalisms in Software Architecture", Mary Shaw and David Garlan, *Computer Science Today: Recent Trends and Developments*, Springer-Verlag Lecture Notes in Computer Science, No.1000, 1996, p.307.

[30] "Succeedings of the Second International Software Architecture Workshop (ISAW-2)", Alexander Wolf, *ACM SIGSOFT Software Engineering Notes*, **Vol.22, No.1** (January 1997), p.42

[31] "Test and Analysis of Software Architectures", Will Tracz, *Proceedings of the 1996 International Symposium on Software Testing and Analysis (ISSTA'96)*, ACM, January 1996, p.1.

[32] "Foundations for the Study of Software Architecture", Dewayne Perry and Alexander Wolf, *ACM SIGSOFT Software Engineering Notes*, **Vol.17, No.4** (October 1992), p.40.

[33] "Essays on Object-Oriented Software Engineering", Edward Bernard, Simon and Schuster, 1993.

[34] "The Elements of Networking Style and other Essays and Animadversions on the Art of Intercomputer Networking", Mike Padlipsky, Prentice-Hall, 1985.

[35] "Security Service API: Cryptographic API Recommendation, Updated and Abridged Edition", NSA Cross Organization CAPI Team, National Security Agency, 25 July 1997.

[36] "Microsoft Cryptographic Application Programming Interface (CryptoAPI)", Version 2, Microsoft Corporation, 22 December 1998.

[37] "A programmer's view of the Intel 432 system", Elliott Organick, McGraw-Hill, 1985.

[38] "An Architecture Supporting Security and Persistent Object Stores", M.Reitenspieß, *Proceedings of the International Workshop on Computer Architectures to Support Security and Persistence of Information (Security and Persistence '90)*, Springer-Verlag, 1990, p.202.

[39] "Rekursiv: Object-Oriented Computer Architecture", David Harland, Ellis Horwood/Halstead Press, 1988.

[40] "AS/400 Architecture and Application: The Database Machine", Jill Lawrence, QED Publishing Group, 1993.

[41] "OpenPGP Message Format", Jon Callas, Lutz Donnerhacke, Hal Finney, and Rodney Thayer, RFC 2440, November 1998.

[42] "Building a High-Performance Programmable, Secure Coprocessor", Sean Smith and Steve Weingart, *Computer Networks and ISDN Systems*, **Vol.31**, **No.4** (April 1999), p.831.

[43] "SKIPJACK and KEA Algorithm Specification", Version 2.0, National Security Agency, 29 May 1998.

[44] "Object-Oriented Requirements Analysis and Logical Design: A Software Engineering Approach", Donald Firesmith, John Wiley and Sons, 1993.

[45] "Problems in Object-Oriented Software Reuse", David Taenzer, Murhty Ganti, and Sunil Podar, *Proceedings of the 1989 European Conference on Object-Oriented Programming (ECOOP'89)*, Cambridge University Press, July 1989, p.25.

[46] "Virtual Cut-Through: A New Computer Communication Switching Technique", Parviz Kermani and Leonard Kleinrock, *Computer Networks*, **Vol.3**, **No.4** (September 1979), p.267.

[47] "A Survey of Wormhole Routing Techniques in Direct Networks", Lionel Ni and Philip McKinley, *IEEE Computer*, **Vol.26**, **No.2** (February 1993), p.62.

[48] "Wormhole routing techniques for directly connected multicomputer systems", Prasant Mohapatra, *ACM Computing Surveys*, **Vol.30**, **No.3** (September 1998), p.374.

[49] "Design of a Computer: The Control Data 6600", J.E.Thornton, Scott, Foresman and Co., 1970.

[50] "Paradigms for Process Interation in Distributed Programs", Gregory Andrews, *ACM Computing Surveys* **Vol.23**, **No.1** (March 1991), p.49.

[51] "Conducting an Object Reuse Study", David Wichers, *Proceedings of the 13th National Computer Security Conference*, October 1990, p.738.

[52] "The Art of Computer Programming, Vol.1: Fundamental Algorithms", Donald Knuth, Addison-Wesley, 1998.

[53] "Garbage collection of linked data structures", Jacques Cohen, *ACM Computing Surveys*, **Vol.13**, **No.3** (September 1981), p.341.

[54] "Uniprocessor Garbage Collection", Paul Wilson, *Proceedings of the International Workshop on Memory Management (IWMM 92)*, Springer-Verlag Lecture Notes in Computer Science, No.637, 1992, p.1.

[55] "Reference Counting Can Manage the Circular Environments of Mutual Recursion", Daniel Friedman and David Wise, *Information Processing Letters*, **Vol.8**, **No.1** (2 January 1979), p.41.

[56] "Garbage Collection: Algorithms for Automatic Dynamic Memory Management", Richard Jones and Rafael Lins, John Wiley and Sons, 1996

[57] "Message Sequence Chart (MSC)", ITU-T Recommendation Z.120, International Telecommunication Union, March 1993.

[58] "The Standardization of Message Sequence Charts", Jens Grabowski, Peter Graubmann, and Ekkart Rudolph, *Proceedings of the IEEE Software Engineering Standards Symposium (SESS'93)*, September 1993.

[59] "Tutorial on Message Sequence Charts", Ekkart Rudolph, Peter Graubmann, and Jens Grabowski, *Computer Networks and ISDN Systems*, **Vol.28**, **No.12** (December 1996), p.1629.

[60] "Integrating an Object-Oriented Data Model with Multilevel Security", Sushil Jajodia and Boris Kogan, *Proceedings of the 1990 IEEE Symposium on Security and Privacy*, IEEE Computer Society Press, 1990, p.76.

[61] "Inside Windows 95", Adrian King, Microsoft Press, 1994.

[62] "Unauthorised Windows 95", Andrew Schulman, IDG Books, 1994.

[63] "Java Security Architecture", JDK 1.2, Sun Microsystems Corporation, 1997.

2 The Security Architecture

2.1 Security Features of the Architecture

Security-related functions that handle sensitive data pervade the architecture, which implies that security needs to be considered in every aspect of the design and must be designed in from the start (it's very difficult to bolt on security afterwards). The standard reference on the topic [1] recommends that a security architecture have the properties listed below, with annotations explaining the approach towards meeting them used in cryptlib:

- Permission-based access: The default access/use permissions should be deny-all, with access or usage rights being made selectively available as required. Objects are only visible to the process that created them, although the default object-access setting makes it available to every thread in the process. This arises from the requirement for ease of use — having to explicitly hand an object off to another thread within the process would significantly reduce the ease of use of the architecture. For this reason, the deny-all access is made configurable by the user, with the option of making an object available throughout the process or only to one thread when it is created. If the user specifies this behaviour when the object is created, then only the creating thread can see the object unless it explicitly hands off control to another thread.

- Least privilege and isolation: Each object should operate with the least privileges possible to minimise damage due to inadvertent behaviour or malicious attack, and objects should be kept logically separate in order to reduce inadvertent or deliberate compromise of the information or capabilities that they contain. These two requirements go hand in hand since each object only has access to the minimum set of resources required to perform its task and can only use them in a carefully controlled manner. For example, if a certificate object has an encryption object attached to it, the encryption object can only be used in a manner consistent with the attributes set in the certificate object. Typically, it might be usable only for signature verification, but not for encryption or key exchange, or for the generation of a new key for the object.

- Complete mediation: Each object access is checked each time that the object is used — it's not possible to access an object without this checking since the act of mapping an object handle to the object itself is synonymous with performing the access check.

- Economy of mechanism and open design: The protection system design should be as simple as possible in order to allow it to be easily checked, tested, and trusted, and should not rely on security through obscurity. To meet this requirement, the security kernel is contained in a single module, which is divided into single-purpose functions of a dozen or so lines of code that were designed and implemented using design-by-contract principles

[2], making the kernel very amenable to testing using mechanical verifiers such as ADL [3]. This is covered in more detail in Chapters 5.

• Easy to use: In order to promote its use, the protection system should be as easy to use and transparent as possible to the user. In almost all cases, the user isn't even aware of the presence of the security functionality, since the programming interface can be set up to function in a manner that is almost indistinguishable from the conventional collection-of-functions interface.

A final requirement is separation of privilege, in which access to an object depends on more than one item such as a token and a password or encryption key. This is somewhat specific to user access to a computer system or objects on a computer system and doesn't really apply to an encryption architecture.

The architecture employs a security kernel to implement its security mechanisms. This kernel provides the interface between the outside world and the architecture's objects (intra-object security) and between the objects themselves (inter-object security). The security-related functions are contained in the security kernel for the following reasons [4]:

• Separation: By isolating the security mechanisms from the rest of the implementation, it is easier to protect them from manipulation or penetration.

• Unity: All security functions are performed by a single code module.

• Modifiability: Changes to the security mechanism are easier to make and test.

• Compactness: Because it performs only security-related functions, the security kernel is likely to be small.

• Coverage: Every access to a protected object is checked by the kernel.

The details involved in meeting these requirements are covered in this and the following chapters.

2.1.1 Security Architecture Design Goals

Just as the software architecture is based on a number of design goals, so the security architecture, in particular the cryptlib security kernel, is also built on top of a number of specific principles. These are:

• Separation of policy and mechanism. The policy component deals with context-specific decisions about objects and requires detailed knowledge about the semantics of each object type. The mechanism deals with the implementation and execution of an algorithm to enforce the policy. The exact context and interpretation are supplied externally by the policy component. In particular it is important that the policy not be hardcoded into the enforcement mechanism, as is the case for a number of Orange Book-based systems. The advantage of this form of separation is that it then becomes possible to change the policy to suit individual applications (an example of which is given in the next chapter) without requiring the re-evaluation of the entire system.

• Verifiable design. It should be possible to apply formal verification techniques to the security-critical portion of the architecture (the security kernel) in order to provide a high degree of confidence that the security measures are implemented as intended (this is a standard Orange Book requirement for security kernels, although rarely achieved). Furthermore, it should be possible to perform this verification all the way down to the running code (this has never been achieved, for reasons covered in a Chapter 4).

- Flexible security policy. The fact that the Orange Book policy was hardcoded into the implementation has already been mentioned. A related problem was the fact that security policies and mechanisms were defined in terms of a fixed hierarchy that led users who wanted somewhat more flexibility to try to apply the Orange Book as a Chinese menu in which they could choose one feature from column A and two from column B [5]. Since not all users require the same policy, it should be relatively easy to adapt policy details to user-specific requirements without either a great deal of effort on the part of the user or a need to re-evaluate the entire system whenever a minor policy change is made.

- Efficient implementation. A standard lament about security kernels built during the 1980s was that they provided abysmal performance. It should therefore be a primary design goal for the architecture that the kernel provide a high level of performance, to the extent that the user isn't even aware of the presence of the kernel.

- Simplicity. A simple design is required indirectly by the Orange Book in the guise of minimising the trusted computing base. Most kernels, however, end up being relatively complex, although still simpler than mainstream OS kernels, because of the necessity to implement a full range of operating system services. Because cryptlib doesn't require such an extensive range of services, it should be possible to implement an extremely simple, efficient, and easy-to-verify kernel design. In particular, the decision logic implementing the system's mandatory security policy should be encapsulated in the smallest and simplest possible number of system elements.

This chapter covers the security-relevant portions of the design, with later chapters covering implementation details and the manner in which the design and implementation are made verifiable.

2.2 Introduction to Security Mechanisms

The cryptlib security architecture is built on top of a number of standard security mechanisms that have evolved over the last three decades. This section contains an overview of some of the more common ones, and the sections that follow discuss the details of how these security mechanisms are employed as well as detailing some of the more specialised mechanisms that are required for cryptlib's security.

2.2.1 Access Control

Access control mechanisms are usually viewed in terms of an access control matrix [6] which lists active subjects (typically users of a computer system) in the rows of the matrix and passive objects (typically files and other system resources) in the columns as shown in Figure

2.1. Because storing the entire matrix would consume far too much space once any realistic quantity of subjects or objects is present, real systems use either the rows or the columns of the matrix for access control decisions. Systems that use a row-based implementation work by attaching a list of accessible objects to the subject, typically implemented using capabilities. Systems that use a column-based implementation work by attaching a list of subjects allowed access to the object, typically implemented using access control lists (ACLs) or protection bits, a cut-down form of ACLs [7].

	Object1	Object2	Object3	
Subject1	Read/Write	Read	Execute	Capability
Subject2		Read	Execute	
Subject3	Read	Read		
		ACL		

Figure 2.1. Access control matrix.

Capability-based systems issue capabilities or tickets to subjects that contain access rights such as read, write, or execute and that the subject uses to demonstrate their right to access an object. Passwords are a somewhat crude form of capability that give up the fine-grained control provided by true capabilities in order to avoid requiring the user to remember and provide a different password for each object for which access is required. Capabilities have the property that they can be easily passed on to other subjects, and can limit the number of accessible objects to the minimum required to perform a specific task. For example, a ticket could be issued that allowed a subject to access only the objects needed for the particular task at hand, but no more. The ease of transmission of capabilities can be an advantage but is also a disadvantage because the ability to pass them on cannot be easily controlled. This leads to a requirement that subjects maintain very careful control over any capabilities that they possess, and makes revocation and access review (the ability to audit who has the ability to do what) extremely tricky.

ACL-based systems allow any subject to be allowed or disallowed access to a particular object. Just as passwords are a crude form of capabilities, so protection bits are a crude form of ACLs that are easier to implement but have the disadvantage that allowing or denying access to an object on a single-subject basis is difficult or impossible. For the most commonly encountered implementation, Unix access control bits, single-subject control works only for the owner of the object, but not for arbitrary collections of subjects. Although groups of subjects have been proposed as a partial solution to this problem, the combinatorics of this solution make it rather unworkable, and they exhibit a single-group analog of the single-subject problem.

A variation of the access-control-based view of security is the information-flow-based view, which assigns security levels to objects and only allows information to flow to a destination object of an equal or higher security level than that of the source object [8]. This concept is the basis for the rules in the Orange Book, discussed in more detail below. In addition there exist a number of hybrid mechanisms that combine some of the best features of capabilities and ACLs, or that try to work around the shortcomings of one of the two. Some of the approaches include using the cached result of an ACL lookup as a capability [9], providing per-object exception lists that allow capabilities to be revoked [10], using subject restriction lists (SRLs) that apply to the subject rather than ACLs that apply to the object [11], or extending the scope of one of the two approaches to incorporate portions of the other approach [12][13].

2.2.2 Reference Monitors

A reference monitor is the mechanism used to control access by a set of subjects to a set of objects as depicted in Figure 2.2. The monitor is the subsystem that is charged with checking the legitimacy of a subject's attempts to access objects, and represents the abstraction for the control over the relationships between subjects and objects. It should have the properties of being tamper-proof, always invoked, and simple enough to be open to a security analysis [14]. A reference monitor implements the "mechanism" part of the "separation of policy and mechanism" requirement.

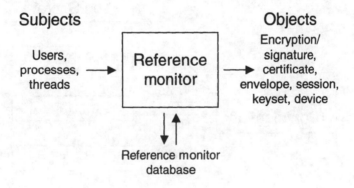

Figure 2.2. Reference monitor.

2.2.3 Security Policies and Models

The security policy of a system is a statement of the restrictions on access to objects and/or information transfer that a reference monitor is intended to enforce, or more generally any formal statement of a system's confidentiality, availability, or integrity requirements. The security policy implements the "policy" part of the "separation of policy and mechanism" requirement.

The first widely accepted formal security model, the Bell–LaPadula model [15], attempted to codify standard military security practices in terms of a formal computer security model. The impetus for this work can be traced back to the introduction of timeshared mainframes in the 1960s, leading to situations such as one where a large defence contractor wanted to sell time on a mainframe used in a classified aircraft project to commercial users [16].

The Bell–LaPadula model requires a reference monitor that enforces two security properties, the Simple Security Property and the *-Property (pronounced "star-property"[1] [17]) using an access control matrix as the reference monitor database. The model assigns a fixed security level to each subject and object and only allows read access to an object if the subject's security level is greater than or equal to the object's security level (the simple security property, "no read up") and only allows write access to an object if the subject's security level is less than or equal to that of the object's security level (the *-property, "no write down"). The effect of the simple security property is to prevent a subject with a low security level from reading an object with a high security level (for example, a user cleared for Secret data to read a Top Secret file). The effect of the *-property is to prevent a subject with a high security level from writing to an object with a low security level (for example, a user writing Top Secret data to a file readable by someone cleared at Secret, which would allow the simple security property to be bypassed). An example of how this process would work for a user cleared at Confidential is shown in Figure 2.3.

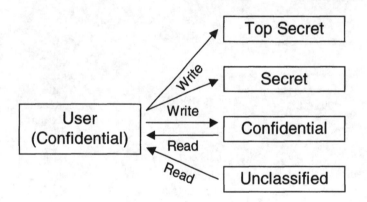

Figure 2.3. Bell–LaPadula model in operation.

The intent of the Bell–LaPadula model beyond the obvious one of enforcing multilevel security (MLS) controls was to address the confinement problem [18], which required preventing the damage that could be caused by trojan horse software that could transmit sensitive information owned by a legitimate user to an unauthorised outsider. In the original threat model (which was based on multiuser mainframe systems), this involved mechanisms such as writing sensitive data to a location where the outsider could access it. In a commonly

---

[1] When the model was initially being documented, no-one could think of a name so "*" was used as a placeholder to allow an editor to quickly find and replace any occurrences with whatever name was eventually chosen. No name was ever chosen, so the report was published with the "*" intact.

encountered more recent threat model, the same goal is achieved by using Outlook Express to send it over the Internet. Other, more obscure approaches were the use of timing or covert channels, in which an insider modulates certain aspects of a system's performance such as its paging rate to communicate information to an outsider.

The goals of the Bell–LaPadula model were formalised in the Orange Book (more formally the Department of Defense Trusted Computer System Evaluation Criteria or TCSEC [19][20][21][22]), which also added a number of other requirements and various levels of conformance and evaluation testing for implementations. A modification to the roles of the simple security and *- properties produced the Biba integrity model, in which a subject is allowed to write to an object of equal or lower integrity level and read from an object of equal or higher integrity level [23]. This model (although it reverses the way in which the two properties work) has the effect on integrity that the Bell–LaPadula version had on confidentiality. In fact the Bell–LaPadula *-property actually has a negative effect on integrity since it leads to blind writes in which the results of a write operation cannot be observed when the object is at a higher level than the subject [24]. A Biba-style mandatory integrity policy suffers from the problem that most system administrators have little familiarity with its use, and there is little documented experience on applying it in practice (although the experience that exists indicates that it, along with a number of other integrity policies, is awkward to manage) [25][26].

2.2.4 Security Models after Bell–LaPadula

After the Orange Book was introduced the so-called military security policy that it implemented was criticised as being unsuited for commercial applications which were often more concerned with integrity (the prevention of unauthorised data modification) than confidentiality (the prevention of unauthorised disclosure) — businesses equate trustworthiness with signing authority, not security clearances. One of the principal reactions to this was the Clark–Wilson model, whose primary target was integrity rather than confidentiality (this follows standard accounting practice — Wilson was an accountant). Instead of subjects and objects, this model works with constrained data items (CDIs), which are processed by two types of procedures: transformation procedures (TPs) and integrity verification procedures (IVPs). The TP transforms the set of CDIs from one valid state to another, and the IVP checks that all CDIs conform to the system's integrity policy [27]. The Clark–Wilson model has close parallels in the transaction-processing concept of ACID properties [28][29][30] and is applied by using the IVP to enforce the precondition that a CDI is in a valid state and then using a TP to transition it, with the postcondition that the resulting state is also valid.

Another commercial policy that was targeted at integrity rather than confidentiality protection was Lipner's use of lattice-based controls to enforce the standard industry practice of separating production and development environments, with controlled promotion of programs from development to production and controls over the activities of systems programmers [31]. This type of policy was mostly just a formalisation of existing practice, although it was shown that it was possible to shoehorn the approach into a system that followed a standard MLS policy. Most other models were eventually subject to the same reinterpretation since during the 1980s and early 1990s it was a requirement that any new security model be shown to eventually map to Bell–LaPadula in some manner (usually via a lattice-based model, the ultimate expression of which was the Universal Lattice Machine or ULM [32]) in the same way that the US island-hopping campaign in WWII showed that you could get to Tokyo from anywhere in the Pacific if you were prepared to jump over enough islands on the way[2]. More recently, mapping via lattice models has been used to get to role-based access controls (RBAC) [33][34].

Another proposed commercial policy is the Chinese Wall security policy [35][36] (with accompanying lattice interpretation [37][38]), which is derived from standard financial institution practice and is designed to ensure that objects owned by subjects with conflicting interests are never accessible by subjects from a conflicting interest group. In the real world, this policy is used to prevent problems such as insider trading from occurring. The Chinese Wall policy groups objects into conflict-of-interest classes (that is, classes containing object groups for which there is a conflict of interest between the groups) and requires that subjects with access to a group of objects in a particular conflict-of-interest class cannot access any other group of objects in that class, although they can access objects in a different conflict-of-interest class. Initially, subjects have access to all objects in the conflict-of-interest class, but once they commit to one particular object, access to any other object in the class is denied to them.

In real-world terms, a market analyst might be allowed to work with Oil Company A (from the "Oil Company" conflict-of-interest class) and Bank B (from the "Bank" conflict-of-interest class), but not Oil Company B, since this would conflict with Oil Company A from the same class. A later modification made the conflict-of-interest relations somewhat more dynamic to correct the problem that a subject obtains write access mostly during early stages of the system and this access is restricted to only one object even if the conflict is later removed, for example through the formerly restricted information becoming public. This modification also proposed building multiple Chinese walls to prevent indirect information flows when multiple subjects interact with multiple objects; for example, a subject with access to Bank A and Oil Company A might expose information about Bank A to a subject with access to Bank B and Oil Company A [39].

These basic models were intended to be used as general-purpose models and policies, applicable to all situations for which they were appropriate. Like other flexible objects such as rubber screwdrivers and foam rubber cricket bats, they give up some utility and practicality in exchange for their flexibility, and in practice tend to be extremely difficult to work with. The implementation problems associated in particular with the Bell–LaPadula/Orange Book model, with which implementers have the most experience, are covered in Chapter 4, and newer efforts such as the Common Criteria (CC) have taken this flexibility-at-any-cost

---

[2] Readers with too much spare time on their hands may want to try constructing a security model that requires two passes through (different views of) the lattice before arriving at Bell-LaPadula.

approach to a whole new level so that a vendor can do practically anything and still claim enough CC compliance to assuage the customer [40][3].

Another problem that occurs with information-flow-based models used to implement MLS policies is that information tends to flow up to the highest security level (a problem known as over-classification [41]), from which it is prevented from returning by the mandatory security policy. Examples of the types of problems that this causes include users having to maintain multiple copies of the same data at different classification levels since once it is contaminated through access at level m it cannot be moved back down to level n, the presence of inadvertent and annoying write-downs arising from the creation of temporary files and the like (MLS Unix systems try to get around this with multiple virtual /tmp directories, but this doesn't really solve the problem for programs that attempt to write data to the user's home directory or a custom location specified in the TMPDIR variable), problems with email where a user logged in at level m isn't even made aware of the presence of email at level n (when logged in at a low level, a user can't see messages at high levels, and when logged in at a high level they can see messages at low levels but can't reply to them), and so on [42].

Although there have been some theoretical approaches made towards mitigating these problems [43] as well as practical suggestions such as the use of floating labels that record real versus effective security levels of objects and the data they contain [44] (at the expense of introducing potential covert channels [45]), the standard solution is to resort to the use of trusted processes (pronounced "kludges"), technically a means of providing specialised policies outside the reach of kernel controls but in practice "a rug under which all problems not easily solved are swept" [46]. Examples of such trusted functions include an ability to violate the *-property in the SIGMA messaging system to allow users to downgrade over-classified messages (or portions of messages) without having to manually retype them at a lower classification level (leading to users leaking data down to lower classification levels because they didn't understand the policy being applied) [47][48], the ability for the user to act as if simultaneously at multiple security levels under Multics in order to avoid having to log out at level m and in again at level n whenever they needed to effect a change in level (a solution which was also adopted later in GEMSOS [49]), and the use of non-kernel security-related (NKSR) functions in KSOS and downgrading functions in the Guard message filter to allow violation of the *-property so that functions such as printing could work [50]. cryptlib contains a single such mechanism, which is required in order to exchange session keys and to save keys held in encryption action objects (which are normally inaccessible) to persistent storage. This mechanism and an explanation of its security model are covered in Section 2.7.

Even systems with discretionary rather than mandatory access controls don't solve this problem in a truly satisfactory manner. For example Unix, the best-known DAC system, assigns default access modes for files on a per-session basis, via the umask shell variable. The result is applied uniformly to all files created by the user, who is unlikely to remember to change the setting as they move from working with public files to private files and back.

---

[3] One of the problems with the CC is that it's so vague — it even has a built-in metalanguage to help users try and describe what they are trying to achieve — that it is difficult to make any precise statement about it, which is why it isn't mentioned in this work except to say that everything presented herein is bound to be compliant with some protection profile or other.

Other systems such as Multics and VMS (and its derivative Windows NT) mitigate the problem to some extent by setting permissions on a per-directory basis, but even this doesn't solve the problem entirely.

Alongside the general-purpose models outlined above and various other models derived from them [51][52][53][54], there are a number of application-specific models and adaptations that do not have the full generality of the previous models but in exchange offer a greatly reduced amount of implementation difficulty and complexity. Many of these adaptations came about because it was recognised that an attempt to create a one-size-fits-all model based on a particular doctrine such as mandatory secrecy controls didn't really work in practice. Systems built along such a model ended up being both inflexible (hardcoding in a particular policy made it impossible to adapt the system to changing requirements) and unrealistic (it was very difficult to try to integrate diverse and often contradictory real-world policies to fit in with whatever policy was being used in the system at hand). As a result, more recent work has looked at creating blended security models or ones that incorporate more flexible, multi-policy mechanisms that allow the mixing and matching of features taken from a number of different models [55][56]. These multipolicy mechanisms might allow the mixing of mandatory and discretionary controls, Bell–LaPadula, Clark–Wilson, Chinese Wall, and other models, with a means of changing the policies to match changing real-world requirements when required. The cryptlib kernel implements a flexible policy of this nature through its kernel filter mechanisms, which are explained in more detail in the next chapter.

The entire collection of hardware, firmware, and software protection mechanisms within a computer system that is responsible for enforcing security policy is known as the trusted computing base or TCB. In order to obtain the required degree of confidence in the security of the TCB, it needs to be made compact and simple enough for its security properties to be readily verified, which provides the motivation for the use of a security kernel, as discussed in the next section.

2.2.5 Security Kernels and the Separation Kernel

Having covered security policies and mechanisms, we need to take a closer look at how the mechanism is to be implemented, and examine the most appropriate combination of policy and mechanism for our purposes. The practical expression of the abstract concept of the reference monitor is the security kernel, the motivation for use of which is the desire to isolate all security functionality, with all critical components in a single place that can then be subject to analysis and verification. Since all non-kernel software is irrelevant to security, the immense task of verifying and securing an entire system is reduced to that of securing only the kernel [57]. The kernel provides the property that it "enforces security on the system as a whole without requiring the rest of the system to cooperate towards that end" [58].

The particular kernel type used in cryptlib is the separation kernel in which all objects are isolated from one another. This can be viewed as a variant of the noninterference requirement, which in its original form was intended for use with MLS systems and stipulated that high-level user input could not interfere with low-level user output [59] but in this case requires that no input or output interfere with any other input or output.

The principles embodied in the separation kernel date back to the early 1960s with the concept of decomposable systems, where the components of the system have no direct interactions or only interact with similar components [60]. A decomposable system can be decomposed into two smaller systems with non-interacting components, which can in turn be recursively decomposed into smaller and smaller systems until they cannot be decomposed any further. The separation kernel itself was first formalised in 1981 (possibly by more than one author [46]) with the realisation that secure systems could be modelled as a collection of individual distributed systems (in other words, a completely decomposed system) in which security is achieved through the separation of the individual components, with mediation performed by a trusted component. The separation kernel allows such a virtually distributed system to be run within a single physical system and provides the ability to compose a single secure system from individual modules that do not necessarily need to be as secure as the system as a whole [61][62]. Separation kernels are also known as separation machines or virtual machine monitors [63][64][65]. Following the practice already mentioned earlier, the separation kernel policy was mapped to the Bell–LaPadula model in 1991 [63].

The fundamental axiom of the separation kernel's security policy is the isolation policy, in which a subject can only access objects that it owns. There is no inherent concept of information sharing or security levels, which greatly simplifies many implementation details. In Orange Book terms, the separation kernel implements a number of virtual machines equal to the number of subjects, running at system high. The separation kernel ensures that there is no communication between subjects by means of shared system objects (communications may, if necessary, be established using normal communications mechanisms, but not security-relevant functions). In this model, each object is labelled with the identity of the subject that owns it (in the original work on the subject, these identifying attributes were presented as colours) with the only check that needs to be applied to it being a comparison for equality rather than the complex ordering required in Bell–LaPadula and other models.

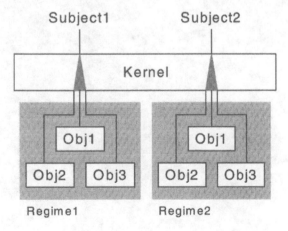

Figure 2.4. Separation kernel.

An example of a separation kernel is shown in Figure 2.4, in which the kernel is controlling two groups of objects (referred to as regimes in the original work) owned by two different subjects. The effect of the separation kernel is that the two subjects cannot distinguish the shared environment (the concrete machine) from two physically separated ones with their resources dedicated to the subject (the abstract machines). The required security property for a separation kernel is that each regime's view of the concrete machine should correspond to the abstract machine, which leads to the concept of a proof of separability for separation kernels: If all communications channels between the components of a system are cut then the components of a system will become completely isolated from one another. In the original work, which assumed the use of shared objects for communication, this required a fair amount of analysis and an even longer formal proof [66], but the analysis in cryptlib's case is much simpler. Recall from the previous chapter that all interobject communication is handled by the kernel, which uses its built-in routing capabilities to route messages to classes of objects and individual objects. In order to cut the communications channels, all we need to do is disable routing either to an entire object class (for example, encryption action objects) or an individual object, which can be implemented through a trivial modification to the routing function. In this manner, the complex data-flow analysis required by the original method is reduced to a single modification, namely removing the appropriate routing information from the routing table used by the kernel routing code.

An early real-life implementation of the separation kernel concept is shown in Figure 2.5. This configuration connects multiple untrusted workstations through a LAN, with communications mediated by trusted network interface units (TNIUs) that perform the function of the separation kernel. In order to protect communications between TNIUs, all data sent over the LAN is encrypted and MACd by the TNIUs. The assumption made with this configuration is that the workstations are untrusted and potentially insecure, so that security is enforced by using the TNIUs to perform trusted mediation of all communication between the systems.

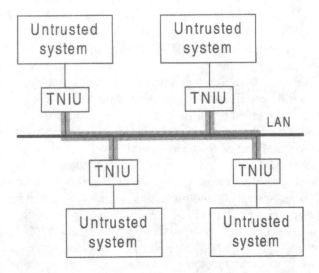

Figure 2.5. Separation kernel implemented using interconnected workstations.

The advantage of a separation kernel is that complete isolation is much easier to attain and assure than the controlled sharing required by kernels based on models such as Bell–LaPadula, and that it provides a strong foundation upon which further application-specific security policies can be constructed. The reason for this, as pointed out in the work that introduced the separation kernel, is that "a lot of security problems just vanish and others are considerably simplified" [61]. Another advantage of the separation model over the Bell–LaPadula one is that it appears to provide a more rigorous security model with an accompanying formal proof of security [66], while some doubts have been raised over some of the assumptions made in, and the theoretical underpinnings of, the Bell–LaPadula model [67][68].

2.2.6 The Generalised TCB

The concept of the separation kernel has been extended into that of a generalised trusted computing base (GTCB), defined as a system structured as a collection of protection domains managed by a separation kernel [69]. In the most extreme form of the GTCB, separation can be enforced through dedicated hardware, typically by implementing the separation kernel using a dedicated processor. This is the approach that is used in the LOCK machine (LOgical Coprocessor Kernel), formerly known as the Secure Ada Target or SAT, before that the Provably Secure Operating System or PSOS, and after LOCK the Secure Network Server or SNS and Standard Mail Guard or SMG. As the naming indicates, this project sheds its skin every few years in order to obtain funding for the "new" project. Even in its original PSOS incarnation it was clearly a long-term work, for after seven years of effort and the creation of a 400-page formal specification it was described by its creators as a "potentially secure operating system […] it might some day have both its design and its implementation subject to rigorous proof" [70].

The LOCK design uses a special SIDEARM (System Independent Domain Enforcing Assured Reference Monitor) coprocessor, which for performance reasons may consist of more than one physical CPU, which plugs into the system backplane to adjudicate access between the system CPU and memory [71][72]. Although originally used for performance reasons, this approach also provides a high level of security since all access control decisions are made by dedicated hardware that is inaccessible to any other code running on the system. However, after LOCK was moved from Honeywell Level 6 minicomputers to 68000-based systems around 1990, SIDEARM moved from access enforcement to a purely decision-making role, since its earlier incarnation relied on the Level 6's use of attached processors that administered memory mapping and protection facilities, a capability not present on the 68000 system. An approach similar to SIDEARM was used in the M^2S machine, which used a 68010 processor to perform access mediation for the main 68020 processor [73], the MUTABOR (Mapping Unit for The Access By Object References) approach which used semi-custom Weitek processors to mediate memory accesses by acting as a coprocessor in a 68020 system [74][75], and the use of Transputers to mediate access to "active memory" modules [76].

This type of implementation can be particularly appropriate in security-critical situations where the hardware in the host system is not completely trusted. In practice, this situation occurs (once a fine enough microscope is applied) with almost all systems and is exacerbated by the fact that, whereas the software that comprises a trusted system is subject to varying levels of scrutiny, the hardware is generally treated as a black box, usually because there is no alternative available (the very few attempts to build formally verified hardware have only succeeded in demonstrating that this approach isn't really feasible [77][78][79][80]). Whereas in the 1970s and 1980s trusted systems, both hardware and software, were typically built by one company and could be evaluated as part of the overall system evaluation process, by the 1990s companies had moved to using commodity hardware, usually 80x86 architecture processors, while retaining the 1970s assumption that the hardware was implicitly safe. As a result, anyone who can exploit one of the known security-relevant problem areas on a given CPU, take advantage of a bug in a particular CPU family, or even discover a new flaw, could compromise an otherwise secure software design [81].

An example of this type of problem is the so-called unreal mode, in which a task running in real mode on an Intel CPU can address the entire 4 GB address space even though it should only be able to see 1 MB + 64 kB (the extra 64 kB is due to another slight anomaly in the way addressing is handled that was initially present as an 80286 quirk used to obtain another 64 kB of memory under DOS and is now perpetuated for backwards-compatibility) [82]. Unreal mode became so widely used after its initial discovery on the 80386 that Intel was forced to support it in all later processors, although its presence was never documented. Potential alternative avenues for exploits include the use of the undocumented ICEBP (in-circuit emulation breakpoint) instruction to drop the CPU into the little-documented ICE mode, from which the system again looks like a 4 GB DOS box, or the use of the somewhat less undocumented system management mode (SMM). These could be used to initialise the CPU into an otherwise illegal state; for example, one that allows such oddities as a program running in virtual x86 mode in ring 0 [83]. This kind of trickery is possible because, when the CPU reloads the saved system state to move back into normal execution mode, it doesn't perform any checks on the saved state, allowing the loading of otherwise illegal values.

Although no exploits using these types of tricks and other, similar ones are currently known, this is probably mostly due to their obscurity and the lack of motivation for anyone to misuse them given that far easier attacks are possible. Once appropriate motivation is present, the effects of a compromise can be devastating. For example the QNX operating system for years used its own (very weak) password encryption algorithm rather than the standard Unix one, but because of its use in embedded devices there was little motivation for anyone to determine how it worked or to try to attack it. Then, in 2000, a vendor introduced a $99 Internet terminal that ran a browser/mailer/news reader on top of QNX on embedded PC hardware. The security of the previously safely obscure OS was suddenly exposed to the scrutiny of an army of hackers attracted by the promise of a $99 general-purpose PC. Within short order, the password encryption was broken [84][85], allowing the terminals to be sidegraded to functionality never intended by the original manufacturer [86][87][88][89][90]. Although the *intent* of the exercise was to obtain a cheap PC, the (entirely unintentional) *effect* was to compromise the security of every embedded QNX device ever shipped. There is no guarantee that similar motivation won't one day lead to the appearance of an equally devastating attack on obscure x86 processor features.

By moving the hardware that implements the kernel out of reach of any user code, the ability of malicious users to subvert the security of the system by taking advantage of particular features of the underlying hardware is eliminated, since no user code can ever run on the hardware that performs the security functions. With a kernel whose interaction with the outside world consists entirely of message passing (that is, one that doesn't have to manage system resources such as disks, memory pages, I/O devices, and other complications), such complete isolation of the security kernel is indeed possible.

2.2.7 Implementation Complexity Issues

When building a secure system for cryptographic use, there are two possible approaches that can be taken. The first is to build (or buy) a general-purpose kernel-based secure operating system and run the crypto code on top of it, and the second is to build a special-purpose kernel that is designed to provide security features that are appropriate specifically for cryptographic applications. Building the crypto code on top of an existing system is explicitly addressed by FIPS 140 [91], the one standard that specifically targets crypto modules. This requires that, where the crypto module is run on top of an operating system that is used to isolate the crypto code from other code, it be evaluated at progressively higher Orange Book (later Common Criteria) levels for each FIPS 140 level, so that security level 2 would require the software module to be implemented on a C2-rated operating system (or its CC equivalent). This provides something of an impedance mismatch between the actual security of equivalent hardware and software crypto module implementations. It's possible that these security levels were set so low out of concern that setting them any higher would make it impossible to implement the higher FIPS 140 levels in software due to a lack of systems evaluated at that level. For example, trying to source a B2 or more realistically a B3 system to provide an adequate level of security for the crypto software is almost impossible (the practicality of employing an OS in this class, whose members include Trusted Xenix, XTS 300, and Multos, speaks for itself).

Another work that examines crypto software modules also recognises the need to protect the software through some form of security-kernel-based mechanism, but views implementation in terms of a device driver protected by an existing operating system kernel. The suggested approach is to modify an existing kernel to provide cryptographic support [92].

Two decades of experience in building high-assurance secure systems have conclusively shown that an approach that is based on the use of an application-specific rather than general-purpose kernel is the preferred one. For example, in one survey of secure systems carried out during the initial burst of enthusiasm for the technology, most of the projects discussed were special-purpose filter or guard systems, and for the remaining general-purpose systems a recurring comment is of poor performance, occasional security problems, and frequent mentions of verification being left incomplete because it was too difficult (although this occurs for some of the special-purpose systems as well, and is covered in more detail in Chapter 4) [93]. Although some implementers did struggle with the problem of kernel size and try to keep things as simple as possible (one paper predicted that "the KSOS, SCOMP, and KVM kernels will look enormous compared to our kernel" [94]), attempts to build general-purpose secure OS kernels appear to have foundered, leaving application-specific and special-purpose kernels as the best prospects for successful implementation.

One of the motivations for the original separation kernel design was the observation that other kernel design efforts at the time were targeted towards producing MLS operating systems on general-purpose hardware, whereas many applications that required a secure system would be adequately served by a (much easier to implement) special-purpose, single-function system. One of the features of such a single-purpose system is that its requirements are usually very different from those of a general-purpose MLS one. In real-world kernels, many processes require extra privileges in order to perform their work, which is impeded by the MLS controls enforced by the kernel. Examples of these extra processes include print spoolers, backup software, networking software, and assorted other programs and processes involved in the day-to-day running of the system. The result of this accumulation of extra processes is that the kernel is no longer the sole arbiter of security, so that all of the extra bits and pieces that have been added to the TCB now also have to be subject to the analysis and verification processes. The need for these extra trusted processes has been characterised as "a mismatch between the idealisations of the MLS policy and the practical needs of a real user environment" [95].

An application-specific system, in contrast, has no need for any of the plethora of trusted hangers-on that are required by a more general-purpose system, since it performs only a single task that requires no further help from other programs or processes. An example of such a system is the NRL Pump, whose function is to move data between systems of different security levels under control of a human administrator, in effect transforming multiple single-level secure systems into a virtual MLS system without the pain involved in actually building an MLS system. Communication with the pump is via non-security-critical wrappers on the high and low systems, and the sole function of the pump itself is that of a secure one-way communications channel that minimises any direct or indirect communications from the high system to the low system [96][97]. Because the pump performs only a single function, the complexity of building a full Orange Book kernel is avoided, leading to a much simpler and more practical design.

Another example of a special-purpose kernel is the one used in Blacker, a communications encryption device using an A1 application-specific kernel that in effect constitutes the entire operating system and acts as a mediator for interprocess communication [98]. At a time when other, general-purpose kernels were notable mostly for their lack of performance, the Blacker kernel performed at a level where its presence was not even noticed by users when it was switched in and out of the circuit for testing purposes [99].

There is only one (known) system that uses a separation kernel in a cryptographic application, the NSA/Motorola Mathematically Analysed Separation Kernel (MASK), which is roughly contemporary with the cryptlib design and is used in the Motorola Advanced Infosec Machine (AIM) [100][101]. The MASK kernel isolates data and threads (called strands) in separate cells, with each subject seeing only its own cell. In order to reduce the potential for subliminal channels, the kernel maintains very careful control over the use of resources such as CPU time (strands are non-preemptively multitasked, in effect making them fibers rather than threads) and memory (a strand is allocated a fixed amount of memory that must be specified at compile time when it is activated), and has been carefully designed to avoid situations where a cell or strand can deplete kernel resources. Strands are activated in response to receiving messages from other strands, with message processing consisting of a one-way dispatch of an allocated segment to a destination under the control of the kernel [102]. The main concern for the use of MASK in AIM was its ability to establish separate cryptographic channels each with its own security level and cryptographic algorithm, although AIM also appears to implement a form of RPC mechanism between cells. Apart from the specification system used to build it [103], little else is known about the MASK design.

2.3 The cryptlib Security Kernel

The security kernel that implements the security functions outlined earlier is the basis of the entire architecture. All objects are accessed and controlled through it, and all object attributes are manipulated through it. The security kernel is implemented as an interface layer that sits on top of the objects, monitoring all accesses and handling all protection functions. The previous chapter presented the cryptlib kernel in terms of a message forwarding and routing mechanism that implements the distributed process software architectural model, but this only scratches the surface of its functionality: The kernel, the general role of which is shown in Figure 2.6, is a full-scale Orange Book-style security kernel that performs the security functions of the architecture as a whole.

As was mentioned earlier, the cryptlib kernel doesn't conform to the Bell–LaPadula paradigm because the types of objects that are present in the architecture don't correspond to the Bell–LaPadula notion of an object, namely a purely passive information repository. Instead, cryptlib objects combine both passive repositories and active agents represented by invocations of the object's methods. In this type of architecture information flow is represented by the flow of messages between objects, which are the sole source of both information and control flow [104].

The security kernel, the system element charged with enforcing the systemwide security policy, acts as a filter for this message flow, examining the contents of each message and allowing it to pass through to its destination (a forward information flow) or rejecting it as inappropriate and returning an error status to the sender. The replies to messages (a backwards information flow) are subject to the same scrutiny, guaranteeing the enforcement of the security contract both from the sender to the recipient and from the recipient back to the sender. The task of the kernel/message filter is to prevent illegal information flows, as well as enforcing certain other object access controls, which are covered in a Sections 2.5 and 2.6.

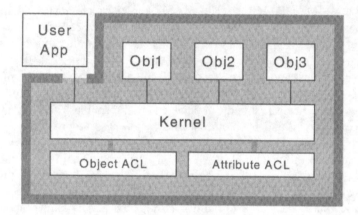

Figure 2.6. Architecture security model.

The cryptlib kernel, serving as the reference monitor for a message-based architecture, has some similarities to the Trusted Mach kernel [105][106]. In both cases objects (in the Mach case these are actually tasks) communicate by passing messages via the kernel. However, in the Mach kernel a task sends a message intended for another task to a message port for which the sender has send rights and the receiver has receive rights. The Mach kernel then checks the message and, if all is OK, moves it to the receiver's message queue, for which the receiver itself (rather than the kernel) is responsible for queue management. This system differs from the one used in cryptlib in that access control is based on send and receive rights to ports, leading to a number of complications as some message processing such as the queue management described above, that might be better handled by the kernel, is handed off to the tasks involved in the messaging. For example, port rights may be transferred between the time the message is sent and the time it is received, or the port on which the message is queued may be deallocated before the message is processed, requiring extra interactions between the tasks and the kernel to resolve the problem. In addition, the fact that Mach is a general-purpose operating system further complicates the message-passing semantics, since messages can be used to invoke other communications mechanisms such as kernel interface commands (KICs) or can be used to arrange shared memory with a child process. In the cryptlib kernel, the only interobject communications mechanism is via the kernel, with no provision for alternate command and control channels or memory sharing. Further problems with the Mach concept of basing access control decisions on port rights, and some proposed solutions, are discussed in the next chapter.

Another design feature that distinguishes the cryptlib kernel from many other kernels is that it doesn't provide any ability to run user code, which vastly simplifies its implementation and the verification process since there is no need to perform much of the complicated protection and isolation that is necessary in the presence of executable code supplied by the user. Since the user can still supply data that can affect the operation of the cryptlib code, this doesn't do away with the need for all checking or security measures, but it does greatly simplify the overall implementation.

2.3.1 Extended Security Policies and Models

In addition to the basic message-filtering-based access control mechanism, the cryptlib kernel provides a number of other security services that can't be expressed using any of the security models presented thus far. The most obvious shortcoming of the existing models is that none of them can manage the fact that some objects require a fixed ordering of accesses by subjects. For example, an encryption action object can't be used until a key and IV have been loaded, but none of the existing security models provide a means for expressing this requirement. In order to constrain the manner in which subjects can use an object, we require a means of specifying a sequence of operations that can be performed with the object, a mechanism first introduced in the form of transaction control expressions, which can be used to enforce serialisability of operations on and with an object [107][108][109]. Although the original transaction control expression model required the additional property of atomicity of operation (so that either none or all of the operations in a transaction could take effect), this property isn't appropriate for the operations performed by cryptlib and isn't used. Another approach that can be used to enforce serialisation is to incorporate simple boolean expressions into the access control model to allow the requirement for certain access sequences to be expressed [110][111] or even to build sequencing controls using finite state automata encoded in state transition tables [112][113], but again these aren't really needed in cryptlib.

Since cryptlib objects don't provide the capability for performing arbitrary operations, cryptlib can use a greatly simplified form of serialisability control that is tied into the object life cycle described in Section 2.4. This takes advantage of the fact that an object is transitioned through a number of discrete states by the kernel during its life cycle so that only operations appropriate to that state can be allowed. For example, when an encryption action object is in the "no key loaded" state, encryption is disallowed but a key load is possible, whereas an object in the "key loaded" state can be used for encryption but can't have a new key loaded over the top of the existing one. The same serialisability controls are used for other objects; for example, a certificate can have its attributes modified before it is signed but not after it is signed.

Another concept that is related to transaction control expressions is that of transaction authorisation controls, which were designed to manage the transactions that a user can perform against a database. An example of this type of control is one in which a user is authorised to run the "disburse payroll" transaction, but isn't authorised to perform an individual payroll disbursement [114]. cryptlib includes a similar form of mechanism that is applied when lower-layer objects are controlled by higher-layer ones; for example, a user might be permitted to process data through an envelope container object but wouldn't be permitted to directly access the encryption, hashing, or signature action objects that the envelope is using to perform its task. This type of control is implicit in the way the higher-level objects work and doesn't require any explicit mechanism support within cryptlib besides the standard security controls.

With the benefit of 20/20 hindsight coming from other researchers who have spent years exploring the pitfalls that inevitably accompany any security mechanism, cryptlib takes precautions to close certain security holes that can crop up in existing designs. One of the problems that needs to be addressed is the general inability of ACL-based systems to constrain the use of the privilege to grant privileges, which gives capability fans something to respond with when ACL fans criticise capability-based systems on the basis that they have problems tracking which subjects have access to a given object (that is, who holds a capability). One approach to this problem has been to subdivide ACLs into two classes, regular and restricted, and to greatly constrain the ability to manipulate restricted ACLs in order to provide greater control over the distribution of access privileges, and to provide limited privilege transfer in which the access rights that are passed to another subject are only temporary [115] (this concept of restricted and standard ACL classes was reinvented about a decade later by another group of researchers [116]). Another approach is that of owner-retained access control (ORAC) or propagated access control (PAC), which gives the owner of an object full control over it and allows the later addition or revocation of privileges that propagate through to any other subjects who have access to it, effectively making the controls discretionary for the owner and mandatory for everyone else [117][118]. This type of control is targeted specifically for intelligence use, in particular NOFORN and ORCON-type controls on dissemination, and would seem to have little other practical application, since it both requires the owner to act as the ultimate authority on access control decisions and gives the owner (or a trojan horse acting for the owner) the ability to allow anyone full access to an object.

cryptlib objects face a more general form of this problem because of their active nature, since not only access to the object but also its use needs to be controlled. For example, although there is nothing much to be gained from anyone reading the key-size attribute of a private-key object (particularly since the same information is available through the public key), it is extremely undesirable for anyone to be able to repeatedly use it to generate signatures on arbitrary data. In this case, "anyone" also includes the key owner, or at least trojan horse code acting as the owner.

In order to provide a means of controlling these problem areas, the cryptlib kernel provides a number of extra ACLs that can't be easily expressed using any existing security model. These ACLs can be used to restrict the number of times that an object can be used (for example, a signature object might be usable to generate a single signature, after which any further signature operations would be disallowed), restrict the types of operations that an object can perform (for example, an encryption action object representing a conventional encryption algorithm might be restricted to allowing only encryption or only decryption of data), provide a dead-man timer to disable the object after a given amount of time (for example, a private-key object might disable itself five minutes after it was created to protect against problems when the user is called away from their computer after activating the object but before being able to use it), and a number of other special-case circumstances. These object usage controls are rather specific to the cryptlib architecture and are relatively simple to implement since they don't require the full generality or flexibility of controls that might be needed for a general-purpose system.

2.3.2 Controls Enforced by the Kernel

As the previous sections have illustrated, the cryptlib kernel enforces a number of controls adapted from a variety of security policies, as well as introducing new application-specific ones that apply specifically to the cryptlib architecture. Table 2.1 summaries the various types of controls and their implications and benefits, alongside some more specialised controls which are covered in Sections 2.5 and 2.6.

Table 2.1. Controls and policies enforced by the cryptlib kernel.

Policy	Separation
Section	2.2.5. Security Kernels and the Separation Kernel
Type	Mandatory
Description	All objects are isolated from one another and can only communicate via the kernel.
Benefit	Simplified implementation and the ability to use a special-purpose kernel that is very amenable to verification.
Policy	No ability to run user code
Section	2.3. The cryptlib Security Kernel
Type	Mandatory
Description	cryptlib is a special-purpose architecture with no need for the ability to run user-supplied code. Users can supply data to be acted upon by objects within the architecture but cannot supply executable code.
Benefit	Vastly simplified implementation and verification.

Policy	Single-level object security
Section	2.3. The cryptlib Security Kernel
Type	Mandatory
Description	There is no information sharing between subjects so there is no need to implement an MLS system. All objects owned by a subject are at the same security level, although object attributes and usages are effectively multilevel.
Benefit	Simplified implementation and verification.
Policy	Multilevel object attribute and object usage security
Section	2.6. Object Usage Control
Type	Mandatory
Description	Objects have individual ACLs indicating how they respond to messages that affect attributes or control the use of the object from subjects or other objects.
Benefit	Separate controls are allowed for messages coming from subjects inside and outside the architecture's security perimeter, so that any potentially risky operations on objects can be denied to subjects outside the perimeter.
Policy	Serialisation of operations with objects
Section	2.3.1 Extended Security Policies and Models, 2.4. The Object Life Cycle
Type	Mandatory
Description	The kernel controls the order in which messages may be sent to objects, ensuring that certain operations are performed in the correct sequence.
Benefit	Kernel-mandated control over how objects are used, removing the need for explicit checking in each object's implementation.
Policy	Object usage controls
Section	2.3.1 Extended Security Policies and Models
Type	Mandatory/discretionary
Description	Extended control over various types of usage such as whether an object can be used for a particular purpose and how many times an object can be used before access is disabled.
Benefit	Precise user control over the object so that, for example, a signing key can only be used to generate a single signature under the direct control of the user rather than an uncontrolled number of signatures under the control of a trojan horse.

2.4 The Object Life Cycle

Each object goes through a series of distinct stages during its lifetime. Initially, the object is created in the uninitialised state by the kernel, after which it hands it off to the object-type-specific initialisation routines to perform object-specific initialisation and set any attributes that are supplied at object creation (for example, the encryption algorithm for an encryption action object or the certificate type for a certificate object). The attributes that are set at object creation time can't be changed later on. Once the kernel and object-specific initialisation are complete, the object is in the low state, in which object attributes can be read, written, or deleted but the object can't generally be used for its intended purpose. For example, in this state a conventional encryption action object can have its encryption mode and IV set, but it can't be used to encrypt data because no key is loaded.

At some point, the object receives a trigger message that causes the kernel to move it into the high state, in which access to attributes is greatly restricted but the object can be used for its intended purpose. For the aforementioned object, the trigger message would be one that loads or generates a key in the object, after which encryption with the object becomes possible but operations such as loading a new key over the top of the existing one are disallowed. The object life cycle is shown in Figure 2.7. As indicated by the arrows, the progression through these stages is strictly one-way, with the kernel ensuring that, like military security levels, the object progresses to higher and higher levels of security until it is eventually destroyed by the kernel at the end of its life. The pre-use and post-use states that exist outside the normal concept of object states have also been described as alpha and omega states, being respectively C++ objects before their constructor is called and after their destructor is called: "the object declaration before it is constructed and the carcass of an object after it has been deleted" [119].

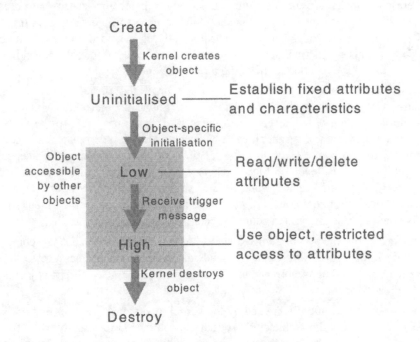

Figure 2.7. The object life cycle.

Similar life cycles occur with other objects; for example, a certificate is transitioned into the high state when it is signed by a CA key, and a session object is transitioned into the high state once a connection with a peer is established.

Although the cryptlib architecture doesn't restrict the number of states to only two (low and high), in practice only these two are used in order to avoid the combinatorial explosion of states that would occur if every change in an object's internal state were to be mapped to a cryptlib state. Even something as simple as an encryption action object could have states corresponding to various combinations of encryption mode set or not set, IV set or not set, and key loaded or not loaded, and the number of states attainable by more complex object types such as envelope or session container objects doesn't bear thinking about. For this reason objects are restricted to having only two states. Experience with cryptlib has shown that this is adequate for handling all eventualities.

2.4.1 Object Creation and Destruction

When an object is created, it is identified to the entity that requested its creation through an arbitrary handle, an integer value that has no connection to the object's data or associated code. The handle represents an entry in an internal object table that contains information such as a pointer to the object's data and ACL information for the object. The handles into the table are allocated in a pseudorandom manner not so much for security purposes but to avoid the problem of the user freeing a handle by destroying an object and then immediately having the handle reused for the next object allocated, leading to problems if some of the user's code still expects to find the previous object accessible through the handle. If the object table is full, it is expanded to make room for more entries.

Both the object table and the object data are protected through locking and ACL mechanisms. Creation of a new object proceeds as shown in Figure 2.8, which creates an object of the given type with the given attributes, adds an entry for it to the object table, marks it as under construction so that it can't be accessed in the incomplete state, and returns a pointer to the object data to the caller (the caller being code within cryptlib itself, the user never has access to this level of functionality). The object can also have a variety of attributes specified for its creation such as the type of memory used; for example, some systems can allocate limited amounts of protected, non-pageable memory, which is preferred for sensitive data such as encryption action objects.

The object is now in the uninitialised state. At this point, the caller can complete any object-specific initialisation, after which it sends an "init complete" message to the kernel, which sets the object's state to normal and returns its handle to the user. The object is now in the low state ready for use.

When the object was initially created by the kernel, it set an ACL entry that marked it as being visible only within the architecture, so that the calling routine has to explicitly make it accessible outside the architecture by changing the ACL. In other words, it defaults to deny-all rather than permit-all, a standard feature of the cryptlib security architecture. It has been observed that an additional benefit of the deny-all default is that errors in which legitimate access is refused will be reported by users much faster than errors in which unauthorised access is allowed [120].

```
caller requests object creation by kernel

lock object table;
create new object with requested type and attributes;
if( object was created successfully )
    add object to object table;
    set object state = under construction;
unlock object table;

caller completes object-specific initialisation
caller sends initialisation complete message to kernel

lock object table;
set object state = normal;
unlock object table;
```

Figure 2.8. Object creation.

An object is usually destroyed by having its reference count decremented sufficiently that it drops to zero, which causes the kernel to destroy the object. Before the object itself is destroyed, any dependent objects (for example a public-key action object attached to a certificate) also have their reference counts decremented, with the process continuing recursively until leaf objects are reached. Destruction of an object proceeds as shown in Figure 2.9, which signals any dependent objects that may be present, marks the object as being in the process of being destroyed so that it can't be accessed any more while this is in progress, sends a destroy object message to the object's message handler to allow it to perform object-specific cleanup, and finally removes the object from the kernel object table.

```
caller requests decrement of object's reference count

lock object table;
decrement reference count of any dependent objects;
set object state = being destroyed;
unlock object table;

send destroy object message to object's message handler

lock object table;
dequeue any further messages for this object;
clear entry in object table;
unlock object table;
```

Figure 2.9. Object destruction.

At this point, the object's slot in the object table is ready for reuse. As has been mentioned previously, in order to avoid problems where a newly created object would be entered into a recently-freed slot and be allocated the same handle as the previous object in that slot, leading to a potential for confusion if the user's code is not fully aware that such a replacement has taken place and that the handle now belongs to a new object, the kernel cycles through the slots to ensure that handles aren't reused for the longest time possible. This is similar to the manner in which Unix process IDs are cycled to give the longest possible time before ID reuse. An alternative approach, used in the LOCK kernel, is to encrypt the unique IDs (UIDs) that it uses, although this is motivated mainly by a need to eliminate the potential for covert channel signalling via UIDs (which isn't an issue with cryptlib) and by the ready availability of fast crypto hardware, which is an integral portion of the LOCK system.

Note that for both object creation and object destruction, the object-specific processing is performed with the object table unlocked, which ensures that if the object-specific processing takes a long time to complete or even hangs altogether, the functioning of the kernel isn't affected.

2.5 Object Access Control

Each object within the cryptlib architecture is contained entirely within its security perimeter, so that data and control information can only flow in and out in a very tightly controlled manner, and objects are isolated from each other within the perimeter by the security kernel. Associated with each object is a mandatory access control list (ACL) that determines who can access a particular object and under which conditions the access is allowed. Mandatory ACLs control features such as whether an object can be accessed externally (by the user) or only via other objects within the architecture (for example an encryption action object associated with an envelope can only be used to encrypt data by the envelope, not by the user who owns the envelope), the way in which an object can be used (for example a private key may be usable for decryption but not for signing), and so on.

A somewhat special-case ACL entry is the one that is used to determine which processes or threads can access an object. This entry is set by the object's owner either when it is created or at a later point when the security properties of the object are changed, and it provides a much finer level of control than the internal/external access ACL. Since an object can be bound to a process or a thread within a process by an ACL, it will be invisible to other processes or threads, resulting in an access error if an attempt is made to access it from another process or thread.

A typical example of this ACL's use is shown in Figure 2.10, which illustrates the case of an object created by a central server thread setting up a key in the object and then handing it off to a worker thread, which uses it to encrypt or decrypt data. This model is typical of multithreaded server processes that use a core server thread to manage initial connections and then hand further communications functions off to a collection of active threads.

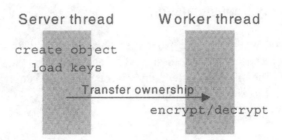

Figure 2.10. Object ownership transfer.

Operating at a much finer level of control than the object ACL is the discretionary access control (DACL) mechanism through which only certain capabilities in an object may be enabled. For example once an encryption action object is established, it can be restricted to only allow basic data encryption and decryption, but not encrypted session key export. In this way a trusted server thread can hand the action object off to a worker thread without having to worry about the worker thread exporting the session key contained within it[4]. Similarly, a signature object can have a DACL set that allows it to perform only a single signature operation before it is automatically disabled by the security kernel, closing a rather troublesome security hole in which a crypto device such as a smart card can be used to authenticate arbitrary numbers of transactions by a rogue application.

These ACLs are not true DACLs in the sense that they can't be arbitrarily changed by the owner once set. Some of the DACLs are one-shot so that once set they can't be unset, and others can be altered initially but can then be locked down using a one-shot ACL, at which point they can no longer be changed. For example, a subject can set properties such as controls on object usage as required and then lock them down so that no further changes can be made. This might be done when a keyset or device is used to instantiate a certificate object and wishes to place controls on the way it can be used before making the object accessible to the user. Since the ACLs are now mandatory, they can't be reset by the user. In this way, they somewhat resemble ORAC/PAC controls, which are discretionary for the originator and mandatory for later recipients, except that these controls become mandatory for everyone so that the originator can't later reverse restrictions again as they can with ORAC/PAC controls.

ACLs are inherited across objects so that retrieving a private key encryption object from a keyset container object will copy the container object's ACL across to the private-key encryption object.

---

[4] Obviously, chosen-plaintext and similar attacks are still possible, but this is something that can never be fully prevented, and provides an attacker far less opportunity than the presence of a straight key export facility.

2.5.1 Object Security Implementation

The actions performed when the user passes an object's handle to cryptlib are shown in Figure 2.11. This performs the necessary ACL checking for the object in an object-independent manner. The link from external handles through the kernel object table and ACL check to the object itself is shown in Figure 2.12.

```
lock object table;
verify that the handle is valid;
verify that the ACL allows this type of access;
if( access allowed )
   set object state = processing message;
   further messages will be enqueued for later processing
   unlock object table;
   forward message to object;
   lock object table;
   set object state = normal;
unlock object table;
```

Figure 2.11. Object access during message processing.

The kernel begins by performing a number of general checks such as whether the message target is a valid object, whether the message is appropriate for this object type, whether this type of access is allowed, and a variety of other checks for which more details are given in later sections and in the next chapter. It then sets a flag in the object table to indicate that the object is busy processing a message, which ensures that further messages that arrive will be enqueued. Finally, it unlocks the object table so that other messages may be processed, and forwards the message to the object. When the object has finished processing the message, the kernel resets its state so that it may process further messages. Again, there are a range of security controls applied during this process which are described later.

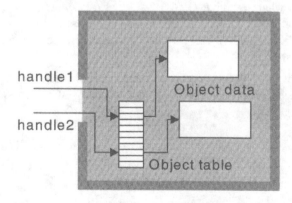

Figure 2.12. Object ACL checking.

The access check is performed each time an object is used, and the ACL used is attached to the object itself rather than to the handle. This means that if an ACL is changed, the change immediately affects all users of the object rather than just the owner of the handle that changed the ACL. This is in contrast to the Unix security model, where an access check is performed once when an object is instantiated (for example, when a file is created or opened) and the access rights that were present at that time remain valid for the lifetime of the handle to the object, and in an even more extreme case the Windows security model where some changes aren't updated until the user logs off and on again. For example, if a file is temporarily made world-readable and a user opens it, the handle remains valid for read access even if read permission to the file is subsequently removed — the security setting applies to the handle rather than to the object and can't be changed after the handle is created. In contrast, cryptlib applies its security to the object itself, so that a change in an object's ACL is immediately reflected to all users of the object. Consider the example in Figure 2.13, in which an envelope contains an encryption action object accessed either through the internal handle from the envelope or the external handle from the user. If the user changes the ACL for the encryption action object the change is immediately reflected on all users of the context, so that any future use of the context by the envelope will result in access restrictions being enforced using the new ACL.

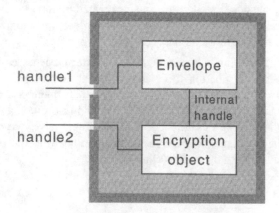

Figure 2.13. Objects with multiple references.

Each object can be accessible to multiple threads or to a single thread. The thread access ACL is handled as part of the thread locking mechanism that is used to make the architecture thread-safe, and tracks the identity of the thread that owns the object. By setting the thread access ACL, a thread can claim an un-owned object, relinquish a claim to an owned object, and transfer ownership of an object to another thread. In general, critical objects such as encryption action objects will be claimed by the thread that created them and will never be relinquished until the object is destroyed. To all other threads in the process, the object doesn't appear to exist.

2.5.2 External and Internal Object Access

cryptlib distinguishes between two types of object access: accesses from within the cryptlib security perimeter, and accesses from outside the perimeter. When an object is created, its ACLs are set so that it is only visible from within the security perimeter. This means that even if code outside the perimeter can somehow guess the object's handle and try to send a message to it, the message will be blocked by the kernel, which will report that the object doesn't exist (as far as the outside user is concerned, it doesn't, since it can't be accessed in any way).

Objects that are used by other objects (for example, a public- or private-key action object attached to a certificate, or a hash or encryption action object attached to an envelope or session object) are left in this state and can never be directly manipulated by the user, but can only be used in the carefully controlled manner permitted by the object that owns them. This is usually done by having the owning object set appropriate ACLs for the dependent object and letting the kernel enforce access controls rather than having the owning object act as an arbitrator, although in the case of very fine-grained and not particularly security-critical controls that the kernel doesn't manage, examples being the certificate expiry date and extended certificate usage such as emailProtection, the control would be handled by the owning object. Objects created directly by the user, on the other hand, have their ACLs set to allow access from the outside. In addition, objects created by internal objects but destined for use by the user (for example, public-key or certificate objects instantiated via a keyset object) also have their ACLs set to allow external access.

In addition to distinguishing between internal and external accesses to objects as a whole, cryptlib also applies this distinction to object attributes and usage. Although the objects themselves inherently exist at a single security level since there is no way for cryptlib to control data sharing among subjects so there is little need to provide an MLS mechanism for objects, the actual attributes and usage modes for the object have two distinct sets of ACLs, one for attribute manipulation and usage messages coming from the outside (the user) and one for messages coming from the inside (other objects).

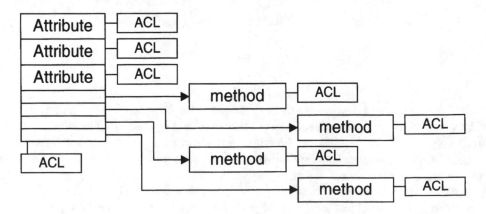

Figure 2.14. Annotated object internal structure indicating presence of ACLs.

The object ACLs can best be visualised by annotating the object internal structure diagram from the previous chapter in the manner shown in Figure 2.14, which illustrates that not only the object as a whole but each individual attribute and method (in other words, the way in which the object can be used) have their own individual ACLs. These controls, although conceptually a part of the object, are maintained and enforced entirely by the kernel, and are discussed in the following sections.

2.6 Object Usage Control

As Figure 2.14 indicates, every action that can be performed by an action object has its own ACL associated with it. The ACL defines the conditions under which the action can be performed, or more precisely the permission that the sender must have in order for the kernel to allow the corresponding message through to the object.

The default setting for an ACL is ACTION_PERM_NOTAVAIL, which indicates that this action isn't available for the object (for example, an encrypt action message for a hash action object would have an ACL set to ACTION_PERM_NOTAVAIL). This setting corresponds to an all-zero value for the ACL, so that the default initialised-to-zero value constitutes a deny-all ACL.

The next level is ACTION_PERM_NONE, which means that the action is in theory available but has been disallowed. An example of this is a private key that could normally be used for signing and decryption but which has been constrained to allow only signing, so that the decrypt action message will have an ACL setting of ACTION_PERM_NONE.

The final two levels enable the action message to be passed on to the object. The more restrictive setting is ACTION_PERM_NONE_EXTERNAL, which means that the action is only permitted if the message originates from another object within the cryptlib security perimeter. If the message comes from the outside (in other words, from the user), the result is the same as if the ACL were set to ACTION_PERM_NONE. This ACL setting is used in cases such as signature envelopes, where the envelope can send a sign data message to an attached private-key action object to sign the data that it contains but the user can't directly send the same message to the action object.

The least restrictive permission is ACTION_PERM_ALL, which means that the action is available for anyone.

The cryptlib kernel enforces a ratchet for these settings that implements the equivalent of the *-property for permissions in that it only allows them to be set to a more restrictive value than their existing one. This means that if an ACL for a particular action is currently set to ACTION_PERM_NONE_EXTERNAL, it can only be changed to ACTION_PERM_NONE, but never to ACTION_PERM_ALL. Once set to ACTION_PERM_NONE, it can never be returned to its original (less restrictive) setting.

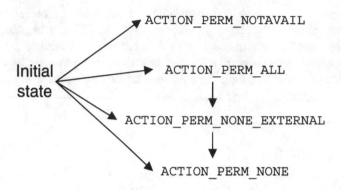

Figure 2.15. State machine for object action permissions.

The finite state machine in Figure 2.15 indicates the transitions that are allowed by the cryptlib kernel. Upon object creation, the ACLs may be set to any level, but after this the kernel-enforced *-property applies and the ACL can only be set to a more restrictive setting.

2.6.1 Permission Inheritance

The previous chapter introduced the concept of dependent objects in which one object, for example a public-key encryption action object, was tied to another, in this case a certificate. The certificate usually specifies, among various other things, constraints on the manner in which the key can be used; for example, it might only allow use for encryption or for signing or key agreement. In a conventional implementation, an explicit check for which types of usage are allowed by the certificate needs to be made before each use of the key. If the programmer forgets to make the check, gets it wrong, or never even considers the necessity of such a check (there are implementations that do all of these), the certificate is useless because it doesn't provide any guarantees about the manner in which the key is used.

The fact that cryptlib provides ACLs for all messages sent to objects means that we can remove the need for programmers to explicitly check whether the requested access or usage might be constrained in some way since the kernel can perform the check automatically as part of its reference monitor functionality. In order to do this, we need to modify the ACL for an object when another object is associated with it, a process that is again performed by the kernel. This is done by having the kernel check which way the certificate constrains the use of the action object and adjust the object's access ACL as appropriate. For example, if the certificate responded to a query of its signature capabilities with a permission denied error, then the action object's signature action ACL would be set to ACTION_PERM_NONE. From then on, any attempt to use the object to generate a signature would be automatically blocked by the kernel.

There is one special-case situation that occurs when an action object is attached to a certificate for the first time when a new certificate is being created. In this case, the object's access ACL is not updated for that one instantiation of the object because the certificate may constrain the object in a manner that makes its use impossible. Examples of instances where this can occur are when creating a self-signed encryption-only certificate (the kernel would disallow the self-signing operation) or when multiple mutually exclusive certificates are associated with a single key (the kernel would disallow any kind of usage). The semantics of both of these situations are in fact undefined, falling into one of the many black holes that X.509 leaves for implementers (self-signed certificates are generally assumed to be version 1 certificates, which don't constrain key usage, and the fact that people would issue multiple conflicting certificates for a single key was never envisaged by X.509's creators). As the next section illustrates, the fact that cryptlib implements a formal, consistent security model reveals these problems in a manner that a typical ad hoc design would never be able to do. Unfortunately in this case the fact that the real world isn't consistent or rigorously defined means that it's necessary to provide this workaround to meet the user's expectations. In cases where users are aware of these constraints, the exception can be removed and cryptlib can implement a completely consistent policy with regard to ACLs.

One additional security consideration needs to be taken into account when the ACLs are being updated. Because a key with a certificate attached indicates that it is (probably) being used for some function which involves interaction with a relying party, the access permission for allowed actions is set to ACTION_PERM_NONE_EXTERNAL rather than ACTION_-PERM_ALL. This ensures both that the object is only used in a safe manner via cryptlib internal mechanisms such as enveloping, and that it's not possible to utilise the signature/encryption duality of public-key algorithms like RSA to create a signature where it has been disallowed by the ACL. This means that if a certificate constrains a key to being usable for encryption only or for signing only, the architecture really will only allow its use for this purpose and no other. Contrast this with approaches such as PKCS #11, where controls on object usage are trivially bypassed through assorted creative uses of signature and encryption mechanisms, and in some cases even appear to be standard programming practice. By taking advantage of such weaknesses in API design and flaws in access control and object usage enforcement, it is possible to sidestep the security of a number of high-security cryptographic hardware devices [121][122].

2.6.2 The Security Controls as an Expert System

The object usage controls represent an extremely powerful means of regulating the manner in which an object can be used. Their effectiveness is illustrated by the fact that they caught an error in smart cards issued by a European government organisation that incorrectly marked a signature key stored on the cards as a decryption key. Since the accompanying certificate identified it as a signature-only key, the union of the two was a null ACL which didn't allow the key to be used for anything. This error had gone unnoticed by other implementations. In a similar case, another European certification authority (CA) marked a signature key in a smart card as being invalid for signing, which was also detected by cryptlib because of the resulting null ACL. Another CA marked its root certificate as being invalid for the purpose of issuing certificates. Other CAs have marked their keys as being invalid for any type of usage. There have been a number of other cases in which users have complained about cryptlib "breaking" their certificates; for example, one CA issued certificates under a policy that required that they be used strictly as defined by the key usage extension in the certificate, and then set a key usage that wasn't possible with the public-key algorithm used in the certificate. This does not provide a very high level of confidence about the assiduity of existing certificate processing software, which handled these certificates without noticing any problems.

The complete system of ACLs and kernel-based controls in fact extends beyond basic error-checking applications to form an expert system that can be used to answer queries about the properties of objects. Loading the knowledge base involves instantiating cryptlib objects from stored data such as certificates or keys, and querying the system involves sending in messages such as "sign this data". The system responds to the message by performing the operation if it is allowed (that is, if the key usage allows it and the key hasn't been expired via its associated certificate or revoked via a CRL and passes whatever other checks are necessary) or returning an appropriate error code if it is disallowed. Some of the decisions made by the system can be somewhat surprising in the sense that, although valid, they come as a surprise to the user, who was expecting a particular operation (for example, decryption with a key for which some combination of attributes disallowed this operation) to function but the system disallowed it. This again indicates the power of the system as a whole, since it has the ability to detect problems and inconsistencies that the humans who use it would otherwise have missed.

A variation of this approach was used in the Los Alamos Advisor, an expert system that could be queried by the user to support "what-if" security scenarios with justification for the decisions reached [123]. The Advisor was first primed by rewriting a security policy originally expressed in rather informal terms such as "Procedures for identifying and authenticating users must be addressed" in the form of more precise rules such as "IF a computer processes classified information THEN it must have identification and authentication procedures", after which it could provide advice based on the rules that it had been given. The cryptlib kernel provides a similar level of functionality, although the justification for each decision that is reached currently has to be determined by stepping through the code rather than having the kernel print out the "reasoning" steps that it applies.

2.6.3 Other Object Controls

In addition to the standard object usage access controls, the kernel can also be used to enforce a number of other controls on objects that can be used to safeguard the way in which they are used. The most critical of these is a restriction on the manner in which signing keys are used. In an unrestricted environment, a private-key object, once instantiated, could be used to sign arbitrary numbers of transactions by a trojan horse or by an unauthorised outsider who has gained access to the system while the legitimate user was away or temporarily distracted. This problem is recognised by some digital signature laws, which require a distinct authorisation action (typically the entry of a PIN) each time that a private key is used to generate a signature. Once the single signature has been generated, the key cannot be used again unless the authorisation action is performed for it.

In order to control the use of an object, the kernel can associate a usage count with it that is decremented each time the object is successfully used for an operation such as generating a signature. Once the usage count drops to zero, any further attempts to use the object are blocked by the kernel. As with the other access controls, enforcement of this mechanism is handled by decrementing the count each time that an object usage message (for example, one that results in the creation of a signature) is successfully processed by the object, and blocking any further messages that are sent to it once the usage count reaches zero.

Another type of control mechanism that can be used to safeguard the manner in which objects are used is a trusted authentication path, which is specific to hardware-based cryptlib implementations and is discussed in Chapter 7.

2.7 Protecting Objects Outside the Architecture

Section 2.2.4 commented on the fact that the cryptlib security architecture contains a single trusted process equivalent that is capable of bypassing the kernel's security controls. In cryptlib's case the "trusted process" is actually a function of half a dozen lines of code (making verification fairly trivial) that allow a key to be exported from an action object in encrypted form. Normally, the kernel will ensure that, once a key is present in an action object, it can never be retrieved; however, strict enforcement of this policy would make both key transport mechanisms that exchange an encrypted session key with another party and long-term key storage impossible. Because of this, cryptlib contains the equivalent of a trusted downgrader that allows keys to be exported from an action object under carefully controlled conditions.

Although the key export and import mechanism has been presented as a trusted downgrader (because this is the terminology that is usually applied to this type of function), in reality it acts not as a downgrader but as a transformer of the sensitivity level of the key, cryptographically enforcing both the Bell–LaPadula secrecy and Biba integrity model for the keys [124].

The key export process as viewed in terms of the Bell–LaPadula model is shown in Figure 2.16. The key, with a high sensitivity level, is encrypted with a key encryption key (KEK), reducing it to a low sensitivity level since it is now protected by the KEK. At this point, it can be moved outside the security architecture. If it needs to be used again, the encrypted form is decrypted inside the architecture, transforming it back to the high-sensitivity-level form. Since the key can only leave the architecture in a low-sensitivity form, this process is not a true downgrading process but actually a transformation that alters the form of the high-sensitivity data to ensure the data's survival in a low-sensitivity environment.

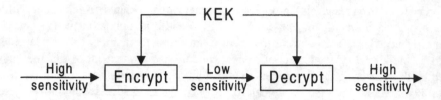

Figure 2.16. Key sensitivity-level transformation.

Although the process has been depicted as encryption of a key using a symmetric KEK, the same holds for the communication of session keys using asymmetric key transport keys.

The same process can be used to enforce the Biba integrity model using MACing, encryption, or signing to transform the data from its internal high-integrity form in a manner that is suitable for existence in the external, low-integrity environment. This process is shown in Figure 2.17.

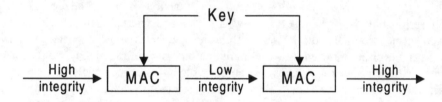

Figure 2.17. Key integrity-level transformation.

Again, although the process has been depicted in terms of MACing, it also applies for digitally signed and encrypted[5] data.

We can now look at an example of how this type of protection is applied to data when leaving the architecture's security perimeter. The example that we will use is a public key, which requires integrity protection but no confidentiality protection. To enforce the transformation required by the Biba model, we sign the public key (along with a collection of user-supplied data) to form a public-key certificate which can then be safely exported outside the architecture and exist in a low-integrity environment as shown in Figure 2.18.

---

[5] Technically speaking encryption with a KEK doesn't provide the same level of integrity protection as a MAC, however what is being encrypted with a KEK is either a symmetric session key or a private key for which an attack is easily detected when a standard key wrapping format is used.

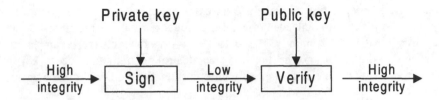

Figure 2.18. Public-key integrity-level transformation via certificate.

When the key is moved back into the architecture, its signature is verified, transforming it back into the high-integrity form for internal use.

2.7.1 Key Export Security Features

The key export operation, which allows cryptovariables to be moved outside the architecture (albeit only in encrypted form), needs to be handled especially carefully, because a flaw or failure in the process could result in plaintext keys being leaked. Because of the criticality of this operation, cryptlib takes great care to ensure that nothing can go wrong.

A standard feature of critical cryptlib operations such as encryption is that a sample of the output from the operation is compared to the input and, if they are identical, the output is zeroised rather than risk having plaintext present in the output. This means that even if a complete failure of the crypto operation occurs, with no error code being returned to indicate this, no plaintext can leak through to the output.

Because encryption keys are far more sensitive than normal data, the key-wrapping code performs its own additional checks on samples of the input data to ensure that all private-key components have been encrypted. Finally, a third level of checking is performed at the keyset level, which checks that the (supposedly) encrypted key contains no trace of structured data, which would indicate the presence of plaintext private key components. Because of these multiple, redundant levels of checking, even a complete failure of the encryption code won't result in an unprotected private key being leaked.

cryptlib takes further precautions to reduce any chance of keying material being inadvertently leaked by enforcing strict red/black separation for key handling code. Public and private keys, which have many common components, are traditionally read and written using common code, with a flag indicating whether only public, or public and private, components should be handled. Although this is convenient from an implementation point of view, it carries with it the risk that an inadvertent change in the flag's value or a coding error will result in private key components being written where the intent was to write a public key.

In order to avoid this possibility, cryptlib completely separates the code to read and write public and private keys at the highest level, with no code shared between the two. The key read/write functions are implemented as C static functions (only visible within the module in which they occur) to further reduce chances of problems, for example, due to a linker error resulting in the wrong code being linked in.

Finally, the key write functions include an extra parameter that contains an access key which is used to identify the intended effect of the function, such as a private-key write. In this way if control is inadvertently passed to the wrong function (for example, due to a compiler bug or linker error), the function can determine from the access key that the programmer's intent was to call a completely different function and disallow the operation.

2.8 Object Attribute security

The discussion of security features has thus far concentrated on object security features; however, the same security mechanisms are also applied to object attributes. An object attribute is a property belonging to an object or a class of objects; for example, encryption, signature, and MAC action objects have a key attribute associated with them, certificate objects have various validity period attributes associated with them, and device objects typically have some form of PIN attribute associated with them.

Just like objects, each attribute has an ACL that specifies how it can be used and applied, with ACL enforcement being handled by the security kernel. For example, the ACL for a key attribute for a triple DES encryption action object would have the entries shown in Figure 2.19. In this case, the ACL requires that the attribute value be exactly 192 bits long (the size of a three-key triple DES key), and it will only allow it to be written once (in other words, once a key is loaded it can't be overwritten, and can never be read). The kernel checks all data flowing in and out against the appropriate ACL, so that not only data flowing from the user into the architecture (for example, identification and authentication information) but also the limited amount of data allowed to flow from the architecture to the user (for example, status information) is carefully monitored by the kernel. The exact details of attribute ACLs are given in the next chapter.

```
attribute label = CRYPT_CTXINFO_KEY
type = octet string
permissions = write-once
size = 192 bits minimum, 192 bits maximum
```

Figure 2.19: Triple DES key attribute ACL.

Ensuring that external software can't bypass the kernel's ACL checking requires very careful design of the I/O mechanisms to ensure that no access to architecture-internal data is ever possible. Consider the fairly typical situation in which an encrypted private key is read from disk by an application, decrypted using a user-supplied password, and used to sign or decrypt data. Using techniques such as patching the systemwide vectors for file I/O routines (which are world-writeable under Windows NT) or debugging facilities such as truss and ptrace under Unix, hostile code can determine the location of the buffer into which the encrypted key is copied and monitor the buffer contents until they change due to the key being decrypted, at which point it has the raw private key available to it. An even more serious situation occurs when a function interacts with untrusted external code by supplying a pointer to information located in an internal data structure, in which case an attacker can take the returned pointer and add or subtract whatever offset is necessary to read or write other information that is stored nearby. With a number of current security toolkits, something as simple as flipping a single bit is enough to turn off some of the encryption (and in at least one case turn on much stronger encryption than the US-exportable version of the toolkit is supposed to be capable of), cause keys to be leaked, and have a number of other interesting effects.

In order to avoid these problems, the architecture never provides direct access to any internal information. All object attribute data is copied in and out of memory locations supplied by the external software into separate (and unknown to the external software) internal memory locations. In cases where supplying pointers to memory is unavoidable (for example where it is required for `fread` or `fwrite`), the supplied buffers are scratch buffers that are decoupled from the architecture-internal storage space in which the data will eventually be processed.

This complete decoupling of data passing in or out means that it is very easy to run an implementation of the architecture in its own address space or even in physically separate hardware without the user ever being aware that this is the case; for example, under Unix the implementation would run as a dæmon owned by a different user, and under Windows NT it would run as a system service. Alternatively, the implementation can run on dedicated hardware that is physically isolated from the host system as described in Chapter 7.

2.9 References

[1] "The Protection of Information in Computer Systems", Jerome Saltzer and Michael Schroeder, *Proceedings of the IEEE*, **Vol.63, No.9** (September 1975), p.1278.

[2] "Object-Oriented Software Construction, Second Edition", Bertrand Meyer, Prentice Hall, 1997.

[3] "Assertion Definition Language (ADL) 2.0", X/Open Group, November 1998.

[4] "Security in Computing", Charles Pfleeger, Prentice-Hall, 1989.

[5] "Why does Trusted Computing Cost so Much", Susan Heath, Phillip Swanson, and Daniel Gambel, *Proceedings of the 14th National Computer Security Conference*, October 1991, p.644. Republished in the *Proceedings of the 4th Annual Canadian Computer Security Symposium*, May 1992, p.71.

[6] "Protection", Butler Lampson, *Proceedings of the 5th Princeton Symposium on Information Sciences and Systems*, Princeton, 1971, p.437.

[7] "Issues in Discretionary Access Control", Deborah Downs, Jerzy Rub, Kenneth Kung, and Carole Joran, *Proceedings of the 1985 IEEE Symposium on Security and Privacy*, IEEE Computer Society Press, 1985, p.208.

[8] "A lattice model of secure information flow", Dorothy Denning, *Communications of the ACM*, **Vol.19. No.5** (May 1976), p.236.

[9]   "Improving Security and Performance for Capability Systems", Paul Karger, PhD Thesis, University of Cambridge, October 1988.

[10]   "A Secure Identity-Based Capability System", Li Gong, *Proceedings of the 1989 IEEE Symposium on Security and Privacy*, IEEE Computer Society Press, 1989, p.56.

[11]   "Mechanisms for Persistence and Security in BirliX", W.Kühnhauser, H.Härtig, O.Kowalski, and W.Lux, *Proceedings of the International Workshop on Computer Architectures to Support Security and Persistence of Information*, Springer-Verlag, May 1990, p.309.

[12]   "Access Control by Boolean Expression Evaluation", Donald Miller and Robert Baldwin, *Proceedings of the 5th Annual Computer Security Applications Conference*, December 1989, p.131.

[13]   "An Analysis of Access Control Models", Gregory Saunders, Michael Hitchens, and Vijay Varadharajan, *Proceedings of the Fourth Australasian Conference on Information Security and Privacy (ACISP'99)*, Springer-Verlag Lecture Notes in Computer Science, No.1587, April 1999, p.281.

[14]   "Designing the GEMSOS Security Kernel for Security and Performance", Roger Schell, Tien Tao, and Mark Heckman, *Proceedings of the 8th National Computer Security Conference*, September 1985, p.108.

[15]   "Secure Computer Systems: Mathematical Foundations and Model", D.Elliott Bell and Leonard LaPadula, M74-244, MITRE Corporation, 1973.

[16]   "Mathematics, Technology, and Trust: Formal Verification, Computer Security, and the US Military", Donald MacKenzie and Garrel Pottinger, *IEEE Annals of the History of Computing*, **Vol.19, No.3** (July-September 1997), p.41.

[17]   "Secure Computing: The Secure Ada Target Approach", W.Boebert, R.Kain, and W.Young, *Scientific Honeyweller*, **Vol.6, No.2** (July 1985).

[18]   "A Note on the Confinement Problem", Butler Lampson, *Communications of the ACM*, **Vol.16, No.10** (October 1973), p.613.

[19]   "Trusted Computer Systems Evaluation Criteria", DOD 5200.28-STD, US Department of Defence, December 1985.

[20]   "Trusted Products Evaluation", Santosh Chokhani, *Communications of the ACM*, **Vol.35, No.7** (July 1992), p.64.

[21]   "NOT the Orange Book: A Guide to the Definition, Specification, and Documentation of Secure Computer Systems", Paul Merrill, Merlyn Press, Wright-Patterson Air Force Base, 1992.

[22]   "Evaluation Criteria for Trusted Systems", Roger Schell and Donald Brinkles, "Information Security: An Integrated Collection of Essays", IEEE Computer Society Press, 1995, p.137.

[23]   "Integrity Considerations for Secure Computer Systems", Kenneth Biba, ESD-TR-76-372, USAF Electronic Systems Division, April 1977.

[24] "Fundamentals of Computer Security Technology", Edward Amoroso, Prentice-Hall, 1994.

[25] "Operating System Integrity", Greg O'Shea, *Computers and Security*, **Vol.10, No.5** (August 1991), p.443.

[26] "Risk Analysis of 'Trusted Computer Systems'", Klaus Brunnstein and Simone Fischer-Hübner, *Computer Security and Information Integrity*, Elsevier Science Publishers, 1991, p.71.

[27] "A Comparison of Commercial and Military Computer Security Policies", David Clark and David Wilson, *Proceedings of the 1987 IEEE Symposium on Security and Privacy*, IEEE Computer Society Press, 1987, p.184.

[28] "Transaction Processing: Concepts and Techniques" Jim Gray and Andreas Reuter, Morgan Kaufmann, 1993.

[29] "Atomic Transactions", Nancy Lynch, Michael Merritt, William Weihl, and Alan Fekete, Morgan Kaufmann, 1994.

[30] "Principles of Transaction Processing", Philip Bernstein and Eric Newcomer, Morgan Kaufman Series in Data Management Systems, January 1997.

[31] "Non-discretionary controls for commercial applications", Steven Lipner, *Proceedings of the 1982 IEEE Symposium on Security and Privacy*, IEEE Computer Society Press, 1982, p.2.

[32] "Putting Policy Commonalities to Work", D.Elliott Bell, *Proceedings of the 14th National Computer Security Conference*, October 1991, p.456.

[33] "Modeling Mandatory Access Control in Role-based Security Systems", Matunda Nyanchama and Sylvia Osborn, *Proceedings of the IFIP WG 11.3 Ninth Annual Working Conference on Database Security (Database Security IX)*, Chapman & Hall, August 1995, p.129.

[34] "Role Activation Hierarchies", Ravi Sandhu, *Proceedings of the 3rd ACM Workshop on Role-Based Access Control (RBAC'98)*, October 1998, p.33.

[35] "The Chinese Wall Security Policy", David Brewer and Michael Nash, *Proceedings of the 1989 IEEE Symposium on Security and Privacy*, IEEE Computer Society Press, 1989, p.206.

[36] "Chinese Wall Security Policy — An Aggressive Model", T.Lin, *Proceedings of the 5th Annual Computer Security Applications Conference*, December 1989, p.282.

[37] "A lattice interpretation of the Chinese Wall policy", Ravi Sandhu, *Proceedings of the 15th National Computer Security Conference*, October 1992, p.329.

[38] "Lattice-Based Enforcement of Chinese Walls", Ravi Sandhu, *Computers and Security*, **Vol.11, No.8** (December 1992), p.753.

[39] "On the Chinese Wall Model", Volker Kessler, *Proceedings of the European Symposium on Resarch in Computer Security (ESORICS'92)*, Springer-Verlag Lecture Notes in Computer Science, No.648, November 1992, p.41.

[40] "A Retrospective on the Criteria Movement", Willis Ware, *Proceedings of the 18th National Information Systems Security Conference* (formerly the National Computer Security Conference), October 1995, p.582.

[41] "Certification of programs for secure information flow", Dorothy Denning, *Communications of the ACM*, **Vol.20, No.6** (June 1977), p.504.

[42] "Computer Security: A User's Perspective", Lenora Haldenby, *Proceedings of the 2nd Annual Canadian Computer Security Conference*, March 1990, p.63.

[43] "Some Extensions to the Lattice Model for Computer Security", Jie Wu, Eduardo Fernandez, and Ruigang Zhang, *Computers and Security*, **Vol.11, No.4** (July 1992), p.357.

[44] "Exploiting the Dual Nature of Sensitivity Labels", John Woodward, *Proceedings of the 1987 IEEE Symposium on Security and Privacy*, IEEE Computer Society Press, 1987, p.23.

[45] "A Multilevel Security Model for Distributed Object Systems", Vincent Nicomette and Yves Deswarte, *Proceedings of the 4th European Symposium on Research in Computer Security (ESORICS'96)*, Springer-Verlag Lecture Notes in Computer Science, No.1146, September 1996, p.80.

[46] "Security Kernels: A Solution or a Problem", Stanley Ames Jr., *Proceedings of the 1981 IEEE Symposium on Security and Privacy*, IEEE Computer Society Press, 1981, p.141.

[47] "A Security Model for Military Message Systems", Carl Landwehr, Constance Heitmeyer, and John McLean, *ACM Transactions on Computer Systems*, **Vol.2, No.3** (August 1984), p.198.

[48] "A Security Model for Military Message Systems: Restrospective", Carl Landwehr, Constance Heitmeyer, and John McLean, *Proceedings of the 17th Annual Computer Security Applications Conference (ACSAC'01)*, December 2001, p.174.

[49] "Development of a Multi Level Data Generation Application for GEMSOS", E.Schallenmuller, R.Cramer, and B.Aldridge, *Proceedings of the 5th Annual Computer Security Applications Conference*, December 1989, p.86.

[50] "A Security Model for Military Message Systems", Carl Landwehr, Constance Heitmeyer, and John McLean, *ACM Transactions on Computer Systems*, **Vol.2, No.3** (August 1984), p.198.

[51] "Formal Models for Computer Security", Carl Landwehr, *ACM Computing Surveys*, **Vol. 13, No. 3** (September 1981), p.247

[52] "A Taxonomy of Integrity Models, Implementations, and Mechanisms", J.Eric Roskos, Stephen Welke, John Boone, and Terry Mayfield, *Proceedings of the 13th National Computer Security Conference*, October 1990, p.541.

[53] "An Analysis of Application Specific Security Policies" Daniel Sterne, Martha Branstad, Brian Hubbard, Barbara Mayer, and Dawn Wolcott, *Proceedings of the 14th National Computer Security Conference*, October 1991, p.25.

[54] "Is there a need for new information security models?", S.A.Kokolakis, *Proceedings of the IFIP TC6/TC11 International Conference on Communications and Multimedia Security (Communications and Security II)*, Chapman & Hall, 1996, p.256.

[55] "The Multipolicy Paradigm for Trusted Systems", Hilary Hosmer, *Proceedings of the 1992 New Security Paradigms Workshop*, ACM, 1992, p.19.

[56] "Metapolicies II", Hilary Hosmer, *Proceedings of the 15th National Computer Security Conference*, October 1992, p.369.

[57] "Security Kernel Design and Implementation: An Introduction", Stanley Ames Jr, Morrie Gasser, and Roger Schell, *IEEE Computer*, **Vol.16, No.7** (July 1983), p.14.

[58] "Kernels for Safety?", John Rushby, *Safe and Secure Computing Systems*, Blackwell Scientific Publications, 1989, p.210.

[59] "Security policies and security models", Joseph Goguen and José Meseguer, *Proceedings of the 1982 IEEE Symposium on Security and Privacy*, IEEE Computer Society Press, 1982, p.11.

[60] "The Architecture of Complexity", Herbert Simon, *Proceedings of the American Philosophical Society*, **Vol.106, No.6** (December 1962), p.467.

[61] "Design and Verification of Secure Systems", John Rushby, *ACM Operating Systems Review*, **Vol.15, No.5** (December 1981), p.12.

[62] "Developing Secure Systems in a Modular Way", Qi Shi, J.McDermid, and J.Moffett, *Proceedings of the 8th Annual Conference on Computer Assurance (COMPASS'93)*, IEEE Computer Society Press, 1993, p.111.

[63] "A Separation Model for Virtual Machine Monitors", Nancy Kelem and Richard Feiertag, *Proceedings of the 1991 IEEE Symposium on Security and Privacy*, IEEE Computer Society Press, 1991, p.78.

[64] "A Retrospective on the VAX VMM Security Kernel", Paul Karger, Mary Ellen Zurko, Douglas Bonin, Andrew Mason, and Clifford Kahn, *IEEE Transactions on Software Engineering*, **Vol.17, No.11** (November 1991), p1147.

[65] "Separation Machines", Jon Graff, *Proceedings of the 15th National Computer Security Conference*, October 1992, p.631.

[66] "Proof of Separability: A Verification Technique for a Class of Security Kernels", John Rushby, *Proceedings of the 5th Symposium on Programming*, Springer-Verlag Lecture Notes in Computer Science, No.137, August 1982.

[67] "A Comment on the 'Basic Security Theorem' of Bell and LaPadula", John McLean, *Information Processing Letters*, **Vol.20, No.2** (15 February 1985), p.67.

[68] "On the validity of the Bell-LaPadula model", E.Roos Lindgren and I.Herschberg, *Computers and Security*, **Vol.13, No.4** (1994), p.317.

[69] "New Thinking About Information Technology Security", Marshall Abrams and Michael Joyce, *Computers and Security*, **Vol.14, No.1** (January 1995), p.57.

[70] "A Provably Secure Operating System: The System, Its Applications, and Proofs", Peter Neumann, Robert Boyer, Richard Feiertag, Karl Levitt, and Lawrence Robinson, SRI Computer Science Laboratory report CSL 116, SRI International, May 1980.

[71] "Locking Computers Securely", O.Sami Saydari, Joseph Beckman, and Jeffrey Leaman, *Proceedings of the 10th Annual Computer Security Conference*, 1987, p.129.

[72] "Constructing an Infosec System Using the LOCK Technology", W.Earl Boebert, *Proceedings of the 8th National Computer Security Conference*, October 1988, p.89.

[73] "M²S: A Machine for Multilevel Security", Bruno d'Ausbourg and Jean-Henri Llareus, *Proceedings of the European Symposium on Research in Computer Security (ESORICS'92)*, Springer-Verlag Lecture Notes in Computer Science, No.648, November 1992, p.373.

[74] "MUTABOR, A Coprocessor Supporting Memory Management in an Object-Oriented Architecture", Jörg Kaiser, *IEEE Micro*, **Vol.8**, **No.5** (September/October 1988), p.30.

[75] "An Object-Oriented Approach to Support System Reliability and Security", Jörg Kaiser, *Proceedings of the International Workshop on Computer Architectures to Support Security and Persistence of Information*, Springer-Verlag, May 1990, p.173.

[76] "Active Memory for Managing Persistent Objects", S.Lavington and R.Davies, *Proceedings of the International Workshop on Computer Architectures to Support Security and Persistence of Information*, Springer-Verlag, May 1990, p.137.

[77] "Programming a VIPER", T.Buckley, P.Jesty, *Proceedings of the 4th Annual Conference on Computer Assurance (COMPASS'89)*, IEEE Computer Society Press, 1989, p.84.

[78] "Report on the Formal Specification and Partial Verification of the VIPER Microprocessor", Bishop Brock and Warren Hunt Jr., *Proceedings of the 6th Annual Conference on Computer Assurance (COMPASS'91)*, IEEE Computer Society Press, 1991, p.91.

[79] "User Threatens Court Action over MoD Chip", Simon Hill, *Computer Weekly*, 5 July 1990, p.3.

[80] "MoD in Row with Firm over Chip Development", *The Independent*, 28 May 1991.

[81] "The Intel 80x86 Processor Architecture: Pitfalls for Secure Systems", Olin Sibert, Phillip Porras, and Robert Lindell, *Proceedings of the 1995 IEEE Symposium on Security and Privacy*, IEEE Computer Society Press, 1995, p.211.

[82] "The Segment Descriptor Cache", Robert Collins, *Dr.Dobbs Journal*, August 1998.

[83] "The Caveats of Pentium System Management Mode", Robert Collins, *Dr.Dobbs Journal*, May 1997.

[84] "QNX crypt() broken", Peter Gutmann, posting to the cryptography@c2.net mailing list, message-ID 95583323401676@kahu.cs.auckland.ac.nz, 16 April 2000.

[85] "qnx crypt comprimised" [sic], 'Sean', posting to the bugtraq@securityfocus.com mailing list, message-ID 20000415030309.6007.qmail@securityfocus.-com, 15 April 2000.

[86] "Adam's Guide to the Iopener", http://www.adamlotz.com/iopener.html.

[87] "Hacking The iOpener", http://iopener.how.to/.

[88] "Iopener as a Thin Client!", http://www.ltsp.org/documentation/-iopener.php.

[89] "I-Opener FAQ", http://fastolfe.net/misc/i-opener-faq.html.

[90] "I-Opener Running Linux", http://www.linux-hacker.net/imod/-imod.html.

[91] "Security Requirements for Cryptographic Modules", FIPS PUB 140-2, National Institute of Standards and Technology, June 2001.

[92] "Cryptographic Application Programming Interfaces (APIs)", Bill Caelli, Ian Graham, and Luke O'Connor, *Computers and Security*, **Vol.12, No.7** (November 1993), p.640.

[93] "The Best Available Technologies for Computer Security", Carl Landwehr, *IEEE Computer*, **Vol.16, No 7** (July 1983), p.86.

[94] "A GYPSY-Based Kernel", Bret Hartman, *Proceedings of the 1984 IEEE Symposium on Security and Privacy*, IEEE Computer Society Press, 1984, p.219.

[95] "KSOS — Development Methodology for a Secure Operating System", T.Berson and G.Barksdale, *National Computer Conference Proceedings*, **Vol.48** (1979), p.365.

[96] "A Network Pump", Myong Kang, Ira Moskowitz, and Daniel Lee, *IEEE Transactions on Software Engineering*, **Vol.22, No.5** (May 1996), p.329.

[97] "Design and Assurance Strategy for the NRL Pump", Myong Kang, Andrew Moore, and Ira Moskowitz, *IEEE Computer*, **Vol.31, No.4** (April 1998), p.56.

[98] "Blacker: Security for the DDN: Examples of A1 Security Engineering Trades", Clark Weissman, *Proceedings of the 1992 IEEE Symposium on Security and Privacy*, IEEE Computer Society Press, 1992, p.286.

[99] "Panel Session: Kernel Performance Issues", Marvin Shaefer (chairman), *Proceedings of the 1981 IEEE Symposium on Security and Privacy*, IEEE Computer Society Press, 1981, p.162.

[100] "AIM — Advanced Infosec Machine", Motorola Inc, 1999.

[101] "AIM — Advanced Infosec Machine — Multi-Level Security", Motorola Inc, 1998.

[102] "Formal Construction of the Mathematically Analyzed Separation Kernel", W.Martin, P.White, F.S.Taylor, and A.Goldberg, *Proceedings of the 15th International Conference on Automated Software Engineering (ASE'00)*, IEEE Computer Society Press, September 2000, p.133.

[103] "An Avenue for High Confidence Applications in the 21st Century", Timothy Kremann, William Martin, and Frank Taylor, *Proceedings of the 22nd National Information Systems Security Conference* (formerly the National Computer Security Conference), October 1999, CDROM distribution.

[104] "Integrating an Object-Oriented Data Model with Multilevel Security", Sushil Jajodia and Boris Kogan, *Proceedings of the 1990 IEEE Symposium on Security and Privacy*, IEEE Computer Society Press, 1990, p.76.

[105] "Security Issues of the Trusted Mach System", Martha Branstad, Homayoon Tajalli, and Frank Meyer, *Proceedings of the 1988 IEEE Symposium on Security and Privacy*, IEEE Computer Society Press, 1988, p.362.

[106] "Access Mediation in a Message Passing Kernel", Martha Branstad, Homayoon Tajalli, Frank Meyer, and David Dalva, *Proceedings of the 1989 IEEE Symposium on Security and Privacy*, IEEE Computer Society Press, 1989, p.66.

[107] "Transaction Control Expressions for Separation of Duties", Ravi Sandhu, *Proceedings of the 4th Aerospace Computer Security Applications Conference*, December 1988, p.282.

[108] "Separation of Duties in Computerised Information Systems", Ravi Sandhu, *Database Security IV: Status and Prospects*, Elsevier Science Publishers, 1991, p.179.

[109] "Implementing Transaction Control Experssions by Checking for Absence of Access Rights", Paul Ammann and Ravi Sandhu, *Proceedings of the 8th Annual Computer Security Applications Conference*, December 1992, p.131.

[110] "Enforcing Complex Security Policies for Commercial Applications", I-Lung Kao and Randy Chow, *Proceedings of the 19th Annual International Computer Software and Applications Conference (COMPSAC'95)*, IEEE Computer Society Press, 1995, p.402.

[111] "Enforcement of Complex Security Policies with BEAC", I-Lung Kao and Randy Chow, *Proceedings of the 18th National Information Systems Security Conference* (formerly the National Computer Security Conference), October 1995, p.1.

[112] "A TCB Subset for Integrity and Role-based Access Control", Daniel Sterne, *Proceedings of the 15th National Computer Security Conference*, October 1992, p.680.

[113] "Regulating Processing Sequences via Object State", David Sherman and Daniel Sterne, *Proceedings of the 16th National Computer Security Conference*, October 1993, p.75.

[114] "A Relational Database Security Policy", Rae Burns, *Computer Security and Information Integrity*, Elsevier Science Publishers, 1991, p.89.

[115] "Extended Discretionary Access Controls", Stephen Vinter, *Proceedings of the 1988 IEEE Symposium on Security and Privacy*, IEEE Computer Society Press, 1988, p.39.

[116] "Protecting Confidentiality against Trojan Horse Programs in Discretionary Access Control Systems", Adrian Spalka, Armin Cremers, and Hurtmut Lehmler, *Proceedings of the 5th Australasian Conference on Information Security and Privacy (ACISP'00)*, Springer-Verlag Lecture Notes in Computer Science No.1841, July 200, p.1.

[117] "On the Need for a Third Form of Access Control", Richard Graubart, *Proceedings of the 12th National Computer Security Conference*, October 1989, p.296.

[118] "Beyond the Pale of MAC and DAC — Defining New Forms of Access Control", Catherine McCollum, Judith Messing, and LouAnna Notargiacomo, *Proceedings of the*

1990 IEEE Symposium on Security and Privacy, IEEE Computer Society Press, 1990, p.190.

[119] "Testing Object-Oriented Systems", Robert Binder, Addison-Wesley, 1999.

[120] "Operating Systems: Design and Implementation (2nd ed)", Andrew Tanenbaum and Albert Woodhull, Prentice-Hall, 1997.

[121] "Attacks on Cryptoprocessor Transaction Sets", Mike Bond, *Proceedings of the 3rd International Workshop on Cryptographic Hardware and Embedded Systems (CHES'01)*, Springer-Verlag Lecture Notes in Computer Science No.2162, 2001, p.220.

[122] "API-Level Attacks on Embedded Systems", Mike Bond and Ross Anderson, *IEEE Computer*, **Vol.34**, **No.10** (October 2001), p.67.

[123] "Knowledge-Based Computer Security Advisor", W.Hunteman and M.Squire, *Proceedings of the 14th National Computer Security Conference*, October 1991, p.347.

[124] "Integrating Cryptography in the Trusted Computing Base", Michael Roe and Tom Casey, *Proceedings of the 1990 IEEE Symposium on Security and Privacy*, IEEE Computer Society Press, 1990, p.50.

3 The Kernel Implementation

3.1 Kernel Message Processing

The cryptlib kernel acts as a filtering mechanism for all messages that pass through it, applying a configurable set of filtering rules to each message. These rules are defined in terms of pre- and post-dispatch actions that are performed for each message. In terms of the separation of mechanism and policy requirement given in the previous chapter, the filter rules provide the policy and the kernel provides the mechanism. The advantage of using a rule-based policy is that it allows the system to be configured to match user needs and to be upgraded to meet future threats that had not been taken into account when the original policy for the system was formulated. In a conventional approach where the policy is hardcoded into the kernel, a change in policy may require the redesign of the entire kernel. Another advantage of a rule-based policy of this type is that it can be made fairly flexible and dynamic to account for the requirements of particular situations (for example, allowing the use of a corporate signing key only during normal business hours, or locking down access or system functionality during a time of heightened risk). A final advantage is that an implementation of this type can be easier to verify than more traditional implementations, an issue that is covered in more detail in Chapter 5.

3.1.1 Rule-based Policy Enforcement

The advantage of a kernel that is based on a configurable ruleset is that it is possible to respond to changes in requirements without having to redesign the entire kernel. Each rule functions as a check on a given operation, specifying which conditions must hold in order for the operation to execute without breaching the security of the system. When the kernel is presented with a request to perform a given operation, it looks up the associated rule and either allows or denies the operation. The cryptlib kernel also applies rules to the result of processing the request, although it appears to be fairly unique in this regard.

The use of a fixed kernel implementing a configurable rule-based policy provides a powerful mechanism that can be adapted to meet a wide variety of security requirements. One implementation of this concept, the Security Model Development Environment (SMDE), uses a rule-based kernel to implement various security models such as the Bell–LaPadula model, the military message system (MMS) model which is based on mandatory controls on information flow, and the MAC portion of the SeaView relational database model. These policies are enforced by expressing each one in a common notation, an example of which is shown in Figure 3.1, which is then parsed by a model translator tool and fed to a rule generator that creates rules for use by the kernel based on the parsed policy information. Finally, the kernel itself acts as an interpreter for the rule generator [1].

```
static constraint Simple_Security_Policy
begin
    -- for all subjects and objects it must be true that
    for all sub : Subjects; ob : Objects |
    -- current read or write access between a subject and an object
    -- implies that
    ( read in current_access( sub, ob ) or
      write in current_access( sub, ob ) ) -->
      -- the current security label of the subject dominates the object
      current_security_label( sub ) >= security_label( ob );
end Simple_Security_Policy;
```

Figure 3.1. Bell–LaPadula simple security policy expressed as SMDE rule.

Another, more generalised approach, the Generalised Framework for Access Control (GFAC), proposed the use of a TCB-resident rule base that is queried by an access decision facility (ADF), with the decision results enforced by an access enforcement facility (AEF). The GFAC implements both MAC and DAC controls, which can be configured to match a particular organisation's requirements [2][3][4][5][6]. Closely related work in this area is the ISO access control framework (from which the ADF/AEF terminology originates) [7][8], although this was presented in a very abstract sense intended to be suitable for a wide variety of situations such as network access control. There are indeed a number of commonly-used network access control mechanisms such as COPS [9], RADIUS [10], and DIAMETER [11] that follow this model, although these are independent inventions rather than being derived from the ISO framework. These approaches may be contrasted with the standard policy enforcement mechanism, which relies on the policy being hardcoded into the kernel implementation.

A similar concept is used in the integrity-lock approach to database security, in which a trusted front-end (equivalent to the cryptlib kernel) mediates access between an untrusted front-end (the user) and the database back-end (the cryptlib objects) [12][13], although the main goal of the integrity-lock approach is to allow security measures to be bolted onto an existing (relatively) insecure commercial database.

3.1.2 The DTOS/Flask Approach

A slightly different approach is taken by the Distributed Trusted Operating System (DTOS), which provides security features based on the Mach microkernel [14][15]. The DTOS policy enforcement mechanism is based on an enforcement manager that enforces security decisions made by a decision server, as shown in Figure 3.2. This approach was used because of perceived shortcomings in the original trusted Mach approach (which was described in the previous chapter) in which access control decisions were based on port rights, so that someone who gained a capability for a port had full access to all capabilities on the associated object. Because trusted Mach provides no object-service-specific security mechanisms, it provides no direct control over object services. The potential solution of binding groups of object services to ports has severe scalability and flexibility problems as the number of groups is increased to provide a more fine-grained level of control, and isn't really practical.

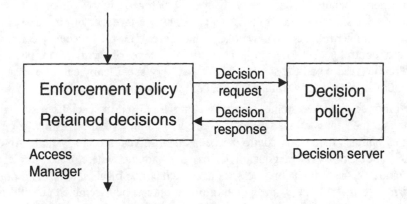

Figure 3.2. DTOS security policy management architecture.

The solution to the problem was to develop a mechanism that could ensure that each type of request made of the DTOS kernel is associated with a decision that has to be made by the decision server before the request can be processed by the kernel. The enforcement manager represents the fixed portion of the system, which identifies where in the processing a security decision is needed and what type of decision is needed, and the decision server represents the variable portion of the system, which can be configured as required to support particular user needs. A final component of the system is a cache of retained decisions that have been made by the decision server, which is required for efficiency reasons in order to speed access in the distributed Mach system [16].

As Figure 3.2 indicates, this architecture bears some general resemblance to the cryptlib kernel message-processing mechanism, although in cryptlib security decisions are made directly by the kernel based on a built-in ruleset rather than by an external decision component. Another difference between this and the cryptlib implementation is that DTOS doesn't send the parameters of each request to the decision server, which somewhat limits its decision-making abilities. In contrast in the cryptlib kernel, all parameters are available for review, and it is an expected function of the kernel that it subject them to close scrutiny.

One feature of DTOS, which arose from the observation that most people either can't or won't read a full formal specification of the security policy, is the use of a simple, table-based policy specification approach. This was used in DTOS to implement a fairly conventional MLS policy and the Clark–Wilson policy (as far as it's possible), with enforcement of other policies such as ORCON being investigated. cryptlib takes a similar approach, using a familiar C-like notation to define tables of policy rules and ACLs.

A later refinement of DTOS was Flask, which, like cryptlib, has a reference monitor that interposes atomically on each operation performed by the system in order to enforce its security policy [17]. Flask was developed in order to correct some shortcomings in DTOS, mostly having to do with dynamic policy changes. Although the overall structure is similar to its ancestor DTOS, Flask includes a considerable amount of extra complexity, which is required in order to handle sudden policy changes (which can involve undoing the results of previous policy decisions and aren't made any easier by the presence of the retained decision cache, which no longer reflects the new policy), and a second level of security controls which are required to control access to the policies for the first level of security controls. Since the cryptlib policy is fixed when the system is built and very specifically can't be changed after this point, there's no need for a similar level of complexity in cryptlib.

An even more extreme version of this approach that is used in specialised systems where the subjects and their interactions with objects are known at system build time compiles not only the rules but also the access control decisions themselves into the system. An example of such a situation occurs in integrated avionics environments where, due to the embedded and fixed nature of the application, the roles and interactions of all subjects and objects are known *a priori* so that all access mediation information can be assembled at build time and loaded into the target system in preset form [18]. Taking this approach has little benefit for cryptlib since its main advantage is to allow for faster startup and initialisation, which in the application mentioned above leads to "faster turnaround and takeoff" which isn't generally a consideration for the situations where cryptlib is used.

3.1.3 Object-based Access Control

An alternative to having security policy enforcement controlled directly by the kernel that has been suggested for use with object-oriented databases is for a special interface object to mediate access to a group of objects. This scheme divides objects into protected groups and only allows communication within the group, with the exception of a single interface object that is allowed to communicate outside the group. Other objects, called implementation objects, can only communicate within the group via the group's interface object. Intergroup communication is handled by making the interface object for one group an implementation object for a second group [19][20]. Figure 3.3 illustrates an example of such a scheme, with object 3 being an implementation object in group 1 and the interface object in group 2, and object 2 being the interface object for group 1.

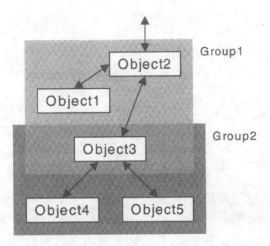

Figure 3.3. Access mediation via interface objects.

Although this provides a means of implementing security measures where none would otherwise exist, it distributes enforcement of security policy across a potentially unbounded number of interface objects, each of which has to act as a mini-kernel to enforce security measures. In contrast, the cryptlib approach of using a single, centralised kernel means that it is only necessary to get it right once, and allows a far more rigorous, controlled approach to security than the distributed approach involving mediation by interface objects.

A variant of this approach encapsulates objects inside a resource module (RM), an extended form of an object that controls protection, synchronisation, and resource access for network objects. The intent of an RM of this type, shown in Figure 3.4, is to provide a basic building block for network software systems [21]. As each message arrives, it is checked by the protection component to ensure that the type of access it is requesting is valid, has integrity checks (for example, prevention of simultaneous access by multiple messages) enforced by the synchronisation component, and is finally processed by the access component.

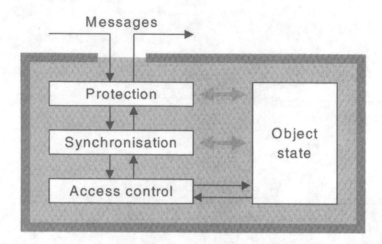

Figure 3.4. Object resource module.

This approach goes even further than the use of interface objects since it makes each object/RM responsible for access control and integrity control/synchronisation. Again, with the cryptlib approach this functionality is present in the kernel, which avoids the need to re-implement it (and get it right) for each individual object.

3.1.4 Meta-Objects for Access Control

Another access control mechanism that has some similarity to the one implemented in the cryptlib kernel is that of security meta-objects (SMOs), meta-objects that are attached to object references to control access to the corresponding object and that can be used to implement arbitrary and user-defined policies. SMOs are objects that are attached to an object reference (in cryptlib terms, an object's handle) and that control access to the target object via this reference. An example of an object with an SMO attached to its reference is shown in Figure 3.5. The meta-object has the ability to determine whether a requested type of access via the reference is permissible or not, and can perform any other types of special-case processing that may be required [22][23]. This is an extension of a slightly earlier concept that used special-purpose objects as a container to encapsulate ACLs for other objects [24].

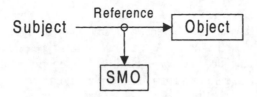

Figure 3.5. Security meta-object attached to an object reference.

If a subject tries to access an object via the protected reference, the SMO is implicitly invoked and can perform access checking based on the subject identity and the parameters being passed across in the access to the protected object. If the SMO allows the access, everything continues as normal. If it denies the access, the invocation is terminated with an error result.

The filter rules used in the cryptlib kernel differ from the SMOs discussed above in several ways, the main one being that whereas SMOs are associated with references to an object, kernel filter rules are associated with messages and are always invoked. In contrast, SMOs are invoked on a per-reference basis so that one reference to an object may have an SMO attached while a second reference is free of SMOs. In addition the kernel contains filter rules for both pre- and post-access states whereas SMOs only apply for the pre-access state (although this would be fairly easy to change if required). A major feature of SMOs is that they provide an extended form of capability-based security, fixing many of the problems of capability-based systems such as revocation of capabilities (implemented by having the SMO disallow access when the capability is revoked) and control over who has a given capability (implemented by having the SMO copied across to any new reference that is created, thus propagating its security policy across to the new reference) [25]. Because of these mechanisms, it is not possible for a subject to obtain an unprotected reference to an object.

3.1.5 Access Control via Message Filter Rules

The principal interface to the cryptlib kernel is the krnlSendMessage function, which provides the means through which subjects interact with objects. When a message arrives through a call to krnlSendMessage, the kernel looks up the appropriate pre- and post-processing rules and information based on the message type and applies the pre-dispatch filtering rule to the message before dispatching it to the target object. When the message is returned from the object, it applies the post-dispatch filtering rule and returns the result to the caller. This message-filtering process is shown in Figure 3.6.

The processing that is being performed by the kernel is driven entirely by the filter rules and doesn't require that the kernel have any built-in knowledge of object types, attributes, or object properties. This means that although the following sections describe the processing in terms of checks on objects, access and usage permissions, reference and usage counts, and the various other controls that are enforced by the kernel, the checking is performed entirely under the control of the filter rules and the kernel itself doesn't need to know about (say) an object's usage count or what it signifies. Because of this clear separation between policy and mechanism, new functionality can be added at any point by adding new filter rules or by amending or extending existing ones. An example of this type of change is given in Section 3.6 when the rules are amended to enforce the FIPS 140 security requirements, but they could just as easily be applied to enforce a completely different, non-cryptographic policy.

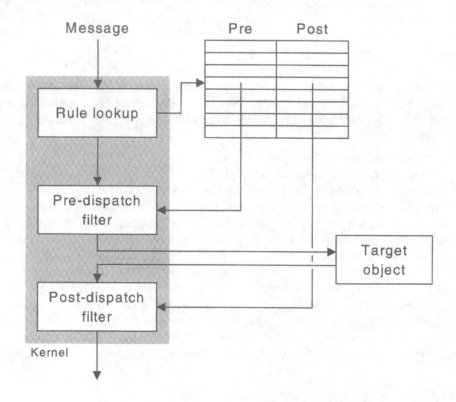

Figure 3.6. Kernel message filtering.

The general similarities of this arrangement and the one used by DTOS/Flask are fairly obvious; in both cases, a fixed kernel consults an external rule base to determine how to react to a message. As has been pointed out earlier, cryptlib provides somewhat more complete mediation by examining the message parameters and not just the message itself and by providing post-dispatch filtering as well as the pre-dispatch filtering used in DTOS/Flask.

```
krnlSendMessage( object, message, ... );
```

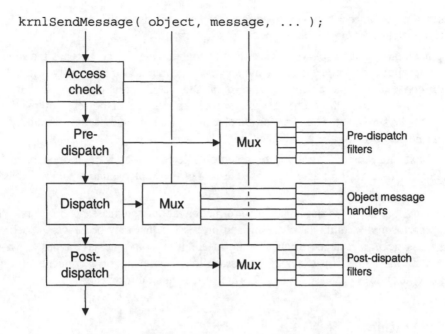

Figure 3.7. Filter rule application.

The manner in which the filter rules are applied to each message being processed is shown in Figure 3.7. The first check that is applied is a general access check on the object to which the message is addressed, the details of which were given in the previous chapter. Once this check has been passed, the pre-dispatch filter rule, selected by the type of the message being processed, is applied. The message is then dispatched to the appropriate object handler, after which the post-dispatch filter, again selected by message type, is applied. Finally, the result of the processing is returned to the caller.

3.2 Filter Rule Structure

Each filter rule begins with an indication of the message type to which it applies. This information is not required for the implementation itself since the kernel performs the rule lookup via a simple table lookup based on the message type, but it is used as part of the internal consistency checks that are performed by the kernel when it is initialised.

The next series of entries contains routing information for the message. If the message has an implicit target type (for example, a generate-key message is always routed to an encryption action object), then the type is specified here. If the message has special-case routing requirements then a handler that performs this routing is specified here. As was mentioned earlier, the filtering code has no explicit knowledge of object types, but just applies the routing mechanism described in a Chapter 1 to ensure that whatever type is given in the rule matches the target object type.

The next entry is used for type checking, and contains the object subtypes for which this message is valid; for example, the generate key message mentioned previously would only be valid for conventional and public-key encryption and MAC action objects. As with object types used for routing, the kernel has no explicit knowledge of object subtypes but just checks to make sure that the subtype for the object to which the message is eventually routed matches one of the subtypes given in the filter rule.

The next entry defines the type of assertion checking that is performed on message parameters. This is used for assertion-based testing of the implementation and is discussed in Chapter 5.

The final series of entries contains information about the message handlers. These handlers perform any additional checking and processing that may be necessary before and after a message is dispatched to an object. In addition, some message types are handled internally by the kernel (for example, a message that increments or decrements an object's reference count), in which case the handlers are kernel-internal mechanisms.

3.2.1 Filter Rules

The message filtering policy definitions are best illustrated with examples of actual filtering rules. The simplest rule is for messages that are handled internally by the kernel without being forwarded to the target object. These include messages to increment and decrement an object's reference count and to manipulate dependent objects. The rules for changing an object's reference count are shown in Figure 3.8.

```
{ MESSAGE_INCREFCOUNT,                  /* Increment object ref.count */
  ROUTE_NONE,
  SUBTYPE_ANY,
  PARAMTYPE_NONE_NONE,
  HANDLE_INTERNAL( incRefCount ) },
{ MESSAGE_DECREFCOUNT,                  /* Decrement object ref.count */
  ROUTE_NONE,
  SUBTYPE_ANY,
  PARAMTYPE_NONE_NONE,
  HANDLE_INTERNAL( decRefCount ) }
```

Figure 3.8. Rules for messages handled by the kernel.

The first entry in each rule contains the message type that is used for internal consistency checking by the kernel at startup. Following this is the routing information, in this case ROUTE_NONE, which indicates that this message is addressed directly to its final destination. The next entry contains the object subtypes for which this message is valid. In this case the messages are valid for all object subtypes. The next entry is used for assertion-based testing of the implementation and specifies that the message has no parameters.

Finally, the last entry specifies the use of an internal handler that increments or decrements the objects reference count.

When the kernel receives one of these messages, it performs the appropriate checks specified by the filtering rules (in this case none apart from the standard object validity and accessibility checks that are always performed), bypasses the routing stage since the rules indicate that the messages aren't routed, and passes control over to the appropriate internal handler, from which it returns to the caller.

A slightly more complex rule that results in a message being passed on to a destination object is the destroy object message, which is usually not invoked directly but results from an object having its reference count decremented to zero. The rule for the destroy object message is shown in Figure 3.9, and is almost identical to the ones in Figure 3.8 except that the use of a pre-dispatch handler is specified that signals any dependent objects that their controlling object is about to have its reference count decremented and places the object in the signalled state to ensure that no further messages will be dispatched to it.

```
{ MESSAGE_DESTROY,                    /* Destroy the object */
  ROUTE_NONE,
  SUBTYPE_ANY,
  PARAMTYPE_NONE_NONE,
  PRE_DISPATCH( SignalDependentObjects ) }
```

Figure 3.9. Destroy object filter rule.

The messages thus far have been ones that are sent directly to their target object. However, there are many messages that are routed by the kernel based on their type. An example of this type of message is shown in Figure 3.10. The encrypt data and decrypt data messages are routed to encryption action objects with an object subtype of conventional or public-key encryption object. As was mentioned earlier, the kernel doesn't need to know about the exact semantics of the objects involved (the message could just as easily be routed to objects of type cat with subtypes Siamese and Persian); all it needs to do is correctly apply the rule definitions.

```
{ MESSAGE_CTX_ENCRYPT,              /* Context: Action = encrypt */
  ROUTE( OBJECT_TYPE_CONTEXT ),
  SUBTYPE_CTX_CONV | SUBTYPE_CTX_PKC,
  PARAMTYPE_DATA_LENGTH,
  PRE_POST_DISPATCH( CheckActionAccess, UpdateUsageCount ) },
{ MESSAGE_CTX_DECRYPT,              /* Context: Action = decrypt */
  ROUTE( OBJECT_TYPE_CONTEXT ),
  SUBTYPE_CTX_CONV | SUBTYPE_CTX_PKC,
  PARAMTYPE_DATA_LENGTH,
  PRE_POST_DISPATCH( CheckActionAccess, UpdateUsageCount ) }
```

Figure 3.10. Rules for messages routed by object type

These rules also contain extra functionality in areas other than message routing. Since the encrypt data message requires as parameters the data to be encrypted and its length, the entry for the assertion-based verification specifies this instead of the null parameters used for the previous messages. In addition, the pre- and post-dispatch filtering for these messages is more complex than it was for the earlier ones. In each case, the pre-dispatch rule applies the access checks that were described in the previous chapter, and the post-dispatch rule updates the object's usage count if the object returns an indication that the message was processed successfully.

Some messages can change an object's state, resulting in a transition from the low to the high state if the object reports that they were successfully processed (object states were discussed in the previous chapter). Examples of two such messages are shown in Figure 3.11, with the first one being a message that generates a key in a conventional, public-key, or MAC action object and the second one being a message that signs a certificate or some variant thereof (a certification request, certificate chain, or attribute certificate), a CRL, or an OCSP request or response.

```
{ MESSAGE_CTX_GENKEY,                   /* Context: Generate a key */
  ROUTE( OBJECT_TYPE_CONTEXT ),
  SUBTYPE_CTX_CONV | SUBTYPE_CTX_PKC | SUBTYPE_CTX_MAC,
  PARAMTYPE_NONE_BOOLEAN,
  PRE_POST_DISPATCH( CheckState, ChangeState ) },
{ MESSAGE_CRT_SIGN,                      /* Cert: Action = sign cert */
  ROUTE( OBJECT_TYPE_CERTIFICATE ),
  ST_CERT_ANY_CERT | ST_CERT_ATTRCERT | ST_CERT_CRL | ST_CERT_OCSP_REQ |
   ST_CERT_OCSP_RESP,
  PARAMTYPE_NONE_ANY,
  PRE_POST_DISPATCH( CheckStateParamHandle, ChangeState ) }
```

Figure 3.11. Rules for messages which change an object's state.

These messages are again automatically routed to the appropriate object type. Before being dispatched, a filter rule is applied that checks to ensure that the object isn't already in the high state and (in the case of the certificate) also checks that the signing key parameter is valid for this type of operation. If the target object reports the successful processing of the message, the kernel applies a post-dispatch filter that moves the object into the high state.

Some messages aren't routed (in the same way as if they had a routing entry of ROUTE_NONE) but don't apply to all object types, being specific to only one or occasionally two object types. Examples of two such messages that create an object in a device and get a key from a keyset or device are shown in Figure 3.12. The first rule specifies that the message to create an object must be targeted specifically at a device and that the assertion-based verification will require a parameter indicating the object type that is to be created. The second rule specifies that the message to get a key (which results in the instantiation of encryption action objects and/or certificates) must be targeted at a standard device (one capable of storing keys such as a smart card or encryption hardware) or a keyset and that the assertion-based verification will require a parameter indicating the item type that is to be fetched. The process of fetching a key can be fairly complex; further checking of the access conditions is handled by the mechanism ACLs described in Section 3.4.

```
{ MESSAGE_DEV_CREATEOBJECT,              /* Device: Create object */
  ROUTE_FIXED( OBJECT_TYPE_DEVICE ),
  SUBTYPE_DEVICE_ANY,
  PARAMTYPE_DATA_OBJTYPE },
{ MESSAGE_KEY_GETKEY,                    /* Keyset: Instantiate ctx/cert */
  ROUTE_FIXED_ALT( OBJECT_TYPE_KEYSET, OBJECT_TYPE_DEVICE ),
  SUBTYPE_KEYSET_ANY | SUBTYPE_DEVICE_ANY_STD,
  PARAMTYPE_DATA_ITEMTYPE,
  PRE_DISPATCH( CheckKeysetAccess ) }
```

Figure 3.12. Rules for messages with fixed routing and alternative targets.

In theory, we could allow routing of such messages; for example, a "get key" message sent to a certificate could be interpreted to mean "get another key from the same location that this one came from". With the appropriate rule changes, the kernel would indeed perform this action; however, this type of functionality is probably stretching the orthogonality of the message-based implementation a bit too far and would only cause confusion among users.

Some message types are internal to cryptlib and are used to invoke mechanisms and actions that can never be directly accessed by the user. Examples of rules for two such messages are shown in Figure 3.13. These rules apply to messages that are used to wrap one key in another (for example, a session key in a public key) and to perform the corresponding unwrapping action. The rules are fairly straightforward, requiring that a valid wrapping or unwrapping mechanism be used as part of the message and checking that the supplied object types and parameters are appropriate for the mechanism, again handled through the mechanism ACLs described in Section 3.4.

```
{ MESSAGE_DEV_EXPORT,                    /* Device: Action = export key */
  ROUTE( OBJECT_TYPE_DEVICE ),
  SUBTYPE_DEVICE_ANY,
  PARAMTYPE_DATA_MECHTYPE,
  PRE_DISPATCH( CheckMechanismWrapAccess ) },
{ MESSAGE_DEV_IMPORT,                    /* Device: Action = import key */
  ROUTE( OBJECT_TYPE_DEVICE ),
  SUBTYPE_DEVICE_ANY,
  PARAMTYPE_DATA_MECHTYPE,
  PRE_DISPATCH( CheckMechanismWrapAccess ) }
```

Figure 3.13. Rules for messages that invoke internal mechanisms.

Examples of a final class of processing rules, which apply to messages that manipulate object attributes, are given in Figure 3.14. These messages are routed implicitly by attribute type so that, for example, a message that manipulates an encryption key attribute would be implicitly routed to an encryption action object and a message that manipulates a signature creation time attribute would be implicitly routed to a certificate object.

```
{ MESSAGE_GETATTRIBUTE,                /* Get numeric object attribute */
  ROUTE_IMPLICIT,
  SUBTYPE_ANY,
  PARAMTYPE_DATA_ANY,
  PRE_DISPATCH( CheckAttributeAccess ) },
{ MESSAGE_SETATTRIBUTE,                /* Set numeric object attribute */
  ROUTE_IMPLICIT,
  SUBTYPE_ANY,
  PARAMTYPE_DATA_ANY,
  PRE_POST_DISPATCH( CheckAttributeAccess, ChangeStateOpt ) },
{ MESSAGE_DELETEATTRIBUTE,             /* Delete object attribute */
  ROUTE_IMPLICIT,
  SUBTYPE_CTX_ANY | SUBTYPE_CERT_ANY,
  PARAMTYPE_NONE_ANY,
  PRE_DISPATCH( CheckAttributeAccess ) }
```

Figure 3.14. Rules for attribute-manipulation messages.

In each case the pre-dispatch filter rule that is applied is one that checks the attribute data and ensures that the access is valid. For the set attribute message, the attribute being set may result in the object being transitioned into the high state (for example, this would happen if the attribute was a key being set for an encryption action object), so a post-dispatch rule is applied that performs the state change if required.

3.3 Attribute ACL Structure

As with the message filter rules, each attribute ACL begins with an indication of the attribute type to which it applies. This is used as part of the internal consistency checking performed by the kernel when it is initialised.

The next series of entries is used for type checking and specifies the type of the attribute (whether it's a boolean, a numeric value, a time value, an object, a string, or various other types) and the object subtype for which the attribute is valid. As with the type information for messages, the kernel has no explicit knowledge of object subtypes but just checks to make sure that the subtype for the object for which the attribute is being manipulated matches one of the subtypes given in the ACL.

The next series of entries contains the access restrictions for the attribute and a series of flags that define additional handling restrictions and conditions for the attribute. The access restrictions are a standard bitmap of read/write/delete (RWD) permissions for internal and external access with a one bit indicating that this type of access is allowed. There are two sets of permissions, one for the object when it is in the high state and one when it is in the low state. If an attribute is accessible both internally and externally, then the RWD permissions are identical for internal and external access. If the attribute is only visible internally, then the RWD permissions for external access are set to all zeroes. Some example permissions and the attributes to which they might apply are given in Table 3.1. The RWD permissions are divided into two groups, with the first group applying when the object is in the high state and the second group applying when it is in the low state.

Table 3.1. Examples of attribute access permissions.

Permission	Description
ACCESS_xxx_xxx	No access from anywhere in any state. This is used for placeholder attributes that represent functionality that will be added at a later date.
ACCESS_xxx_Rxx	Read-only access in the low state, no access in the high state. This is used for status information when the object is in the low state that no longer has any meaning once it has been moved into the high state; for example, the details of a key that is required in order to move the object into the high state.
ACCESS_Rxx_xxx	Read-only access in the high state, no access in the low state. This is used for information that is created when the object changes states; for example, a certificate fingerprint (hash of the encoded certificate) that only exists once the certificate has been signed and is in the high state.
ACCESS_xxx_RWx	Read/write access in the low state, no access in the high state. This is a variant of ACCESS_xxx_Rxx and is used for information that has no meaning in the high state but is required in the low state.
ACCESS_Rxx_RWD	Full access in the low state, read-only access in the high state. This is used for information that can be manipulated freely in the low state but that becomes immutable once the object has been moved into the high state, typical examples being certificate attributes.
ACCESS_RWD_xxx	Full access in the high state, no access in the low state. This is used for information pertaining to fully initialised objects (for example signed certificates) that doesn't apply when the object is in the low state where the details of the object are still subject to change.
ACCESS_INT_xxx_Rxx	Internal read-only access in the low state, no external access or access in the high state. This is identical to ACCESS_xxx_Rxx except that it is used for attributes that are only visible internally.
ACCESS_INT_Rxx_RWx	Internal read/write access in the low state, internal read-only access in the high state, no external access. This is mostly identical to ACCESS_Rxx_RWD (except for the lack of delete access) but is used for attributes that are only visible internally.

The flags that accompany the access permissions indicate any additional handling that must be performed by the kernel. There are only two of these flags, the first one being ATTRIBUTE_FLAG_PROPERTY which indicates that the attribute applies to the object itself rather than being an attribute of the object. Examples of attribute properties include the object type, whether the object is externally visible, whether the object is in the low or high state, and so on (all of these properties are internal attributes, so that the corresponding access permissions are ACCESS_INT_*xxx*). The second flag is ATTRIBUTE_FLAG_TRIGGER, which indicates that setting this attribute triggers a change from the low to the high state. As with messages that initiate this change, if the object reports that a message that sets an attribute with the ATTRIBUTE_FLAG_TRIGGER flag set was processed successfully, the kernel will move the object into the high state. Examples of trigger attributes are ones that contain key components such as public keys, user passwords, or conventional encryption keys.

The next series of entries contains routing information for the message that affects the attribute. If the message has an implicit target type that is given via the attribute type then the target type is specified here. If the message has special-case routing requirements then a handler that performs this routing is specified here. As with the message-routing code, the kernel has no explicit knowledge of object types but just applies the routing mechanism described in Chapter 1 to ensure that whatever type is given in the ACL entry matches the target object type.

The final series of entries is used for type checking and contains range information for the attribute data (for example a range of 192...192 bits for triple DES keys or 1...64 characters for many X.509 certificate strings) and any additional checking information that may be required. This includes things such as sequences of allowed values for the attribute, limits on sub-ranges rather than a single continuous range, an indication that the attribute value must correspond to a valid object, and so on.

In addition to these general-purpose range checks, ACLs can be applied recursively to subranges of objects. For example, a request submitted to a session object is handled using a sub-ACL that contains details of valid request types matched to session types, so that a timestamping session would require a timestamping request and an online certificate status protocol (OCSP) session would require an OCSP request. cryptlib first applies the main ACL which covers the entire class of session and request types, and then recursively applies the sub-ACL that is appropriate for the particular session type.

3.3.1 Attribute ACLs

As with the message filtering rules, the attribute ACLs are best illustrated through examples. One of the simplest of these is a basic boolean flag indicating the status of a certain condition. The ACL for the CRYPT_CERTINFO_SELGSIGNED attribute, which indicates whether a certificate is self-signed (that is, whether the public key contained in it can be used to verify the signature on it) is shown in Figure 3.15. This ACL indicates that the attribute is a boolean flag that is valid for any type of certificate, that it can be read or written when the certificate is in the low (unsigned) state but only read when it is in the high (signed) state, and that the message that manipulates it is routed to certificate objects.

```
MKACL_B(                                  /* Cert is self-signed */
    CRYPT_CERTINFO_SELFSIGNED,
    SUBTYPE_CERT_ANY_CERT,
    ACCESS_Rxx_RWx,
    ROUTE( OBJECT_TYPE_CERTIFICATE ) )
```

Figure 3.15. ACL for boolean attribute.

Two slightly more complex entries that apply for attributes with numeric values are shown in Figure 3.16. Both are for encryption action objects, and both are read-only, since the attribute value is set implicitly when the object is created. The first ACL is for the encryption algorithm that is used by the object, and the allowable range is defined in terms of the predefined constants CRYPT_ALGO_NONE and CRYPT_ALGO_LAST. The attribute is allowed to take any value within these two limits. The second ACL is for the block size of the algorithm used by the action object. The allowable range is defined in terms of the largest block size used by any algorithm, which in this case is the size of the hash value produced by a hash algorithm. As was mentioned earlier, the allowable range could also be specified in terms of a sequence of permitted values, a set of subranges, or in a variety of other ways.

```
MKACL_N(                                  /* Algorithm */
    CRYPT_CTXINFO_ALGO,
    SUBTYPE_CTX_ANY,
    ACCESS_Rxx_Rxx,
    ROUTE( OBJECT_TYPE_CONTEXT ),
    RANGE( CRYPT_ALGO_NONE + 1, CRYPT_ALGO_LAST - 1 ) ),
MKACL_N(                                  /* Block size in bytes */
    CRYPT_CTXINFO_BLOCKSIZE,
    SUBTYPE_CTX_ANY,
    ACCESS_Rxx_Rxx,
    ROUTE( OBJECT_TYPE_CONTEXT ),
    RANGE( 1, CRYPT_MAX_HASHSIZE ) )
```

Figure 3.16. ACL for numeric attributes.

The two examples shown above illustrate the way in which the kernel is kept isolated from any low-level object implementation considerations. If it knew every nuance of every object's implementation it would know that (for example) a DES object can only have a CRYPT_CTXINFO_ALGO attribute value of CRYPT_ALGO_DES and a CRYPT_CTXINFO_BLOCKSIZE value of 8; however, the kernel shouldn't be required to be aware of these details since all that it's enforcing is a general set of rules, with any object-specific details being handled by the objects themselves (going back to the cat analogy from earlier on, the rules could just as well be specifying cat fur colours and lengths as encryption algorithms and key sizes). What the kernel guarantees to subjects and objects in terms of message parameters is that the messages it allows through have parameters within the ranges that are permitted for the object as defined by the filter rules that it enforces.

An example of ACLs for general-purpose string attributes is shown in Figure 3.17. The first entry is for the IV for an encryption action object, which is a general-purpose string attribute with no restrictions on access so that it can be read or written when the object is in the low or high state. Since only conventional encryption algorithms have IVs, the permitted object subtype range is conventional encryption action objects only. As with the algorithm block size in Figure 3.16, the allowed size is given in terms of the predefined constant CRYPT_MAX_IVSIZE, with the object itself taking care of the exact details. In practice this means that it pads short IVs out as required and truncates long ones; the semantics of mismatched IV sizes are undefined in any crypto standards which provide for the use of variable-length IVs, so in practice cryptlib is generous with what it accepts.

```
MKACL_S(                                /* IV */
    CRYPT_CTXINFO_IV,
    SUBTYPE_CTX_CONV,
    ACCESS_RWx_RWx,
    ROUTE( OBJECT_TYPE_CONTEXT ),
    RANGE( 8, CRYPT_MAX_IVSIZE ) ),
MKACL_S(                                /* Label for private key */
    CRYPT_CTXINFO_LABEL,
    SUBTYPE_CTX_PKC,
    ACCESS_Rxx_RWD,
    ROUTE( OBJECT_TYPE_CONTEXT ),
    RANGE( 1, CRYPT_MAX_TEXTSIZE ) )
```

Figure 3.17. ACL for a string attribute.

The second entry is for the label for a private key, with an object subtype allowing its use only with private-key action objects. This attribute contains a unique label that is used to identify a key when it is stored to disk or to a crypto token such as a smart card, typical labels being "My encryption key" or "My signature key". cryptlib enforces the uniqueness requirement by sending a message to the keyset or device in which the object will be held, inquiring whether something with this label already exists. If the keyset or device indicates that an object with the given label is already present then a duplicate value error is returned to the user. Because the user could bypass this check by changing the label after the object is stored in or associated with the keyset or device, the label is made read-only once the object is in the high state.

As with numeric attributes, cryptlib allows subranges, sets of permitted values, and other types of specifiers to be used with string attributes. For example, the CRYPT_CERTINFO_-IPADDRESS attribute is allowed a length of either four or sixteen bytes, corresponding to IPv4 and IPv6 addresses respectively.

```
MKACL_S(                             /* Ctx: Key ID */
    CRYPT_IATTRIBUTE_KEYID,
    SUBTYPE_CTX_PKC,
    ACCESS_INT_Rxx_Rxx,
    ROUTE( OBJECT_TYPE_CONTEXT ),
    RANGE( 20, 20 ) )
```

Figure 3.18. ACL for internal attribute.

Having looked at some of the more generic attribute ACLs, we can now look at the more special-case ones. The first of these is shown in Figure 3.18, and constitutes the ACL for the key identifier for a public- or private-key object. The key identifier (also known under a variety of other names such as thumbprint, key hash, subjectPublicKeyIdentifier, and various other terms) is an SHA-1 hash of the public-key components and is used to uniquely identify a public key both within cryptlib and externally when used with data formats such as X.509 and S/MIME version 3. Since this value is not something that is of any use to the user, its ACL specifies it as being accessible only within cryptlib. As a result of this ACL setting, any message coming from outside cryptlib cannot access the attribute. If an outside user does try to access it, an error code will be returned indicating that the attribute doesn't exist. Note that this is in contrast to many systems where the error would be permission denied. In cryptlib's case, it's not even possible to determine the existence of an internal attribute from the outside, since its presence is completely hidden by the kernel. cryptlib takes the view that "What you want doesn't exist" provides less temptation for a potentially malicious user than "It's here, but you can't have it".

```
MKACL_S_EX(                          /* Key */
    CRYPT_CTXINFO_KEY,
    SUBTYPE_CTX_CONV | SUBTYPE_CTX_MAC,
    ACCESS_xxx_xWx,
    ATTRIBUTE_FLAG_TRIGGER,
    ROUTE( OBJECT_TYPE_CONTEXT ),
    RANGE( bitsToBytes( MIN_KEYSIZE_BITS ), CRYPT_MAX_KEYSIZE ) )
```

Figure 3.19. ACL for an attribute that triggers an object state change.

Figure 3.19 indicates another special-case attribute, this time one that, when set, triggers a change in the object's state from the low to the high state. This attribute, the encryption key, is valid for conventional and MAC encryption action objects (public-key action objects have composite public-key parameters that are somewhat different from standard keys) and when set causes the kernel to transition the object into the high state. An attempt to set it if the object is already in the high state is disallowed, thus enforcing the write-once semantics for encryption keys.

Some security standards don't allow plaintext keys to pass over an external interface, a rule that can be enforced through the ACL change shown in Figure 3.20. Previously, the attribute could be set from inside and outside the architecture; with this change it can only be set from within the architecture. In order to load a key into an action object, it is now necessary to send in an encrypted key from the outside that can be unwrapped internally and loaded into the action object from there, but plaintext keys can no longer be loaded. This example illustrates the flexibility of the rule-based policy enforcement, which allows an alternative security policy to be employed by a simple change to an ACL entry that then takes effect across the entire architecture.

```
MKACL_S_EX(                              /* Key */
    CRYPT_CTXINFO_KEY,
    SUBTYPE_CTX_CONV | SUBTYPE_CTX_MAC,
    ACCESS_INT_xxx_xWx,
    ATTRIBUTE_FLAG_TRIGGER,
    ROUTE( OBJECT_TYPE_CONTEXT ),
    RANGE( bitsToBytes( MIN_KEYSIZE_BITS ), CRYPT_MAX_KEYSIZE ) )
```

Figure 3.20. Modified trigger attribute ACL which disallows plaintext key loads.

3.4 Mechanism ACL Structure

In addition to ACLs for messages and attributes, the cryptlib kernel also enforces ACLs for crypto and keyset mechanisms. A crypto mechanism can be an operation such as creating or checking a signature, wrapping or unwrapping an encryption key, or deriving an encryption key from keying material such as a password or shared secret information. In addition, storing or fetching keys from keyset or device objects also represent mechanisms that are controlled through ACLs.

As with the message and attribute ACLs, each mechanism ACL is identified by the crypto or keyset mechanism or operation to which it applies. This is used by the kernel to select the appropriate ACL for a given mechanism.

The remainder of the crypto mechanism ACL consists of information that is used to check the parameters for the mechanism. The first parameter is the output parameter (the result of the crypto operation), and the remaining parameters are input parameters (the action objects or data used to produce the result). For example, a PKCS #1 signature operation takes as parameters a private-key and hash action object and produces as output a byte string approximately equal in size to the private-key modulus size (the exact size varies somewhat depending on whether the result is normalised or not).

Keyset mechanism ACLs have a slightly different structure than crypto mechanism ACLs. Rather than working with a variable-length list of parameters that can handle arbitrary crypto mechanisms, the keyset mechanisms ACLs apply to specific operations on keysets (and, by extension, devices that can store keys and certificates). Because of this, the ACL structure resembles that of the message filter rules, with one ACL for each type of operation that can be performed and the ACL itself specifying the details of the operation.

As with message ACLs, the first entry specifies the operation to which the ACL applies, for example public-key (and by extension certificate) access or certificate request access.

The next set of entries specify the keyset types for which general read/write/delete access, enumeration access (reading a sequence of connected entries), and query access (for example wildcard matching on an email address) are valid. Enumeration is used to build certificate chains by fetching a leaf certificate and then fetching successive issuer certificates until a root certificate is reached, or to assemble CRLs. The data returned from queries and enumeration operations are handled through get-first and get-next calls, where get-first returns the initial result and get-next returns successive results until no more values are available.

The next entry specifies cryptlib object types such as public keys, certificates, and private keys that are valid for the mechanism.

The next entry specifies valid key-management flags for the mechanism. These include KEYMGMT_FLAG_CHECK_ONLY (which checks for the existence of an item without returning it, and is useful for checking for revocation entries in a CRL), KEYMGMT_FLAG_LABEL_ONLY (which returns the label attached to a private key for use in user prompts requesting a password or PIN for the key), and KEYMGMT_FLAG_USAGE_SIGN, which indicates that if multiple keys/certificates match the given key ID, then the most current signing key/certificate should be returned.

The next two entries indicate the access types for which a key ID parameter and password or related information are required. For example, a public-key read requires a key ID parameter to identify the key being read but not a password, and a private-key write requires a password but not a key ID, since it is included with the key being written. Enumeration operations don't require a password but do require somewhere to store enumeration state information that records the current progress of the enumeration operation. This requirement is also specified in the password-or-related-information entry.

Finally, the last two (optional) entries specify specific object types that are required in some cases for specific keysets. For example a public-key action object may be valid for the overall class of public-key mechanisms and keysets, but a certificate will be required if the mechanism is being used to manipulate a certificate-based keyset such as a CA certificate store.

3.4.1 Mechanism ACLs

As with the message and attribute ACLs, the mechanism ACLs are best illustrated with examples taken from the different mechanism types. The ACL for the PKCS #1 signature creation mechanism, shown in Figure 3.21, is one of the simplest. This takes as input a hash and signature action object and produces as output a byte string equal in length to the signing key modulus size, from 64 bytes (512 bits) up to the maximum allowed modulus size. Both the signature and hash objects must be in the high state, and the signature action is routed to the signature action object if the value being passed in is a certificate object with an associated action object. The ACL for PKCS #1 signature checking is almost identical.

```
MECHANISM_PKCS1,
{ MKACM_S_OPT( 64, CRYPT_MAX_PKCSIZE ),
  MKACM_O( SUBTYPE_CTX_HASH, ACL_FLAG_HIGH_STATE ),
  MKACM_O( SUBTYPE_CTX_PKC, ACL_FLAG_HIGH_STATE | ACL_FLAG_ROUTE_TO_CTX ) }
```

Figure 3.21. ACL for PKCS #1 signatures.

The type of each parameter, either a boolean, numeric, string, or object, is defined by the MKACM_x definition, where the letter indicates the type. String parameters can be marked optional as in the ACL in Figure 3.21, in which case passing in a null destination value returns only length information while passing in a destination buffer returns the data and its length. This is used to determine how much space the mechanism output value will consume without actually invoking the mechanism.

The ACL for CMS (Cryptographic Message Syntax) key wrapping is shown in Figure 3.22. This wraps a session key for an encryption or MAC action object using a second encryption action object. The ACL for key unwrapping is almost identical, except that the action object for the unwrapped key must be in the low rather than high state, since it has a key loaded into it by the unwrapping process.

```
MECHANISM_CMS,
{ MKACM_S_OPT( 8 + 8, CRYPT_MAX_KEYSIZE + 16 ),
  MKACM_O( SUBTYPE_CTX_CONV | SUBTYPE_CTX_MAC, ACL_FLAG_HIGH_STATE ),
  MKACM_O( SUBTYPE_CTX_CONV, ACL_FLAG_HIGH_STATE ) }
```

Figure 3.22. ACL for CMS key wrap.

As with the PKCS #1 signature ACL, the output parameter is a byte string containing the session key encrypted with the key encryption key, and the input parameters are the action objects containing the session key and key-encryption key, respectively. The length of the output parameter is defined by the CMS specification, and falls within the range given in the ACL.

The most complex crypto mechanism ACLs are those for key derivation. The key derivation mechanisms take as input keying material, a salt value, and an iteration count, and produce as output processed keying material ready for use. Depending on the protocol being used, it is sometimes loaded as a key into an action object but is usually processed further to create keys or secret data for multiple action objects (for example, to encrypt and MAC incoming and outgoing data streams in secure sessions).

In the case of SSL derivation, the mechanism is used to convert the premaster secret that is exchanged during the SSL handshake process into the master secret and then to convert the master secret into the actual keying material that is used to protect the SSL session. The ACL for SSL keying material derivation is shown in Figure 3.23. Again, the first parameter is the output data, from 48 to 512 bytes of keying material. The remaining three parameters are the input keying material, the salt (64 bytes), and the number of iterations of the derivation function to use (1 iteration).

```
MECHANISM_SSL,
{ MKACM_S( 48, 512 ),
  MKACM_S( 48, 512 ),
  MKACM_S( 64, 64 ),
  MKACM_N( 1, 1 ) }
```

Figure 3.23. ACL for SSLv3 key derivation.

Keyset mechanism ACLs are somewhat more complex than crypto mechanism ACLs. One of the simpler ones is the ACL for accessing revocation information, shown in Figure 3.24. This ACL specifies that read access to revocation information is valid for certificate keysets and CA certificate stores, write access is only valid for certificate keysets but not CA certificate stores (it has to be entered indirectly through a revocation request which is subject to CA auditing requirements), and delete access is never valid (revocation information is only deleted as part of normal CA management operations once it has expired, but is never deleted directly). Enumeration and query operations (which return connected sequences of objects, which doesn't make sense for per-certificate revocation entries) aren't valid for any keyset types (again, the assembly of CRLs is a CA management operation that can't be performed directly). The permitted object types for this mechanism are CRLs, which can be read or written to the keyset. Use of the presence-check flag is permitted, and (implicitly) encouraged since in most cases users only care about the valid/not valid status of a certificate and don't want to see the entire CRL that caused the given status to be returned.

```
KEYMGMT_ITEM_REVOCATIONINFO,
/*RWD*/      SUBTYPE_KEYSET_DBMS | SUBTYPE_KEYSET_DBMS_STORE,
             SUBTYPE_KEYSET_DBMS, SUBTYPE_NONE,
/*FnQ*/      SUBTYPE_NONE, SUBTYPE_NONE,
/*Obj*/      SUBTYPE_CERT_CRL,
/*Flg*/      KEYMGMT_FLAG_CHECK_ONLY,
KEYMGMT_FLAG_CHECK_ONLY,
ACCESS_KEYSET_FxRxD,
ACCESS_KEYSET_FNxxx
```

Figure 3.24. ACL for revocation information access.

Finally, an ID is required for get-first, read, and delete operations, and enumeration state storage is required for get-first and get-next operations. Note that although the ID-required entry specifies the conditions for get-first and delete operations, the operations themselves are disallowed by the permitted-operations entry. All of the ACL entries are consistent, even if some of them are never used.

The ACL for private key access is shown in Figure 3.25. This ACL specifies that private-key read/write/delete access is valid for private key files and Fortezza and PKCS #11 crypto devices. In this case there's only a single entry, since the read/write/delete access settings are identical. Similarly, query and enumeration operations (which would return connected sequences of objects, which doesn't make sense for private keys) are not valid and have a single setting of 'no access'. The mechanism operates on private-key action objects and allows optional flags specifying a presence check only without returning data and a label read only that returns the label associated with the key but doesn't try to retrieve the key itself. Key reads and deletes require a key ID, and key reads and writes require a password. Since devices are typically session-based, with the user providing a PIN only when initially establishing the session with the device, the password-required entry is marked as optional rather than mandatory for read/write (XX rather than RW).

```
KEYMGMT_ITEM_PRIVATEKEY,
/*RWD*/      SUBTYPE_KEYSET_FILE | SUBTYPE_DEV_FORT | SUBTYPE_DEV_P11,
/*FnQ*/      SUBTYPE_NONE,
/*Obj*/      SUBTYPE_CTX_PKC,
ACCESS_KEYSET_xxRWD,
KEYMGMT_FLAG_CHECK_ONLY | KEYMGMT_FLAG_LABEL_ONLY,
ACCESS_KEYSET_xxXXx
```

Figure 3.25. ACL for private-key access.

The most complex ACL is the one for public-key, and by extension certificate, access. This ACL, shown in Figure 3.26, permits public-key access for any keyset type and any device type that is capable of storing keys, and query and enumeration access for any keyset and device type that supports this operation. The mechanism operates on public key action objects and any certificate type that contains a public key. Some operations are disallowed in specific cases, for example as with the revocation information ACL earlier it's not possible to directly inject arbitrary certificates into a CA certificate store. This can only be done indirectly through a certification request which is subject to CA auditing requirements. The result is complex enough that each access type is specified using its own ACL rather than collecting them into common groups them as with the other keyset mechanism ACLs.

```
KEYMGMT_ITEM_PUBLICKEY,
/* R */      SUBTYPE_KEYSET_ANY | SUBTYPE_DEV_FORT | SUBTYPE_DEV_P11,
/* W */      SUBTYPE_KEYSET_FILE | SUBTYPE_KEYSET_DBMS |
             SUBTYPE_KEYSET_HTTP | SUBTYPE_KEYSET_LDAP |
             SUBTYPE_DEV_FORT | SUBTYPE_DEV_P11,
/* D */      SUBTYPE_KEYSET_FILE | SUBTYPE_KEYSET_DBMS |
             SUBTYPE_KEYSET_HTTP | SUBTYPE_KEYSET_LDAP |
             SUBTYPE_DEV_FORT | SUBTYPE_DEV_P11,
/* Fn*/      SUBTYPE_KEYSET_DBMS | SUBTYPE_KEYSET_DBMS_STORE |
             SUBTYPE_KEYSET_FILE | SUBTYPE_DEV_FORT,
/* Q */      SUBTYPE_KEYSET_DBMS | SUBTYPE_KEYSET_DBMS_STORE |
             SUBTYPE_KEYSET_LDAP,
/*Obj*/      SUBTYPE_CTX_PKC | SUBTYPE_CERT_CERT |
             SUBTYPE_CERT_CERTCHAIN,
/*Flg*/      KEYMGMT_FLAG_CHECK_ONLY | KEYMGMT_FLAG_LABEL_ONLY |
             KEYMGMT_MASK_CERTOPTIONS,
ACCESS_KEYSET_FxRxD,
ACCESS_KEYSET_FNxxx
SUBTYPE_KEYSET_DBMS | SUBTYPE_KEYSET_DBMS_STORE |
   SUBTYPE_KEYSET_LDAP | SUBTYPE_DEV_FORT | SUBTYPE_DEV_P11,
SUBTYPE_CERT_CERT | SUBTYPE_CERT_CERTCHAIN
```

Figure 3.26. ACL for public-key/certificate access.

This ACL also contains the optional pair of entries specifying that applying the mechanism to certain keyset types requires the use of a specific object type. For example applying a public-key write to a file keyset such as a PKCS #15 soft-token or PGP keyring can be done with a generic public-key item (which may be a public- or private-key action object or certificate), but applying the same operation to a certificate store specifically requires a certificate object.

3.5 Message Filter Implementation

The previous sections have covered the filter rules that are applied to messages and, at a more fine-grained level, the attributes that are manipulated by messages. This section covers the implementations of some of the filters that are applied by the kernel filtering rules.

3.5.1 Pre-dispatch Filters

One of the simplest filters is the one that is invoked before dispatching a destroy object message, the implementation of which is shown in Figure 3.27. This decrements the reference count for any dependent objects that may exist and moves the object being destroyed into the signalled state, which indicates to the kernel that it should not dispatch any further messages to it. Once these actions have been taken, the message is dispatched on to the object for processing.

```
preDispatchSignalDependentObjects ::=
    if( objectInfoPtr->dependentDevice != CRYPT_ERROR )
        decRefCount( objectInfoPtr->dependentDevice, 0, NULL );
    if( objectInfoPtr->dependentObject != CRYPT_ERROR )
        decRefCount( objectInfoPtr->dependentObject, 0, NULL );
    objectInfoPtr->flags |= OBJECT_FLAG_SIGNALLED;
```

Figure 3.27. Destroy object message filter.

When the object finishes processing the message, the kernel dequeues all further messages for it and clears the object table entry. This is the one message that has an implicit rather than explicit post-dispatch action, since the act of dequeueing messages is logically part of the kernel dispatcher rather than an external filter rule.

```
preDispatchCheckState ::=
    if( isInHighState( objectHandle ) )
        return( CRYPT_ERROR_PERMISSION );
```

Figure 3.28. Check object state filter.

The pre-dispatch filter that checks an object's state in response to a message that would transition it into the high state is shown in Figure 3.28. This is an extremely simple rule that should be self-explanatory.

One of the more complex pre-dispatch filters, which checks that an action that is being requested for an object is permitted, is shown in Figure 3.29. This begins by ensuring that the object is in the high state (if it isn't, it can't perform any action) and that if the requested action is one that caused a transition into the high state, that it can't be applied a second time. In addition, it ensures that if the object has a usage count set and it has gone to zero, it can't be used any more.

```
preDispatchCheckActionAccess ::=
    /* If the object is in the low state, it can't be used for any action */
    if( !isInHighState( objectHandle ) )
        return( CRYPT_ERROR_NOTINITED );

    /* If the object is in the high state, it can't receive another message
       of the kind that causes the state change */
    if( message == RESOURCE_MESSAGE_CTX_GENKEY )
        return( CRYPT_ERROR_INITED );

    /* If there's a usage count set for the object and it's gone to zero, it
       can't be used any more */
    if( objectInfoPtr->usageCount != CRYPT_UNUSED && \
        objectInfoPtr->usageCount <= 0 )
        return( CRYPT_ERROR_PERMISSION );

    /* Determine the required level for access.  Like protection rings, the
       lower the value, the higher the privilege level.  Level 3 is all-
       access, level 2 is internal-access only, level 1 is no access, and
       level 0 is not-available (e.g. encryption for hash contexts) */
    requiredLevel = \
        objectInfoPtr->actionFlags & \
            MK_ACTION_PERM( message, ACTION_PERM_MASK );

    /* Make sure the action is enabled at the required level */
    if( message & RESOURCE_MESSAGE_INTERNAL )
        /* It's an internal message, the minimal permissions will do */
        actualLevel = MK_ACTION_PERM( message, ACTION_PERM_NONE_EXTERNAL );
    else
        /* It's an external message, we need full permissions for access */
        actualLevel = MK_ACTION_PERM( message, ACTION_PERM_ALL );
    if( requiredLevel < actualLevel )
        {
        /* The required level is less than the actual level (e.g. level 2
           access attempted from level 3), return more detailed information
           about the problem */
        return( ( ( requiredLevel >> ACTION_PERM_SHIFT( message ) ) == \
                                            ACTION_PERM_NONE ) ? \
                CRYPT_ERROR_NOTAVAIL : CRYPT_ERROR_PERMISSION );
        }
```

Figure 3.29. Check requested action permission filter.

Once the basic security checks have been performed, it then checks whether the requested action is permitted at the object's current security setting. This is a simple comparison between the permission level of the message (in other words the permission level of the subject that sent it) and the permission level set for the object. If the message's permission level is insufficient, the request is denied. Since there are two different ways of saying no, ACTION_PERM_NOTAVAIL (it's not there) and ACTION_PERM_NONE (it's there but you can't use it), the filter performs a check for why the request was denied and returns the appropriate error code to the caller.

3.5.2 Post-dispatch Filters

The post-dispatch filters are all very simple, mostly performing housekeeping and cleanup tasks after a message has been processed by an object. The one implicit filter, which is invoked after an object has processed a destroy object message, has already been covered. Another post-dispatch filter is the one that updates an object's usage count if it has one set and if the object has successfully processed the message that was sent to it (for example, if an encryption action object returns a success status in response to a message instructing it to encrypt data). This filter is shown in Figure 3.30, and simply decrements the object's usage count if this is being used. Although it would appear that this filter can decrement the usage count past zero, this can never occur because the pre-dispatch filter shown earlier will prevent further messages from being dispatched to it once the usage count reaches zero. Not shown in the code snippet presented here are the assertion-based testing rules that ensure that this is indeed the case. The testing and verification of the filter rules (and the kernel as a whole) are covered in Chapter 5.

```
postDispatchUpdateUsageCount ::=
    /* If there's an active usage count present, update it */
    if( objectInfoPtr->usageCount != CRYPT_UNUSED )
        objectInfoPtr->usageCount--;
```

Figure 3.30. Decrement object usage count filter.

Another filter, which moves an object into the high state, is shown in Figure 3.31. This rule should need no further comment.

```
postDispatchChangeState ::=
    /* The state change message was successfully processed, the object is
       now in the high state */
    objectInfoPtr->flags |= OBJECT_FLAG_HIGH;
```

Figure 3.31. Transition object into high-state filter.

In practice, this filter is used as part of the PRE_POST_DISPATCH(CheckState, ChangeState) rule shown in earlier examples.

3.6 Customising the Rule-Based Policy

As was mentioned in Section 3.1, one of the advantages of the rule-based policy used in cryptlib is that it can be easily adapted to meet a particular set of requirements without requiring the redesign, rebuilding, and revalidation of the entire security kernel upon which the system is based. This section looks at the changes that would be required in order to make cryptlib comply with policies such as the FIPS 140 crypto module security requirements [26].

This task is made relatively easy by the fact that both cryptlib and FIPS 140 represent a commonsense cryptographic security policy containing requirements such as "plaintext keys shall not be accessible from outside the cryptographic module" (FIPS 140 Section 4.7.5), so that the native cryptlib policy already complies with most of FIPS 140. Other requirements such as "if a cryptographic module supports concurrent operators then the module shall internally maintain the separation of the roles and services performed by each operator" (FIPS 140 Section 4.3) and "the output data path shall be logically disconnected from the circuitry and processes performing key generation, manual key entry or key zeroization" (FIPS 140 Section 4.2) are met through the use of the separation kernel. The reason for the disconnection requirement in FIPS 140 is to ensure that there is no chance that the currently active keying material could be interfered with through the arrival of new keying material on shared circuits. The cryptlib kernel actually goes much further than the mere isolation of key handling by isolating all operations which take place.

In addition to the design requirements, several of the FIPS 140 documentation and specification requirements are already addressed through the use of the rule-based policy. Some of these include the requirement that the "precise specification of the security rules under which a cryptographic module shall operate, including the security rules derived from the requirements of this standard and the additional security rules imposed by the vendor" (FIPS 140 appendix C.1), which is provided by the kernel filter rules, and the ability to "provide answers to the following questions: what access does operator X, performing service Y while in role Z, have to data item W?" (FIPS 140 appendix C.1), which is provided by the expert-system nature of the kernel which was discussed in the previous chapter.

The FIPS 140 requirements that remain to be addressed by cryptlib are relatively few and relate to the separation of I/O ports for data and cryptovariables (critical security parameters or CSPs in FIPS-140-speak) and the use of role-based authentication for users. Both of these requirements, which are present at the higher FIPS 140 security levels, are meant for hardware-based crypto modules and aren't addressed in the current cryptlib implementation because it is used almost exclusively in its software-only form. Updating the current implementation to meet the FIPS 140 requirements requires three sets of changes, two fairly simple ones to kernel filter rules and ACLs and one slightly more complex one to the access check performed for object attributes.

The first and simplest change arises from the requirement that "all encrypted secret and private keys entered into or output from the cryptographic module and used in an approved mode of operation shall be encrypted using an approved algorithm" (FIPS 140 Section 4.7.4). Currently, cryptlib allows keys to be loaded in plaintext form since this is what's usually done in software-only implementations. Meeting the requirement above involves changing the key attribute ACLs from ACCESS_*xxx* to ACCESS_INT_*xxx* as described in Section 3.3.1, which removes the ability to load plaintext keys into the module exactly as required. Because the new ACL is enforced centrally by the kernel, this change immediately takes effect throughout the entire architecture rather than having to be implemented in every location where a key load might take place. This again demonstrates the advantage of having standardised, rule-based controls enforced by a security kernel, since in a more conventional design a single security check omitted from any of the many functions that typically manage key import and export would result in the FIPS 140 requirement not being met. Incredibly, one vendor actually provides detailed step-by-step instructions complete with sample code telling users how to bypass the security of their cryptographic API and extract plaintext keys [27].

The second change arises from the requirement that "a cryptographic module shall support the following authorized roles for operators: User role, the role assumed to obtain security services and to perform cryptographic operations or other authorised functions. Crypto officer role, the role assumed to perform a set of cryptographic initialization or management functions" (FIPS 140 Section 4.3.1). Again, the use of roles doesn't make much sense in a software-only implementation where cryptlib is being controlled by a single user who takes all roles; however, it can be added fairly easily through a simple ACL change. In addition to the internal and external access bits, each ACL can be extended to include an indication of whether it applies to the user or crypto officer; for example, the encryption key attributes would be marked as being accessible only by the crypto officer, whereas the encrypt/decrypt/sign/verify object usage would be marked as being usable only by the user. In actual fact, cryptlib already enforces roles internally, but this is invisible when a single user is acting in multiple roles.

The final change, which is specific to hardware implementations, is that "the data input and output physical port(s) used for plaintext cryptographic key components, plaintext authentication data, and other unprotected CSPs shall be physically separated from all other ports of the cryptographic module" (FIPS 140 Section 4.2). Since this requirement is very specific to the underlying hardware implementation, there is no general-purpose solution to the problem, although one approach would be to use the standard filter rule mechanism to ensure that CSP-related attributes can only be set through a safe I/O channel or trusted I/O path. An example of this type of mechanism is presented in Chapter 7, which uses a trusted I/O path with an implementation of cryptlib running in embedded cryptographic hardware. Another approach that eliminates most of the problem is to disallow most forms of unprotected CSP load (which the ACL change described earlier has the effect of doing), although some form of I/O channel over which the user or crypto officer can authenticate themselves to the crypto module will still be required.

A set of requirements that predates the FIPS 140 ones is the British Telecom cryptographic equipment security code of practice [28], which suggests measures such as checking for attempts to scan for all legal commands and options (a standard technique for finding interesting things in ISO 7816-4 smart cards), detection of commands issued outside normal operating conditions (for example an attempt to create a contract signature at 3 am), and detection of a mismatch in the number of commands submitted versus the number of commands authorised. cryptlib already performs the last check, and the first two can be implemented without too much trouble through the use of filter rules for appropriate commands such as object usage actions in combination with a retry counter and a mechanism for recording the conditions (for example, the time of day) under which an action is permitted.

The ease with which cryptlib can be adapted to meet the FIPS 140 and BT code of practice requirements demonstrates the flexibility of the rule-based policy and kernel implementation, which allow the policy change to be handled through a few minor changes in a centralised location that are immediately reflected throughout the entire cryptlib architecture. In contrast, a more conventional security kernel with hardcoded policies would require at least a partial kernel redesign, and a conventional crypto toolkit implementation would require a potentially huge number of changes scattered throughout the code, with accompanying verification and assurance difficulties.

3.7 Miscellaneous Implementation Issues

Making each object thread-safe across multiple operating systems is somewhat tricky. The locking capabilities in cryptlib are implemented as a collection of preprocessor macros that are designed to allow them to be mapped to appropriate OS-specific user- and system-level thread synchronisation and locking functions. Great care has been taken to ensure that this locking mechanism is as fine-grained as possible, with locks typically covering no more than a dozen or so lines of code before they are relinquished, and the code executed while the lock is active being carefully scrutinised to ensure that it can never become the cause of a bottleneck (for example, by executing a long-running loop while the lock is active).

Under Windows, the locking is handled by critical sections, which aren't really critical sections at all but a form of fast mutex. If a thread enters one of these pseudocritical sections, all other threads continue running normally unless one of them tries to enter the same pseudocritical section, at which point it is suspended until the first thread exits the section. For the Windows kernel-mode version, the locking variables have somewhat more accurate names and are implemented as kernel mutexes. Otherwise, their behaviour is the same as the user-level pseudocritical sections.

Under Unix, the implementation is somewhat more complex since there are a number of threading implementations available. The most common is the Posix pthreads one, but the mechanism used by cryptlib allows any vaguely similar threading mechanism (for example, Solaris or Mach threads) to be employed. Under other OSes such as BeOS, OS/2, and the variety of embedded operating systems that cryptlib runs under, the locking is handled by mutexes in a manner similar to the Unix version.

In addition to handling object locking, we need a way to manage the ACL's that tie an object to a thread. This is again built on top of preprocessor macros that map to the appropriate OS-specific data structures and functions. If the ownership variable is set to the predefined constant CRYPT_ERROR (a value equivalent to the floating-point NaN constant) then the object is not owned by any particular thread. The getCurrentIdentity macro is used to check object ownership. If the object's owner is CRYPT_ERROR or is the same as getCurrentIdentity, then the object is accessible. If the object is unowned, then setting the owner to getCurrentIdentity binds it to the current thread. The object can also be bound to another thread by setting the owner to the given thread ID (provided the object's ACL allows the thread that is trying to set the new owner to do so).

3.8 Performance

There are a number of factors that make an assessment of the overall performance impact of the cryptlib kernel implementation rather difficult. Firstly, the access controls and parameter checking that are performed by the kernel take the place of the parameter checking that is usually performed by functions used in conventional implementations (at least in properly implemented ones), so that much of the apparent overhead imposed by the kernel would also exist in more conventional implementations.

A second factor that makes the performance impact difficult to assess is the fact that although the kernel appears to contain mechanisms such as the message queue and message routing code that could add some amount of overhead to each message that is processed, the stunt box eliminates any use of the queue except under very heavy loads, and the message routing for most messages sent to objects only takes one or two compares and a branch, again having almost no overhead.

A final factor that makes performance assessment difficult is the fact that the nature of the cryptlib implementation changes the way in which code is written. Whereas normal code might require a variety of checks around a function call to ensure that everything is as required and to handle special-case conditions by the caller, with cryptlib it's quite safe to fire off a message since the kernel will ensure that no inappropriate outcome arises.

Although the kernel would appear to impose a certain amount of extra overhead on all operations that it manages, its overall effect is probably more or less neutral when compared to a more conventional implementation (for example the kernel greatly simplifies a number of areas, such as checks on key usage, that would otherwise need to be performed explicitly either by the caller or by the called code). Without rewriting most of cryptlib in a more conventional manner for use in a performance comparison, the best performance assessment that can be made is the one described in the previous chapter for Blacker in which users couldn't detect the presence of the security mechanisms (in this case, the cryptlib kernel) when they were activated.

3.9 References

[1]   "Evaluation of Security Model Rule Bases", John Page, Jody Heaney, Marc Adkins, and Gary Dolsen, *Proceedings of the 12th National Computer Security Conference*, October 1989, p.98.

[2]   "A Generalized Framework for Access Control: An Informal Description", Marshall Abrams, Leonard LaPadula, Kenneth Eggers, and Ingrid Olson, *Proceedings of the 13th National Computer Security Conference*, October 1990, p.135.

[3]   "A Generalized Framework for Database Access Controls", Marshall Abrams and Gary Smith, *Database Security IV: Status and Prospects*, North-Holland, 1991, p.171.

[4]   "Generalized Framework for Access Control: Towards Prototyping the ORGCON Policy", Marshall Abrams, Jody Heaney, Osborne King, Leonard LaPadula, Manette Lazear, and Ingrid Olson, *Proceedings of the 14th National Computer Security Conference*, October 1991, p.257.

[5]   "A Framework for Access Control Models", Burkhard Lau, *Proceedings of the IFIP TC11 11th International Conference on Information Security (IFIP/Sec'95)*, 1995, p.513.

[6]   "Rule-Set Modeling of a Trusted Computer System", Leonard LaPadula, "Information Security: An Integrated Collection of Essays", IEEE Computer Society Press, 1995, p.187.

[7]   "Mediation and Separation in Contemporary Information Technology Systems", Marshall Abrams, Jody Heaney, and Michael Joyce, *Proceedings of the 15th National Computer Security Conference*, October 1992, p.359.

[8]   "Information Retrieval, Transfer and Management for OSI: Access Control Framework", ISO 10181-3, 1993.

[9]   "The COPS (Common Open Policy Service) Protocol", RFC 2748, Jim Boyle, Ron Cohen, David Durham, Raju Rajan, Shai Herzog, and Arun Sastry, January 2000.

[10] "Remote Authentication Dial In User Service (RADIUS)", RFC 2138, Carl Rigney, Allan C. Rubens, William Allen Simpson, and Steve Willens, April 1997.

[11] "Diameter Base Protocol", Pat R. Calhoun, Jari Arkko, Erik Guttman, Glen Zorn, and John Loughney, `draft-ietf-aaa-diameter-11.txt`, June 2002.

[12] "The Integrity-Lock Approach to Secure Database Management", Richard Graubart, *Proceedings of the 1984 IEEE Symposium on Security and Privacy*, IEEE Computer Society Press, 1984, p.62.

[13] "Towards Practical MLS Database Management Systems using the Integrity Lock Technology", Rae Burns, *Proceedings of the 9th National Computer Security Conference*, September 1986, p.25.

[14] "Providing Policy Control Over Object Operations in a Mach Based System", Spencer Minear, *Proceedings of the 5th Usenix Security Symposium*, June 1995, p.141.

[15] "A Comparison of Methods for Implementing Adaptive Security Policies", Michael Carney and Brian Loe, *Proceedings of the 7th Usenix Security Symposium*, January 1998, p.1.

[16] "Developing and Using a 'Policy Neutral' Access Control Policy", Duane Olawsky, Todd Fine, Edward Schneider, and Ray Spencer, *Proceedings of the 1996 ACM New Security Paradigms Workshop*, September 1996, p.60.

[17] "The Flask Security Architecture: System Support for Diverse Security Policies", Ray Spencer, Stephen Smalley, Peter Loscocco, Mike Hibler, David Andersen, and Jay Pepreau, *Proceedings of the 8th Usenix Security Symposium*, August 1999, p.123.

[18] "The Privilege Control Table Toolkit: An Implementation of the System Build Approach", Thomas Woodall and Roberta Gotfried, *Proceedings of the 19th National Information Systems Security Conference* (formerly the National Computer Security Conference), October 1996, p.389.

[19] "Protected Groups: An Approach to Integrity and Secrecy in an Object-oriented Database", James Slack and Elizabeth Unger, *Proceedings of the 15th National Computer Security Conference*, October 1992, p.513.

[20] "Security In An Object-Oriented Database", James Slack, *Proceedings of the 1993 New Security Paradigms Workshop*, ACM, 1993, p.155.

[21] "An Access Control Language for Object-Oriented Programming Systems", Masaaki Mizuno and Arthur Oldehoeft, *The Journal of Systems and Software*, **Vol.13**, **No.1** (September 1990), p.3.

[22] "Meta Objects for Access Control: Extending Capability-Based Security", Thomas Riechmann and Franz Hauck, *Proceedings of the 1997 ACM New Security Paradigms Workshop*, September 1997, p.17.

[23] "Meta Objects for Access Control: Role-Based Principals", Thomas Riechmann and Jürgen Kleinöder, *Proceedings of the 3rd Australasian Conference on Information Security and Privacy (ACISP'98)*, Springer-Verlag Lecture Notes in Computer Science, No.1438, July 1998, p.296.

[24] "Discretionary access control by means of usage conditions", Eike Born and Helmut Steigler, *Computers and Security*, **Vol.13**, **No.5** (October 1994), p.437.

[25] "Meta Objects for Access Control: A Formal Model for Role-Based Principals", Thomas Riechmann and Franz Hauck, *Proceedings of the 1998 ACM New Security Paradigms Workshop*, September 1998, p.30.

[26] "Security Requirements for Cryptographic Modules", FIPS PUB 140-2, National Institute of Standards and Technology, July 2001.

[27] "HOWTO: Export/Import Plain Text Session Key Using CryptoAPI", Microsoft Knowledge Base Article Q228786, Microsoft Corporation, 11 January 2000.

[28] "Cryptographic Equipment Security: A Code of Practice", Stephen Serpell, *Computers and Security*, **Vol.4**, **No.1** (March 1985), p.47.

4 Verification Techniques

4.1 Introduction

In 1987, Fred Brooks produced his seminal and oft-quoted paper "No Silver Bullet: Essence and Accidents of Software Engineering" [1]. Probably the single most important point made in this article is one that doesn't directly touch on the field of computer software at all, but comes from the field of medicine. Before modern medicine existed, illness and disease were believed to be the fault of evil spirits, angry gods, demons, and all manner of other causes. If it were possible to find some magic cure that would keep the demons at bay, then a great many medical problems could be solved. Scientific research into the real reasons for illness and disease destroyed these hopes of magical cures. There is no single, universal cure since there is no single problem, and each new problem (or even variation of an existing problem) needs to be addressed via a problem-specific solution.

When the message in the article is reduced to a simple catchphrase, its full meaning often becomes lost: There really is no silver bullet, no rubber chicken that can be waved over a system to make it secure. This chapter examines some of the attempts that have been made to find (or decree) a silver bullet and looks at some of the problems that accompany them. The next chapter will then look at alternative approaches towards building secure systems.

As did an earlier paper on this topic that found that "proclaiming that the gods have clay feet or that the emperor is naked [...] are never popular sentiments" [2] (another paper that pointed out problems in a related area found that it had attracted "an unusually large number of anonymous reviewers" [3]), this chapter provides a somewhat higher number of references than usual in order to substantiate various points made in the text and to provide leads for further study.

4.2 Formal Security Verification

The definition and the promise of formal methods is that they provide a means to "allow the specification, development, and verification of a computer system using a rigorous mathematical notation. Using a formal specification language to specify a system allows its consistency, completeness, and correctness to be assessed in a systematic fashion" [4]. The standard approach towards trying to achieve this goal for security-relevant systems is through the use of formal program verification techniques that make use of mathematical logic to try to prove the correctness of a piece of software or hardware. There are two main classes of tools used in this task, proof checkers (sometimes called theorem provers), which apply laws from logic and set theory to a set of assumptions until a desired goal is reached, and model checkers, which enumerate all of the possible states that a system can be in and check each state against rules and conditions specified by the user [5][6][7]. In terms of reporting problems, proof checkers (which work with symbolic logic) will report which step in a particular proof is invalid, whereas model checkers (which work with finite state machines, FSMs) will report the steps that lead to an invalid state.

Proof checkers are named thus because they don't generate the entire proof themselves but only aid the user in constructing a proof from an algebraic specification, performing many of the tedious portions of the proving process automatically. This means that users must still know how to perform the proof themselves, and are merely assisted in the process by the proof checker. This requires some level of skill from the users, not only because they need to know enough mathematics to construct the proof and drive the checker, but also because they need to be able to recognise instances where the checker is being sent down the wrong path, in which case the checker cannot complete the proof. The user can't distinguish (from the actions of the checker) the case of a proof that is still in the process of being completed, and a proof which can never be completed (for example because it is based on an invalid assumption). This can make proof checkers somewhat frustrating to use.

Another problem that arises with proof checking is with the specifications themselves. Algebraic specifications work with a predefined type of abstraction of the underlying system in which functions are defined indirectly in terms of their interaction with other functions (that is, the functions are transformational rewrite statements). Because of this, they can require a fair amount of mental gymnastics by anyone working with them in order to understand them. A slightly different specification approach, the abstract model approach, defines functions in terms of an underlying abstraction (lists, arrays, and sets being some examples) selected by the user, as well as a set of preconditions and postconditions for each function being specified. This has the advantage that it's rather easier to work with than an algebraic specification because it's closer to the way programmers think, but has the corresponding disadvantage that it strongly influences the final implementation towards using the same data representation as the one used in the abstract specification.

In contrast to proof checkers, model checkers operate on a particular model of a system (usually a finite-state machine), enumerating each state that the system can enter and checking it against certain constraints (can the state be reached, can the state be exited once reached, and so on). A state machine is defined in terms of two things, states that have V-functions (value returning functions) which provide the details of the state, and transitions that have O-functions (observation functions) which define the transitions [8][9]. Other methodologies use the terms "state" or "variable" for V-functions and "transform" for O-functions. An exception to this is FIPS 140, which reverses the standard terminology so that "state" corresponds to the execution of a piece of code and another term has to be invented to describe what is being transformed by a "state".

An O-function works by taking a V-function and changing the details that it will return about the state. In verification systems such as InaJo (which uses the "transform" terminology) the O-functions are then used to provide input and output assertions for a verification condition generator. Because the number of states grows exponentially with the complexity of the system, model checkers tend to be incredibly resource-hungry. One solution to this problem is to fall back on the use of a proof checker when the model checker can't find any problem because it has run out of memory, or to use two different, complementary formal methods in the hope that one will cover any blind spots present in the other [10] (other variations of this technique are examined in Section 4.3.4). Failing the availability of this safety device, it's unsafe to draw any real conclusions since the model checker may have found problems had it been able to search more of the state space [11]. Proof checkers have an analogous problem in that they can't detect all possible inconsistent ways to write a specification, so that with a little effort and ingenuity it's possible to persuade the system to prove a false theorem [12].

An alternative approach is to apply further amounts of abstraction to try to manage the state explosion. In one example a model with a state space of 2^{87} states that would have taken 10^{12} years to search was further abstracted by partitioning the system into equivalence classes, separating the validation of portions that were assumed to be independent from one another so that they could be validated in isolation, and removing information from the model that was held to be non-germane to the validation. This refinement process finally resulted in six validations that checked around 100,000 states each [13]. This type of manipulation of the problem domain has the disadvantage that the correspondence between the new abstraction and the original specification is lost, leading to the possible introduction of errors in the specification-to-new-abstraction mapping phase. A second potential problem area is that some of the techniques being applied (for example validating different portions in isolation) may miss faults if it turns out that there were actually interactions present between some of the portions. An example of this occurred during the analysis of the Viper ALU (which first cropped up in Chapter 2), which was analysed as a set of eight 4-bit slices because viewing it as a single 32-bit unit would have made analysis intractable. Since a proof used at another level of the attempted verification of the Viper CPU assumed a complete 32-bit ALU rather than a collection of 4-bit slices, no firm conclusion could be drawn as to whether one corresponded to the other [14]. The controversy over exactly what was evaluated in Viper and what constituted a "proven correct design" eventually resulted in the demise of the company that was to exploit it commercially in a barrage of finger-pointing and legal action [15][16]. A similar problem had beset the Autodin II upgrade in the late 1970s, leading to a court battle over the definition of the term "formal specification" [59]. The work was eventually abandoned in favour of a more conventional design that just added encryption to the existing system.

All of these approaches suffer from something called the hidden function problem, which is the inability of the system to retain any state from previous invocations. The solution to this problem is to use hidden functions that are not directly visible to the user but that can retain state information from previous invocations. These hidden functions manage information that is not part of the visible behaviour of the abstract machine being specified but is required for its operation. Algebraic specifications in particular, the functions of which are true functions in the mathematical sense that they can have no side effects, are plagued by the need to use hidden functions. In some cases, the specification can contain more hidden functions (that is, artefacts of the specification language) than actual functions that specify the behaviour of the system being modelled [17].

4.2.1 Formal Security Model Verification

The use of formal methods for security verification arose from theoretical work performed in the 1970s, which was followed by some experimental tools in the late 1970s and early 1980s. The belief then, supported by the crusading efforts of a number of formal methods advocates, was that it would only be a matter of time before the use of formal methods in industry was widespread, and that at some point it would be possible to extend formal-methods-based verification techniques all the way down to the code level. It was this background that led to the emphasis on formal methods in the Orange Book.

The formal security model that is being verified is typically based on a finite state machine model of the system, which has an initial state that is shown (or at least decreed) to be secure, and a number of successor states that can be reached from the initial state which should also be secure. One representation of the security model for such a system consists of a collection of mathematical expressions that, when proven true, verify that the state transitions preserve the initial secure state [18].

In order to perform this verification, the system's security policy (in Orange Book terms, its top-level specification or TLS) must be rephrased as a formal top-level specification (FTLS) containing the security policy expressed in a mathematically verifiable form. Once the FTLS has been proven, it (or more usually the TLS, since the FTLS will be incomprehensible to anyone but its authors) is rephrased as a sequence of progressively lower-level specifications until a level is reached at which implementation becomes practical (sometimes the FTLS itself needs to be progressively decomposed in order to make analysis possible [19]). The translation from lower-level formal specification to code must then be verified in some manner, traditionally through the use of a verification system such as Gypsy or InaJo that has been designed for this stage of the process. In addition to an FTLS, the Orange Book also allows for a descriptive TLS (DTLS) that is written in plain English and gets around the problem that no-one who wasn't involved in producing it can understand the FTLS. The Orange Book requires the use of a DTLS for classes B2 and higher and an FTLS for class A1. B1 only requires an informal model of the security policy and was added at a late stage in the Orange Book process because it was felt that the jump from C2 to B2, then known as levels 2 and 3 [20], was too large.

After the FTLS is verified, the verification process generally stops. Specifically, there is no attempt to show that the code being executed actually corresponds to the high-level specification from which it is built, although at least one effort, the LOCK project, attempted to go one step beyond the FTLS with a formal interface level specification (FILS) [21]. Formal-methods purists such as the creators of the Boyer–Moore theorem prover have attacked this lack of lower-level proof with comments such as "This travesty of mathematical proof has been defended with the claim that it at least gives the government better documentation. The Department of Defense has published official standards authorising this nonsense" [22]. On the other hand, other authors disagree: "We took the attitude that the code proofs were absolutely irrelevant if the specifications were wrong, and that the immediate payoff would come from showing that the design was no good" [23]. This is something of a religious issue, and a variety of other opinions on the subject exist.

There have been some limited, mostly experimental attempts made to address this problem. These include attempts to build trusted compilers using correctness-preserving transformations [24], the use of a translator from an implementation in Modula-1 (to which the verification was applied) to C (which wasn't verified), from which it could finally be compiled for the target platform [25], the use of a lambda-calculus-based functional language that is compiled into code for an experimental, special-purpose computer [26], the use of low-level instruction transformations for restricted virtual machines (one a stack machine, the other with a PDP-11 like instruction set) [27], the use of a subset of the Intel 8080 instruction set (in work performed in 1988 (!!)) [28], a minimal subset of C that doesn't contain loops, function calls, or pointers [29], a template-like translation of a description of a real-time control system into C (with occasional help from a human) [30], and a version of Ada modified to remove problem areas such as dynamic memory allocation and recursion [31]. All of these efforts either require making a leap of faith to go from verified code to a real-world system, or require the use of an artificially restricted system in order to function (the Newspeak approach: create a language in which it's impossible to think bad thoughts). This indicates that formal verification down to the binary code level is unlikely to be practical in any generally accepted formal-methods sense.

4.3 Problems with Formal Verification

Formal methods have been described as "an example of a revolutionary technique that has gained widespread appeal without rigorous experimentation" [32]. Like many software engineering techniques covered in the next section, much work on formal methods is analytical advocacy research (characterised as "conceive an idea, analyse the idea, advocate the idea" [33]), in which the authors describe a technique in some detail, discuss its potential benefits, and recommend that the concept be transferred into practice. Empirical studies of the results of applying these methods, however, have had some difficulty in finding any correlation between their use and any gains in software quality [34], with no hard evidence available that the use of formal methods can deliver reliability more cost-effectively than traditional structured methods with enhanced testing [35]. Even in places where there has been a concerted push to apply formal methods, penetration has been minimal and the value of their use has been difficult to establish, especially where high quality can be achieved through other methods [36].

This section will examine some of the reasons why formal methods have failed to provide the silver bullet that they initially seemed to promise.

4.3.1 Problems with Tools and Scalability

The tools used to support formal methods arose from an academic research environment characterised by a small number of highly skilled users (usually the developers of the tools) and by extension an environment in which it didn't really matter if the tools weren't quite production grade, difficult to use, slow, or extremely resource-hungry — they were only research prototypes, after all. The experimental background of the tools used often led to a collection of poorly-integrated components built by different researchers, with specification languages that varied over time and contained overlapping and unclear features contributed by various sources, or that differed depending on which researcher's verification tool was being employed. In systems such as HDM, this led to assessments by independent observers that "at present an outsider can not use HDM to design, implement, and verify a program from beginning to end" [37]. In addition, the tools were tested on small problems (usually referred to somewhat disparagingly as "toy problems") that were targeted more at exercising the tools than at exercising the problem. This section covers some of the issues that arose because of this.

Both of the formal methods endorsed for use with the Orange Book, Ina Jo/Ina Mod (collectively known as the Formal Development Methodology, FDM) [38][39][40] and Gypsy (as part of the Gypsy Verification Environment, GVE) [41][42][43] date from the 1970s and have seen little real development since then. Both are interactive environments, which isn't a feature but a polite way of indicating that they require a lot of tedious user intervention and manual effort in order to function. Furthermore, not only do they require extensive assistance from the user, but the difficult nature of the tools and task requires expert users to work with it, and once they're finished it requires another set of expert users to verify and evaluate the results [44][45][46][47].

Another early effort, the Boyer–Moore theorem prover, has been described as "like trying to make a string go in a certain direction by pushing it [...] Proof becomes a challenge: to beat the machine at its own game (the designers and some others have chalked up some very high scores though)" [48]. Attempts to use the BM prover in practice led to the observation that "the amount of effort required to verify the system was very large. The tools were often very slow, difficult to use, and unable to completely process a complex specification. There were many areas where tedious hand analysis had to be used" [49].

Many of the tools originate from a research environment and are of a decidedly experimental nature, which contributes to the difficulty in using them. Several kernel verifications have had to be abandoned (or at least restarted so that they could be approached in a different manner) because the tools being used for the verification were not quite up to handling the problem. This wasn't helped by the fact that they were often built using whatever other tools happened to be available or handy rather than the tools that would typically be found in a production environment. For example, the Gypsy compiler that was used in some kernel validations was originally implemented as a cross-compiler into Bliss, which was only available on a limited number of DEC platforms, making it extremely difficult even to get access to the right tools for the job. Similarly, tools endorsed for Orange Book use had to be converted to run on the Multics system used by the Computer Security Evaluation Center, a distinctly nontrivial undertaking. As an added bonus, the endorsed tools then became subject to export controls, making it effectively impossible to supply them to overseas customers.

Working at a very high level of abstraction can produce a (hopefully) correct and (more or less) verifiable specification that then needs to be completely rewritten by system developers in order to make it implementable [50]. This is somewhat problematic since "we are barely up to the task of building large and complex systems that almost work; we are certainly not up to building such systems twice — once in a programming language and once in a logic — without any flaws at all" [51].

Some researchers have suggested performing the implementation directly in a specification language; however, this is equivalent to a standard implementation created with an even-higher-level-language. Although this may eliminate many specification bugs, what will be left is a class of even tougher specification bugs that require an even higher-level specification system to expose [52]. In addition, in order to make it workable, the specification language will typically have been modified in order to remove features that are considered unsafe, but the downside of removing unsafe features such as pointer variables is that all data structures that are manipulated by a routine will need to be passed in and out explicitly as parameters, resulting in huge parameter lists for each routine and a high overhead from moving all of the data around.

Another approach that has been suggested is to automatically verify (in the "formal proof of correctness" sense) the specification against the implementation as it is compiled [53]. This has the disadvantage that is can't be done using any known technology.

4.3.2 Formal Methods as a Swiss Army Chainsaw

Formal methods have in the past been touted as the ultimate cure for all security software assurance problems, a "panacea with unbounded applicability and potency" [54]. It has been pointed out that although it is recognised that some formal methods are more suited for use in certain areas than others, "these qualities are no more than discreetly acknowledged minimal departures from a default presumption of universal applicability. No mainstream formal method carries a maker's disclaimer that it is useful only for a small and narrowly defined class of problem" [55]. For example, one paper on formal verification begins with a long list of language features that had to be removed, and changes made to the semantics of what remained, and then concludes with "The proposed translation scheme is universally applicable" [56].

One of the reasons for their perceived failure to perform as required is the desire to apply them as a universal elixir, a silver bullet capable of slaying the security bugbear in all its forms. In problem-solving terminology this is a "weak method", a general-purpose approach intended to be applied to many types of problems: "A strong method, like a specific size of wrench, is designed to fit and do an optimal job on one kind of problem; a weak method, like a monkey wrench, is designed to adjust to a multiplicity of problems, but solve none of them optimally" [57].

Related to this problem was the desire to build a complete, general-purpose secure operating system kernel, something that is now known to be infeasible if efficiency and time/budgetary constraints are also present. The reason for this is that a general-purpose kernel is required to support any number of functions that are extremely difficult to analyse from a security point of view. For example, various types of I/O devices, DMA, and interrupts all cause severe headaches for security architects, to the point where they have been disallowed in some designs because they cannot be managed in a secure manner. The extra complexity of handling all of the required generality adds more overhead to the system, which drags performance down. One almost universal byline of 1980s papers on high-security kernels was some sort of lament about their lack of performance [58][59]. This has also been blamed on the close correspondence between the TLS and the actual implementation since the formal specification system by its very nature is typically incapable of describing any sort of efficient implementation (all of the features that make an implementation efficient also make it dangerous and/or unverifiable using formal methods).

Another reason for the poor performance was that kernel design and implementation were usually driver by the verifiers, so that if the tools couldn't manage some aspect of the kernel, the response was to require that the kernel be redesigned to fit what the tools could do. The performance problem was finally solved with the VAX VMM security kernel, which was driven by performance rather than verification considerations. In contrast to the "A1 at any cost" of earlier efforts, the VAX VMM kernel philosophy was "A1 if possible, B3 if it would impact performance too much", so that if the tools failed the response was to change the tools rather than the kernel [60]. A similar approach was later taken in other kernels such as MASK, where efficiency measures in the C implementation were migrated back into the formal specification [61].

The complexity of a general-purpose kernel puts a great burden on the formal verification tools. As the previous section indicated, these are often already fragile enough when faced with toy problems without having to try to cope with extremely complex, general-purpose security models and mechanisms. One attempt to mitigate this problem is by choosing a subset of the overall problem and applying formal methods only to this subset, avoiding the high cost and effort required to apply the formal methods. In security-critical systems this subset is the security kernel, but even this (relatively) small subset has proven to be very difficult to manage, and applying formal methods to even reasonable-sized systems appears to be infeasible [62].

Another factor that complicates the use of formal methods is that the mathematical methods available to software engineers are often very difficult to use (much more so than the mathematics employed in other areas of engineering) and plagued by notation that is cumbersome and hard to read and understand, with substantial effort being required to present the ideas in a manner that is understandable to non-cognoscenti [63]. As an example of the types of problems this can lead to, a medical instruments project at Hewlett-Packard ran into difficulties because no-one outside the project group was willing or able to review the formal specifications [36].

One study of the comprehensibility of formal specifications found that the most common complaint among users was that the specification was incomprehensible. When asked to provide an absolute comprehensibility rating of a Z specification, subjects rated the specification at either "hard" or "incomprehensible" *after a week of intensive training in using the language* [64]. Another survey, again related to the comprehensibility of Z, found that even subjects trained in discrete mathematics who had completed a course in formal methods found it very difficult to understand any of a 20-line snippet from a Z specification, with nearly a third of the test group being unable to answer any questions relating to the specification, which they found incomprehensible [65].

Concerns about the write-only nature of many specification languages were echoed by many other groups who had tried to apply formal methods in real life. This problem arises from the fact that understandability appears to be inversely proportional to the level of complexity and formality present [66]. One survey of techniques that used as one criterion the understandability of the resulting document rated the language surveyed, PAISLey [67], as the least understandable of all of the techniques covered (and PAISLey is downright comprehensible compared to many of its peers) [68]. This legibility problem isn't restricted just to tools that support program proving, for example the specification language GIST was designed to allow the specification of the states in a system and its behaviour based on stimulus-response rules [69][70], but resulted in specifications that were so hard to read that a paraphraser had to be written to translate them back into something that could be understood. In another experiment which compared the use of the formal specification language OBJ with the non-formal specification language PDL and the even less formal specification language English, one unanimous piece of feedback from users was their dislike of the formal specification language's syntax, even though it had been post-processed with a text editor in order to make it more palatable [71].

The results obtained from real-world kernel verifications are even more depressing. One paper, which examined the possibility of creating a "beyond A1" system, contained figures of 2–6 lines of verified code being produced per day per highly trained verification specialist, of which the entire worldwide community was estimated at around 200 individuals, of which only a small fraction were actually available for this kind of work. To put this into perspective, the verification of a portion of the system mentioned in the paper required three pages of specification and 200-odd pages of proof logs [72]. Another paper was even more pessimistic: "The national technology base for A1-level systems is essentially non-existent. There do not appear to be even 20 people in the world [in 1985] that have undertaken the essential steps of building an A1 system" [73]. A third makes the rather dry observation that "in order to get a system with excellent system integrity, you must ensure that it is designed and built by geniuses. Geniuses are in short supply" [74].

4.3.3 What Happens when the Chainsaw Sticks

A previous chapter pointed out that security kernels are generally accompanied by a collection of camp followers in the guise of trusted processes, privileged processes that can bypass the system's security policy in order to perform their intended task. This presents something of a problem in terms of formal verification since it's not really possible to verify the security of a system once these trusted processes, which exist solely to bypass the system's security, are taken into account. The workaround to this problem is to provide an informal (in the sense of it being DTLS-style rather than FTLS-style) argument capable of convincing the evaluators that the trusted process isn't really a problem, which in its defence at least forces the developer to think about the problem before leaping in and violating the formal model.

In some cases, however, it doesn't even take a trusted process to introduce problems into the proof process. During the SCOMP validation, the theorem prover failed to prove several formulae, which then had to be justified using English/informal explanations [75]. In another verification, it was found that a significant proportion of the system's assurance argument wasn't amenable to formal specification because the specification system model was based on CSP, which wasn't capable of expressing some of the characteristics of the system and required the use of informal specification and verification methods [76] (this is a problem that seems to be common among other CSP-based models [77]). In the LOCK verification effort, 61% of the Gypsy code consisted of lemmas whose sole purpose was to automate the proof [130]. This can lead to problems that occur when a proof has to be manually augmented with "self-evident" axioms that the prover isn't capable of deriving itself since "self-evident" truths sometimes turn out to be false and end up misguiding the prover, a problem explored in more detail in Section 4.3.4.

Another problem with formal methods is the lack of allowance for feature creep (although much of this is likely to be outside the TCB). The average project goes through roughly 25% change between the point at which the requirements are complete and the first release [78], which causes severe problems for formal methods, which assume that everything can be specified in advance, or, even if they don't explicitly assume it, at least require it, since once the formal proof process has begun a single change can entail restarting it from scratch [79][80]. This is particularly problematic in cases where multiple layers of abstraction are required to go from FTLS to implementation, since a change in any of the layers can result in a ripple effect as changes propagate up and down the hierarchy, requiring a lot of tedious re-proving and analysis, which may in turn result in further changes being made. If a change manages to propagate its way into a formally proven section of the design, either the entire proof must be redone or the affected portions of the proof must somehow be undone so that they can be re-proven, with the hope that some portion that hasn't yet been re-proven isn't mistakenly regarded as still being valid.

Even if the formal specification can somehow be frozen so that the implementation is based on the same specification as the one that is evaluated, the need to use trusted processes, which are almost required in order to make a system based on the Bell–LaPadula model workable [81], results in a system where it's difficult to determine the exact nature of the security rules that the system is enforcing, since what's actually being enforced isn't the same as the axioms present in the formal security model. Because the actual policy being enforced differs from the Bell–LaPadula axioms, any formal proof that the system provides certain properties (for example that it maintains a secure state) can only apply to one portion of the system rather than the system as a whole.

The assumption that a particular system will be used exactly in the manner and situation for which it was designed is rather unrealistic, especially since history has demonstrated that systems will always end up in unanticipated environments, an example being the interconnection of formerly isolated systems into a single heterogenous environment [82]. The inability of formal methods to adapt to such changes means that either the systems are run in a manner for which they were never evaluated, or the evaluation is subject to increasingly tortuous "interpretations" in order to try to adapt it for each new environment that crops up (it is for this reason that the Orange Book has also been referred to as the Orange Bible, with interpretations being "ministerial treatments derived from the Orange Bible" [83]).

Once a program exists, there is an irresistible pressure to modify it, either to correct real or perceived defects or because of feature creep. This maintenance is usually done with far less care than was used when the program was originally created, and once even a single change is made to the system all bets are off [84][85]. What is running now isn't what was formally specified or what was verified. This type of problem is almost inevitable because user requirements are extremely volatile, which means that the formal specification technique can only work if it assumes that users know exactly what they want in advance. Real-world surveys have shown that this isn't the case, with specification being an incremental, iterative process and most development being maintenance rather than so-called greenfields (starting from scratch) development [86][87]. This has led to a constant revision of software engineering methodologies from the initial waterfall model through to the spiral model and finally "development on Internet time" or "extreme programming" (this last stage is still being worked on and doesn't have a generic label yet. It is examined in Section 4.5.1).

In the case of software designed for the mass market, this problem is even worse, since with custom software development there is at least some interaction with the eventual user and/or customer, whereas with mass-market software the first chance for customer feedback on the design occurs when they install a buggy and unstable beta release on their system, or even later when they buy the finished product (possibly still in the buggy and unstable state). This is made more difficult by the fact that the developers of the applications often lack relevant domain knowledge; for example, someone implementing a portion of a word processor probably hasn't had any formal training in typesetting or page layout requirements (a fact which is obvious in some widely-used Word processors), resulting in a product that fairly promptly needs to be adapted to meet the user's requirements in an $x.1$ and $x.2$ release update. As a result of this style of development, there is a strong need to handle late changes to the design and to allow for customisation and other adaptations to the implementation late in the development cycle [88].

Unfortunately, most formal methods never made it past the waterfall model, with no flexibility or provision for change later on in the development process. Although this issue isn't generally addressed in publications describing the results of applying formal methods to security system evaluations, one paper that did touch on this issue reported that the planned waterfall-model development became instead very iterative, with many update cycles being necessary in order to nail down the precise details of the model [89]. Another paper commented that "even very simple models can entail significant costs of time and effort over the verification phase. The effect of incrementally adding new modules to a stable (i.e. proven) body of modules introduces the obligation to integrate all new variables and data structures into the old module proofs, and thus multiply their length. As more models are integrated in this way, the effect appears to be significantly non-linear" [77]. This sentiment was echoed in yet another paper that described a real-world implementation, the eventually cancelled Autodin II upgrade effort (first mentioned in Section 4.2) in which "the code deviated from the DTLS and the DTLS was not updated. In the end, the FTLS was being developed from the code, a terrible form of 'reverse engineering'" [23]. In the LOCK project, the FTLS was developed at the same time as the source code, and the formal proofs weren't performed until the system testing phase, after coding was essentially complete. The proof process often detected requirements and design flaws, necessitating larger changes to the system [130].

This iterative development process mirrors real-world engineering experience in which a new product (for example, a car or appliance) is almost never a greenfields development, but is very similar to its predecessors and shares the same structuring of problem and solution. The traditional engineer doesn't start with a clean slate (or monitor) but instead bases their work on successful designs that have evolved over many product generations through the contribution of a community of other engineers.

Although there have been attempts at allowing for a limited amount of design change and maintenance, in general these haven't been very successful; for example, the Orange Book Rating Maintenance Program (RAMP) has been described as leading to "a plethora of paperwork, checking, bureaucracy and mistrust" being imposed on vendors who participate in it [90]. As a result, SCOMP, the first A1 system, was re-evaluated at B3 rather than A1 when it was moved to newer hardware because it simply wasn't worth the effort to do another A1. Even the initial A1 SCOMP had never broken even, selling less than 30 units, and the Honeywell sales team estimated they would sell at most 5% more units with an A1 rather than a B3 rating.

Other approaches to the maintenance problem include TCB subsetting, which involve hanging a bag on the side of the existing TCB rather than changing it in order to avoid having to go through the evaluation process again [91][92][93], and trying to combine bits and pieces evaluated at various levels for which some sort of composite rating can then be claimed [94][95], a variation of the Chinese menu approach mentioned in Chapter 2, which is bound to cause uncertainty and confusion for all involved. A more interesting proposed approach to the problem involves having new modules evaluated under ITSEC or the Common Criteria and digitally signed by the evaluators, whereupon a kernel could grant them certain privileges based on the evaluation level [96]. This approach has the downside that it requires that a high degree of confidence be placed in the efficacy of the evaluation and the evaluators.

4.3.4 What is being Verified/Proven?

Since current verification techniques can't generally reach down any further than the high-level specification (that is, all that they can do is verify consistency between some formal model and the design), they result in large amounts of time and energy being poured into producing a design specification that by its very nature is void of any implementation detail [97]. Formal methods typically view a system as a set of operations on a state or a collection of communicating sequential processes, offering a designer almost no guidance in how to approach a particular problem. This means that a verified design doesn't ensure that the completed system is error-free or functioning correctly, but merely that it meets the requirements set out in some user-defined model. Because of this, it isn't terribly meaningful to claim that an implementation is "correct" (in terms of satisfying some requirement) without including as a rider the requirement that it satisfies. In its purest technical sense, correct doesn't mean "good" or "useful" or "appropriate" or any other similar approbatory adjective, but merely "consistent with its specification". As with ISO 9000, it's possible to produce an arbitrarily bad product but still claim it's correct, since it complies with the paperwork.

Determining the appropriate point at which to stop the modelling process can be difficult because in a real system information can be accessed in so many ways that don't obey the formal security model that the result is a system that can contain many apparent exceptions to the formal security model. Such exceptions can occur due to any number of hardware or software mechanisms; for example, DMA or I/O device access or at a more subtle level, interrupts being used as a subliminal channel all add extra complexity to a security model if an attempt is made to express the security-relevant property of each operation that can occur in a system. The choice then is either to abstract the system to a level which makes analysis tractable, or to try to model every relevant property and end up with an unworkably complex model.

Another problem with formal proofs is that although they can show with some certainty (that is, provided there are no mistakes made in any calculations and the supporting tools are bug-free) that a given specification is "correct", what can't be shown is that the assumptions that are being made in the specification are a correct description of the actual physical system. If the code that is supposed to implement the formal specification doesn't quite conform to it or the compiler can't produce an executable that quite matches what was intended in the code, then no amount of formal proving will be able to guarantee the execution behaviour of the code. Just as Newton's laws don't work well close to the speed of light or for objects that are not in inertial frames of reference, so formal proofs have problems with issues such as arithmetic overflow and underflow (the most famous example of this being the Ariane 5 disaster), division by zero, and various language and compiler bugs and quirks [98]. Even if the compiler is formally verified, this only moves the problem to a lower level. No matter how thoroughly an application is formally verified, at some point the explanations must come to an end and users must assume that the physical system satisfies the axioms used in the proof [99]. It is perhaps in recognition of this that Common Criteria certificates contain at the bottom a disclaimer that "Certification is not a guarantee of freedom from security vulnerabilities [...] It is the responsibility of users to check whether any security vulnerabilities have been discovered since the date shown on this certificate". This is a sound precaution, since the product covered by the certificate from which this text was taken was subsequently found to have a flaw that completely voided its security [100][101] (one news story even devoted more coverage to the product's EAL4 certification than to the hole itself [102]).

Although the design documents for security systems are not usually made public, one of the few that has been provides a good example of how easily errors can creep into a specification. In this case the specification for the control software for a smart card as published at a security conference was presented in three locations: as a sidebar to the main text in plain English, in the main text in a formal notation with English annotations to explain what was happening, and again in separate paragraphs with more English text to provide further detail. All three versions are different [103]. In addition since the software exists as a full FTLS in InaJo, a DTLS, and finally a concrete implementation, there are likely to be at least six varying descriptions of what the card does, of which at least three differ (the full FTLS, DTLS, and software were never published, so it's not possible to determine whether they correspond to each other).

A similar problem was found during an attempt to formally verify the SET protocol. This protocol is specified in three separate parts: a business description targeted at managers ("Book 1"), a programmer's guide ("Book 2"), and a so-called formal protocol definition ("Book 3"), which in this case describes the SET protocol in ASN.1 (a data format description language) rather than in an FTLS-style language (in other words, it's more a formal description of the message format than of the protocol semantics). Not only are all three books inconsistent ("there are 600 pages spread over three documents which do not agree with each other [...] all the documents disagree with each other and it is not a lot of fun reading 600 pages of extremely boring material" [104]), but the "formal definition" in Book 3 contains ambiguities that need to be explained with textual annotations, occasionally from Book 1 and 2. In response to one particular statement that pertains to an ambiguity in Book 3 but which itself appears in Book 2, the exasperated evaluators commented that "It is difficult to believe that such a statement could be part of the specification of a security protocol" [105]. In defence of the SET specification, it must be mentioned that the problem of imprecise and inconsistent specifications is endemic to Internet security protocols, an issue that has been pointed out by other authors [106]. SET probably represents one of the better-specified of these protocols.

The evaluators eventually had to assemble the protocol details from all three books, making various common-sense assumptions and simplifications in cases where it wasn't possible to determine what was intended, or where the books contradicted each other, with the observation that "ambiguities can be resolved by discussion and reflection, but there is no guarantee that other readers of the specification will interpret it the same way" [107]. Eventually, they were able to verify some portions of their interpretation of a subset of the SET protocol, although beyond discovering a few potential problem areas it's not certain how valuable the overall results of the effort really are.

In another example of problems with the specification used to drive the verification effort, a system targeted at Orange Book A1 contained a flaw that would allow users to violate the Bell–LaPadula *-property, even though the verification process for the system had been completed without discovering the error. This error was present in the implementation because it faithfully followed the specification that contained the same error, although it was corrected using a two-line fix when discovered by the implementers. The same specification contained further errors in sections that had no meaning other than to guide the verification tool, one of which misguided it to the point of failing to find the flaw [108]. In another example, the Autodin II specification contained an internal inconsistency in the FTLS that would have allowed any arbitrary formula to be proved as a theorem [109]. In contrast, when a C standards committee published an incorrect specification for the snprintf() function most of the implementers made sure that the function behaved correctly rather than behaving as per the specification, so the implementation was correct (in the sense of doing the right thing) only because it explicitly *didn't* comply with the specification [110]. The issue of correctness versus correctness is examined in more detail in the next chapter, which introduces the concept of conceptual and teleological bugs in specifications and implementations.

In some cases, the assumptions that underlie a security system or protocol can alter the security claims that can be made about it. One case that garnered some attention due to the debate it generated among different groups who examined it was the security proofs of the Needham–Schroeder public-key protocol, which was first proven secure using BAN logic [111], then found to have a flaw under a slightly different set of assumptions using the FDR model checker [112][113], and finally found to have further problems when subject to analysis by the NRL protocol analyser, a proof checker that switches to model checking for the final stage [114]. It can be argued that both of the initial analyses were correct, since the first analysis assumed that principals wouldn't divulge secrets while the flaw found in the second analysis relied on the fact that if a principal revealed a secret nonce then an attacker could (depending on various other protocol details) impersonate one or either of the two principals. The third analysis used slightly different assumptions again, and found problems in cases such as one where a participant is communicating with itself (there were also other problems that were found using the NRL protocol analyser which weren't found by the FDR model checker for slightly different reasons that are explained further on). The differences arose in part because BAN logic contains a protocol idealisation step in which messages exchanged as part of the protocol are transformed into formulae about the messages so that inferences can be made within the logic, which requires assigning certain meanings to the messages that may not be present in the actual protocol. Such an idealisation step isn't present in the FDR or NRL analysis. In addition the BAN logic analysis contained a built-in assumption that all principals are honest, whereas the others did not. The situation was summed up in a later analysis of the various attacks with the observation that "The model has to describe the behaviour of principals. Protocol goals are often formalized as if agents could engage in a protocol run only by following the rules of the protocol" [115].

Even when the formal specification provides an accurate model of the physical system, real-world experience has shown that great care has to be devoted to ensuring that what is being proven is what was intended to be proven [116][117]. In other words, even if the formal specification accurately modelled the actual system, was there some way to breach security that was not covered by the proof? An example of this was in the SCOMP verification, where discrepancies were found during the specification-to-implementation mapping process that had been missed by the formal verification tools because they weren't addressed in the FTLS. Another system was verified to be correct and then "compiled, tested, and run with remarkably few errors discovered subsequent to the verification" [72].

These sorts of problems can arise from factors such as narrowing of the specification caused by restrictions in the specification language (for example, the fact that the specification language was much more restrictive than the implementation language), widening of the specification caused by the nature of the specification language (for example, some special-case conditions might be assigned a magic meta-value in the specification language that is treated quite differently from, say, an empty string or a null pointer in the implementation language), or an inability to accurately express the semantics of the specification in the implementation language. This type of specification modification arises because the specification writers aren't omnipotent and can't take into account every eventuality that will arise. As a result, an implementation of a specification doesn't just implement it, but alters it in order to fit real-world constraints that weren't foreseen by the original designers or couldn't be expressed in the specification. The resulting not-quite-to-spec implementation therefore represents a lower-level form of the specification that has been elaborated to match real-world constraints [118].

Just as it has been observed that spreading the task of building a compiler across n programming teams will result in an n-pass compiler, so the syntax and semantics associated with a formal specification language can heavily influence the final implementation. For example, Estelle's model of a system consists of a collection of FSMs that communicate via asynchronous messaging, SDL's model consists of FSMs connected together through FIFO message queues, and LOTOS' model consists of multiple independent processes that communicate via events occurring at synchronisation points. None of these resemble anything that is present in any common implementation language like C.

The effects of this lack of matching between specification and implementation languages are evident in real-world experiences in which an implementation of the same concept (a layer of the OSI model) specified in the three specification languages mentioned above closely mirrored the system model used by the specification language, whether this was appropriate for the situation or not [119]. In one case, an implementation contained a bug relating to message ordering that was an artefact of the specification language's view of the system and that was only discovered by running it against an implementation derived from one of the other specifications, the system model of which did not assume that messages were in any particular order. This problem arose due to the particular weltanschauung of the formal specification language rather than any error in the specification or implementation itself. In the analysis of the Needham–Schroeder public-key protocol mentioned earlier, the NRL protocol analyser was able to locate problems that had not been found by the FDR model checker because the model checker took a CSP specification and worked forwards while the NRL analyser took a specification of state transitions and worked backwards, and because the model checker couldn't verify any properties that involved an unbounded number of executions of the protocol whereas the analyser could. This allowed it to detect odd boundary conditions such as one where the two participants in the protocol were one and the same [114].

The use of FDR to find weaknesses in a protocol that was previously thought to be secure triggered a wave of other analyses. These included the use of the Isabelle theorem prover [120], the Brutus model checker (with the same properties and limitations as FDR but using various reduction techniques to try to combat the state-space explosion that is experienced by model checkers) [121], the Murφ model checker and typography stress tester [122], and the Athena model checker combined with a new modelling technique called the strand space model, which attempts to work around the state space explosion problem and restrictions on the number of principals (although not the number of protocol runs) that beset traditional model checkers [123][124][125] (some of the other model checkers run out of steam once three or four principals participate). These further analyses that confirmed the findings of the initial work are an example of the analysis technique being a social process that serves to increase our confidence in the object being examined, something that is examined in more detail in the next section.

4.3.5 Credibility of Formal Methods

From a mathematical point of view, the attractiveness of formal methods, and specifically formal proofs of correctness, is that they have the potential to provide a high degree of confidence that a certain method or mechanism has the properties that it is intended to have. This level of confidence often can't be obtained through other methods, for example something as simple as the addition operation on a 32-bit CPU would require 2^{64} or 10^{19} tests (and a known good set of test vectors against which to verify the results), which is infeasible in any real design. The solution, at least in theory, is to construct a mathematical proof that the correct output will be produced for all possible input values. However, the use of mathematical proofs is not without its problems. One paper gives an example of American and Japanese topologists who provided complex (and contradictory) proofs concerning a certain type of topological object. The two sides swapped proofs, but neither could find any flaws in the other side's argument. The paper then goes on to give further examples of "proofs" that in some cases stood for years before being found to be flawed. In some cases the (faulty) proofs are so beguiling that they require footnotes and other commentary to avoid entrapping unwary readers [126].

An extreme example of a complex proof was Wiles' proof of Fermat's last theorem, which took seven years to complete and stretched over 200 pages, and then required another year of peer-review (and a bugfix) before it was finally published [127]. Had it not been for the fact that it represented a solution to a famous problem, it is unlikely that it would have received much scrutiny; in fact, it's unlikely that any journal would have wanted to publish a 200-page proof. As DeMillo et al point out, "mathematical proofs increase our confidence in the truth of mathematical statements only after they have been subject to the social mechanisms of the mathematical community". Many of these proofs are never subject to much scrutiny, and of the estimated 200,000 theorems published each year, most are ignored [128]. A slightly different view of the situation covered by DeMillo et al (but with the same conclusion) is presented by Fetzer, who makes the case that programs represent conjectures, and the execution of the program is an attempted refutation of the conjecture (the refutation is all too often successful, as anyone who has used commercial software will be aware) [129].

Security proofs and analyses for systems targeted at A1 or equivalent levels are typically of a size that makes the Fermat proof look trivial by comparison. It has been suggested that perhaps the evaluators use the 1000+ page monsters produced by the process as a pillow in the hope that they will absorb the contents by osmosis, or perhaps only check every tenth or twentieth page in the hope that a representative spot check will weed out any potential errors. It is almost certain that none of them are ever subject to the level of scrutiny that the proof of Fermat's last theorem, at a fraction of the size, was. For example although the size of the Gypsy specification for the LOCK kernel cast doubts on the correctness of its automated proof, it was impractical for the mathematicians involved to double-check the automated proof manually [130].

The problems inherent in relying purely on a correctness proof of code may be illustrated by the following example. In 1969, Peter Naur published a paper containing a very simple 25-line text-formatting routine that he informally proved correct [131]. When the paper was reviewed in *Computing Reviews*, the reviewer pointed out a trivial fault in the code that, had the code been run rather than proven correct, would have been quickly detected [132]. Subsequently, three more faults were detected, some of which again would have been quickly noticed if the code had been run on test data [133].

The author of the second paper presented a corrected version of the code and formally proved it correct (Naur's paper only contained an informal proof). After it had been formally proven correct, three further faults were found that, again, would have been noticed if the code had been run on test data [134].

This episode underscores three important points made earlier. The first is that even something as apparently simple as a 25-line piece of code took some effort (which eventually stretched over a period of five years) to fully analyse. The second point is that, as pointed out by DeMillo et al, the process only worked because it was subject to scrutiny by peers. Had this analysis by outsiders not occurred, it is quite likely that the code would have been left in its original form, with an average of just under one fault for every three lines of code, until someone actually tried to use it. Finally, and most importantly, the importance of actually testing the code is shown by the fact that four of the seven defects could have been found immediately simply by running the code on test data.

A similar case occurred in 1984 with an Orange Book A1 candidate for which the security-testing team recommended against any penetration testing because the system had an A1 security kernel based on a formally verified FTLS. The government evaluators questioned this blind faith in the formal verification process and requested that the security team attempt a penetration of the system. Within a short period, the team had hypothesised serious flaws in the system and managed to exploit one such flaw to penetrate its security. Although the team had believed that the system was secure based on the formal verification, "there is no reason to believe that a knowledgeable and sceptical adversary would have failed to find the flaw (or others) in short order" [109]. A similar experience occurred with the LOCK kernel, where the formally verified LOCK platform was too unreliable for practical use while the thoroughly tested SMG follow-on was deployed worldwide [130].

In a related case, a program that had been subjected to a Z proof of the specification and a code-level proof of the implementation in SPARK (an Ada dialect modified to remove problematic areas such as dynamic memory allocation and recursion) was shipped with run-time checking disabled in the code (!!) even though testing had revealed problems such as numeric overflows that could not be found by proofs (just for reference, it was a numeric overflow in Ada code that brought down Ariane 5). Furthermore, the fact that the compiler had generated code that employed dynamic memory allocation (although this wasn't specified in the source code) required that the object code be manually patched to remove the memory allocation calls [31].

The saga of Naur's program didn't end with the initial set of problems that were found in the proofs. A decade later, another author analysed the last paper that had been published on the topic and found twelve faults in the program specification which was presented therein [135]. Finally (at least as far as the current author is aware, the story may yet unfold further), another author pointed out a problem in that author's corrected specification [136]. The problems in the specifications arose because they were phrased in English, a language rather unsuited for the task due to its imprecise nature and the ease with which an unskilled practitioner (or a politician) can produce results filled with ambiguities, vagueness, and contradictions. The lesson to be drawn from the second part of the saga is that natural language isn't very well suited to specifying the behaviour of a program, and that a somewhat more rigorous method is required for this task. However, many types of formal notation are equally unsuited, since they produce a specification that is incomprehensible to anyone not schooled in the particular formal method which is being applied. This issue is addressed further in the next chapter.

4.3.6 Where Formal Methods are Cost-Effective

Is there any situation in which formal methods are worth the cost and effort involved in using them? There is one situation where they are definitely cost-effective, and that is for hardware verification. The first of the two reasons for this is that hardware is relatively easy to verify because it has no pointers, no unbounded loops, no recursion, no dynamically created processes, and none of the other complexities that make the verification of software such a joy to perform.

The second reason why hardware verification is more cost-effective is because the cost of manufacturing a single unit of hardware is vastly greater than that of manufacturing (that is, duplicating) a single unit of software, and the cost of replacing hardware is outrageously more so than replacing software. As an example of the typical difference, compare the $400 million that the Pentium FDIV bug cost Intel to the negligible cost to Microsoft of a hotfix and soothing press release for the Windows bug du jour. Possibly inspired by Intel's troubles,

AMD spent a considerable amount of time and money subjecting their FDIV implementation to formal analysis using the Boyer–Moore theorem prover, which confirmed that their algorithm was OK.

Another factor that contributes to the relative success of formal methods for hardware verification is the fact that hardware designers typically use a standardised language, either Verilog or VHDL, and routinely use synthesis tools and simulators, which can be tied into the use of verification tools, as part of the design process. An example of how this might work in practice is that a hardware simulator would be used to explore a counterexample to a design assertion that was revealed by a model checker (assertion-based verification of Verilog/VHDL is touched on in the next chapter). In software development, this type of standardisation and the use of these types of tools doesn't occur.

These two factors — the fact that hardware is much more amenable to verification than software and the fact that there is a much greater financial incentive to do so — are what make the use of formal methods for hardware verification cost-effective, and the reason why most of the glowing success stories cited for the use of formal methods relate to their use in verifying hardware rather than software [137][138][139][47]. One paper on the use of formal methods for developing high-assurance systems only cites hardware verification in its collection of formal methods successes [140], and another paper concludes with the comment that several of the participants in the formal evaluation of an operating system then went on to find work formally verifying integrated circuits [130].

4.3.7 Whither Formal Methods?

Apart from their use in validating hardware, a task for which they are ideally suited, the future doesn't look too promising for formal methods. It is not in general a good sign when a paper presented at the tenth annual conference for users of Z, probably the most popular formal method (at least in Europe) and one of the few with university courses that teach it, opens with "Z is in trouble" [141]. A landmark paper on software technology maturity that looked at the progress of technologies initiated in the 1960s and 1970s (including formal methods) found that it typically takes 15–20 years for a new technology to gain mainstream acceptance, with the mean time being 17 years [142]. Formal methods have been around for nearly twice that span and yet their current status is that the most popular ones have an acceptance level of "in trouble" (the referenced paper goes on to mention that there is "pathetically little use of Z in industry"). Somewhat more concrete figures are given in a paper that contains figures intending to point out the low penetration of OO methods in industry [143], but which show the penetration of formal methods as being only a fraction of that, coming in slightly above the noise level.

One of the most compelling demonstrations of the conflict of formal methods with real-world practice can be found by examining how a programmer would implement a typical algorithm, for example one to find the largest entry in an array of integers. The formal-methods advocates would present the implementation of an algorithm to solve this problem as a process of formulating a loop invariant for a loop that scans through the array ($\forall j \in [0...i]$, max >= array[j]), proving it by induction, and then deriving an implementation from it. The problem with this approach is that no-one (except perhaps for the odd student in an introductory programming course) ever writes code this way. Anyone who knows how to program will never generate a program in this manner because they can recognise the problem and pull a working solution from existing knowledge [144]. This style of program creation represents a completely unnatural way of working with code, a problem that isn't helping the adoption of formal methods by programmers (the way in which code creation actually works is examined in some detail in the next chapter).

This general malaise in the use of formal methods for software engineering purposes (which has been summed up with the comment that they are perceived as "merely an academic exercise, a form of mental masturbation that has no relation to real-world problems" [145]), as well as the evidence presented in the preceding sections, indicates that formal proofs of correctness and similar techniques make for a less than ideal way to build a secure system since, like a number of other software engineering methodologies, they constitute belief systems rather than an exact science, and "attempts to prove beliefs are bottomless pits" [146]. A rather different approach to this particular problem is given in the next chapter.

4.4 Problems with other Software Engineering Methods

As with formal methods, the field of software engineering contains a great many miracle cures, making it rather difficult to determine which techniques are worthy of further investigation. There are currently around 300 software engineering standards, and yet the state of most software currently being produced indicates that they either don't work or are being ignored (the number of faults per 1000 lines of code, a common measure of software quality, has remained almost constant over the last 15 years). This is of little help to someone trying to find techniques suitable for constructing trustworthy systems.

For example, two widely-touted software engineering panaceas are the Software Engineering Institute's capability maturity model (CMM) and the use of CASE tools. Studies are only now being carried out to determine whether organisations at level $n + 1$ of the CMM produce software that is any better than organisations at level n (in other words, whether the CMM actually works) [147]. One study that has been completed could find "no relationship between any dimension of maturity and the quality of RE [Requirements Engineering] products. [...] These findings do not adequately support the hypothesised strong relationship between organisational maturity and RE success" [148]. Another report cites management's "decrease in motivation from lack of a clear link between their visions of the business and the progress achieved" after they initiated CMM programs [149]. Of particular relevance to implementers wanting to build trustworthy systems, a book on safe programming techniques for safety-critical and high-integrity systems found only a weak relationship between the presence of faults and either the level of integrity of the code or its process certification [150].

An additional problem with methods such as the CMM is the manner in which they are applied. Although the original intent was laudable enough, the common approach of using the CMM levels simply as a pass/fail filter to determine who is awarded a contract results in at least as much human ingenuity being applied to bypassing them as is applied to areas such as tax law. Some of the tricks that are used include overwhelming the auditors with detail, or alternatively underwhelming them with vague and misleading information in the knowledge that they'll never have time to follow things up, using misleading documentation (one example that is mentioned is a full-page diagram of a peer review process that in real life amounted to "find some technical people and get them to look at the code"), and general tricks such as asking participants to carry a CMM manual in the presence of the auditors and "scribble in the book, break the spine, and make it look well used" [151]. As a result, when the evaluation is just another hurdle to be jumped in order to secure a contract, all guarantees about the validity of the process become void. In practice, so much time and money is frequently invested that the belief, be it CC, CMM, or ISO 9000, often becomes an end in itself.

The propensity for organising methodologies into hierarchies with no clear indication as to what sort of improvement can be expected by progressing from one level to the next isn't constrained entirely to software engineering. It has been pointed out that the same issue affects security models as well, with no clear indication that penetrating or compromising a system with a sequence of properties $P_1...P_n$ is easier than penetrating one where P_{n+1} has been added, or (of more importance to the people paying for it) that a system costing $2n$ is substantially more difficult to exploit than one costing only n [152][153][154] (there have been efforts recently to leverage the security community's existing experience in lack of visible difference between security levels by applying the CMM to security engineering [155][156][157]). The lack of assurance that spending twice as much gives you twice as much security is troubling because the primary distinction between the various levels given in standards such as the Orange Book, ITSEC, and Common Criteria is the amount of money that needs to be spent to attain each level. The lead hardware engineer for one of the few A1 evaluated products has reported that there was no evidence (from his experience in working with high-assurance systems) that higher-assurance products were better built [158]. His observation that "quality comes from what the developer does, not what the evaluator measures" is borne out by the experience with the evaluated LOCK versus tested SMG covered in Section 4.3.5.

Another observer has pointed out that going to a higher level can even lead to a decrease in security in some circumstances; for example, an Orange Book B1 system conveniently labels the most damaging data for an attacker to target whereas C2 doesn't. This type of problem was first exploited more than a decade before the Orange Book appeared in an attack that targeted classified data that was treated differently from lower-value unclassified data by the operating environment [159]. The same type of attack is still possible today under Windows NT to target valuable data such as user passwords (by adding the name of a DLL to the HKEY_LOCAL_MACHINE\SYSTEM\CurrentControlSet\Control\Lsa\Notification Packages key which is fed any new or updated passwords by the system [160]) and private keys (by adding the name of a DLL to the HKEY_LOCAL_MACHINE\SOFTWARE\-Microsoft\Cryptography\Offload\ExpoOffload key, which is fed all private keys that are in use by CryptoAPI [161]).

One alternative approach to the CMM levels that has been suggested in an attempt to match the real world is the use of a capability immaturity model with rankings of (progressively) foolish, stupid, and lunatic to match the CMM levels initial, repeatable, defined, managed, and optimising, providing levels 0 to –2 of the CMM [162]. Level –1 of the anti-CMM involves the use of "complex processes involving the use of arcane languages and inappropriate documentation standards [requiring] significant effort and a substantial proportion of their resources in order to impose these" (this seems to be describing the eventual result of applying the positive-valued levels of the CMM). Level –2 mentions the hope of "automatically generating a program from the specification", which has been proposed by a number of formal methods advocates. A similar approach was taken some years earlier by another publication when it published an alternative series of levels for guaranteed-to-fail projects [163], and (on a slightly less pessimistic note) as a pragmatic alternative to existing security models that examines security in terms of allowable failure modes rather than absolute restrictions [164].

For CASE tools (which have been around for somewhat longer than the CMM), a study by the CASE Research Corporation found (contrary to the revolutionary improvements claimed through the use of CASE tools) that productivity dropped markedly in the first year of use as users adjusted to whatever CASE process was in use, and then returned to more or less the original, pre-CASE level (the study found some very modest gains, but wasn't able to determine whether this arose from factors other than the CASE tools, or that it lay outside the margin of error) [165]. Another survey carried out in three countries and covering some hundreds of organisations found that it was "very difficult to quantify overall gains in the areas of productivity, efficiency, and quality arising from the use of CASE [...] Currently it would appear that any gains in one area are often offset by problems in another" [166]. Some of the blame for this may lie in the fact that CASE tools, like many other methodologies, were over-hyped when it came to be their turn at being the silver bullet candidate (as with formal methods, no CASE tool vendor would admit that there might be certain application domains for which their product was somewhat more suited than others) with the result that most of them ended up as shelfware [167] or were only used when the client specifically demanded it [168].

The reasons for the failure of these methodologies may lie in the assumptions that they make about how software development works. The current model has been compared to nineteenth-century physics, in which energy is continuous, matter is particulate, and the luminiferous ether fills space and is the medium through which light and radio waves travel. The world as a whole works in a rational way, and if we can find the rules by which things happen we can find out which ones apply when good things happen and use those to make sure that the good things keep happening [169]. Unfortunately, real software development doesn't work like this. Attempts to treat software production as just another industrial mass-production process cannot work because software is the result of a creative design and engineering process, not of a conventional manufacturing activity [170]. This means that although it makes sense to try to perfect the process for reliably cranking out car parts or light bulbs or refrigerators, the creation of software is not a mass production process but instead is based on the cloning of the result of a one-off development effort that is the product of the creativity, skill, and co-operation of developers and users.

Certainly there are special cases such as assembling web storefronts, where number 27 looks and works exactly the same as the previous 26, that can be addressed through a process-based methodology. However, if the problem to be solved is of unknown scope, hasn't been solved before, has an unclear solution, and has an analysis that is incomplete or even nonexistent, then no standard methodology will be of much help. Software production of this type is more like research or mathematical theorem-proving than light bulb manufacturing, and no-one has ever tried proposing a process quality model for theorem-proving. When someone can produce a process methodology of a type that can help solve Goldbach's conjecture, then we can also start applying it to one-off software projects.

Methodologies such as the CMM and related production-process-based techniques, which assume that software can be cranked out like car parts, are therefore doomed to failure (or at least lack of success) because software engineering isn't like any other type of engineering process.

4.4.1 Assessing the Effectiveness of Software Engineering Techniques

Section 4.3 described formal methods as "a revolutionary technique that has gained widespread appeal without rigorous experimentation", however this problem is not unique to formal methods but extends to many software engineering practices in general. For example, one independent study found that applying a variety of software-engineering techniques had only a minor effect on code quality, and none on productivity [171]. Another study, this one specifically targeting formal methods and based on a detailed record of faults encountered in a large software program, could find no compelling evidence that formal methods improved code quality (although they did find a link to the programming team size, with smaller teams leading to fewer faults) [172]. The editor of Elsevier's *Journal of Systems and Software* reports seeing many papers that conclude that the techniques presented in them are of enormous value, but very little in the way of studies to support these claims [173], as did the author of a survey paper that examined the effects of a variety of techniques claimed to be revolutionary, who concluded that "the findings of this article present a few glimmers of light in an otherwise dark universe" [174]. The situation was summed up by one commentator with the observation that "software engineering owes more to the fashion industry than it does to the engineering industry [...] creativity is unconstrained, beliefs are unsupported and progress is either erratic or nonexistent. It is not for nothing that we have hundreds of programming languages, hundreds of paradigms, and essentially the same old problems. [...] In each case the paradigm arises without measurement, subsists without analysis, and usually disappears without comment" [175].

The same malaise that besets the study of the usefulness of formal methods afflicts software engineering in general, to the extent that one standard text on the subject has an entire chapter devoted to the topic of "Experimentation in Software Engineering" to alert readers to the fact that many of the methods described therein may not have any real practical foundation [136]. Some of the problems that have been identified in the study of software engineering methods are:

- Use of students as subjects. Experiments are carried out on conveniently available subjects, which generally means university students, with problems that can be solved in the available time span, usually a few weeks or a semester. In the standard student tradition, the software engineering task will be completed the night before the deadline. It has also been suggested that the use of software produced by inexperienced student programmers is so buggy that it will produce an overabundance of results when subject to analysis [176]. This produces results that indicate how the methodology applies to toy problems executed by students, but not how it will fare in the real world.

- Scale of experimentation. Real-world studies are chosen, but because of various real-world constraints such as cost and release schedules, no control group is available. One of the references cited above mentions a methodology that is based on an experiment that has been performed only once, and with a sample size of one (Fleischman and Pons were not involved). An example of this type of experimentation was one that was used to justify the use of formal methods carried out once using a single subject who for good measure was also a student [177]. Other experiments have been carried out by the developers of the methodology being tested, or where the project was a flagship project being carried out with elite developers with access to effectively unlimited resources, and where the process was highly susceptible to the Hawthorne Effect (in which an improvement in a production process is caused by the intrusive observation of that process). This sort of testing produces results from which no valid conclusion can be drawn, since a single positive result can be trivially refuted by a negative result in the next test.

- Blind belief in experts. In many cases researchers will blindly accept statements made by proponents of a new methodology without ever questioning or challenging them. For example, one researcher who was looking for empirical data on the use of the widely-accepted principle of module coupling (ranked as data coupling, stamp coupling, control coupling, common coupling, and content coupling) and cohesion (ranging from functional through communicational, procedural, temporal, and logical through to coincidental) for software design was initially unable to identify any company that used this scheme, and after some prodding found that the ranking of five of the classes was misleading [178] (these classes have been used elsewhere as a measure of "goodness" for Orange Book kernel implementations [179]).

The problem of a lack of experimental evidence to support claims made by researchers exists for software engineering techniques other than the formal methods already mentioned above. One author who tried to verify claims made at a software engineering seminar found it impossible to obtain access to any of the evidence that would be required to support the claims, the reasons being given for the lack of evidence including the fact that the data was proprietary, unavailable, or had not been analysed properly, leading him to conclude that "as an industry we collect lots of data about practices that are poorly described or flawed to start with. These data then get disseminated in a manner that makes it nearly impossible to confirm or validate their significance" [180].

An example of where this can lead is provided by IBM's CICS redevelopment, which won the Queen's Award for Technological Achievement in 1992 for its application of formal methods and is frequently used as a rare example of why the use of Z is a Good Thing. The citation stated that "The use of Z reduced development costs significantly and improved reliability and quality", however when a group of researchers not directly involved in the project attempted to verify these claims, they could find no evidence to support them [181]. Although some papers that were published on the work contained various (occasionally difficult to quantify) comments that the new code contained fewer problems than expected, the reason for this was probably due more to the fact that they constituted rewrites of a number of known failure-prone modules than any magic worked by the use of Z.

A more recent work that claims to show that Z and code-level proofs were more effective at finding faults than testing contains figures that show the exact opposite (testing found 66%

of all faults, the Z proof — done at the specification stage — found 16%, and the code proof found 5¼%). The reason why the paper is able to make the claim that proofs are more effective at finding faults is because Z was more *efficient* at finding problems than testing was (even though it didn't find most of the problems) [31]. In other words, Z is the answer provided you phrase the question very carefully. The results presented in the paper, written by the developers of the tools that were used to carry out the proofs, have not (yet) been subject to outside analysis. More comments on the work in this paper are given in Section 4.3.5 above.

Another effort that compared the relative merits of formal evaluation and testing found that the latter was far more productive at finding flaws, where productivity was evaluated in terms of the number of flaws found for the amount of time and money invested. The work also pointed out that any high-tech community will contain a large population of experienced testers, and beginning testers can be produced with minimal training, whereas formal evaluation teams are exceedingly rare and very difficult to create. The author concluded that as a result of this situation "the costs of formal assurance will outstrip the resources of most software development projects" [130].

Other software engineering success stories also arise in cases where everything else has failed, so that any change at all from whatever methodology is currently being followed will lead to some measure of success. One work mentions formal methods being applied to an existing design that consisted of "a hodge-podge of modules with patches in various languages that dated back to the late 1960s" [36], where it is quite likely that anything at all when used in this situation would have resulted in some sort of improvement (this work was probably the CICS redevelopment, although it is never named explicitly). Just because leaping from a speeding car which is heading for the edge of a cliff is a good idea for that particular situation doesn't mean that the concept should be applied as a general means of exiting vehicles.

Another problem, not specifically mentioned above since it plagues many other disciplines as well, is the misuse of statistics, although specific complaints about their misuse in the field of software metrics have been made [182][183]. Serving as a complement to the misuse of statistics is a complete lack thereof. One investigation into the number of computer science research papers containing experimentally validated results found that nearly half of the papers taken from a random sample of refereed computer science journals that contained statements that would require empirical validation contained none, with software engineering papers in particular leading the others in a lack of evidence to support claims made therein. In contrast, the figure for optical engineering and neuroscience journals that were used for comparison had just over one tenth of the papers lacking experimental evidence. The authors concluded that "there is a disproportionately high percentage of design and modelling work without any experimental evaluation in the CS samples [...] Samples related to software engineering are worse than the random CS sample" [184].

The reason why these techniques are used isn't always because of sloppiness on the part of the researchers involved, but because it is generally impractical to conduct the standard style of experiment involving control subjects, real-world applications, and testing over a long period of time. For example, if a real-world project were to be subject to experimental evaluation, it might require three or four independent teams (to get a reasonable sample size) and perhaps five other groups of teams performing the same task using different methodologies. This would raise the cost to around fifteen to twenty times the original cost, making it simply too expensive to be practical. In addition, since the major effects of the methodology won't really be felt until the maintenance phase, the evaluation would have to continue over the next several years to determine which methodology produced the best result in the long term. This would require maintaining a large collection of parallel products for the duration of the experiment, which is clearly infeasible.

4.5 Alternative Approaches

Since the birth of software engineering in the late 1960s/early 1970s, the tendency has been to solve problems by adding rules and building methodologies to cover every eventuality, in the hope that eventually all possible situations would be covered and perfect, bug-free software would materialise on time and within budget. Alternative approaches lead to meta-methodologies such as ISO 9000, which aren't software engineering methodologies in and of themselves but represent meta-methodologies with which a real methodology is meant to be created — the bureaucrat's dream which allows the production of infinite amounts of paperwork and the illusion of progress without actually necessitating the production of an end product.

These juggernaut approaches to software engineering run into problems because the very term "software engineering" is itself something of a misnomer. The standard engineering processes operate within the immutable laws of nature, so that, for example, an electrical engineer designing a circuit is eventually constrained by the laws of physics, and more directly by the real physical and electrical limits of the devices with which they are working. Software engineering, on the other hand, has no such fixed framework within which to operate. Unlike the world of non-software-engineering, there are no laws of nature to serve as a *ne plus ultra*.

Limits on software beyond basic resource-usage constraints arise entirely from artificial design requirements that can be changed at the drop of a hat (see Section 4.5.1), so that the software equivalent of "natural laws" are the design requirements for the project [185]. As a result of this, there is considerable difficulty in establishing across-the-board guidelines for software design. Since the natural laws of software change across projects and even within them, it is impossible to set universal rules that apply in all (or even most) cases. Imagine the effect on the electrical engineering design mentioned above if the direction, or velocity, or resistance to, electron flow could change from one day to the next!

The response to this problem is backlash methodologies such as extreme programming (XP[1]) whose principal feature is that they are everything their predecessors were not: lightweight, easy to use, and flexible. It's instructive to take a look at XP in order to compare it with traditional alternatives.

---

[1] This methodology has no relation to a Microsoft product with a similar name.

4.5.1 Extreme Programming

XP is a slightly more rigorous form of an ad-hoc methodology that has been termed "development on Internet time" which begins with a general functional product specification which is revised as the product evolves and is only complete when the product itself is complete. Development is broken up into sub-cycles at the end of which the product is stabilised by fixing major errors and freezing certain features. Schedule slip is handled by deleting features. In addition developers are (at least in theory) given the power to veto some requirements on technical grounds [186][187].

XP follows the general pattern of "development on Internet time" but is far more rigorous [188][189][190]. It also doesn't begin with the traditional mountain of design documentation. Instead, the end user is asked to provide a collection of user stories, short statements on what the finished product is expected to do. The intent of the user stories is to provide just enough detail to allow the developers to estimate how long the story will take to implement. Each story describes only the user's needs; implementation details are left to the developers who (presumably) will understand the technical capabilities and limitations far better than the end user, leaving them with the freedom to choose the most appropriate solution to the problem. The relationship to earlier methodologies such as the waterfall model (characterised by long development cycles) and the spiral model (with slightly shorter cycles) is shown in Figure 4.1.

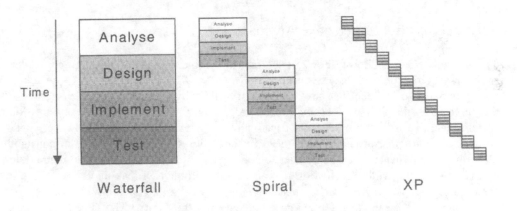

Figure 4.1. Comparison of software development life cycles.

The development process is structured around the user stories, ordered according to their value to the user and their risk to the developers. The selection of which stories to work with first is performed by the end user in collaboration with the programmers. In this way, the most problematic and high-value problems are handled first, and the easy or relatively inconsequential ones are left for later. The end user is kept in the loop at all times during the development process, with frequent code releases to allow them to determine whether the product meets their requirements. This both allows the end user to ensure that it will work as required in its target environment, and avoids the "it's just what I asked for but not what I want" problem that plagues software developed using traditional methodologies in which the customer signs off on a huge, only vaguely understood design specification and doesn't get to play with the deliverables until it's too late to make any changes. The general concept behind XP is that if it's possible to make change cheap, then all sorts of things can be achieved that wouldn't be possible with other methodologies.

XP also uses continuous testing as part of the development process, actually moving the creation of unit testing code to before the creation of the code itself, so that it's easy to determine whether the program code works as required as soon as it's written. If a bug is found, a new test is created to ensure that it won't recur later.

Practitioners of "real" methodologies who are still reading at this point will no doubt be horrified by this description of XP; however, it's an example of what can be done by adapting the methodology to the environment rather than trying to force-fit the environment to match the methodology. XP also incorporates a strong measure of pragmatism, which is frequently absent from other methodologies. One XP practitioner has summed up the approach as "use a technique where it works, ignore it where it doesn't. XP has never been described as a panacea" [191]. A remarkable feature of XP that arises from this is the level of enthusiasm displayed for it by its users (as opposed to its advocates, vendors, authors of books expounding its benefits, and other hangers-on), something that is hard to find for alternatives such as ISO 9000, CASE tools, and so on [192] (the popularity of XP is such that it has its own conference and a number of very active web forums).

4.5.2 Lessons from Alternative Approaches

The previous section showed how, in the face of problems with traditional approaches, a problem-specific approach may be successful. Note that XP isn't a general-purpose solution, and it remains to be seen just how effective it will really be in the long term (one of its assumptions is that it'll be used by skilled programmers who know what they are doing, which generally isn't the case once a methodology goes mainstream). However, it does address one particular problem — the need for rapid development in the face of constantly-changing requirements — and only tries to solve this particular problem. The methodology evolved by starting with a real-world approach to the problem of making change cheap and then codifying it as XP, rather than beginning with a methodology based on (say) mathematical theory and then forcing development to fit the theory. The same approach, this time with the goal of developing secure systems, is taken in the next chapter.

4.6 References

[1]   "No Silver Bullet: Essence and Accidents of Software Engineering", Frederick Brooks Jr., *IEEE Computer*, **Vol.20**, **No.4** (April 1987), p.10.

[2]   "Striving for Correctness", Marshall Abrams and Marvin Zelkowitz, *Computers and Security*, **Vol.14**, **No.8** (1995), p.719.

[3]   "Does OO Sync with How We Think?", Les Hatton, *IEEE Software*, **Vol.15**, **No.3** (May/June 1998), p.46.

[4]   "Software Engineering: A Practitioners Approach (3rd ed)", Roger Pressman, McGraw-Hill International Edition, 1992.

[5]   "A Specifier's Introduction to Formal Methods", Jeannette Wing, *IEEE Computer*, **Vol.23**, **No.9** (September 1990), p.8.

[6]   "Strategies for Incorporating Formal Specifications in Software Development", Martin Fraser, Kuldeep Kumar, and Vijay Vaishnavi, *Communications of the ACM*, **Vol.37**, **No.10** (October 1994), p.74.

[7]   "Formal Methods and Models", James Willams and Marshall Abrams, "Information Security: An Integrated Collection of Essays", IEEE Computer Society Press, 1995, p.170.

[8]   "A Technique for Software Module Specification with Examples", David Parnas, *Communications of the ACM*, **Vol.15**, **No.5** (May 1972), p.330.

[9]   "Implications of a Virtual Memory Mechanism for Implementing Protection in a Family of Operating Systems", William Price, PhD thesis, Carnegie-Mellon University, June 1973.

[10] "An Experiment with Affirm and HDM", Jonathan Millen and David Drake, *The Journal of Systems and Software*, **Vol.2**, **No.2** (June 1981), p.159.

[11] "Applying Formal Methods to an Information Security Device: An Experience Report", James Kirby Jr., Myla Archer, and Constance Heitmeyer, *Proceedings of the 4th International Symposium on High Assurance Systems Engineering (HASE'99)*, IEEE Computer Society Press, November 1999, p.81.

[12] "Building a Secure Computer System", Morrie Gasser, Van Nostrand Reinhold, 1988.

[13] "Validating Requirements for Fault Tolerant Systems using Model Checking", Francis Schneider, Steve Easterbrook, John Callahan, and Gerard Holzman, *Proceedings of the 3rd International Conference on Requirements Engineering*, IEEE Computer Society Press, April 1998, p.4.

[14] "Report on the Formal Specification and Partial Verification of the VIPER Microprocessor", Bishop Brock and Warren Hunt Jr., *Proceedings of the 6th Annual Conference on Computer Assurance (COMPASS'91)*, IEEE Computer Society Press, 1991, p.91.

[15] "User Threatens Court Action over MoD Chip", Simon Hill, *Computer Weekly*, 5 July 1990, p.3.

[16] "MoD in Row with Firm over Chip Development", *The Independent*, 28 May 1991.

[17] "Formal Methods of Program Verification and Specification", H.Berg, W.Boebert, W.Franta, and T.Moher, Prentice-Hall Inc, 1982.

[18] "A Description of a Formal Verification and Validation (FVV) Process", Bill Smith, Cynthia Reese, Kenneth Lindsay, and Brian Crane, *Proceedings of the 1988 IEEE Symposium on Security and Privacy*, IEEE Computer Society Press, August 1988, p.401.

[19] "An InaJo Proof Manager for the Formal Development Method", Daniel Barry, *ACM SIGSOFT Software Engineering Notes*, **Vol.10**, **No.4** (August 1985), p.19.

[20] "Proposed Technical Evaluation Criteria for Trusted Computer Systems", Grace Nibaldi, MITRE Technical Report M79-225, The MITRE Corporation, 25 October 1979.

[21] "Locking Computers Securely", O.Sami Saydari, Joseph Beckman, and Jeffrey Leaman, *Proceedings of the 10th National Computer Security Conference*, September 1987, p.129.

[22] "Program Verification", Robert Boyer and J.Strother Moore, *Journal of Automated Reasoning*, **Vol.1**, **No.1** (1985), p.17.

[23] "Mathematics, Technology, and Trust: Formal Verification, Computer Security, and the US Military", Donald MacKenzie and Garrel Pottinger, *IEEE Annals of the History of Computing*, **Vol.19**, **No.3** (July-September 1997), p.41.

[24] "Do You Trust Your Compiler", James Boyle, R.Daniel Resler, Victor Winter, *IEEE Computer*, **Vol.32**, **No.5** (May 1999), p.65.

[25] "Integrating Formal Methods into the Development Process", Richard Kemmerer, *IEEE Software*, **Vol.7**, **No.5** (September 1990), p.37.

[26] "Towards a verified MiniSML/SECD system", Todd Simpson, Graham Birtwhistle, and Brian Graham, *Software Engineering Journal*, **Vol.8**, **No.3** (May 1993), p.137.

[27] "Formal Verification of Transformations for Peephole Optimisation", A.Dold, F.von Henke, H.Pfeifer, and H.Rueß, *Proceedings of the 4th International Symposium of Formal Methods Europe (FME'97)*, Springer-Verlag Lecture Notes in Computer Science, No.1313, p.459.

[28] "The verification of low-level code", D.Clutterbuck and B.Carré, *Software Engineering Journal*, **Vol.3**, **No.3** (May 1988), p.97.

[29] "Automatic Verification of Object Code Against Source Code", Sakthi Subramanian and Jeffrey Cook, *Proceedings of the 11th Annual Conference on Computer Assurance (COMPASS'96)*, IEEE Computer Society Press, June 1996, p.46.

[30] "Automatic Generation of C++ Code from an ESCRO2 Specification", P.Grabow and L.Liu, *Proceedings of the 19th Computer Software and Applications Conference (COMPSAC'95)*, September 1995, p.18.

[31] "Is Proof More Cost-Effective Than Testing", Steve King, Jonathan Hammond, Rod Chapman, and Andy Pryor, *IEEE Transactions on Software Engineering*, **Vol.26**, **No.8** (August 2000), p.675.

[32] "Science and Substance: A Challenge to Software Engineers", Norman Fenton, Shari Lawrence Pfleeger, and Robert L.Glass, *IEEE Software*, **Vol.11**, **No.4** (July 1994), p.86.

[33] "The Software-Research Crisis", Robert Glass, *IEEE Software*, **Vol.11**, **No.6** (November 1994), p.42.

[34] "Observation on Industrial Practice Using Formal Methods", Susan Gerhart, Dan Craigen, and Ted Ralston, *Proceedings of the 15th International Conference on Software Engineering (ICSE'93)*, 1993, p.24.

[35] "How Effective Are Software Engineering Methods?", Norman Fenton, *The Journal of Systems and Software*, **Vol.22**, **No.2** (August 1993), p.141.

[36] "Industrial Applications of Formal Methods to Model, Design, and Analyze Computer Systems: An International Survey", Dan Craigen, Susan Gerhart, and Ted Ralston, Noyes Data Corporation, 1994 (originally published by NIST).

[37] "The Evaluation of Three Specification and Verification Methodologies", Richard Platek, *Proceedings of the 4th Seminar on the DoD Computer Security Initiative* (later the National Computer Security Conference), August 1981, p.X-1.

[38] "Ina Jo: SDC's Formal Development Methodology", *ACM SIGSOFT Software Engineering Notes*, **Vol.5**, **No.3** (July 1980).

[39] "FDM — A Specification and Verification Methodology", Richard Kemmerer, *Proceedings of the 3rd Seminar on the DoD Computer Security Initiative Program* (later the National Computer Security Conference) November 1980, p.L-1.

[40] "INATEST: An Interactive System for Testing Formal Specifications", Steven Eckmann and Richard Kemmerer, *ACM SIGSOFT Software Engineering Notes*, **Vol.10**, **No.4** (August 1985), p.17.

[41] "Gypsy: A Language for Specification and Implementation of Verifiable Programs", Richard Cohen, Allen Ambler, Donald Good, James Browne, Wilhelm Burger, Charles Hoch, and Robert Wells, *SIGPLAN Notices*, **Vol.12**, **No.3** (March 1977), p.1.

[42] "A Report on the Development of Gypsy", Richard Cohen, Donald Good and Lawrence Hunter, *Proceedings of the 1978 National ACM Conference*, December 1978, p.116.

[43] "Building Verified Systems with Gypsy", Donald Good, *Proceedings of the 3rd Seminar on the DoD Computer Security Initiative Program* (later the National Computer Security Conference), November 1980, p.M-1.

[44] "Industrial Use of Formal Methods", Steven Miller, *Dependable Computing and Fault-Tolerant Systems*, **Vol.9**, Springer-Verlag, 1995, p.33.

[45] "Can we rely on Formal Methods?", Natarajan Shankar, *Dependable Computing and Fault-Tolerant Systems*, **Vol.9**, Springer-Verlag, 1995, p.42.

[46] "Applications of Formal Methods", Mike Hinchey and Jonathan Bowen, Prentice-Hall International, 1995.

[47] "A Case Study in Model Checking Software Systems", Jeannette Wing and Mondonna Vaziri-Farahani, *Science of Computer Programming*, **Vol.28**, **No.2-3** (April 1997), p.273.

[48] "A survey of mechanical support for formal reasoning", Peter Lindsay, *Software Engineering Journal*, **Vol.3**, **No.1** (January 1988), p.3.

[49] "Verification Technology and the A1 Criteria", Terry Vickers Benzel, *ACM SIGSOFT Software Engineering Notes*, **Vol.10**, **No.4** (August 1985), p.108.

[50] "Verifying security", Maureen Cheheyl, Morrie Gasser, George Huff, and Jonathan Millen, *ACM Computing Surveys*, **Vol.13**, **No.3** (September 1981), p.279.

[51] "A Role for Formal Methodists", Fred Schneider, *Dependable Computing and Fault-Tolerant Systems*, **Vol.9**, Springer-Verlag, 1995, p.54.

[52] "Software Testing Techniques (2nd ed)", Boris Beizer, Van Nostrand Reinhold, 1990.

[53] "Engineering Requirements for Production Quality Verification Systems", Stephen Crocker, *ACM SIGSOFT Software Engineering Notes*, **Vol.10**, **No.4** (August 1985), p.15.

[54] "Problems, methods, and specialisation", Michael Jackson, *Software Engineering Journal*, **Vol.9**, **No.6** (November 1994), p.249.

[55] "Formal Methods and Traditional Engineering", Michael Jackson, *The Journal of Systems and Software*, **Vol.40**, **No.3** (March 1998), p.191.

[56] "Verifying the Specification-to-Code Correspondence for Abstract Data Types", Daniel Schweizer and Christoph Denzler, *Dependable Computing and Fault-Tolerant Systems*, **Vol.11**, Springer-Verlag, 1998, p.33.

[57] "Strong vs. Weak Approaches to Systems Development", Iris Vessey and Robert Glass, *Communications of the ACM*, **Vol.41**, **No.4** (April 1998), p.99

[58] "Panel Session: Kernel Performance Issues", Marvin Shaefer (chairman), *Proceedings of the 1981 IEEE Symposium on Security and Privacy*, IEEE Computer Society Press, August 1981, p.162.

[59] "The Best Available Technologies for Computer Security", Carl Landwehr, *IEEE Computer*, **Vol.16**, **No 7** (July 1983), p.86.

[60] "A Retrospective on the VAX VMM Security Kernel", Paul Karger, Mary Ellen Zurko, Douglas Bonin, Andrew Mason, and Clifford Kahn, *IEEE Transactions on Software Engineering*, **Vol.17**, **No.11** (November 1991), p.1147.

[61] "Formal Construction of the Mathematically Analyzed Separation Kernel", W.Martin, P.White, F.S.Taylor, and A.Goldberg, *Proceedings of the 15th International Conference on Automated Software Engineering (ASE'00)*, IEEE Computer Society Press, September 2000, p.133.

[62] "Formal Methods Reality Check: Industrial Usage", Dan Craigen, Susan Gerhart, and Ted Ralston, *IEEE Transactions on Software Engineering*, **Vol.21**, **No.2** (February 1995), p.90.

[63] "Mathematical Methods: What we Need and Don't Need", David Parnas, *IEEE Computer*, **Vol.29**, **No.4** (April 1996), p.28.

[64] "Literate Specifications", C.Johnson, *Software Engineering Journal*, **Vol.11**, **No.4** (July 1996), p.225.

[65] "Mathematical Notation in Formal Specification: Too Difficult for the Masses?", Kate Finney, *IEEE Transactions on Software Engineering*, **Vol.22**, **No.2** (February 1996), p.158.

[66] "The Design of a Family of Applications-oriented Requirements Languages", Alan Davis, *IEEE Computer*, **Vol.15**, **No.5** (May 1982), p.21.

[67] "An Operational Approach to Requirements Specification for Embedded Systems", *IEEE Transactions on Software Engineering*, **Vol.8**, **No.3** (May 1982), p.250.

[68] "A Comparison of Techniques for the Specification of External System Behaviour", Alan Davis, *Communications of the ACM*, **Vol.31**, **No.9** (September 1988), p.1098.

[69] "A 15 Year Perspective on Automatic Programming", *IEEE Transactions on Software Engineering*, **Vol.11, No.11** (November 1985), p.1257.

[70] "Operational Specification as the Basis for Rapid Prototyping", Robert Balzer, Neil Goldman, and David Wile, *ACM SIGSOFT Software Engineering Notes*, **Vol.7, No.5** (December 1982), p.3.

[71] "Fault Tolerance by Design Diversity: Concepts and Experiments", Algirdas Avižienis and John Kelly, *IEEE Computer*, **Vol.17, No.8** (August 1984), p.67.

[72] "Coding for a Believable Specification to Implementation Mapping", William Young and John McHugh, , *Proceedings of the 1987 IEEE Symposium on Security and Privacy*, IEEE Computer Society Press, August 1987, p.140.

[73] "DoD Overview: Computer Security Program Direction", Colonel Joseph Greene Jr., *Proceedings of the 8th National Computer Security Conference*, September 1985, p.6.

[74] "The Emperor's Old Armor", Bob Blakley, *Proceedings of the 1996 New Security Paradigms Workshop*, ACM, 1996, p.2.

[75] "Analysis of a Kernel Verification", Terry Vickers Benzel, *Proceedings of the 1984 IEEE Symposium on Security and Privacy*, IEEE Computer Society Press, August 1984, p.125.

[76] "Increasing Assurance with Literate Programming Techniques", Andrew Moore and Charles Payne Jr., *Proceedings of the 11th Annual Conference on Computer Assurance (COMPASS'96)*, National Institute of Standards and Technology, June 1996.

[77] "Formal Verification Techniques for a Network Security Device", Hicham Adra and William Sandberg-Maitland, *Proceedings of the 3rd Annual Canadian Computer Security Symposium*, May 1991, p.295.

[78] "Assessment and Control of Software", Capers Jones, Yourdon Press, 1994.

[79] "An InaJo Proof Manager", Daniel Berry, *ACM SIGSOFT Software Engineering Notes*, **Vol.10, No.4** (August 1985), p.19.

[80] "Formal Methods: Promises and Problems", Luqi and Joseph Goguen, *IEEE Software*, **Vol.14, No.1** (January 1997), p.73.

[81] "A Security Model for Military Message Systems", Carl Landwehr, Constance Heitmeyer, and John McLean, *ACM Transactions on Computer Systems*, **Vol.2, No.3** (August 1984), p.198.

[82] "Risk Analysis of 'Trusted Computer Systems'", Klaus Brunnstein and Simone Fischer-Hübner, *Computer Security and Information Integrity*, Elsevier Science Publishers, 1991, p.71.

[83] "A Retrospective on the Criteria Movement", Willis Ware, *Proceedings of the 18th National Information Systems Security Conference* (formerly the National Computer Security Conference), October 1995, p.582.

[84] "Are We Testing for True Reliability?", Dick Hamlet, *IEEE Software*, **Vol.9, No.4** (July 1992), p.21.

[85] "The Limits of Software: People, Projects, and Perspectives", Robert Britcher and Robert Glass, Addison-Wesley, 1999.

[86] "A Review of the State of the Practice in Requirements Modelling", Mitch Lubars, Colin Potts, and Charlie Richter, *Proceedings of the IEEE International Symposium on Requirements Engineering*, IEEE Computer Society Press, January 1993, p.2.

[87] "Software-Engineering Research Revisited", Colin Potts, *IEEE Software*, **Vol.10**, **No.5** (September 1993), p.19.

[88] "Invented Requirements and Imagined Customers: Requirements Engineering for Off-the-Shelf Software", Colin Potts, *Proceedings of the 2nd IEEE International Symposium on Requirements Engineering*, IEEE Computer Society Press, March 1995, p.128.

[89] "Validating a High-Performance, Programmable Secure Coprocessor", Sean Smith, Ron Perez, Steve Weingart, and Vernon Austel, *Proceedings of the 22nd National Information Systems Security Conference* (formerly the National Computer Security Conference), October 1999.

[90] "A New Paradigm for Trusted Systems", Dorothy Denning, *Proceedings of the New Security Paradigms Workshop '92*, 1992, p.36.

[91] "TCB Subsets for Incremental Evaluation", William Shockley and Roger Schell, *Proceedings of the 3rd Aerospace Computer Security Conference*, December 1987, p.131.

[92] "Does TCB Subsetting Enhance Trust?", Richard Feiertag, *Proceedings of the 5th Annual Computer Security Applications Conference*, December 1989, p.104.

[93] "Considerations in TCB Subsetting", Helena Winkler-Parenty, *Proceedings of the 5th Annual Computer Security Applications Conference*, December 1989, p.105.

[94] "Requirements for Market Driven Evaluations for Commercial Users of Secure Systems", Peter Callaway, *Proceedings of the 3rd Annual Canadian Computer Security Symposium*, May 1991, p.207.

[95] "Re-Use of Evaluation Results", Jonathan Smith, *Proceedings of the 15th National Computer Security Conference*, October 1992, p.534.

[96] "Using a Mandatory Secrecy and Integrity Policy on Smart Cards and Mobile Devices", Paul Karger, Vernon Austel, and David Toll, *Proceedings of the EuroSmart Security Conference*, June 2000, p.134.

[97] "The Need for an Integrated Design, Implementation, Verification, and Testing Methodology", R.Alan Whitehurst, *ACM SIGSOFT Software Engineering Notes*, **Vol.10**, **No.4** (August 1985), p.97.

[98] "SELECT — A Formal System for Testing and Debugging Programs by Symbolic Execution", Robert Boyer, Bernard Elspas, and Karl Levitt, *ACM SIGPLAN Notices*, **Vol.10**, **No.6** (June 1975), p.234.

[99] "A Review of Formal Methods", Robert Vienneau, *A Review of Formal Methods*, Kaman Science Corporation, 1993, p.3.

[100] "CERT Advisory CA-2001-25 Buffer Overflow in Gauntlet Firewall allows intruders to execute arbitrary code", CERT, `http://www.cert.org/advisories/CA-2001-25.html`, 6 September 2001.

[101] "Security hole found in Gauntlet: NAI firewall suffers second serious hole. Experts ask, is anything safe?", Kevin Poulsen, *SecurityFocus News*, `http://www.-securityfocus.com/news/248`, 4 September 2001.

[102] "PGP's Gauntlet Firewall Vulnerable", George Hulme, *Wall Street and Technology*, `http://www.wallstreetandtech.com/story/itWire/IWK20010911S0 003`, 11 September 2001.

[103] "Formal Specification and Verification of Control Software for Cryptographic Equipment", D.Richard Kuhn and James Dray, *Proceedings of the 1990 IEEE Symposium on Security and Privacy*, IEEE Computer Society Press, August 1990, p.32.

[104] "Making Sense of Specifications: The Formalization of SET (Transcript of Discussion)", Lawrence Paulson, *Proceedings of the 8th International Security Protocols Workshop*, April 2000, Springer-Verlag Lecture Notes in Computer Science, No.2133, p.82.

[105] "Formal Verification of Cardholder Registration in SET", Giampaolo Bella, Fabio Massacci, Lawrence Paulson, and Piero Tramontano, *Proceedings of the 6th European Symposium on Research in Computer Security (ESORICS 2000)*, Springer-Verlag Lecture Notes in Computer Science, No.1895, p.159.

[106] "A Cryptographic Evaluation of IPsec", Niels Ferguson and Bruce Schneier, Counterpane Labs, 1999, `http://www.counterpane.com/ipsec.html`.

[107] "Making Sense of Specifications: The Formalization of SET", Giampaolo Bella, Fabio Massacci, Lawrence Paulson, and Piero Tramontano, *Proceedings of the 8th International Security Protocols Workshop*, April 2000, Springer-Verlag Lecture Notes in Computer Science, No.2133, p.74.

[108] "Information Flow and Invariance", Joshua Guttman, *Proceedings of the 1987 IEEE Symposium on Security and Privacy*, IEEE Computer Society Press, August 1987, p.67.

[109] "Symbol Security Condition Considered Harmful", Marvin Schaefer, *Proceedings of the 1989 IEEE Symposium on Security and Privacy*, IEEE Computer Society Press, August 1989, p.20.

[110] "Re: WuFTPD: Providing *remote* root since at least 1994", Theo de Raadt, posting to the bugtraq mailing list, message-ID `200006272322.e5RNMIv18874@cvs.-openbsd.org`, 27 June 2000.

[111] "A Logic of Authentication", Michael Burrows, Martín Abadi, and Roger Needham, *ACM Transactions on Computer Systems*, **Vol.8**, **No.1** (February 1990), p.18.

[112] "Breaking and fixing the Needham-Schroeder public-key protocol using CSP and FDR", Gavin Lowe, *Proceedings of the 2d International Workshop on Tools and Algorithms for the Construction and Analysis of Systems (TACAS'96)*, Springer-Verlag Lecture Notes in Computer Science, No.1055, March 1996, p.147.

[113] "Casper: A Compiler for the Analysis of Security Protocols", Gavin Lowe, *Proceedings of the 1997 IEEE Symposium on Security and Privacy*, IEEE Computer Society Press, May 1997, p.18.

[114] "Analyzing the Needham-Schroeder Public Key Protocol: A Comparison of Two Approaches", Catherine Meadows, *Proceedings of the 4th European Symposium on Research in Computer Security (ESORICS'96)*, Springer-Verlag Lecture Notes in Computer Science, No.1146, September 1996, p.351.

[115] "On the Verification of Cryptographic Protocols — A Tale of Two Committees", Dieter Gollman, *Proceedings of the Workshop on Secure Architectures and Information Flow*, Electronic Notes in Theoretical Computer Science (ENTCS), **Vol.32**, 2000, `http://www.elsevier.nl/gej-ng/31/29/23/57/23/show/-Products/notes/index.htt`.

[116] "The Logic of Computer Programming", Zohar Manna and Richard Waldinger, *IEEE Transactions on Software Engineering*, **Vol.4**, **No.3** (May 1978), p.199.

[117] "Verifying a Real System Design — Some of the Problems", Ruaridh Macdonald, *ACM SIGSOFT Software Engineering Notes*, **Vol.10**, **No.4** (August 1985), p.128.

[118] "On the Inevitable Intertwining of Specification and Implementation", William Swartout and Robert Balzer, *Communications of the ACM*, **Vol.25**, **No.7** (July 1982), p.438.

[119] "An Empirical Investigation of the Effect of Formal Specifications on Program Diversity", Thomas McVittie, John Kelly, and Wayne Yamamoto, *Dependable Computing and Fault-Tolerant Systems*, **Vol.6**, Springer-Verlag, 1992, p.219.

[120] "Proving Properties of Security Protocols by Induction", Lawrence Paulson, *Proceedings of the 10th Computer Security Foundations Workshop (CSFW'97)*, June 1997, p.70.

[121] "Verifying Security Protocols with Brutus", E.M.Clarke, S.Jha, and W.Marrero, *ACM Transactions on Software Engineering and Methodology*, **Vol.9**, **No.4** (October 2000), p.443.

[122] "Automated Analysis of Cryptographic Protocols Using Murφ", John Mitchell, Mark Mitchell, and Ulrich Stern, *Proceedings of the 1997 IEEE Symposium on Security and Privacy*, IEEE Computer Society Press, May 1997, p.141.

[123] "Strand Spaces: Why is a Security Protocol Correct", F.Javier Thayer Fábrega, Jonathan Herzog, and Joshua Guttman, *Proceedings of the 1998 IEEE Symposium on Security and Privacy*, IEEE Computer Society Press, May 1998, p.160.

[124] "Athena: a novel approach to efficient automatic security protocol analysis", Dawn Xiaoding Song, Sergey Berezin, and Adrian Perrig, *Journal of Computer Security*, **Vol.9**, **Nos.1,2** (2000), p.47.

[125] "Dynamic Analysis of Security Protocols", Alec Yasinsac, *Proceedings of the New Security Paradigms Workshop*, September 2000, p.77.

[126] "Social Processes and Proofs of Theorems and Programs", Richard DeMillo, Richard Lipton, and Alan Perlis, *Communications of the ACM*, **Vol.22**, **No.5** (May 1979), p.271.

[127] "Fermat's Last Theorem", Simon Singh, Fourth Estate, 1997.

[128] "Adventures of a Mathematician", Stanislaw Ulam, Scribners, 1976.

[129] "Program Verification: The Very Idea", James Fetzer, *Communications of the ACM*, **Vol.31**, **No.9** (September 1988), p.1048.

[130] "Cost Profile of a Highly Assured, Secure Operating System", Richard Smith, *ACM Transactions on Information and System Security*, **Vol.4**, **No.1** (February 2001), p.72.

[131] "Programming by Action Clusters", Peter Naur, *BIT*, **Vol.9**, **No.3** (September 1969), p.250.

[132] Review No.19,420, Burt Leavenworth, *Computing Reviews*, **Vol.11**, **No.7** (July 1970), p.396.

[133] "Software Reliability through Proving Programs Correct", *Proceedings of the IEEE International Symposium on Fault-Tolerant Computing*, March 1971, p.125.

[134] "Toward a Theory of Test Data Selection", John Goodenough and Susan Gerhart, *IEEE Transactions on Software Engineering*, **Vol.1**, **No.2** (June 1975), p.156.

[135] "On Formalism in Specifications", *IEEE Software*, **Vol.2**, **No.1** (January 1985), p.6.

[136] "Software Engineering (2nd ed)", Stephen Schach, Richard Irwin and Asken Associates, 1993.

[137] "Acceptance of Formal Methods: Lessons from Hardware Design", David Dill and John Rushby, *IEEE Computer*, **Vol.29**, **No.4** (April 1996), p.23.

[138] "Formal Hardware Verification: Methods and systems in comparison", Lecture Notes in Computer Science, No.1287, Springer-Verlag, 1997.

[139] "Formal methods in computer aided design: Second international conference proceedings", Lecture Notes in Computer Science, No.1522, Springer-Verlag, 1998.

[140] "Formal Methods For Developing High Assurance Computer Systems: Working Group Report", Mats Heimdahl and Constance Heitmeyer, *Proceedings of the 2nd Workshop on Industrial-Strength Formal Specification Techniques (WIFT'98)*, IEEE Computer Society Press, October 1998.

[141] "Taking Z Seriously", Anthony Hall, *The Z formal specification notation: Proceedings of ZUM'97*, Springer-Verlag Lecture Notes in Computer Science, No.1212, 1997, p.1.

[142] "Software Technology Maturation", Samuel Redwine and William Riddle, *Proceedings of the 8th International Conference on Software Engineering (ICSE'85)*, IEEE Computer Society Press, August 1985, p.189.

[143] "OO is NOT the Silver Bullet", J.Barrie Thompson, *Proceedings of the 20th Computer Software and Applications Conference (COMPSAC'96)*, IEEE Computer Society Press, 1996, p.155.

[144] "The Psychological Study of Programming", B.Sheil, *Computing Surveys*, **Vol.13**, **No.1** (March 1981), p.101.

[145] "Seven More Myths of Formal Methods" Jonathan Bowen and Michael Hinchey, *IEEE Software*, **Vol.12**, **No.4** (July 1995), p.34.

[146] "Belief in Correctness", Marshall Abrams and Marvin Zelkowitz, *Proceedings of the 17th National Computer Security Conference*, October 1994, p.132.

[147] "Status Report on Software Measurement", Shari Lawrence Pfleeger, Ross Jeffery, Bill Curtis, and Barbara Kitchenham, *IEEE Software*, **Vol.14**, **No.2** (March/April 1997), p.33.

[148] "Does Organizational Maturity Improve Quality?", Khaled El Emam and Nazim Madhavji, *IEEE Software*, **Vol.13**, **No.5** (September 1996), p.209.

[149] "Is Software Process Re-engineering and Improvement the 'Silver Bullet' of the 1990's or a Constructive Approach to Meet Pre-defined Business Targets", Annie Kuntzmann-Combelles, *Proceedings of the 20th Computer Software and Applications Conference (COMPSAC'96)*, 1996, p.435.

[150] "Safer C: Developing for High-Integrity and Safety-Critical Systems", Les Hatton, McGraw-Hill, 1995.

[151] "Can You Trust Software Capability Evaluations", Emilie O'Connell and Hossein Saiedian, *IEEE Computer*, **Vol.33**, **No.2** (February 2000), p.28.

[152] "New Paradigms for High Assurance Systems", John McLean, *Proceedings of the 1992 New Security Paradigms Workshop*, IEEE Press, 1993, p.42.

[153] "Quantitative Measures of Security", John McLean, *Dependable Computing and Fault-Tolerant Systems*, **Vol.9**, Springer-Verlag, 1995, p.223.

[154] "The Feasibility of Quantitative Assessment of Security", Catherine Meadows, *Dependable Computing and Fault-Tolerant Systems*, **Vol.9**, Springer-Verlag, 1995, p.228.

[155] "Determining Assurance Levels by Security Engineering Process Maturity", Karen Ferraiolo and Joel Sachs, *Proceedings of the 5th Annual Canadian Computer Security Symposium*, May 1993, p.477.

[156] "Community Response to CMM-Based Security Engineering Process Improvement", Marcia Zior, *Proceedings of the 18th National Information Systems Security Conference* (formerly the National Computer Security Conference), October 1995 p.404.

[157] "Systems Security Engineering Capability Maturity Model (SSE-CMM), Model Description Document Version 2.0", Systems Security Engineering Capability Maturity Model (SSE-CMM) Project, 1 April 1999.

[158] "RE: [open-source] Market demands for reliable software", Gary Stoneburner, posting to the open-source@csl.sri.com mailing list, message-ID `5.0.0.25.2.-20010404083833.009fd100@mail.nist.gov`, 4 April 2001.

[159] "OS/360 Computer Security Penetration Exercise", S.Goheen and R.Fiske, MITRE Working Paper WP-4467, The MITRE Corporation, 16 October 1972.

[160] "HOWTO: Password Change Filtering & Notification in Windows NT", Microsoft Knowledge Base Article Q151082, June 1997.

[161] "A new Microsoft security bulletin and the OffloadModExpo functionality", Sergio Tabanelli, posting to the `aucrypto` mailing list, message-ID `20000413102943.-OGOB5378.fep03-svc.tin.it@fep11-svc.tin.it`, 13 April 2000.

[162] "A Software Process Immaturity Model", Anthony Finkelstein, *ACM SIGSOFT Software Engineering Notes*, **Vol.17**, **No.4** (October 1992), p.22.

[163] "Rules to Lose By: The Hopeless character class", Roger Koppy, *Dragon Magazine*, **Vol.9, No.11** (April 1985), p.54.

[164] "The Need for a Failure Model for Security", Catherine Meadows, *Dependable Computing and Fault-tolerant Systems*, **Vol.9**, 1995.

[165] "The Second Annual Report on CASE", CASE Research Corp, Washington, 1990.

[166] "An Empirical Evaluation of the Use of CASE Tools", S.Stobart, A.van Reeken, G.Low, J.Trienekens, J.Jenkins, J.Thompson, and D.Jeffery, *Proceedings of the 6th International Workshop on Computer-Aided Software Engineering (CASE'93)*, IEEE Computer Society Press, July 1993, p.81.

[167] "The Methods Won't Save You (but it can help)", Patrick Loy, *ACM SIGSOFT Software Engineering Notes*, **Vol.18, No.1** (January 1993), p.30.

[168] "What Determines the Effectiveness of CASE Tools? Answers Suggested by Empirical Research", Joseph Trienekens and Anton van Reeken, *Proceedings of the 5th International Workshop on Computer-Aided Software Engineering (CASE'92)*, IEEE Computer Society Press, July 1992, p.258.

[169] "Albert Einstein and Empirical Software Engineering", Shari Lawrence Pfleeger, *IEEE Computer*, **Vol.32, No.10** (October 1999), p.32.

[170] "Rethinking the modes of software engineering research", Alfonso Fugetta, *Journal of Systems and Software*, **Vol.47, No.2-3** (July 1999), p.133.

[171] "Evaluating Software Engineering Technologies", David Card, Frank McGarry, Gerald Page, *IEEE Transactions on Software Engineering*, **Vol.13, No.7** (July 1987), p.845.

[172] "Investigating the Influence of Formal Methods", Shari Lawrence Pfleeger and Les Hatton, *IEEE Computer*, **Vol.30, No.2** (February 1997), p.33.

[173] "Formal Methods are a Surrogate for a More Serious Software Concern", Robert Glass, *IEEE Computer*, **Vol.29, No.4** (April 1996), p.19.

[174] "The Realities of Software Technology Payoffs", Robert Glass, *Communications of the ACM*, **Vol.42, No.2** (February 1999), p.74.

[175] "Software failures, follies, and fallacies", Les Hatton, *IEE Review*, **Vol.43, No.2** (March 1997), p.49.

[176] "More Testing Should be Taught", Terry Shepard, Margaret Lamb, and Diane Kelly, *Communications of the ACM*, **Vol.44, No.6** (June 2001), p.103.

[177] "Applying Mathematical Software Documentation: An Experience Report", Brian Bauer and David Parnas, *Proceedings of the 10th Annual Conference on Computer Assurance (COMPASS'95)*, IEEE Computer Society Press, June 1995, p.273.

[178] "What's Wrong with Software Engineering Research Methodology", Franck Xia, *ACM SIGSOFT Software Engineering Notes*, **Vol.23, No.1** (January 1998), p.62.

[179] "Assessing Modularity in Trusted Computing Bases", J.Arnold, D.Baker, F.Belvin, R.Bottomly, S.Chokhani, and D.Downs, *Proceedings of the 15th National Computer Security Conference*, October 1992, p.44. Republished in the *Proceedings of the 5th Annual Canadian Computer Security Symposium*, May 1993, p.351,

[180] "The Sorry State of Software Practice Measurement and Evaluation", William Hetzel, *The Journal of Systems and Software*, **Vol.31**, **No.2** (November 1995), p.171.

[181] "Evaluating the Effectiveness of Z: The Claims Made About CICS and Where We Go From Here", Kate Finney and Norman Fenton, *The Journal of Systems and Software*, **Vol.35**, **No.3** (December 1996), p.209.

[182] "Rigor in Software Complexity Measurement Experimentation", S.MacDonell, *The Journal of Systems and Software*, **Vol.16**, **No.2** (October 1991), p.141.

[183] "The Mathematical Validity of Software Metrics", B.Henderson-Sellers, *ACM SIGSOFT Software Engineering Notes*, **Vol.21**, **No.5** (September 1996), p.89.

[184] "Experimental Evaluation in Computer Science: A Quantitative Study", Walter Tichy, Paul Lukowicz, Lutz Prechelt, and Ernst Heinz, *The Journal of Systems and Software*, **Vol.28**, **No.1** (January 1995), p.9.

[185] "Beware the Engineering Metaphor", Wei-Lung Wang, *Communications of the ACM*, **Vol.45**, **No.5** (May 2002), p.27

[186] "How Microsoft Builds Software", Michael Cusumano and Richard Selby, *Communications of the ACM*, **Vol.40**, **No.6** (June 1997), p.53.

[187] "Software Development on Internet Time", Michael Cusumano and David Yoffie, *IEEE Computer*, **Vol.32**, **No.10** (October 1999), p.60.

[188] "Extreme Programming Explained: Embrace Change", Kent Beck, Addison-Wesley, 1999.

[189] "Embracing Change with Extreme Programming", Kent Beck, *IEEE Computer*, **Vol.32**, **No.10** (October 1999), 70.

[190] "XP", John Vlissides, *C++ Report*, June 1999.

[191] "Pair Programming on the C3 Project", Jim Haungs, *IEEE Computer*, **Vol.34**, **No.2** (February 2001), p.119.

[192] "Bush Threatens ISO Certification on Taliban", Mark Todaro, BBspot International News, `http://bbspot.com/News/2001/10/iso9000.html`, 16 October 2001.

5 Verification of the cryptlib Kernel

5.1 An Analytical Approach to Verification Methods

Having found the traditional methods used to build trusted systems somewhat lacking, we need to determine an alternative that is more suited to the task. The goal is to determine the most suitable means of creating a trustworthy system, one whose design is capable of earning the user's trust, rather than a trusted system, in which the user is required to trust that the designers and evaluation agency got it right, since the users have no real way to determine this for themselves. The previous chapter discussed the conventional approach to this problem, which is to apply an analytical advocacy method (propose a formal theory or set of axioms, develop a theory, and advocate its use). In place of this, we take the highly unconventional approach of applying a mixture of scientific methods (observe the world, propose a model or theory of behaviour, and analyse the results) and engineering methods (observe existing solutions, propose better ones, build or develop, and analyse the results) to the problem.

To meet this goal, we need to go to two very different fields: the field of cognitive psychology, to determine how programmers understand programs, and the field of software engineering, to locate the tools and techniques used to verify the software. By combining knowledge from both of these fields, we can (hopefully) come up with a technique that can be employed by end users to evaluate the system for themselves, making it something that they can trust, rather than something that they are forced to trust. This mirrors real life, in which users base their trust on personal experience and the experiences of others whom they trust. For example, at a time when it was very difficult to build a large bridge that wouldn't fall down within a few years, people trusted the Brooklyn Bridge not because someone had formally proven that it wouldn't fall down but because it was quite obviously constructed like an outdoor convenience of advanced structural integrity. More than a hundred years later people still trust it because it's stood for all that time without collapsing, in the same way that people will trust software that has been in active use and has shown no sign of causing problems, regardless of whether it's been formally proven to be secure or not.

Our goal in building a trustworthy system is a twofold one:

1. The user must be able to examine the code and specifications to be reassured that they perform the functions expected of them. This requires very careful thought about how to present the work in a manner that users will find both palatable and comprehensible, and that doesn't require highly trained, expert users to understand. The success of the assurance argument depends at least as much on presentation as production (possibly more so), so that rigorously produced evidence that is incomprehensible to an average

user or present in such quantity that it can't be effectively assessed contributes little to assurance and user trust. As the previous chapter showed, current formal methods fail miserably in this regard.

2. The user must be able to use the formal specification to verify that the binary executable that they have conforms to the specification. In other words, it must be possible to pull the final, finished product out of the system on which it is running and use an automatic verification process to check that what's running on the system is performing as the specification says it should, a goal that can be termed "Verification all the way down"[1]. As the previous chapter also showed, current formal methods don't do so well here either.

Similar sentiments have been expressed in a paper that lists a set of requirements for practical formal methods, which include a minimisation of the effort and expertise needed to apply the method, use of a language that developers find easy to use and understand, making formal analysis as automatic as possible, and providing a good suite of support tools [1].

This section will cover the approach used to try and meet these goals, with the rest of the chapter containing the actual details.

5.1.1 Peer Review as an Evaluation Mechanism

Encouraging examination of the code should provide the same benefits as peer review of journal articles, and has proven to be an effective way of fixing problems. In terms of the number of problems located, simply reading the code (that is, code inspection) is capable of locating many more defects than alternatives such as black box or white box testing. A variety of studies have found it to be several times more effective than other techniques for finding defects [2][3][4][5][6][7][8]. Although the previous chapter pointed out the somewhat dubious basis of a number of software engineering practices, so that claims made about the particular effectiveness of code review should, as with other practices, be taken with a grain of salt, there exists at least one analysis with broad enough scope and coverage that it avoids the criticisms levelled in the previous chapter [9]. In addition, the fact that peer review is a standard practice for any scholarly journal and the earlier discussion of rather dissimilar techniques such as mathematical theorem-proving being as much a social as mathematical process indicates that extensive review should be encouraged even for systems that have been otherwise "proven to be secure". This claim is backed up by empirical evidence such as that provided from the evaluation of the first system that was certified at the Orange Book A1 level, in which the majority of the security problems (covert channels) were discovered not as a result of the very lengthy and laborious formal proving process, but through reviews and code walkthroughs [10]. Peer review also produced good results in the

---

[1] This terminology was inspired by the following Stephen Hawking anecdote: An elderly lady confronted Bertrand Russell at the end of his lecture on orbiting planets saying "What you have told us is rubbish. The world is really a flat plate supported on the back of a giant tortoise". Russell gave a superior smile before asking what the turtle was standing on. "You're very clever young man, very clever" replied the old woman "but it's turtles all the way down".

VAX VMM kernel implementation, resulting in the detection and fixing of many problems [11].

This type of review is formally defined as N-fold inspection and involves having a number of small teams or individuals examine code or specifications for defects, with results coordinated by a single moderator. N-fold inspection is based on the hypothesis that the N separate reviewers don't significantly duplicate each other's work so that there isn't a large degree of fault-detection overlap. The same concept has been proposed as a means of ensuring that a security subsystem performs as required, with N versions voting on a result [12][13][14], an idea taken from the field of fault-tolerant systems.

N-fold inspection is the same methodology that is used in most open source software development, although there it appears to have evolved naturally rather than as a result of any deliberate design process. In the open-source world the phenomenon has been assigned the mantra "many eyes make bugs shallow", although this only applies if the many eyes really are being applied to the code [15][16]. With the exception of the OpenBSD effort, which has been making deliberate efforts to review the code that they distribute, this type of examination seems to occur mostly for code in which users have a direct interest (for example a driver needed to make a new DVD player work) rather than for security-relevant code. This has been demonstrated by the number of serious security bugs found in widely circulated code years after it was first released.

In terms of its effectiveness, one study of the N-fold inspection process found that, as further parallel inspections were performed (that is, as more individual users or small groups examined the code), the number of faults located increases cumulatively [17]. One study found that whereas individuals would typically locate around 27% of all faults, with five inspections in parallel it went up to 65% [18]. Unfortunately, these percentage figures are of somewhat dubious value since the 100% rate was arbitrarily set as being the number of faults found by ten parallel inspections. A later experiment used a slightly different methodology that took as a baseline a document written by an experienced software project leader that was preprocessed by having it reviewed by approximately 40 people, who found over 70 faults in the specification (this came as a surprise to the original author, who was amazed at their range and severity). The document was then revised and seeded with 99 known faults and subject to another round of N-fold inspection by nine teams, who produced a 78% detection rate of the known faults [19].

This study indicated a wide variation in individual team performance, with detection rates ranging from 22% to 50% and with no one fault being found by every team. These results underline the importance of extensive independent peer review, as well as showing how easy it is even for experienced designers to produce specifications with errors, a problem that was expanded on in the previous chapter.

This form of open peer review isn't even feasible under a number of standard development methodologies for secure systems, which can require measures such as having all development performed in a sensitive compartmented information facility (SCIF), with optional TEMPEST shielding to deter particularly persistent peer reviewers [20]. An even more rigorous approach than this has been proposed that would be even more effective in deterring peer review, since it seems to be structured towards ensuring that no code is ever produced [21]. Although these measures were intended to prevent peer review by the opposition, they do little to inspire public trust in the resulting end product, since it can then require legal action or pressure from government bodies to reveal what the resulting code really does, as opposed to what the vendor claims it does [22][23].

5.1.2 Enabling Peer Review

In contrast to the systems that are designed to make peer review as difficult as possible, the goal of a trustworthy system design is to make review as easy as possible. In order to make peer review (and therefore the ability to detect various classes of faults) easy, we need to structure the code in a manner that makes it easily comprehensible to the typical programmer. Although the connection between code comprehension and the ability to find faults has the potential to be yet another "intuitively obvious" but never verified facet of software engineering, there has in fact been a study carried out that found a strong correlation between code comprehension and fault detection [24].

The standard response to the requirement to make code easily comprehensible is to rattle off a list of rules ("Use meaningful variable names", "Add plenty of comments", "Use structured code", and so on), seasoned to taste with personal preferences ("Use an OO methodology", "Write it in Java", "Document it using *insert name of favourite CASE tool*", and so on). However, instead of basing the code structure on these somewhat arbitrary choices, we can take advantage of the considerable amount of research that has been performed over the last 30 years on the subject of how programmers comprehend code in order to create code of optimum comprehensibility, and therefore code that is ideally suited for peer review. By tuning the code to match the human thought and comprehension process, we both ensure that the chances of any misunderstandings of the code's function and purpose are reduced, and encourage review by third parties by making it easy for them to examine the code. This is a process that needs to be examined from a psychological rather than the traditional software engineering perspective — if we can prove that a spaghetti mess of goto's is logically equivalent to a structured program then why do we need to use structured code? The answer is that humans are better able to understand structured code than spaghetti code, an issue that is examined in more detail in Section 5.2.2.

5.1.3 Selecting an Appropriate Specification Method

The final peer review problem that remains to be solved is the issue of the formal specification. As the previous chapter demonstrated, one almost universal property of formal specification languages is that they are incomprehensible to all but a few cognoscenti (the specification languages used by the two methodologies endorsed by the Orange Book have been described as "difficult to read, the machine language of specification languages" [25]). The end result of this is that the formal specification is never analysed by anyone other than the people who wrote it and possibly the people who were paid to evaluate it. This is exactly the opposite effect of the one desired.

We can address this problem by examining the precise roles of the DTLS (descriptive top-level specification) and FTLS (formal top-level specification). The DTLS is meant to be a natural-language form of the specification; however, this assumes that the "natural language" being used is English. For most programmers the natural language they use to describe the behaviour of a program is not English but a programming language, usually C. The US Ninth Circuit court has defined C source code as something that is "meant to be read and understood by humans and that can be used to express an idea or a method", something that is "meant for human eyes and understanding" [26], in other words the natural language of programmers. Going beyond the legal definition, psychological studies have shown that even complete non-programmers will spontaneously evolve programming-language-like constructs such as control statements when asked to create descriptions of algorithm-like tasks [27], indicating that this is indeed the natural language for use when communicating information about computer tasks. This means that the DTLS should be written in the programmer's natural language (in this case, C or a C-like language) rather than the average person's natural language (in this case, English).

Studies into the understandability of software documentation have indicated that software developers and maintainers find it easier to understand closely related languages than distantly related ones [28] so that the use of a C-like specification language will help their ability to comprehend the resulting specification. In addition since we can now choose a specification language that has a well-defined syntax and a well-defined semantics, all of the details of the specification must be stated explicitly, so that missing or ambiguous information can be easily identified. In contrast, the English specification that is typically used to guide implementers makes it very difficult to write concisely and without ambiguity, making it necessary to produce a small essay at each step in order to ensure that all readers of the specification interpret it correctly. It is for this reason that formal specification languages are sometimes referred to as error avoidance systems, since they reduce the chances of ambiguity or errors in the specification.

Because an English DTLS cannot be applied directly, it first needs to be manually translated into an executable form. This task is "error prone, expensive, time consuming, and contributes little to the standard development process" [29]. Furthermore, "when only a natural language specification is given, it is probable that there will be different interpretations which all meet the specification, although they may logically be different" [30]. There has been a limited amount of experimental work in applying natural language processing (NLP) techniques to English specifications, but the results have been less than spectacular [31][32], and the case has been made that this approach represents, at best, a dangerous illusion since natural language is simply incapable of expressing precisely the exact semantics of a system even if the NLP problem is finally satisfactorily solved [33].

Making the specification directly executable through the use of a C-like specification language avoids this problem, and has the additional benefit that formal reasoning about and mechanical verification of the code to the specification are now possible. It has even been suggested that, since an implementation is the definitive specification of a program's behaviour, the source code itself should serve as the ultimate specification, providing a behavioural as well as conceptual specification of its operation [34]. This ensures that it will always be a correct (or at least current) specification, since only the code itself is guaranteed to be maintained and updated once the initial implementation has been completed. This is particularly critical when the implementation is subject to constant revision and change, but has the downside that implementation languages don't as a rule make terribly good specification languages.

Using this approach ties in to the concept of cognitive fit — matching the tools and techniques that are used to the task to be accomplished [35][36]. If we can perform this matching, we can assist in the creation of a consistent mental representation of the problem and its solution. In contrast, if a mismatch between the representation and the solution occurs then the person examining the code has to first transform it into a fitting representation before applying it to the task at hand, or alternatively formulate a mental representation based on the task and then try and work backwards to the actual representation. By matching the formal representation to the representation of the implementation, we can avoid this unnecessary, error-prone, and typically very labour-intensive step. The next logical step below the formal specification then becomes the ultimate specification of the real system, the source code that describes every detail of the implementation and the one from which the executable system is generated.

Ensuring a close match between the specification and implementation raises the spectre of implementation bias, in which the specification unduly influences the final implementation. For example one source comments that "A specification should describe only *what* is required of the system and not *how* it is achieved [...] There is no reason to include a *how* in a specification: specifications should describe what is desired and no more" [37]. Empirical studies of the effects of the choice of specification language on the final implementation have shown that the specification language's syntax, semantics, and representation style can heavily influence the resulting implementation [38]. When the specification and implementation languages are closely matched, this presents little problem. When the two bear little relation to each other (SDL's connected FSMs, Estelle's communicating FSMs, or LOTOS' communicating sequential processes, and C or Ada), this is a much bigger problem since the fact that the two have very different semantic domains makes their combined use rather difficult. An additional downside, which was mentioned in the previous chapter, is that the need to very closely follow a design presented in a language that is unsuited to specifying implementation details results in extremely inefficient implementations since the implementer needs to translate all of the quirks and shortcomings of the specification language into the final implementation of the design.

However, it is necessary to distinguish implementation bias (which is bad) from designed requirements (which are good). Specifying the behaviour of a C implementation in a C-like language is fine since this provides strong implementation guidance, and doesn't introduce any arbitrary, specification-language-based bias on the implementation since the two are very closely matched. On the other hand, forcing an implementation to be based on communicating sequential processes or asynchronously communicating FSMs does constitute a case of specification bias since this is purely an artifact of the specification language and (in most cases) not at all what the implementation actually requires.

5.1.4 A Unified Specification

Using a programming language for the DTLS means that we can take the process a step further and merge the DTLS with the FTLS, since the two are now more or less identical (it was originally intended that languages such as Gypsy also provide this form of functionality). The result of this process is a unified TLS or UTLS. All that remains is to find a C-like formal specification language (as close to the programmer's native language as possible) in which to write the UTLS. If we can make the specification executable (or indirectly executable by having one that is usable for some form of mechanical code verification), we gain the additional benefit of having not only a conceptual but also a behavioural model of the system to be implemented, allowing immediate validation of the system by execution [39]. Even users who would otherwise be uncomfortable with formal methods can use the executable specification to verify that the behaviour of the code conforms to the requirements. This use of "stealth formal methods" has been suggested in the past in order to make them more palatable to users [40][41], for example, by referring to them as "assertion-based testing" to de-emphasise their formal nature [42].

Both anecdotal evidence from developers who have worked with formal methods [43] and occasional admissions in papers that mention experience with formal methods indicate that the real value of the methods lies in the methodology, the structuring of the requirements and specification for development, rather than the proof steps that follow [44][45][46][47]. It was in recognition of this that early Orange Book drafts contained an entrée[2] class A0 which required an unverified FTLS, but this was later dropped alongside anything more than a discussion of the hypothesised "beyond A1" classes. As was pointed out several times in the previous chapter, the failing of many formal methods is that they cannot reach down deep enough into the implementation phase(s) to provide any degree of assurance that what was implemented is what was actually required. However, by taking the area where formal methods are strongest (the ability of the formal specification to locate potential errors during the specification phase) and combining it with the area where executable specifications are strongest (the ability to locate errors in the implementation phase), we get the best of both worlds while at the same time avoiding the areas where both are weak.

Another advantage to using specifications that can be verified automatically and mechanically is that it greatly simplifies the task of revalidation, an issue that presents a nasty problem for formal methods, as was explained in the previous chapter, but becomes a fairly standard regression testing task when an executable specification is present [48][49]. Unlike standard formal methods, which can require that large portions of the proof be redone every time a change is made, the mechanical verification of conformance to a specification is an automated procedure that, although potentially time-consuming for a computer, requires no real user effort. Attempts to implement a revalidation program using Orange Book techniques (the Rating Maintenance Program or RAMP) in contrast have been far less successful, leading to "a plethora of paperwork, checking, bureaucracy and mistrust" being imposed on vendors [50]. This situation arose in part because RAMP required that A1-level configuration control be applied to a revalidation of (for example) a B1 system, with the

---

[2] Given that the Orange Book comes to us from the US, it would probably have been designated an appetizer rather than an entrée.

result that it was easier to redo the B1 evaluation from scratch than to apply A1-level controls to it.

5.1.5 Enabling Verification All the way Down

The standard way to verify a secure system has been to choose an abstract mathematical modelling method (usually on the basis of being able to find someone on staff who can understand it), repeatedly jiggle and juggle the DTLS until it can be expressed as an FTLS within the chosen mathematical model, prove that it conforms to the requirements, and then hope that functioning code can be magicked into existence based on the DTLS (in theory it should be built from the FTLS, but the implementers won't be able to make head or tail of that).

The approach taken here is entirely different. Instead of choosing a particular methodology and then forcing the system design to fit it, we take the system design and try to locate a methodology that matches it. Since the cryptlib kernel is a filter that acts on messages passing through it, its behaviour can best be expressed in terms of preconditions, postconditions, invariants, and various other properties of the filtering mechanism. This type of system corresponds directly to the design-by-contract methodology [51][52][53][54][55].

Design-by-contract evolved from the concept of defensive programming, a technique created to protect program functions from the slings and arrows of buggy code, and involves the design of software routines that conform to the contract "If you promise to call this routine with precondition x satisfied then the routine promises to deliver a final state in which postcondition x' is satisfied" [56]. This mirrors real-life contracts, which specify the obligations and benefits for both parties. As with real-life contracts, these benefits and obligations are set out in a contract document. The software analog to a real-life contract is a formal specification that contains preconditions that specify the conditions under which a call to a routine is legitimate, and postconditions that specify the conditions that are ensured by the routine on return.

From the discussion in previous chapters, it can be seen that the entire cryptlib kernel implements design-by-contract rules. For example, the kernel enforces design-by-contract on key loads into an encryption action object by ensuring that certain preconditions hold (the initial access check and pre-dispatch filter, which ensures that the caller is allowed to access the action object, the object is an encryption action object, the key is of the appropriate type and size, the object is in a state in which a key load is possible, and so on) and that the corresponding postconditions are fulfilled (the post-dispatch filter, which ensures that the action object is transitioned into the high state ready for use for encryption or decryption). The same contract-based rules can be built for every other operation performed by the kernel, providing a specification against which the kernel can be validated.

By viewing the kernel as the enforcer of a contract, it moves from being just a chunk of code to the implementation of a certain specification against which it can be tested. The fact that the contract defines what is acceptable behaviour for the kernel introduces the concept of incorrect behaviour or failure, which in the cryptlib kernel's case means the failure to enforce a security condition. Determining whether the contract can be voided in some way by external forces is therefore equivalent to determining whether a security problem exists in the kernel, and this is what gives us the basis for verifying the security of the system. If we can find a way in which we can produce a contract for the kernel that can be tested against the finished executable, we can meet the requirement for verification all the way down.

5.2 Making the Specification and Implementation Comprehensible

A standard model of the human information-processing system known as the Atkinson–Shiffrin model [57][58], which indicates how the system operates when information from the real world passes through it, is shown in Figure 5.1. In the first stage of processing, incoming information about a real-world stimulus arrives in the sensory register and is held there for a brief amount of time (the longer it sits in the register, the more it decays). While the information is in the register, it is subject to a pattern recognition process in which it is matched against previously acquired knowledge held in long-term memory. This complex interaction results (hopefully) in the new information being equated with a meaningful concept (for example, the association of the shape **A** with the first letter of the alphabet), which is then moved into short-term memory (STM).

Data held in STM is held in its processed form rather than in the raw form found in the input register, and may be retained in STM by a process known as rehearsal, which recycles the material over and over through STM. If this rehearsal process isn't performed, the data decays just as it does in the input register. In addition to the time limit, there is also a limit on the number of items that can be held in STM, with the total number of items being around seven [59]. These items don't correspond to any particular unit such as a letter, word, or line of code, but instead correspond to chunks, data recoded into a single unit when it is recognised as representing a meaningful concept [60]. A chunk is therefore a rather variable entity containing more or less information depending on the circumstances[3]. People chunk information into higher-order units using knowledge of both meaning and syntax. Thus, for example, the C code corresponding to a while look might be chunked by someone familiar with the language into a single unit corresponding to "a while loop".

---

[3] This leads to an amusing circular definition of STM capacity as "STM can contain seven of whatever it is that STM contains seven of".

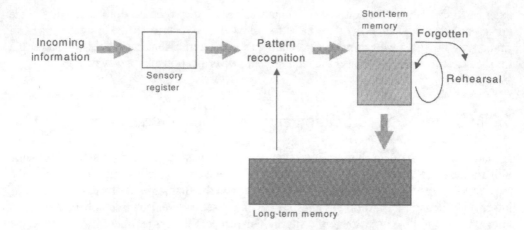

Figure 5.1. The human memory process.

The final element in the process is long-term memory (LTM), into which data can be moved from STM after sufficient rehearsal. LTM is characterised by enormous storage capacity and relatively slow decay [61][62][63].

5.2.1 Program Cognition

Now that the machinery used in the information acquisition and learning process has been covered, we need to examine how the learning process actually works, and specifically how it works in relation to program cognition. One way of doing this is by treating the cognitive process as a virtual communication channel in which errors are caused not by the presence of external noise but by the inability to correctly decode received information. We can model this by looking at the mental information decoding process as the application of a decoder with limited memory. Moving a step further, we can regard the process of communicating information about the functioning of a program via its source code (or, alternatively, a formal specification) as a standard noisy communications channel, with the noise being caused by the limited amount of memory available to the decoding process. The more working storage (STM) that is consumed, the higher the chances of a decoding error or "decoding noise". The result is a discrepancy between the semantics of the information received as input and the semantics present in the decoded information.

An additional factor that influences the level of decoding noise is the amount of existing semantic knowledge that is present in LTM. The more information that is present, the easier it is to recover from "decoding noise".

This model may be used to explain the differences in how novices and experts understand programs. Whereas experts can quickly recognise and understand (syntactically correct) code because they have more data present in LTM to mitigate decoding errors, novices have little or no data on LTM to help them in this regard and therefore have more trouble in recognising and understanding the same code. This theory has been supported by experiments in which experts were presented with plan-like code (code that conforms to generally-accepted programming rules; in other words code, that contained recognisable elements and structures) and unplan-like code (code that doesn't follow the usual rules of discourse). When faced with unplan-like code, expert programmers performed no better than novices when it came to code comprehension because they weren't able to map the code to any schemas they had in LTM [64].

5.2.2 How Programmers Understand Code

Having examined the process of cognition in somewhat more detail, we now need to look at exactly how programs are understood by experts (and, with rather more difficulty, by non-experts). Research into program comprehension is based on earlier work in the field of text comprehension, although program comprehension represents a somewhat specialised case since programs have a dual nature because they can be both executed for effect and read as communications entities. Code and program comprehension by humans involves successive recodings of groups of program statements into successively higher-level semantic structures that are in turn recognised as particular algorithms, and these are in turn organised into a general model of the program as a whole.

One significant way in which this process can be assisted is through the use of clearly structured code that makes use of the scoping rules provided by the programming language. The optimal organisation would appear to be one that contains at its lowest level short, simple code blocks that can be readily absorbed and chunked without overflowing STM and thus leading to an increase in the number of decoding errors [65]. An example of such a code block, taken from the cryptlib kernel, is shown in Figure 5.2. Note that this code has had the function name/description and comments removed for reasons explained later.

```
function ::=
    PRE( isValidObject( objectHandle ) );

    objectTable[ objectHandle ].referenceCount++;

    POST( objectTable[ objectHandle ].referenceCount == \
          ORIGINAL_VALUE( referenceCount ) + 1 );

    return( CRYPT_OK );
```

Figure 5.2. Low-level code segment comprehension.

The amount of effort required to perform successful chunking is directly related to a program's semantic or cognitive complexity, the "characteristics that make it difficult for humans to comprehend software" [66][67]. The more semantically complex a section of code is, the harder it is to perform the necessary chunking. Examples of semantic complexity that go beyond obvious factors such as the choice of algorithm include the fact that recursive functions are harder to comprehend than non-recursive ones, the fact that linked lists are more difficult to comprehend than arrays, and the use of certain OO techniques that lead to non-linear code that is more difficult to follow than non-OO equivalents [68][69], so much so that the presence of indicators such as a high use of method invocation and inheritance has been used as a means of identifying fault-prone C++ classes [70][71].

At this point, the reader has achieved understanding of the code segment, which has migrated into LTM in the form of a chunk containing the information "increment an object's reference count". If the same code is encountered in the future, the decoding mechanism can directly convert it into "increment an object's reference count" without the explicit cognition process that was required the first time. Once this internal semantic representation of a program's code has been developed, the knowledge is resistant to forgetting even though individual details may be lost over time [72]. This chunking process has been verified experimentally by evaluating test subjects reading code and retrogressing through code segments (for example, to find the while at the start of a loop or the if at the head of a block of conditional code). Other rescan points included the start of the current function, and the use of common variables, with almost all rescans occurring within the same function [73].

At this point, we can answer the rhetorical question that was asked earlier: If we can use the Böhm–Jacopini theorem [74] to prove that a spaghetti mess of goto's is logically equivalent to a structured program, then why do we need to use structured code? The reason given previously was that humans are better able to understand structured code than spaghetti code, and the reason that structured code is easier to understand is that large forwards or backwards jumps inhibit chunking since they make it difficult to form separate chunks without switching attention across different parts of the program.

We can now step back one level and apply the same process again, this time using previously understood code segments as our basic building blocks instead of individual lines of code, as shown in Figure 5.3, again taken from the cryptlib kernel. At this level, the cognition process involves the assignment of more meaning to the higher-level constructs than is present in the raw code, including control flow, transformational effects on data, and the general purpose of the code as a whole.

Again, the importance of appropriate scoping at the macroscopic level is apparent: If the complexity grows to the point where STM overflows, comprehension problems occur.

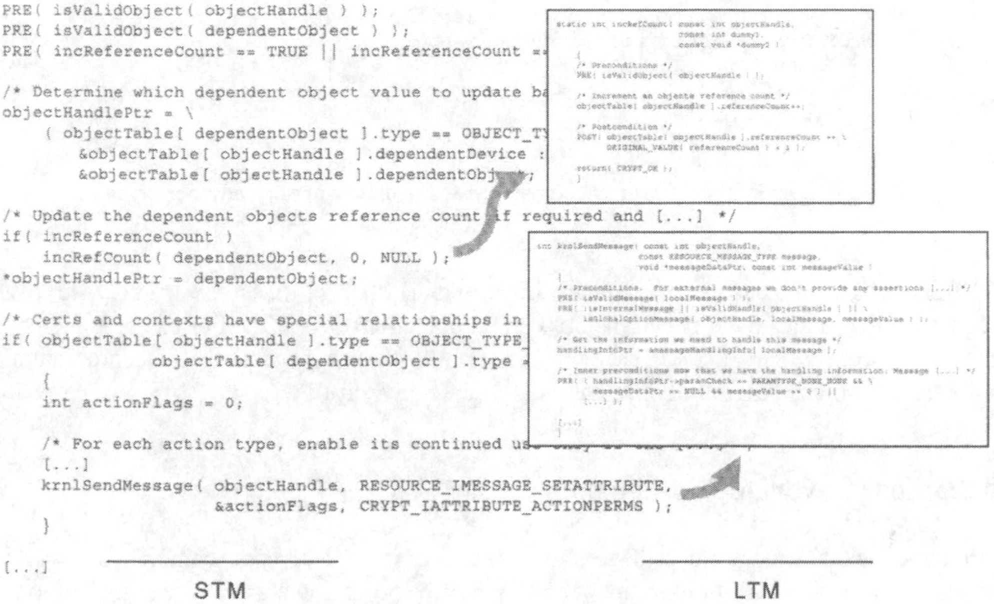

```
PRE( isValidObject( objectHandle ) );
PRE( isValidObject( dependentObject ) );
PRE( incReferenceCount == TRUE || incReferenceCount =

/* Determine which dependent object value to update ba
objectHandlePtr = \
    ( objectTable[ dependentObject ].type == OBJECT_TY
      &objectTable[ objectHandle ].dependentDevice :
      &objectTable[ objectHandle ].dependentObj    ;

/* Update the dependent objects reference count    f required and [...] */
if( incReferenceCount )
    incRefCount( dependentObject, 0, NULL );
*objectHandlePtr = dependentObject;

/* Certs and contexts have special relationships in
if( objectTable[ objectHandle ].type == OBJECT_TYPE
             objectTable[ dependentObject ].type =
    {
    int actionFlags = 0;

    /* For each action type, enable its continued u
    [...]
    krnlSendMessage( objectHandle, RESOURCE_IMESSAGE_SETATTRIBUTE,
                     &actionFlags, CRYPT_IATTRIBUTE_ACTIONPERMS );
    }

[...]
```

STM   LTM

Figure 5.3. Higher-level program comprehension.

A somewhat different view of the code comprehension process is that it is performed through a process of hypothesis testing and refinement in which the meaning of the program is built from the outset by means of features such as function names and code comments. These clues act as "advance organisers", short expository notes that provide the general concepts and ideas that can be used as an aid in assigning meaning to the code [75]. The code section in Figure 5.2 was deliberately presented earlier without its function name. It is presented again for comparison in Figure 5.4 with the name and a code comment acting as an advance organiser.

```
/* Increment/decrement the reference count for an object */

static int incRefCount( const int objectHandle )
    {
    PRE( isValidObject( objectHandle ) );

    objectTable[ objectHandle ].referenceCount++;
```

```
POST( objectTable[ objectHandle ].referenceCount == \
      ORIGINAL_VALUE( referenceCount ) + 1 );

return( CRYPT_OK );
}
```

Figure 5.4. Low-level code segment comprehension with the aid of an advance organiser.

Related to the concept of advance organisers is that of beacons, stereotyped code sequences that indicate the occurrence of certain operations [76][77]. For example the code sequence 'for i = 1 to 10 do { a[i] = 0 }' is a beacon that the programmer automatically translates to 'initialise data (in this case an array)'.

5.2.3 Code Layout to Aid Comprehension

Studies of actual programmers have shown that the process of code comprehension is as much a top-down as a bottom-up one. Typically, programmers start reading from the beginning of the code using a bottom-up strategy to establish overall structure; however, once overall plans are recognised (through the use of chunking, beacons, and advance organisers), they progress to the use of a predictive, top-down mode in which lower levels of detail are skipped if they aren't required in order to obtain a general overview of how the program functions [78][79][80]. The process here is one of hypothesis formation and verification, in which the programmer forms a hypothesis about how a certain section of code functions and only searches down far enough to verify the hypothesis (there are various other models of code comprehension that have been proposed at various times, a survey of some of these can be found elsewhere [81]).

Although this type of code examination may be sufficient for program comprehension, when in-depth understanding is required, experienced programmers go down to the lower levels to fully understand every nuance of the code's behaviour rather than simply assuming that the code works as indicated by documentation or code comments [82]. The reason for this behaviour is that full comprehension is required to support the mental simulation of the code, which is used to satisfy the programmer that it does indeed work as required. This is presumably why most class libraries are shipped with source code even though OO theology would indicate that their successful application doesn't require this, since having programmers work with the source code defeats the concept of code reuse, which assumes that modules will be treated as black box, reusable components. An alternative view is that since documentation is often inaccurate, ambiguous, or out of date, programmers prefer going directly to the source code, which definitively describes its own behaviour.

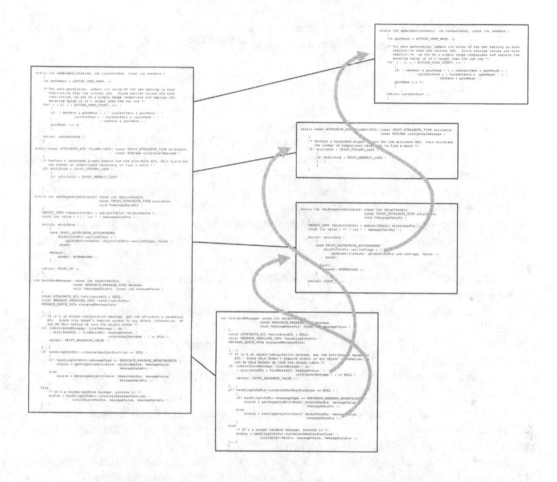

Figure 5.5. Physical (left) and logical (right) program flow.

In order to take advantage of both the top-down and bottom-up modes of program cognition, we can use the fact that a program is a procedural text that expresses the actions of the machine on which it is running [83][84]. Although the code is expressed as a linear sequence of statements, what is being expressed is a hierarchy in which each action is linked to one or more underlying actions. By arranging the code so that the lower-level functions occur first in the listing, the bottom-up chunking mode of program cognition is accommodated for programmers who take the listing and read through it from start to finish. For those who prefer to switch to a top-down mode once they understand enough of the program to handle this, the placement of the topmost routines at the opposite end of the listing allows them to be easily located in order to perform a top-down traversal. In contrast, placing the highest-level routines at the start would force bottom-up programmers to traverse the listing backwards, significantly reducing the ease of comprehension for the code. The code layout that results from the application of these two design principles is shown in Figure 5.5.

Similar presentation techniques have been used in software exploration and visualisation tools that are designed to aid users in understanding software [85].

5.2.4 Code Creation and Bugs

The process of creating code has been described as one of symbolic execution in which a given plan element triggers the generation of a piece of code, which is then symbolically executed in the programmer's mind in order to assign an effect to it. The effect is compared to the intended effect and the code modified if necessary in order to achieve the desired result, with results becoming more and more concrete as the design progresses. The creation of sections of code alternates with frequent mental execution to generate the next code section. The coding process itself may be interrupted and changed as a result of these symbolic execution episodes, giving the coding process a sporadic and halting nature [86][87][88][89].

An inability to perform mental simulation of the code during the design process can lead to bugs in the design, since it is no longer possible to progressively refine and improve the design by mentally executing it and making improvements based on the results. The effect of an inability to perform this mental execution is that expert programmers are reduced to the level of novices [90]. This indicates that great care must be exercised in the choice of formal specification language, since most of them don't allow this mental simulation (or only allow it with great difficulty), effectively reducing the ability of its users to that of novice programmers.

The fact that the coding process can cause a trickle-back effect through various levels of refinement indicates that certain implementation aspects such as programming language features must be taken into account when designing an implementation. For example, specifying a program design in a functional language for implementation in a procedural language creates an impedance mismatch, which is asking for trouble when it comes to implementing the design. Adhering to the principle of cognitive fit when matching the specification to the implementation is essential in order to avoid these mismatches, which have the potential to lead to a variety of specification/implementation bugs in the resulting code.

The types of problems that can occur due to a lack of cognitive fit can be grouped into two classes, conceptual bugs and teleological bugs, illustrated in Figure 5.6. Conceptual bugs arise due to differences between the actual program behaviour as implemented and the required behaviour of the program (for example, as it is specified in a requirements document). Teleological bugs arise due to differences between the actual program behaviour as implemented and the behaviour intended by the implementer [91][92]. There is often some blurring between the two classes, for example if it is intended that private keys be protected from disclosure but the implementation doesn't do this, then it could be due to either a conceptual bug (the program specification doesn't specify this properly) or a teleological bug (the programmer didn't implement it properly).

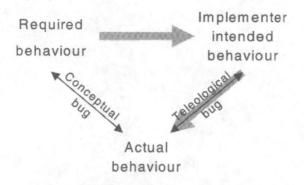

Figure 5.6. Types of implementation bugs.

The purpose of providing a good cognitive fit between the specification and implementation is to minimise conceptual bugs, ones which arise because the implementer had trouble following the specification. Minimising teleological bugs, ones which arise where the programmer had the right intentions but got it wrong, is the task of code verification, which is covered in Section 5.3.

5.2.5 Avoiding Specification/Implementation Bugs

Now that we have looked at the ways in which errors can occur in the implementation, we can examine the ways in which the various design goals and rules presented above act to address them. Before we do this though, we need to extend Figure 5.6 to include the formal specification for the code, since this represents a second layer at which errors can occur. The complete process from specification to implementation is shown in Figure 5.7, along with the errors that can occur at each stage (there are also other error paths that exist, such as the actual behaviour not matching the specifier's intended behaviour, but this is just a generalisation of one of the more specific error types shown in Figure 5.7).

Starting from the top, we have conceptual differences between the specifier and the implementer. We act to minimise these by closely matching the implementation language to the specification language, ensuring that the specifier and implementer are working towards the same goal. In addition to the conceptual bugs we have teleological bugs in the specification, which we act to minimise by making the specification language as close to the specifier's natural language (when communicating information about computer operations) as possible.

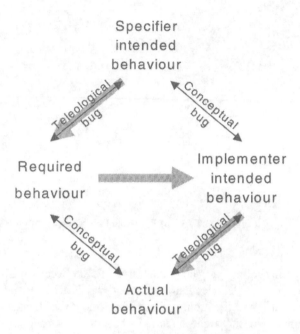

Figure 5.7. Specification and implementation bug types.

At the next level, we have teleological bugs between the implementer and the implementation that they create, which we act to minimise through the use of automated verification of the specification against the code, ensuring that the behaviour of what's actually implemented matches the behaviour described in the specification. Finally, we have conceptual bugs between what's required and what's actually implemented, which we act to minimise by making the code as accessible and easily comprehensible for peer review as possible.

These error-minimisation goals also interact to work across multiple levels; for example, since the specification language closely matches the implementation language, the specifier can check that their intent is mirrored in the details of the implementation, allowing checking from the highest level down to the lowest in a single step.

This concludes the coverage of how the cryptlib kernel has been designed to make peer review and analysis as tractable as possible. The next section examines how automated verification is handled.

5.3 Verification All the Way Down

The contract enforced by the cryptlib kernel is shown in Figure 5.8.

```
ensure that bad things don't happen;
```

Figure 5.8. The overall contract enforced by the cryptlib kernel.

This is something of a tautology, but it provides a basis upon which we can build further refinements. The next level of refinement is to decide what constitutes "bad things" and then itemise them. For example, one standard requirement is that encryption keys be protected in some manner (the details of which aren't important at this level of refinement). Our extended-form contract thus takes the form shown in Figure 5.9.

```
[...]
ensure that keys are protected;
[...]
```

Figure 5.9. Detail from the overall contract enforced by the kernel.

This is still too vague to be useful, but it again provides us with the basis for further refinement. We can now specify how the keys are to be protected, which includes ensuring that they can't be extracted directly from within the architecture's security perimeter, that they can't be misused (for example, using a private key intended only for authentication to sign a contract), that they can't be modified (for example, truncating a 192-bit key to 40 bits), and various other restrictions. This further level of refinement is shown in Figure 5.10.

```
[...]
ensure that conventional encryption keys can't be extracted in plaintext
    form;
ensure that private keys can't be extracted;
ensure that keys can't be used for other than their intended purpose;
ensure that keys can't be modified or altered;
[...]
```

Figure 5.10. Detail from the key-protection contract enforced by the kernel.

The specifications thus far have been phrased in terms of expressing when things cannot happen. In practice, however, the kernel works in terms of checking when things are allowed to happen and only allowing them in that instance, defaulting to deny-all rather than allow-all. In order to accommodate this, we can rephrase the rules as in Figure 5.11.

```
[...]
ensure that conventional encryption keys can only be extracted in encrypted
     form;
ensure that keys can only be used for their intended purpose;
[...]
```

Figure 5.11. Modified key-protection contract.

Note that two of the rules now vanish, since the actions that they were designed to prevent in the Figure 5.10 version are disallowed by default in the Figure 5.11 version. Although the technique of expressing an FTLS as a series of assertions that can be mapped to various levels of the design abstraction has been proposed before for use in verifying a B2 system by translating its FTLS into an assertion list that defines the behaviour of the system that implements the FTLS [93], the mapping from FTLS was done manually and seems to have been used more as an analysis technique than as a means of verifying the actual implementation.

We now have a series of rules that determine the behaviour of the kernel. What remains is to determine how to specify them in a manner that is both understandable to programmers and capable of being used to automatically verify the kernel. The most obvious solution to this problem is to use some form of executable specification or, more realistically, a meta-executable specification that can be mechanically mapped onto the kernel implementation and used to verify that it conforms to the specification. The distinction between executable and meta-executable is made because the term "executable specification" is often taken to mean the process of compiling a formal specification language directly into executable code, a rather impractical approach which was covered in the previous chapter.

Some possible approaches to meta-executable specifications are covered in the following sections.

5.3.1 Programming with Assertions

The simplest way of specifying the behaviour of the kernel is to annotate the existing source code with assertions that check its operation at every step. An assertion is an expression that defines necessary conditions for correct execution, acting as "a tireless auditor which constantly checks for compliance with necessary conditions and complains when the rules are broken" [94]. For general-purpose use, C's built-in assert() macro is a little too primitive to provide anything more than a relatively basic level of checking; however, when applied to a design-by-contract implementation its use to verify that the preconditions and postconditions are adhered to can be quite effective. Since the cryptlib kernel was specifically designed to be verifiable using design-by-contract principles, it's possible to go much further with such a simple verification mechanism than would be possible in a more generalised design.

As the previously presented code fragments have indicated, the cryptlib kernel is comprehensively annotated with C assertions, which function both to document the contract that applies for each function and to verify that the contract is being correctly enforced. Even a mechanism as simple as this has helped to catch problems such as an optimiser bug in the gcc compiler that resulted in an object's reference count not being decremented under some circumstances. The author has resisted the temptation to publish a paper in a software engineering journal advocating the universal use of assert() based on this successful result.

Moving beyond the built-in assertion capability, there exist a number of extensions that provide the more powerful types of assertions needed for design-by-contract programming. The simplest of these just extend the basic assert() macro to support quantifiers such as $\forall$ and $\exists$, provided through the macros forall() and exists(), and access to the value of a variable at the time a function is called, provided through the macro old(). Combined with extensive preprocessor trickery and using special features of the C++ language, it is possible to provide this functionality without requiring any add-on programs or modifications to the C compiler [95]. cryptlib uses these extensions to annotate the kernel, although without resorting to the use of C++ to do so.

Going beyond what's possible using the compiler itself were various efforts that looked at extending the concept of basic assertions to the creation of automatic runtime consistency checks. One of the earliest efforts in this area was the work on Anna (Annotated Ada), which uses annotations to Ada source code to perform runtime consistency checking of the executable code [96][97][98]. A derivative of Anna, GNU Nana [99], exists for C++, but has the disadvantage that it is tied heavily into the GNU software tools, being based on preprocessor macros and using language extensions in the gcc compiler and hooking into the gdb debugger. In terms of legibility, Nana-annotated programs have the unfortunate property of appearing to have been hit by a severe bout of line noise.

A slightly different approach is used with App, the Annotation PreProcessor for C, which is implemented as a preprocessor pass that recognises assertions embedded in source code comments and produces as its output (via the C compiler) an executable with built-in checks against the assertions [100]. Since App annotations exist outside the scope of the C code, they don't have to be implemented as preprocessor macros but can instead be handled through a C-like minilanguage that should be instantly understandable by most C programmers and that doesn't suffer from Nana's line-noise problem. App doesn't appear to be publicly available.

Another effort inspired by Anna was A++ (annotated C++), which allowed methods in C++ classes to be annotated with axioms specifying semantic constraints, with the annotations being of the form [*quantifiers*; require *preconditions*; promise *postconditions*] statement;. The annotations were to be processed by an A++ front-end, which then fed the statement part on to the C++ compiler [101]. Work on A++ was abandoned at an early experimental stage so it's not known how verification would have been performed.

All of the mechanisms that rely on annotating program source code, from simple C assertions through to more sophisticated tools such as Anna/Nana, App, and A++, have two common disadvantages: they require modification of the original source code, reducing the comprehensibility of both the code and the annotations by creating a hybrid mix of the two, and they are all-or-nothing in that they can either be enabled and increase the program size and execution time, or be disabled, with the result that the code runs without any checking. More seriously, the fact that they are implemented as inline code means that their presence can alter the behaviour of the code (for example, by changing the way in which some compiler optimisations are performed) so that the behaviour of code compiled with the built-in checks differs from that compiled without the checks. This leads to a class of faults popularly referred to as Heisenbugs [102], which vanish when attempts are made to observe them.

In order to solve these two problems we need to make two changes to the way that the specification and verification are performed. Firstly, the specification needs to be written as a separate unit rather than being embedded in the code, and secondly the testing process needs to be non-intrusive so that the code under test doesn't need to be recompiled before or after testing.

5.3.2 Specification using Assertions

In order to achieve the two goals given above, we need to have the ability to compile the specification into a separate piece of executable code that, in conjunction with the code under test, forms an oracle that, for any given set of test data, is capable of judging whether the code conforms to the specification. The creation of tools to handle this was inspired by Guttag and Horning's work on the formal specification of the properties of abstract data types that combined a syntactic definition of the data type and a set of axioms that specified the operations that were allowed on the data [103]. This work was contemporary with early efforts such as SELECT, which used symbolic execution of LISP code and tried to automatically determine appropriate test data (falling back to requesting user input if required) [104]. This later led to tools such as the Data Abstraction, Implementation, Specification, and Testing System (DAISTS) that allowed the specification of classes along with a set of axioms for the abstract data type implemented by each class and test data that checked the implementation against the axioms. The testing was performed by using the algebraic specification as an oracle for testing the implementation, utilising the left-hand side of each axiom as a test case that was compared using a user-supplied equality function to the right-hand side [105]. DAISTS was the first tool that allowed the semantics of an ADT to be specified and verified in the manner outlined earlier, but suffered from the problem that both sides of the equation (the formal specification and the implementation) had to be provided in the DAISTS implementation language SIMPL-D.

Although DAISTS itself appears to have faded from view, it did spawn some later (rather distant) derivatives and adaptations for C++ [106] and Eiffel [107]. The latter, A Set of Tools for Object-Oriented Testing (ASTOOT), is based on the concept of observational equivalence for objects. Two objects are said to be observationally equivalent if, after a sequence of operations on them, they end up in the same abstract state (even if their implementation details differ). A specification can be checked against its implementation by applying a sequence of operations and then verifying that both end up in the same abstract state. Although this type of testing system is ideal for abstract data structures such as heaps, queues, lists, and trees, the functionality that it provides doesn't result in a very good match for the operations performed by the cryptlib kernel.

When creating a specification that contains assertions about the behaviour of an implementation, we need to distinguish between definitional and operational specifications. Definitional specifications describe the properties that an implementation should exhibit, whereas operational specifications describe how those properties are to be achieved. For example, a definitional specification for a sort function might be "upon termination the items are sorted in ascending order", whereas an operational specification might be a description of a bubble sort, heap sort, merge sort, or quicksort. In its most extreme form, an operational specification is a direct implementation of an algorithm in a programming language. The pros and cons of definitional versus operational specifications were considered in Section 5.1.3. For the cryptlib kernel, an operational specification is used.

This introduction now leads us to the use of formal specification languages and assertion-based testing/stealth formal methods, of which the sections that follow provide a representative sample.

5.3.3 Specification Languages

The usual way to write specifications for a piece of software is in informal English, a DTLS in Orange Book terms. Unfortunately, a DTLS has the disadvantage that it is written in a language unsuited for the creation of specifications, one in which it is both easy to create a vague and ambiguous specification, and one that is unusable with automated verifiers. This means that such an informal specification cannot be checked for correctness using automated tools, nor can it be processed automatically for input to other tools such as those that check the program code against the specification. Informal specifications condemn developers to manual verification and testing.

In order to express specifications precisely — an FTLS in Orange Book terms — we need to resort to the use of a formal specification language that is capable of capturing semantic rules and working with a precision not possible with plain English. This can then be passed through a language verifier to check that the content of the specification conforms to the rules, and the result passed on to other tools to confirm that the code and/or final program conforms to the specification [108]. Although there has been some debate about the use of executable (or meta-executable) specifications among formal-methods purists [109][39][110], we can take the standard criticism of this type of verification — that it can't be used to prove the absence of errors — and reverse it to show that it can at least demonstrate their presence. This is no more or less useful than what model checkers do when they attempt to find counterexamples to security claims about a system, and indeed reported successful applications of model checkers to find faults often emphasise their use in showing the presence of errors in the same manner as more conventional types of testing would [111]. It should be noted here that the validation being performed goes beyond the standard functional-testing approach, which simply checks that the system works correctly, to also verify that the system doesn't work incorrectly. The overall intent of the validation process then is to accumulate evidence that the implementation matches the specification, something that even a hypothetically perfect formal proof isn't capable of doing.

Another advantage of a formalised rather than descriptive specification is that it makes it rather difficult to fiddle a design decision, since any errors or ambiguities in the designer's thinking will be revealed when an attempt is made to capture it in the form of a formal specification. An example of such an ambiguity is the fairly common practice of using the value –1 (or some similar out-of-band value) to indicate a "don't care" value in cases where a handle to an object is required. This practice was used in one location in the cryptlib kernel, but the semantics couldn't be captured in the specification, which required that the entity that was present at this point be a cryptlib object and not a choice between an object and a special-case magic value with no significance other than to indicate that it had no significance. Redesigning the portion of the kernel that caused the problem in order to eliminate this ambiguity revealed a somewhat artificial constraint (which admittedly had made sense when the code was originally written) that came through from non-kernel code. Removing this constraint considerably simplified the semantics of the code once the kernel design change was made. There were a number of other cases in which the rigorously structured kernel similarly enforced coding discipline in non-kernel code.

The following sections examine some sample specification languages that could potentially be used for specifying the behaviour of and verifying the cryptlib kernel. In each case, a brief overview of a sample from a particular class of language is provided along with an example of how it might be used and an analysis of its applicability to the task at hand. Since many of these languages use an event-based or asynchronously-communicating process model of the world, the example is somewhat contrived in some cases (this also explains many specification language designers' apparent preoccupation with either elevator controllers or stacks when presenting their work, these being examples that fit the language's world view). More extensive surveys of specification languages, including coverage of BagL, Clear, CSP, Larch, PAISLey, Prolog, SEGRAS, SF, Spec, and Z, can be found elsewhere [112][113].

5.3.4 English-like Specification Languages

One standardised specification language is the Semantic Transfer Language (STL) [114], an English-like language for specifying the behaviour of programs. STL was designed to be a tool-manageable language capable of describing actions, information such as data and relationships among data, events, states, and connection paths. A portion of an STL specification for a left-shift function is shown in Figure 5.12.

As a cursory examination of the sample shows, STL is an extremely expressive language, allowing every nuance of the code's behaviour to be expressed. An equally cursory examination will also indicate that it is a language that makes COBOL look concise by comparison. Note that the specification in Figure 5.12 has still not arrived the point of specifying the operation that is being performed (result = value << amount in C), and is also missing a number of supporting lines of specification that are required in order to make the whole thing work.

[...]

```
Action leftshift
   is actiontype internal;
   uses dataitem value;
   uses dataitem amount;
   produces dataitem result;
   is tested exhaustively on dataitem value;
   is tested exhaustively on dataitem amount.

Dataitem value is an instance of datatype bitmask.
Dataitem amount is an instance of datatype integer.

Datatype bitmask
   is datatypeclass integer;
   has value range minimum 1;
   has value range maximum 32767;
   has value range resolution 1;
   has invalid subdomain out_of_bounds;
   has valid subdomain as_specified;
```

[...]

Figure 5.12. Excerpt from an STL specification.

The corresponding advantage gained from all of this verbosity is that it's possible to automatically generate many types of test cases from the specification. An example of a set of test cases generated automatically is given in Table 5.1, and includes high and low bounds, fencepost (off-by-one) errors, above- and below-bounds errors, and a reference value to make sure everything is working as required.

Table 5.1. Test data generated from STL specification.

Subdomain	Equivalence class	Label	Value
invalid	below_bounds	below_bounds	0
valid	as_specified	low_bound	1
valid	as_specified	low_debug	2
valid	as_specified	reference	16384
valid	as_specified	high_debug	32766
valid	as_specified	high_bound	32767
invalid	above_bounds	above_bounds	32768

Although the automatic-test-case-generation ability is a powerful one, the incredible verbosity (and resulting unreadability due to its size) of an STM specification makes it unsuited for use as a specification language for a security kernel, since the huge size of the resulting specification could easily conceal any number of errors or omissions that would never be discovered due to the sheer volume of material that would need to be examined in order to notice them. Other languages that have been designed to look English-like have also ended up with similar problems. For example, the CATS specification language, which was specifically modified to allay the IEEE POSIX community's fears that the pool of potential developers, reviewers, and users who could understand a formal specification language if it were used for POSIX specifications would be severely restricted, ended up being very English-like at the expense of also being very COBOL-like [29].

5.3.5 Spec

Spec is a formal specification language that bears some resemblance to Pascal and uses predicate logic to define a piece of code's required behaviour independently of its internal structure [115][116] (the Spec referred to here shouldn't be confused with another specification language of the same name and vaguely the same goals but that uses an incomprehensible mathematical notation [117]). Whereas other specification languages such as Larch (see below) are intended for use with automated program-verification tools, Spec is intended more as a design tool for large-scale systems specification and development, specifically for use with event-driven real-time systems. An example Spec specification for the left-shift operation is given in Figure 5.13. For clarity this doesn't include constraints on the shift amount, which are specified elsewhere, or the ability to shift by more than a single bit position.

```
FUNCTION left_shift { amount: integer } WHERE amount > 0 & amount < 16

MESSAGE ( value : bitmask )
    WHEN value >= 0                        -- Shifting signed values is tricky
        REPLY ( shifted_value : bitmask )
        WHERE shifted_value >= 0 & shifted_value = value * 2
    OTHERWISE
        REPLY EXCEPTION negative_value
END
```

Figure 5.13. Excerpt from a Spec specification.

Spec functional descriptions describe the response of a function to an external stimulus. The intent is that functions described in Spec provide a single service, with the function description containing the stimulus-response characteristics for the function. An incoming message that fits into a particular when clause triggers the given response, with the otherwise clause giving the response when none of the conditions in a when clause are matched. The reply statement provides the actual response sent to the function that provided the original stimulus.

In addition to these basic properties, Spec also has an extensive range of properties and capabilities that are targeted at use with real-time, event-driven systems, as well as support for defining new types, and a facility for defining "machines" which work a bit like classes in object-oriented methodologies.

Although Spec meets the requirements for a programmer's natural language, it has some drawbacks that make it unsuited for use in specifying the cryptlib kernel. As the description above has indicated, Spec is more suited for working with event-driven stimulus-response models than the procedural model used in the cryptlib kernel. This provides something of an impedance mismatch with what is required for the kernel verification since the functions-as-event-handlers model, although it can be adapted to work with cryptlib, isn't really capable of adequately representing the true functionality present in the kernel, whereas the more sophisticated capabilities such as machines don't match anything in the kernel and aren't required. Another problem with Spec is the lack of any tool support for the language.

5.3.6 Larch

Larch is a two-tiered specification language with the upper tier consisting of a general-purpose shared language, Larch Shared Language or LSL, that provides an implementation-language-independent specification for the properties of the abstract data types being used, and the lower tier consisting of an interface language that describes the mapping to the actual implementation language. For C, the lower-level language is LCL [118][119].

LSL works with sorts, which are roughly equivalent to data types, and operators, which map one or more input values to an output value. Specifications are presented in terms of traits that define an abstract data type or occasionally just a set of operators that aren't tied to any particular data type. The LSL specification doesn't specify things like the ADT representation, algorithms used to manipulate the ADT, or various exception conditions such as the behaviour when an illegal or out-of-bounds value is encountered. These lower-level details are left to the LCL specification. A portion of the Larch specifications for the shift operation are shown in Figure 5.14, although in this case the two-tier nature of the language and the fact that the shift operation is far more simplistic than what would usually be specified as a Larch trait make it somewhat artificial. Sitting at a third layer below LCL is the implementation itself, which in this case will be in C and is even more simplistic.

```
Left_shift: trait                      int left_shift( int Val, int Amt )
   includes Integer                    {
   introduces                          modifies Val;
      shift: Val, Amt → Val            ensures result = ( Val < INT_MAX ∨
   asserts ∀ a: Amt, v: Val                ( Amt < 16 ∧ Amt >= 0 ) ) ∧
      v < INT_MAX ∨ ( a < 16 ∧ a >= 0 );     ( Val' = Val << Amt );
                                       }
```

Figure 5.14. Excerpt from a Larch specification indicating LSL (left) and LCL (right).

Since Larch specifications cannot (with occasional exceptions) be executed, users of LSL are expected to annotate the specification with assertions that can then be verified against the implementation, although some of the tools for this portion of the process are still at a somewhat experimental stage. LCL provides the operators ^ and ', which can be used to obtain the value of an object (locs in Larch-speak) before and after a procedure. In the example above, the ' operator is being used to indicate the state of the loc after the shift operation has been performed.

As the example indicates, the Larch notation, which at the LSL level uses multi-sorted first-order logic, is far more powerful than the verbose and English-like specification languages that have been discussed so far. Unfortunately, despite its C-friendliness, Larch goes too far towards the nature of the formal specification and proof systems discussed in the previous chapter, requiring a considerable amount of mathematical skill from users with an accompanying steep learning curve as they come to terms with traits, locs, sorts, subgoals and proofs, and all of the other paraphernalia that accompanies formal proof tools. As with other provers covered earlier, Larch also requires the use of an interactive proof assistant, the Larch prover (LP), in order to help users reason about conjectures. These problems mean that Larch doesn't meet the requirements given earlier for understandability and automation. In addition, the powerful range of facilities provided by Larch are overkill for our purposes, since a much simpler specification and verification system will also suffice for the task at hand.

5.3.7 ADL

The assertion definition language ADL is a predicate-logic-based specification language that is used to describe the relationship between the inputs and outputs of a program function or module. An ADL specification consists of a set of first-order predicate logic assertions that hold immediately after the completion of a call to a function and which act to constrain the values of the input and output parameters of the function [120][121]. The use of imperative software functions rather than applicative mathematical functions solves one of the major headaches present in many formal methods languages in that software functions can change the state of the computation whereas mathematical functions cannot, avoiding the need to sprinkle the formal specification with hidden functions in the manner described in the previous chapter.

An ADL specification for a function constitutes a formal description of the function's semantics, and usually begins by partitioning the behaviour of the function into normal and abnormal states, identified by the keywords normal and exception which identify what happens when the function behaves normally and what happens when it encounters an exception condition. For example, the behaviour for many Unix system calls, which return the value −1 on encountering an error, would be characterised with exception := (return = -1), normal := !exception, where return is a keyword indicating the return value from the function.

The remainder of the function specification contains a series of assertions that must evaluate to true once the function completes execution. Operators and expressions which are typically used in assertions are the call-state operator @, which provides the state of a variable at the time that the function was called and is equivalent to the old keyword in Eiffel [122], an exception expression <:> (implicitly defined in terms of exception), which characterises error situations by defining the conditions that cause the function to fail and relating them to the error condition that arises, and the keyword `normally` (implicitly defined in terms of `normal`), which lists the behaviour of the function under non-exception conditions. For example, a statement indicating that the function returns –1 (which ADL recognises as an exception condition using the previous definition of `exception`) if a value is nonzero would be given as `value != 0 <:> return = -1`.

There are two types of test conditions that can be derived from ADL specifications, call-state conditions (equivalent to the Eiffel `require` keyword for preconditions), and return-state conditions (equivalent to the Eiffel `ensure` keyword for postconditions). An ADL specification for the shift operation that contains these tests is shown in Figure 5.15, although this is slightly overspecified (having been chosen to illustrate the features described above) since in real life something as simple as a shift operation would probably be expected to throw an exception on encountering a programmer error rather than returning detailed error codes.

```
int left_shift( int value, int amount )

semantics {
    exception := ( return = -1 ),
    normal := !exception,

    amount < 0 || amount > 16
        <:> return == -1,

    normally {
        value == @value << amount
        }
    }
```

Figure 5.15. Excerpt from an ADL specification.

The code fragment used earlier that increments a cryptlib object's reference count is shown again in Figure 5.16, alongside the corresponding ADL specification. Because this is a sample chosen to illustrate an ADL specification and because the concrete C specification only contains a single line of actual code, the size of the abstract specification is about the same as the concrete specification. In practice, the former is much smaller, but this can't be easily illustrated without using an impractically large code example.

Both of these specifications say that, when given a valid cryptlib object, the function will increment its reference count. The ADL version illustrates the use of the call-state operator to obtain the value of a variable when the function is called. In the C version, the same effect is achieved through the use of a C preprocessor macro as described in Section 5.3.1, which also throws an exception if the assertion condition is not met. As the example shows, ADL is close enough in appearance to C that it should be understandable by the typical C programmer after a brief explanation of what ADL is and how it works. Contrast this with more rigorous formal approaches such as Z, where after a week-long intensive course programmers rated a sample Z specification that they were presented with as either hard or impossible to understand [123].

```
int incRefCount( const int objectHandle )     int incRefCount( const int objectHandle )
    {
    PRE( isValidObject( objectHandle ) );     semantics {
                                                  exception := cryptStatusError( return
    objectTable[ objectHandle ].\                     ),
        referenceCount++;                         normal := !exception,

    POST( objectTable[ objectHandle ].\           isValidObject( objectHandle )
        referenceCount == \                           <:> return == CRYPT_ARGERROR_OBJECT,
        ORIGINAL_VALUE( referenceCount ) +
        1 );                                      normally {
                                                      objectTable[ objectHandle ].\
    return( CRYPT_OK );                               referenceCount == \
    }                                                 @objectTable[ objectHandle ].\
                                                      referenceCount + 1,
                                                      return == CRYPT_OK
                                                      }
                                               }
```

Figure 5.16. C and ADL specifications for object reference count increment.

A final ADL operator, which has not been required thus far, is the implication operator
`-->`. In the specification above, we could have added a superfluous statement using the
predefined function `unchanged` to indicate that `exception --> unchanged(`
`objectTable[ objectHandle ].referenceCount )`, but this isn't required since
it's already indicated through the call-state test for a valid object.

ADL specifications are written as separate units that are fed into the ADL translator
(ADLT) and compiled into an executable form that can be used to verify the implementation
against the specification. Because this approach is completely non-intrusive, there is no need
to modify the implementation itself. This allows the code as it is currently running on a
system to be verified against the specification, fulfilling the "verification all the way down"
requirements. Figure 5.17 illustrates the process involved in building a test program to verify
the C specification for a program (in other words, its actual implementation) against its ADL
specification. The output of ADLT is C code, which is compiled alongside cryptlib's C
implementation code and linked into a single test program that can be run to verify that one
matches the other.

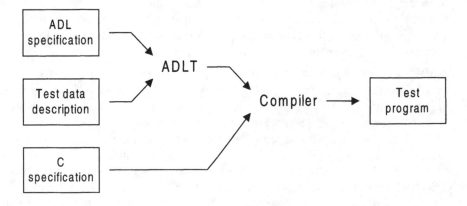

Figure 5.17. Building a test program from ADL and C specifications.

The test program built from this process verifies the functions in the cryptlib C specification against the semantics specified in the ADL specification by first evaluating all expressions qualified by the call-state operator, calling the function under test with the given test values, evaluating all assertions in the ADL version (using the values saved earlier where appropriate), and reporting an error if any of the assertions evaluate to false.

The process of using an ADL specification to verify an existing cryptlib binary is shown in Figure 5.18. In this case, the compiled form of the C specification already exists in the form of the executable code that is being run on the system, so the ADL specification is compiled and linked with the existing binary to produce the final test program.

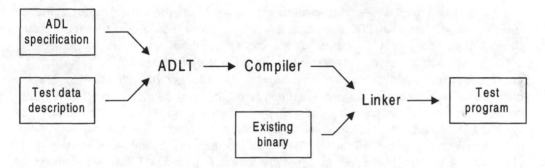

Figure 5.18. Building a test program for an existing binary.

The two cases illustrated above indicate the use of a test data description file, which can either be generated manually or automatically based on the ADL specification. The issue of test data selection is covered in Section 5.4.

An additional facility provided by ADL, which isn't directly useful when verifying cryptlib, is the ability to generate a natural-language document based on annotations in the formal specification. In Orange Book terms, this means that it's possible to generate a DTLS based on extra information added to the FTLS. A similar approach has been used for the specification of a software-based RS232 repeater that used Knuth's literate programming techniques to generate EVES and FDR specifications as well as LaTeX documentation from a single source file [124]. In our case, since the UTLS subsumes the FTLS and DTLS, this extra step isn't necessary, although it could be added if required by third-party evaluators. As with the literate programming approach, ADL provides the capability to mix plain English annotations with the formal specification. These annotations are then combined by ADLT with information extracted from the specification to produce a plain English version of the specification in troff or HTML format.

5.3.8 Other Approaches

Various approaches other than the ADL one used with cryptlib have been suggested for specification-based testing. These build on the idea that the abstract and concrete implementations can be viewed as different versions of the same software with the hope that their differing form and content will keep common-mode errors to a minimum. Similar ideas exist in the form of *N*-version programming, where a particular error will (it is hoped) be caught by at least one of the *N* independently developed program versions [125][126][127][128]. Note that this approach doesn't attempt to verify the entire implementation as do some formal methods but merely seeks to check it for particular cases, in return for a huge improvement in the success rate of the process and a lowering of the time and skill investment that is needed to obtain results. This type of self-checking implementation can be viewed as a special kind of two-version programming that has a high degree of design diversity.

One approach to creating a complementary implementation of this kind builds an abstract specification of various ADTs in a Larch-like language and then uses a parallel concrete implementation in C++ with classes containing an additional `abstract` member that contains the abstract form and a concrete-to-abstract mapping function `concr2abstr()` to map the concrete implementation to its abstract form. Member functions of the class are modified to invoke the abstract form of the implementation and then verify that the result conforms to that of the concrete one [129]. In formal-methods terms, the abstraction represents a V-function, which is modified by an operation, the O-function, to the transformed version of the abstraction. This parallels the modification of the contents of a class instance via a method invocation. The resulting self-checking ADT system is shown in Figure 5.19.

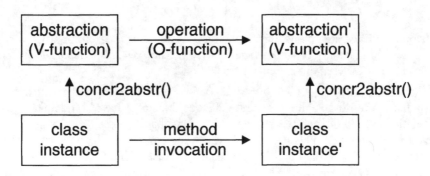

Figure 5.19. Self-checking ADT implementation.

This approach differs from the ADL one in that it requires modification of the source code, although some suggested improvements include the use of a C++-to-C++ preprocessor that inserts the necessary statements into the class implementation and the use of a term rewriting system to help automate the creation of portions of the implementation from the specification. In addition, the approach appears to be limited to C++ (rather than straight C)

---

[4] Readers using these and related references should be aware that there are some ideological differences among researchers involved in *N*-version programming work, which is sometimes reflected in the publications.

and is somewhat tricky to extend beyond checking of ADTs. A final disadvantage relative to ADL is that, as with the simpler types of assertion-based testing, the checks become embedded in the code, bringing with it the disadvantages already covered in Section 5.3.1.

5.4 The Verification Process

In order to verify the kernel implementation using either C assertions or ADL, we need to perform two types of testing, an inherently top-down form that verifies that the implementation follows the intent of the designer, and an inherently bottom-up form that verifies that the implementation follows the specification. As Section 5.2.4 indicated, the purpose of this two-tier verification approach is to catch both teleological and conceptual bugs at every level. The inherently top-down testing is intended to ensure that all of the design requirements are met (for example, that setting certain attributes for an object under appropriate conditions functions as the designer intended). The inherently bottom-up testing is intended to ensure that the implementation corresponds exactly to the specification. This form of testing is generally referred to as specification-based testing. The two forms of testing can be viewed as enforcing the letter of the law (bottom-up or specification-based testing) and the intent of the law (top-down testing).

The top-down verification, which checks that the implementation conforms to the designer's intent, is relatively straightforward (in fact, the kernel performs a core subset of these checks as part of the self-test that is performed to exercise the kernel mechanisms in the last stage of the kernel boot process every time it starts up). The bottom-up verification, which checks that the implementation complies with the letter of the specification, is somewhat more complicated and is covered in the following sections.

5.4.1 Verification of the Kernel Filter Rules

Chapter 3 described the kernel filter mechanism through which the kernel filter rules were implemented, and we can now examine how the implementation is verified. Each message type is subject to three types of processing: the general access check, which is applied to each message, and a message-type-specific pre- and post-dispatch filter, which varies based on message type. Instead of treating the kernel as a monolithic collection of filters and mechanisms, we can decompose it into a number of independent { general, pre-dispatch, post-dispatch } triples and then verify each one individually. This decomposition of the complete set of filter rules into a plurality of discrete paths representing different equivalence classes is shown in Figure 5.20.

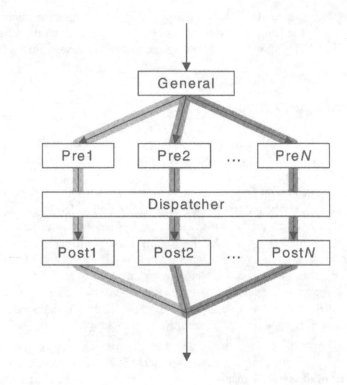

Figure 5.20. Verification of per-message filter rules.

In order to verify that the kernel handles each message correctly, we can verify each path as an independent unit rather than having to verify the kernel as a whole. In many cases, there is no post-dispatch filter (the message simply results in a status value being returned) so only the pre-dispatch step needs to be verified.

Similar techniques are being used to verify ASICs composed of individual IP cores (intellectual property, basic hardware functionality blocks) tied together to form a single composite unit, with assertions inserted into the VHDL or Verilog code for each IP block. In this case the strict separation of modules is motivated not by security concerns but (as the name "IP block" implies) intellectual property considerations in which vendors of each block don't want to reveal their inner workings to anyone else [130]. The use of verification techniques with VHDL and Verilog was covered in more detail in the previous chapter.

5.4.2 Specification-Based Testing

An asserted program p can be viewed as a sequence of assertions $a1$, $a2$, ..., an that, when executed on input i, transforms it to output o while satisfying a single global assertion A that is the sum of all of the satisfied assertions. We can then say that the program is self-checking with respect to A [131]. Since A is typically too complex to test as a single postcondition, we break it down into a number of separate assertions $a1$, $a2$, ..., an that are spread throughout the program, as explained earlier. In order to verify the program with respect to the single global meta-assertion A we need to determine input data i, which causes no assertion to be false and which results in the overall meta-assertion holding during the transformation from i to o.

The traditional functional testing approach is to partition the input domain into equivalence classes and take test data from each class. Each test case consists of an input criterion that describes data that satisfies the test case and an acceptance criterion that describes whether this test case is acceptable or whether it should generate an error. There are a variety of possible selection techniques for test data, including specification-based testing to detect specification-to-implementation mapping errors and oracle-based testing in which the specification acts as an oracle to be violated. Specification-based testing is typically used by selecting test cases that verify that for a given input criterion or assertion the output criterion or assertion is met, and oracle-based testing verifies the opposite. This represents a general overview of formal specification-based testing strategies; in practice, there are many variants that can be used [132][133]. The literature on test case generation is at least as extensive as it is for formal methods, and most of the tools appear to be at a similar level of development as their formal methods counterparts.

The testing task is simplified considerably by the strong separation of policy and mechanism maintained by the cryptlib kernel. For example, instead of specifically verifying that, once a key is loaded into an encryption action object, the kernel moves it into the high state, we only need to verify that the mechanism to manage the transitioning from low to high state is functioning as required in order to determine that it will function correctly not only for key loads but also for key generation, certificate signing, and any other operations that result in an object being transitioned from the low to the high state. This means that the operations performed by the kernel are already pre-partitioned into a set of equivalence classes that correspond to the different filter rules, an issue that was covered in the previous section.

This also explains why the simple boot-time self-test that was mentioned in Section 5.4, which is performed by the kernel as the last part of the boot process, is sufficient to check its critical functionality without requiring exhaustive testing of each filter rule. A single application of the types of test cases shown in Table 5.1 is sufficient to verify the correct functioning of range checking on boolean, integer, time, string, or other parameter types that are passed to any cryptlib object. In contrast, the more conventional collection-of-functions approach requires that every parameter passed to every function be individually checked and correctly handled. As an example of how difficult this is to get right, the recent application of a newly-developed tool that looks for absent or inappropriate range checking for parameters and similar faults found 137 security errors in the Linux and OpenBSD kernels [134]. These problems included missing upper and lower bounds checks, use of unchecked user-supplied pointers and array indices, integer overflow and signed/unsigned data type conflicts, complex code flows that resulted in checks being missed in some cases, and many more. The Linux kernel was found to have 125 faults of this kind, with roughly 1 of every 28 variables being mishandled, and even the heavily-audited OpenBSD kernel contained 12 faults, with 1 of 50 variables mishandled.

To verify the correctness of a loop, we must verify that it iterates the correct number of times and then stops. The necessary conditions for loop termination are given by the loop variant, a boolean expression that relates variables that are increased or decreased on each iteration. Its predicate is true while the loop is within bounds and false if the loop goes out of control. In terms of specifying a concrete assertion, the loop variant is a restatement of the loop control predicate, which contains an integer expression that can be evaluated after each iteration of the loop body, that after each iteration of the body produces a number smaller than at the previous iteration, and that can never go negative. The loop variant for the kernel routing function, along with the function itself, is shown in Figure 5.21. The magic value 3 is the maximum depth of a hierarchy of connected objects, as explained in Chapter 1.

Since the cryptlib kernel is almost entirely loop-free, and the few loops that do exist are guaranteed to terminate after a small, fixed number of iterations (so that they could if necessary be unrolled and expressed as a small number of conditional expressions), verification of this aspect of the code should present no real difficulties.

```
/* Route the request through any dependent objects as required until we
   reach the required target object type */
while( object != ε && object.type != target.type )
    {
    /* Try sending the message to the target */
    [...]

    /* Loop variant */
    INV( 3 - loop_index > 0 );
    }
```

Figure 5.21. Loop variant for the kernel routing function.

5.4.3 Verification with ADL

The formal specification of the behaviour of the cryptlib kernel consists of a set of assertions that constrain the state of the computation being performed. When an assertion evaluates to false during program execution, there exists an incorrect state in the program. This type of full security testing ensures that the implementation both works correctly (corresponding to standard functional testing) and doesn't work incorrectly, a property that doesn't necessarily follow from having it work correctly [135]. In order to test a design-by-contract-based program using assertion-based testing, it is necessary to generate test data that violates assertions, preferably automatically, and then check that the behaviour of the implementation corresponds to that specified by the assertions in the formal specification. The problem of finding program input on which an assertion is violated may be reduced to the problem of finding program input on which a selected statement is executed, so that a number of existing methods of test data selection can be applied [136][137].

In the testing processes shown in Figure 5.17 and Figure 5.18, the input test data was supplied by the user in the form of a test data description (TDD) specification that was fed to

ADLT alongside the ADL specification for the program, from which ADLT generated code to verify the implementation against the specification. The manual creation of TDD specifications is a labour-intensive and error-prone process, and it would be of considerable benefit if this could be done automatically. The earlier discussion of STL indicated that it was possible to specify, in a rather long-winded manner, valid values for various data types defined using STL that allowed the automatic selection of test values to check the handling of conditions such as low- and high-range checking and off-by-one errors.

It turns out that it's possible to do exactly the same thing in ADL without requiring STL's incredibly verbose and long-winded description of what represents permitted values for variables. For an ADL specification, this can be done by examining the call-state and return-state test conditions and creating test data based on the values used in the assertions. For example if an assertion indicated that `val >= 0 && val < 10`, then a test-data-generation tool could use this to choose test values of –1, 0, 5, 9, and 10, corresponding to the earlier STL range checks for `below_bounds`, `low_bound`, `reference`, `high_bound`, and `above_bounds`. Although this technique has the potential to run into problems with arbitrarily complex expressions in assertions, it is quite practical if a small amount of restraint is exercised by the specifier, so that test conditions are specified as a number of discrete assertions rather than as a single enormous obfuscated test statement.

The choice of values is obtained by walking the ADL parse tree and generating call-state test conditions from call-state evaluatable expressions and return-state test conditions from all evaluatable expressions. In order to test the normal behaviour of a function, `exception` must have the value false, which means that all exception assertions must evaluate to false and all `normally` assertions must evaluate to true. In the case of the `incRefCount` function, this means that the exception condition for `isValidObject( objectHandle )` must not be invoked on entry (in other words, that the function must be passed a valid object) and that the normal execution condition for the reference count increment must occur. In order to test the exception behaviour of a function `exception` must have the value true, which means that, for each exception assertion being tested, all previous exception assertions must evaluate to false. Since `incRefCount` is simple enough that it doesn't contain any exception conditions (that is, provided that the precondition holds, it will always increment an object's reference count), there is nothing to test in this particular case.

The exact details of how test values can be automatically derived from the ADL specification are covered elsewhere [138]. Once the test data has been derived, it can be used to generate a set of coverage-checking functions using the ADLscope tool, which augments the test code introduced by ADLT, as shown in Figure 5.17, to produce coverage statistics for the code under test. The resulting coverage information can be used to identify portions of the C specification that require more testing [139].

5.5 Conclusion

This chapter has presented a new approach to building a trusted system, introducing the concept of an (obviously) trustworthy system rather than a trusted (because we say so) system. The verification methodology that is used to construct this system has been specially designed to instil confidence in users by allowing them to verify the design specification and implementation themselves through the use of "all the way down" verification. This is achieved through a combination of design-by-contract and specification-based testing, either with C assertions or ADL. Although this type of verification has long been classed as "beyond A1" (also known as "impossible at the current state of the art"), by carefully matching the verification methodology to the system design it is possible to perform this type of verification in this particular instance. Michael Jackson (the other one) has observed that "It's a good rule of thumb that the value of a method is inversely proportional to its generality. A method for solving all problems can give you very little help with any particular problem" [140]. The method presented here has exactly the opposite properties. Far from trying to be a silver bullet, it constitutes a kryptonite bullet, one that is spectacularly effective against werewolves from Krypton, and not much good against any other kind. However, this doesn't matter to us since all that's important is that it's the right tool for the job. Attacking a werewolf with a Swiss army chainsaw is no more useful. It just makes a bigger mess.

5.6 References

[1]   "On the Need for Practical Formal Methods", Constance Heitmeyer, Proceedings of the 5th International Symposium on Formal Techniques in Real-Time and Real-Time Fault-Tolerant Systems (FTRTFT'98), Springer-Verlag Lecture Notes in Computer Science, No.1486, September 1998, p.18.

[2]   "A Controlled Experiment in Program Testing and Code Walkthroughs/Inspections", Glenford Myers, Communications of the ACM, Vol.21, No.9 (September 1978), p.760.

[3]   "Software Inspection and the Industrial Production of Software", A.Frank Ackerman, Priscilla Fowler, and Robert Ebenau, Proceedings of the Symposium on Software Validation, Elsevier Science Publishers, 1984, p.13.

[4]   "Software Inspections: An Effective Verification Process", A.Frank Ackerman, Lynne Buchwald, and Frank Lewski, IEEE Software, Vol.6, No.3 (May 1989), p.31.

[5]   "Handbook of Walkthroughs, Inspections, and Technical Reviews", Daniel Freedman and Gerald Weinberg, Dorset House, 1990.

[6]   "Practical Software Metrics for Project Management and Process Improvement", Robert Grady, Prentice-Hall, 1992.

[7]   "Software Inspections: An Industry Best Practice", David Wheeler, Bill Brykczynski, and Reginald Meeson Jr., IEEE Computer Society Press, 1996.

[8]   "Software Inspections and the Cost-Effective Production of Reliable Software", A.Frank Ackerman, Software Engineering, IEEE Computer Society Press, 1997, p.235.

[9]   "National Software Quality Experiment: Results 1992-1996", Don O'Neill, Proceedings of the 8th Annual Software Technology Conference, April 1996.

[10] "Analysis of a Kernel Verification", Terry Vickers Benzel, *Proceedings of the 1984 IEEE Symposium on Security and Privacy*, IEEE Computer Society Press, August 1984, p.125.

[11] "A Retrospective on the VAX VMM Security Kernel", Paul Karger, Mary Ellen Zurko, Douglas Bonin, Andrew Mason, and Clifford Kahn, *IEEE Transactions on Software Engineering*, **Vol.17, No.11** (November 1991), p.1147.

[12] "Building Reliable Secure Computing Systems out of Unreliable Insecure Components", John Dobson and Brian Randell, *Proceedings of the 1986 IEEE Symposium on Security and Privacy*, IEEE Computer Society Press, August 1986, p.187.

[13] "Fault Tolerance and Security", Brian Randell, *Dependable Computing and Fault-Tolerant Systems*, **Vol.9**, Springer-Verlag, 1995, p.389.

[14] "Building Reliable Secure Computing Systems out of Unreliable Insecure Components", John Dobson and Brian Randell, *Proceedings of the 17th Annual Computer Security Applications Conference (ACSAC'01)*, December 2001, p.162 (this is an update/retrospective on [12])..

[15] "Building Secure Software", John Viega and Gary McGraw, Addison-Wesley, 2002.

[16] "Open Source Security: Opportunity or Oxymoron", George Lawton, *IEEE Computer*, **Vol.35, No.3** (March 2002), p.18.

[17] "The Performance of the *N*-Fold Requirement Inspection Method", Eliezer Kantorowitz, Arie Guttman, and Lior Arzi, *Requirements Engineering*, **Vol.2, No.3** (1997), p.152.

[18] "*N*-fold inspection: A requirements analysis technique", Johnny Martin and Wei-Tek Tsai, *Communications of the ACM*, **Vol.33, No.2** (February 1990), p.225.

[19] "An Experimental Study of Fault Detection in User Requirements Documents", G.Michael Schneider, Johnny Martin, and W.Tsai, *ACM Transactions on Software Engineering and Methodology*, **Vol.1, No.2** (April 1992), p.188.

[20] "Ensuring Software Integrity", Jonathan Weiss and Edward Amoroso, *Proceedings of the 4th Aerospace Computer Security Applications*, December 1988, p.323.

[21] "Toward an Approach to Measuring Software Trust", Ed Amoroso, Thu Nguyen, Jon Weiss, John Watson, Pete Lapiska, and Terry Starr, *Proceedings of the 1991 IEEE Symposium on Security and Privacy*, IEEE Computer Society Press, August 1991, p.198.

[22] "Mondex Blows Users Anonymity", Gavin Clarke and Madeleine Acey, *Network Week*, 25 October 1995.

[23] "Mondex's double life: E-Cash both 'private' and 'fully auditable'", Niall McKay, *Infoworld Canada*, 7 May 1997.

[24] "The role of comprehension in software inspection", A.Dunsmore, M.Roper, and M.Wood, *The Journal of Systems and Software*, **Vol.52, No.2/3** (1 June 2000), p.121.

[25] "The Evaluation of Three Specification and Verification Methodologies", Richard Platek, *Proceedings of the 4th Seminar on the DoD Computer Security Initiative* (later the National Computer Security Conference), August 1981, p.X-1.

[26] Bernstein vs. USDOJ, U.S. Court of Appeals for the Ninth Circuit, Case Number 97-16686, 6 May 1999.

[27] "What non-programmers know about programming: Natural language procedure specification", Kathleen Galotti and William Ganong III, *International Journal of Man-Machine Studies*, **Vol.22**, **No.1** (January 1985), p.1.

[28] "Estimating Understandability of Software Documents", Kari Laitinen, *ACM SIGSOFT Software Engineering Notes*, **Vol.21**, **No.4** (July 1996), p.81.

[29] "Issues in the Full Scale use of Formal Methods for Automated Testing", J.Crowley, J.Leathrum, and K.Liburdy, *Proceedings of the 1996 International Symposium on Software Testing and Analysis (ISSTA'96)*, ACM, January 1996, p.71.

[30] "The PKI Specification Dilemma: A Formal Solution", Maris Ozols, Marie Henderson, Chichang Liu, and Tony Cant, *Proceedings of the 5th Australasian Conference on Information Security and Privacy (ACISP'00)*, Springer-Verlag Lecture Notes in Computer Science No.1841, July 2000, p.206.

[31] "A Translation Method from Natural Language Specifications into Formal Specifications Using Contextual Dependencies", Yasunori Ishihara, Hiroyuki Seki, and Tadao Kasami, *Proceedings of the IEEE International Symposium on Requirements Engineering*, IEEE Computer Society Press, January 1993, p.232.

[32] "Processing Natural Language Software Requirement Specifications", Miles Osborne and Craig MacNish, *Proceedings of the 2nd International Conference on Requirements Engineering (ICRE'96)*, IEEE Computer Society Press, April 1996, p.229.

[33] "The Role of Natural Language in Requirements Engineering", Kevin Ryan, *Proceedings of the IEEE International Symposium on Requirements Engineering*, IEEE Computer Society Press, January 1993, p.240.

[34] "Lessons Learned in an Industrial Software Lab", Albert Endres, *IEEE Software*, **Vol.10**, **No.5** (September 1993), p.58.

[35] "Cognitive Fit: An Empirical Study of Information Acquisition", Iris Vessey and Dennis Galletta, *Information Systems Research*, **Vol.2**, **No.1** (March 1991), p.63.

[36] "Cognitive Fit: An Empirical Study of Recursion and Iteration", Atish Sinha and Iris Vessey, *IEEE Transactions on Software Engineering*, **Vol.18**, **No.5** (May 1992), p.368.

[37] "On the Nature of Bias and Defects in the Software Specification Process", Pablo Straub and Marvin Zelkowitz, *Proceedings of the 16th International Computer Software and Applications Conference (COMPSAC'92)*, IEEE Computer Society Press, September 1992, p.17.

[38] "An Empirical Investigation of the Effects of Formal Specifications on Program Diversity", Thomas McVittie, John Kelly, and Wayne Yamamoto, *Dependable Computing and Fault-Tolerant Systems*, **Vol.6**, Springer-Verlag, 1992, p.219.

[39] "Specifications are (preferably) executable", Norbert Fuchs, *Software Engineering Journal*, **Vol.7**, **No.5** (September 1992), p.323.

[40] "From Formal Methods to Formally Based Methods: An Industrial Experience", *ACM Transactions on Software Engineering and Methodology*, **Vol.8**, **No.1** (January 1999), p.79.

[41] "An Avenue for High Confidence Applications in the 21st Century", Timothy Kremann, William Martin, and Frank Taylor, *Proceedings of the 21st National Information Systems Security Conference* (formerly the National Computer Security Conference), October 1999, CDROM distribution.

[42] "Formal Methods and Testing: Why the State-of-the Art is Not the State-of-the Practice", ISSTA'96/FMSP'96 panel summary, David Rosenblum, *ACM SIGSOFT Software Engineering Notes*, **Vol.21**, **No.4** (July 1996), p.64.

[43] Personal communications with various developers who have worked on A1 and A1-equivalent systems.

[44] "A Case Study of SREM", Paul Scheffer, Albert Stone, and William Rzepka, *IEEE Computer*, **Vol.18**, **No.3** (April 1985), p.47.

[45] "Seven Myths of Formal Methods", Anthony Hall, *IEEE Software*, **Vol.7**, **No.5** (September 1990), p.11.

[46] "Striving for Correctness", Marshall Abrams and Marvin Zelkowitz, *Computers and Security*, **Vol.14**, **No.8** (1995), p.719.

[47] "Symbol Security Condition Considered Harmful", Marvin Schaefer, *Proceedings of the 1989 IEEE Symposium on Security and Privacy*, IEEE Computer Society Press, August 1989, p.20.

[48] "A Method for Revalidating Modified Programs in the Maintenance Phase", S.Yau and Z. Kishimoto, *Proceedings of the 11th International Computer Software and Applications Conference (COMPSAC'87)*, October 1987, p.272.

[49] "Techniques for Selective Revalidation", Jean Hartman and David Robson, *IEEE Software*, **Vol.7**, **No.1** (January 1990), p.31.

[50] "A New Paradigm for Trusted Systems", Dorothy Denning, *Proceedings of the New Security Paradigms Workshop '92*, 1992, p.36.

[51] "Lesson from the Design of the Eiffel Libraries", Bertrand Meyer, *Communications of the ACM*, **Vol.33**, **No.9** (September 1990), p.69.

[52] "Applying 'Design by Contract'", Bertrand Meyer, *IEEE Computer*, **Vol.25**, **No.10** (October 1992), p.40.

[53] "iContract — The Java Design by Contract Tool", Reto Kramer, *Technology of Object-Oriented Languages and Systems*, IEEE Computer Society Press, 1998, p.295.

[54] "The Object Constraint Language", Jos Warmer and Anneke Kleppe, Addison Wesley, 1999.

[55] "Making Components Contract-aware", Antoine Beugnard, Jean-Marc Jézéquel, Noël Plouzeau, and Damien Watkins, *IEEE Computer*, **Vol.32**, **No.7** (July 1999), p.38.

[56] "Object-oriented Software Construction", Bertrand Meyer, Prentice Hall, 1988.

[57] "Human memory: A proposed system and its control processes", R.Atkinson and R.Shiffrin, *The psychology of learning and motivation: Advances in research and theory, Vol.2*, Academic Press, 1968, p.89.

[58] "The control of short-term memory", R.Atkinson and R.Shiffrin, *Scientific American*, **No.225** (August 1971), p.82

[59] "Über das Gedächtnis", Hermann Ebbinghaus, Duncker and Humblot, 1885.

[60] "The magical number seven, plus or minus two: Some limits on our capacity for processing information", George Miller, *Psychological Review*, **Vol.63**, **No.2** (March 1956), p.81.

[61] "Human Memory: Structures and Processes", Roberta Klatzky, W.H.Freeman and Company, 1980.

[62] "Learning and Memory", William Gordon, Brooks/Cole Publishing Company, 1989.

[63] "Human Memory: Theory and Practice", Alan Baddeley, Allyn and Bacon, 1998.

[64] "Empirical Studies of Programming Knowledge", Elliot Soloway and Kate Ehrlich, *IEEE Transactions on Software Engineering*, **Vol.10**, **No.5** (September 1984), p.68.

[65] "An integrating common framework for measuring cognitive software complexity", Zsolt Öry, *Software Engineering Journal*, **Vol.8**, **No.5** (September 1993), p.263.

[66] "Software Psychology: Human Factors in Computers and Information Systems", Ben Shneiderman, Winthrop Publishers Inc, 1980.

[67] "A study in dimensions of psychological complexity of programs", B.Chaudhury and H.Sahasrabuddhe, *International Journal of Man-Machine Studies*, **Vol.23**, **No.2** (August 1985), p.113.

[68] "Does OO Sync with How We Think?", Les Hatton, *IEEE Software*, **Vol.15**, **No.3** (May/June 1998), p.46.

[69] "Experimental assessment of the effect of inheritance on the maintainability of object-oriented systems", R.Harrison, S.Counsell, and R.Nithi, *The Journal of Systems and Software*, **Vol.52**, **No.2/3** (1 June 2000), p.173.

[70] "Exploring the relationships between design measures and software quality in object-oriented systems", Lionel Brand, Jürgen Wüst, John Daly, and D.Victor Porter, *The Journal of Systems and Software*, **Vol.51**, **No.3** (1 May 2000), p.245.

[71] "An Empirical Investigation of an Object-Oriented Software System", Michelle Cartwright and Martin Shepperd, *IEEE Transactions on Software Engineering*, **Vol.26**, **No.8** (August 2000), p.786.

[72] "A effect of semantic complexity on the comprehension of program modules", Barbee Mynatt, *International Journal of Man-Machine Studies*, **Vol.21**, **No.2** (August 1984), p.91.

[73] "Program Comprehension Beyond the Line", Scott Robertson, Erle Davis, Kyoko Okabe, and Douglas Fitz-Randolf, *Proceedings of Human-Computer Interaction — INTERACT'90*, Elsevier Science Publishers, 1990, p.959.

[74] "Flow Diagrams, Turing Machines And Languages With Only Two Formation Rules", Corrado Böhm and Guiseppe Jacopini, *Communications of the ACM*, **Vol.9**, **No.5** (May 1966), p.336.

[75] "The Psychology of How Novices Learn Computer Programming", Richard Mayer, *Computing Surveys*, **Vol.13**, **No.1** (March 1981), p.121.

[76] "Towards a theory of the comprehension of computer programs", Ruven Brooks, *International Journal of Man-Machine Studies*, **Vol.8**, **No.6** (June 1983), p.543.

[77] "Beacons in computer program comprehension", Susan Weidenbeck, *International Journal of Man-Machine Studies*, **Vol.25**, **No.6** (December 1986), p.697.

[78] "Syntactic/Semantic Interactions in Programmer Behaviour: A Model and Experimental Results", Ben Shneiderman and Richard Mayer, *International Journal of Computer and Information Sciences*, **Vol.8**, **No.3** (June 1979), p.219.

[79] "Expertise in debugging computer programs: A process analysis", Iris Vessey, *International Journal of Man-Machine Studies*, **Vol.23**, **No.5** (November 1985), p.459.

[80] "Knowledge and Process in the Comprehension of Computer Programs", Elliott Soloway, Beth Adelson, and Kate Erhlich, *The Nature of Expertise*, Lawrence Erlbaum and Associates, 1988, p.129.

[81] "Program Comprehension During Software Maintenance and Evolution", Anneliese von Mayrhauser and A.Marie Vans, *IEEE Computer*, **Vol.28**, **No.8** (August 1995), p.44.

[82] "The Programmer's Burden: Developing Expertise in Programming", Robert Campbell, Norman Brown, and Lia DiBello, *The Psychology of Expertise: Cognitive Research and Empirical AI*, Springer-Verlag, 1992, p.269.

[83] "Advanced Organisers in Computer Instruction Manuals: Are they Effective?", Barbee Mynatt and Katherine Macfarlane, *Proceedings of Human-Computer Interaction (INTERACT'87)*, Elsevier Science Publishers, 1987, p.917.

[84] "Characteristics of the mental representations of novice and expert programmers: an empirical study", Susan Weidenbeck and Vikki Fix, *International Journal of Man-Machine Studies*, **Vol.39**, **No.5** (November 1993), p.793.

[85] "Cognitive design elements to support the construction of a mental model during software exploration", M.-A. Storey, F.Fracchia, and H.Müller, *The Journal of Systems and Software*, **Vol.44**, **No.3** (January 1999), p.171.

[86] "Towards a theory of the cognitive processes in computer programming", Ruven Brooks, *International Journal of Man-Machine Studies*, **Vol.9**, **No.6** (November 1977), p.737.

[87] "Change-Episodes in Coding: When and How Do Programmers Change Their Code?", Wayne Gray and John Anderson, *Empirical Studies of Programmers: Second Workshop*, Ablex Publishing Corporation, 1987, p,185.

[88] "Cognitive Processes in Software Design: Activities in the Early, Upstream Design", Raymonde Guindon, Herb Krasner, and Bill Curtis, *Proceedings of Human-Computer Interaction (INTERACT'87)*, Elsevier Science Publishers, 1987, p.383.

[89] "A Model of Software Design", Beth Adelson and Elliot Soloway, *The Nature of Expertise*, Lawrence Erlbaum and Associates, 1988, p.185.

[90] "Novice-Export Differences in Software Design", B.Adelson, D.Littman, K.Ehrlich, J.Black, and E.Soloway, *Proceedings of Human-Computer Interaction (INTERACT'84)*, Elsevier Science Publishers, 1984, p.473.

[91] "Stereotyped Program Debugging: An Aid for Novice Programmers", Harald Wertz, *International Journal of Man-Machine Studies*, **Vol.16**, **No.4** (May 1982), p.379.

[92] "Expert Programmers Re-establish Intentions When Debugging Another Programmer's Program", Ray Waddington, *Proceedings of Human-Computer Interaction (INTERACT'90)*, Elsevier Science Publishers, 1990, p.965.

[93] "An Assertion Mapping Approach to Software Testing", Greg Bullough, Jim Loomis, and Peter Weiss, *Proceedings of the 13th National Computer Security Conference*, October 1990, p.266.

[94] "Testing Object-Oriented Systems: Models, Patterns, and Tools", Robert Binder, Addison-Wesley, 1999.

[95] "Powerful Assertions in C++", Harald Mueller, *C/C++ User's Journal*, **Vol.12**, **No.10** (October 1994), p.21.

[96] "An Overview of Anna, a Specification Language for Ada", David Luckham and Friedrich von Henke, *IEEE Software*, **Vol.2**, **No.2** (March 1985), p.9.

[97] "A methodology for formal specification and implementation of Ada packages using Anna", Neel Madhav and Walter Mann, *Proceedings of the 1990 Computer Software and Applications Conference*, IEEE Computer Society Press, 1990, p.491.

[98] "Programming with Specifications: An Introduction to ANNA, A Language for Specifying Ada Programs", David Luckham, *Texts and Monographs in Computer Science*, Springer-Verlag, January 1991.

[99] "Nana — GNU Project — Free Software Foundation (FSF)", http://www.gnu.-org/software/nana/nana.html.

[100] "A Practical Approach to Programming With Assertions", David Rosenblum, *IEEE Transactions on Software Engineering*, **Vol.21**, **No.1** (January 1995), p.19.

[101] "The Behavior of C++ Classes", Marshall Cline and Doug Lea, *Proceedings of the Symposium on Object-Oriented Programming Emphasizing Practical Applications*, ACM, September 1990.

[102] "The New Hacker's Dictionary (3rd Edition)", Eric S.Raymond, MIT Press, 1996.

[103] "The Algebraic Specification of Abstract Data Types", John Guttag and James Horning, *Acta Informatica*, **Vol.10** (1978), p.27.

[104] "SELECT — A Formal System for Testing and Debugging Programs by Symbolic Execution", Robert Boyer, Bernard Elspas, and Karl Levitt, *ACM SIGPLAN Notices*, **Vol.10**, **No.6** (June 1975), p.234.

[105] "Data-Abstraction Implementation, Specification, and Testing", John Gannon, Paul McMullin, and Richard Hamlet, *ACM Transactions on Programming Languages and Systems*, **Vol.3**, **No.3** (July 1981), p.211.

[106] "Daistish: Systematic Algebraic Testing for OO Programs in the Presence of Side-effects", Merlin Hughes and David Stotts, *Proceedings of the 1996 International Symposium on Software Testing and Analysis (ISSTA'96)*, ACM, January 1996, p.53.

[107] "The ASTOOT Approach to Testing Object-Oriented Programs", Roong-Ko Doong and Phyllis Frankl, *ACM Transactions on Software Engineering and Methodology*, Vol.3, No.2 (April 1994), p.101.

[108] "Automating specification-based software testing", Robert Poston, IEEE Computer Society Press, 1996.

[109] "Specifications are not (necessarily) executable", Ian Hayes and Cliff Jones, *Software Engineering Journal*, **Vol.4**, **No.6** (November 1989), p.330.

[110] "Executing formal specifications need not be harmful", Andrew Gravell and Peter Henderson, *Software Engineering Journal*, **Vol.11**, **No.2** (March 1996), p.104.

[111] "Feasibility of Model Checking Software Requirements: A Case Study", Tirumale Sreemani and Joanne Atlee, *Proceedings of the 11th Annual Conference on Computer Assurance (COMPASS'96)*, IEEE Computer Society Press, June 1996, p.77.

[112] "A Practical Assessment of Formal Specification Approaches for Data Abstraction", K.Ventouris and P.Pintelas, *The Journal of Systems and Software*, **Vol.17**, **No.1** (January 1992), p.169.

[113] "Languages for the Specification of Software", Daniel Cooke, Ann Gates, Elif Demirörs, Onur Demirörs, Murat Tanik, and Bernd Krämer, *The Journal of Systems and Software*, **Vol.32**, **No.3** (March 1996), p.269.

[114] "Standard Reference Model for Computing System Engineering Tool Interconnections", IEEE Standard 1175:1992, IEEE, 1992.

[115] "Languages for Specification, Design, and Prototyping", Valdis Berzins and Luqi, *Handbook of Computer-Aided Software Engineering*, Van Nostrand Reinhold, 1990, p.83.

[116] "An Introduction to the Specification Language Spec", Valdis Berzins and Luqi, *IEEE Software*, **Vol.7**, **No.2** (March 1990), p.74.

[117] "Specifying Distributed Systems", Butler Lampson, Working Material for the International Summer School on Constructive Methods in Computing Science, August 1988.

[118] "A Tutorial on Larch and LCL, a Larch/C Interface Language", John Guttag and James Horning, *Proceedings of the 4th International Symposium of VDM Europe (VDM'91), Formal Software Development Methods*, Springer-Verlag Lecture Notes in Computer Science, No.552, 1991, p1.

[119] "Larch: Languages and Tools for Formal Specification", John Guttag and James Horning, Springer-Verlag Texts and Monographs in Computer Science, 1993.

[120] "Preliminary Design of ADL/C++ — A Specification Language for C++", Sreenivasa Viswanadha and Sriram Sankar, *Proceedings of the 2nd Conference on Object-Oriented Technology and Systems (COOTS'96)*, Usenix Association, June 1996, p.97.

[121] "Specifying and Testing Software Components using ADL", Sriram Sankar and Roger Hayes, Sun Microsystems Technical Report TR-94-23, Sun Microsystems Laboratories Inc, April 1994.

[122] "Eiffel: The Language", Bertrand Meyer, Prentice-Hall, 1991.

[123] "Literate specifications", C.Johnson, *Software Engineering Journal*, **Vol.11**, **No.4** (July 1996), p.225.

[124] "Increasing Assurance with Literate Programming Techniques", Andrew Moore and Charles Payne Jr., *Proceedings of the 11th Annual Conference on Computer Assurance (COMPASS'96)*, IEEE Computer Society Press, June 1996, p.187.

[125] "Fault Tolerance by Design Diversity: Concepts and Experiments", Algirdas Avizienis and John Kelly, *IEEE Computer*, **Vol.17**, **No.8** (August 1984), p.67.

[126] "The *N*-version Approach to Fault Tolerant Systems", Algirdas Avizienis, *IEEE Transactions on Software Engineering*, **Vol.11**, **No.12** (December 1985), p.1491.

[127] "The Use of Self Checks and Voting in Software Error Detection: An Empirical Study", Nancy Leveson, Stephen Cha, John Knight, and Timothy Shimeall, *IEEE Transactions on Software Engineering*, **Vol.16**, **No.4** (April 1990), p.432.

[128] "N-version design versus one good version", Les Hatton, *IEEE Software*, **Vol.14**, **No.6** (November/December 1997), p.71.

[129] "Automatically Checking an Implementation against Its Formal Specification", Sergio Antoy and Dick Hamlet, *IEEE Transactions on Software Engineering*, **Vol.26**, **No.1** (January 2000), p.55.

[130] "Checking the Play in Plug-and-Play", Harry Goldstein, *IEEE Spectrum*, **Vol.39**, **No.6** (June 2002), p.50.

[131] "On the Use of Executable Assertions in Structured Programs", Ali Mili, Sihem Guemara, Ali Jaoua, and Paul Torrés, *The Journal of Systems and Software*, **Vol.7**, **No.1** (March 1987), p.15.

[132] "A Method for Test Data Selection", F.Velasco, *The Journal of Systems and Software*, **Vol.7**, **No.2** (June 1987), p.89.

[133] "Approaches to Specification-Based Testing", Debra Richardson, Owen O'Malley, and Cindy Tittle, *Proceedings of the Third ACM SIGSOFT Symposium on Software Testing, Analysis and Verification*, December 1989, p.86.

[134] "Using Programmer-Written Compiler Extensions to Catch Security Holes", Ken Ashcroft and Dawson Engler, *Proceedings of the 2002 IEEE Symposium on Security and Privacy*, May 2002, p.143

[135] "Security Testing as an Assurance Mechanism", Susan Walter, *Proceedings of the 3rd Annual Canadian Computer Security Symposium*, May 1991, p.337.

[136] "Predicate-Based Test Generation for Computer Programs", Kuo-Chung Tai, *Proceedings of the 15th International Conference on Software Engineering (ICSE'93)*, IEEE Computer Society/ACM Press, May 1993, p.267.

[137] "Assertion-Oriented Automated Test Data Generation", Bogdan Korel and Ali Al-Yami, *Proceedings of the 18th International Conference on Software Engineering (ICSE'96)*, IEEE Computer Society Press, 1996, p.71

[138] "Structural Specification-based Testing with ADL", Juei Chang and Debra Richardson, *Proceedings of the 1996 International Symposium on Software Testing and Analysis (ISSTA'96)*, January 1996, p.62.

[139] "Structural Specification-Based Testing: Automated Support and Experimental Evaluation", Juei Chang and Debra Richardson, *Proceedings of the 7th European Software Engineering Conference (ESE/FSE'99)*, Springer-Verlag Lecture Notes in Computer Science, No.1687, November 1999.

[140] "Software Requirements and Specifications: A Lexicon of Practice, Principles, and Prejudices", Michael Jackson, Addison-Wesley, 1995.

6 Random Number Generation

6.1 Introduction

The primary goal of a cryptographic security architecture is to safeguard cryptovariables such as keys and related security parameters from misuse. Sensitive data of this kind lies at the heart of any cryptographic system and must be generated by a random number generator of guaranteed quality and security. If the cryptovariable generation process is insecure then even the most sophisticated protection mechanisms in the architecture will do no good. More precisely, the cryptovariable generation process must be subject to the same high level of assurance as the kernel itself if the architecture is to meet its overall design goals, even though it isn't directly a part of the security kernel.

Because of the importance of this process, this entire chapter is devoted to the topic of generating random numbers for use as cryptovariables. The theoretically best means of doing this is to measure physical phenomena such as radioactive decay, thermal noise in semiconductors, sound samples taken in a noisy environment, and even digitised images of a lava lamp. However, few computers (or users) have access to the kind of specialised hardware required for these sources, and must rely on other means of obtaining random data. The term "practically strong randomness" is used here to represent randomness that isn't cryptographically strong by the usual definitions but that is as close to it as is practically possible.

Existing approaches that don't rely on special hardware have ranged from precise timing measurements of the effects of air turbulence on the movement of hard drive heads [1], timing of keystrokes as the user enters a password [2][3], timing of memory accesses under artificially induced thrashing conditions [4], timing of disk I/O response times [5], and measurement of timing skew between two system timers (generally a hardware and a software timer, with the skew being affected by the 3-degree background radiation of interrupts and other system activity) [6][7]. In addition a number of documents exist that provide general advice on using and choosing random number sources [8][9][10][11][12].

Due to size constraints, a discussion of the nature of randomness, especially cryptographically strong randomness, is beyond the scope of this work. One of the principal problems with randomness and entropy is that neither are really physical quantities, but instead walk a slippery line between being physical and philosophical entities. A good general overview of what constitutes randomness, what types of sources are useful (and not useful), and how to process the data from them, is given in RFC 1750 [13]. Further discussion on the nature of randomness, pseudorandom number generators (PRNGs), and cryptographic randomness is available from a number of sources [14][15][16][17]. Unfortunately, the advice presented by various authors is all too often ignored, resulting in insecure random number generators that produce encryption keys that are far easier to attack than the underlying cryptosystems with which they are used. A particularly popular source of bad random numbers is the current time and process ID. This type of flawed generator, of which an example is shown in Figure 6.1, first gained widespread publicity in late 1995 when it was found that the encryption in Netscape browsers could be broken in around a minute due to the limited range of values provided by this source, leading to some spectacular headlines in the popular press [18]. Because the values used to generate session keys could be established without too much difficulty, even non-crippled browsers with 128-bit session keys carried (at best) only 47 bits of entropy in their session keys [19].

```
a = mixbits( time.tv_usec );
b = mixbits( getpid() + time.tv_sec + ( getppid() << 12 ));
seed = MD5( a, b );

nonce = MD5( seed++ );
key = MD5( seed++ );
```

Figure 6.1. The Netscape generator.

Shortly afterwards, it was found that Kerberos V4, whose generator is shown in Figure 6.2, suffered from a similar weakness (in fact, it was even worse than Netscape since it used random() instead of MD5 as its mixing function) [20].

```
srandom( time.tv_usec ^ time.tv_sec ^ getpid() ^ gethostid() ^ counter++ );
key = random();
```

Figure 6.2. The Kerberos V4 generator.

At about the same time as the Kerberos flaw was discovered, it was announced that the MIT-MAGIC-COOKIE-1 key generation, which created a 56-bit value, effectively only had 256 seed values due to its use of rand(), as shown in Figure 6.3. This flaw had in fact been discovered in January of that year, but the announcement was delayed to allow vendors to fix the problem [21]. A variant of this generator was used in Sesame (which just used the output of rand() directly), the glibc resolver (which used 16 bits of output) [22], and no doubt in many other programs that require a quick source of "random" values. FireWall-1 doesn't even use rand() but instead uses a direct call to time() to generate the secret value for its S/Key authentication and regenerates it after 99 uses, making it a relatively simple task to recover the authentication secret and compromise the firewall [23].

```
Key = rand() % 256;                key = rand();
```

Figure 6.3. The MIT_MAGIC_COOKIE (left) and Sesame (right) generators.

The generator used in the Gauntlet and FWTK firewalls is shown in Figure 6.4. This is yet another time + process-ID generator that has the same problems as the Kerberos V4 generator due to its use of rand(). This generator is used with (and therefore compromises the security of) Cryptocard, SNK (Axent), MD5, and RADIUS CHAP challenge-response authentication to the firewall, since after waiting getpid() seconds the firewall software will reuse a previous challenge value, allowing a response observed earlier to be played back [24].

```
srand( ( ( int ) time( NULL ) % getpid() ) + getppid() );
return( rand() );
```

Figure 6.4. The Gauntlet/FWTK firewall generator.

The PalmOS SysRandom() function, used as a source of randomness in various PalmPilot security programs, is shown in Figure 6.5. This is another rand()-equivalent generator, which uses a default seed value of 0.

```
seed = ( seed * 22695477 ) + 1;
return ( ( seed >> 16 ) & 0x7fff );
```

Figure 6.5. The PalmOS generator.

In some cases, the use of a linear congruential random number generator (LCRNG, which is the type usually used in programming language libraries) can interact with the cryptosystem with which it is used. For example, using an LCRNG or truncated LCRNG with DSA makes it possible to recover the signer's secret key after seeing only three signatures [25]. The DSA code included in Sun's JDK 1.1 was even worse, using a fixed value for the random variable k which is required when generating DSA signatures. This error meant that the DSA private key could be recovered after it had been used to generate anything more than a single signature. Two of these k values (one for 512-bit keys, one for 1024-bit keys) are 66 D1 F1 17 51 44 7F 6F 2E F7 95 16 50 C7 38 E1 85 0B 38 59 and 65 A0 7E 54 72 BE 2E 31 37 8A EA 7A 64 7C DB AE C9 21 54 29 [26]. The use of a fixed k value represented a coding error on the part of the programmers rather than the use of a bad seed value, since it was intended to be used only for testing, but was accidentally left enabled in the release version of the code (continuous testing of the generator output would have detected this as a stuck-at fault). Another product, from a US crypto hardware vendor, had a similar problem, always producing the same "random" number as output. Yet another product, a crypto smart card, always generated the same public/private key pair when requested to generate a new key [27].

Other generators use similarly poor sources and then further reduce what little security may be present through a variety of means such as implementation or configuration errors; for example, Sun derived NFS file handles (which serve as magic tokens to control access to a file and therefore need to be unpredictable) from the traditional process ID and time of day but never initialised the time of day variable (a coding error) and installed the NFS file handle initialisation program using the suninstall procedure, which results in the program running with a highly predictable process ID (a configuration problem). The result of this was that a great many systems ended up using identical NFS file handles [28]. In another example of how the security of an already weak generator can be further reduced, a company that produced online gambling software used the current time to seed the Delphi (a Pascal-like programming language) random() function and used the output to shuffle a deck of cards. Since players could observe the values of some of the shuffled cards, they could predict the output of the generator and determine which cards were being held by other players [29][30]. Another generator can be persuaded to write megabytes of raw output to disk for later analysis, although the fact that it uses an X9.17 generator (described in more detail in Section 6.3.2) makes this less serious than if a weak generator were used [31].

In an attempt to remedy this situation, this chapter provides a comprehensive guide to designing and implementing a practically strong random data accumulator and generator that requires no specialised hardware or access to privileged system services. The result is an easy-to-use random number generator that (currently) runs under BeOS, DOS, the Macintosh, OS/2, OS/400, Tandem NSK, VM/CMS, Windows 3.x, Windows 95/98/ME, Windows NT/2000/XP, Unix, and a variety of embedded operating systems, and which should be suitable even for demanding applications.

6.2 Requirements and Limitations of the Generator

There are several special requirements and limitations that affect the design of a practically strong random number generator. The main requirement (and also limitation) imposed on the generator is that it cannot rely on only one source, or on a small number of sources, for its random data. For example even if it were possible to assume that a system has some sort of sound input device, the signal obtained from it is often not random at all, but heavily influenced by crosstalk with other system components or predictable in nature (one test with a cheap sound card in a PC produced only a single changing bit that toggled in a fairly predictable manner).

An example of the problems caused by reliance on a single source is provided by a security flaw discovered in PGP 5 when used with Unix systems that contain a /dev/random driver (typically Linux and x86 BSD's). Due to the coding error shown in Figure 6.6, the single-byte random-data buffer would be overwritten with the return code from the read() function call, which was always 1 (the number of bytes read). As a result, the "random" input to the PGP generator consisted of a sequence of 1s instead of the expected /dev/random output [32]. The proposed fix for the problem itself contained a bug in that the return status of the read() was never checked, leaving the possibility that nonrandom data would be added to the pool if the read failed. A third problem with the code was that the use of single-byte reads made the generator output vulnerable to iterative-guessing attacks in which an attacker who had somehow discovered the initial pool state could interleave reads with the PGP ones and use the data they were reading to test for the most probable new seed material being added. This would allow them to track changes in pool state over time because only a small amount of new entropy was flowing into the pool between each read, and from this predict the data that PGP was reading [33]. Solutions to this type of problem are covered in the Yarrow generator design [34].

```
RandBuf = read(fd, &RandBuf, 1);        Read (fd, &RandBuf, 1);
pgpRandomAddBytes(&pgpRandomPool,       PgpRandomAddBytes(&pgpRandomPool,
    &RandBuf, 1);                           &RandBuf, 1);
```

Figure 6.6. PGP 5 /dev/random read bug (left) and suggested fix (right).

In addition several of the sources mentioned thus far are very hardware-specific or operating-system specific. The keystroke-timing code used in older versions of PGP relies on direct access to hardware timers (under DOS) or the use of obscure ioctls to allow uncooked access to Unix keyboard input, which may be unavailable in some environments, or function in unexpected ways. For example, under Windows, many features of the PC hardware are virtualised, and therefore provide much less entropy than they appear to, and under Unix the user is often not located at the system console, making keystrokes subject to the timing constraints of the `telnet`, `rlogin`, or `ssh` session, as well as being susceptible to network packet sniffing. Even where direct hardware access for keystroke latency timing is possible, what is being read isn't the closure of a keyswitch on a keyboard but data that has been processed by at least two other CPUs, one in the keyboard and one on the host computer, with the result that the typing characteristics will be modified by the paths over which the data has to travel and may provide much less entropy than they appear to.

This problem can also affect sources that rely on timing techniques such as using a fast software timer to sample a slower hardware one. The problem in this case is that there is no way to fully verify them for all the situations in which they will be used. For example, there may be an undetected correlation between the two sources, or operating system task scheduling or interrupt handling may upset their operation, or they may not function as required when running inside a virtual machine, or under a different operating system version, or at a different process priority, or on a different CPU, or any one of a hundred other things that may affect the timer sampling in a deterministic manner. In other words, just because a timer-based generator appears to perform as required on a system with CPU A stepping B, chipset C stepping D, network card E revision F, operating system kernel G patchlevel H, and so on, doesn't guarantee that running it under exactly the same conditions but with CPU stepping C instead of B won't show strong correlations between samples. It is for this reason that Orange Book security evaluations are carried out on very carefully-defined system configurations, and are only valid for those exact configurations, with any change to the system invalidating the evaluation.

Other traps abound. In the absence of a facility for timing keystrokes, mouse activity is often used as a source of randomness. However, some Windows mouse drivers have a "snap to" capability that positions the mouse pointer over the default button in a dialog box or window. Networked applications may transmit the client's mouse events to a server, revealing information about mouse movements and clicks. Some operating systems will collapse multiple mouse events into a single meta-event to cut down on network traffic or handling overhead, reducing the input from wiggle-the-mouse randomness gathering to a single mousemove event. In addition, if the process is running on an unattended server, there may be no keyboard or mouse activity at all.

Indirect traffic analysis can also reveal details of random seed data; for example, an opponent could observe the DNS queries used to resolve names when netstat is run without the -n flag, lowering its utility as a potential source of randomness. In order to avoid this dependency on a particular piece of hardware, an operating system, or the correct implementation of the data-gathering code, the generator should rely on as many inputs as possible. This is expanded on in Section 6.5.

The generator should also have several other properties:

- It should be resistant to analysis of its input data. An attacker who recovers or is aware of a portion of the input to the generator should be unable to use this information to recover the generator's state.

- As an extension of the above, it should also be resistant to manipulation of the input data, so that an attacker able to feed chosen input to the generator should be unable to influence its state in any predictable manner. An example of a generator that lacked this property was the one used in early versions of the BSAFE library, which could end up containing a very low amount of entropy if fed many small data blocks such as user keystroke information [35].

- It should be resistant to analysis of its output data. An attacker who recovers a portion of the generator's output should be unable to recover any other generator state information from this. For example, recovering generator output such as a session key or PKCS #1 padding for RSA keys should not allow any of the generator state to be recovered.

- It should take steps to protect its internal state to ensure that it cannot be recovered through techniques such as scanning the system swap file for a large block of random data. This is discussed in more detail in Section 6.8.

- The implementation of the generator should make explicit any actions such as mixing the pool or extracting data in order to allow the conformance of the code to the generator design to be easily checked. This is particularly problematic in the code used to implement the PGP 2.x random number pool, which (for example) relies on the fact that a pool index value is initially set to point past the end of the pool so that on the first attempt to read data from it the available byte count will evaluate to zero bytes, resulting in no data being copied out and the code dropping through to the pool mixing function. This type of coding makes the correct functioning of the random pool management code difficult to ascertain, leading to problems such as the ones discussed in Sections 6.3.3 and 6.3.8.

- All possible steps should be taken to ensure that the generator state information never leaks to the outside world. Any leakage of internal state that would allow an attacker to predict further generator output should be regarded as a catastrophic failure of the generator. An example of a generator that fails to meet this requirement is the Netscape one presented earlier, which reveals the hash of its internal state when it is used to generate the nonce used during the SSL handshake. It then increments the state value (typically changing a single bit of data) and hashes it again to produce the premaster secret from which all cryptovariables are generated. Although there are (currently) no known attacks on this, it is a rather unsound practice to reveal generator state information to the world in this manner. Since an attack capable of producing MD5 preimages would allow the premaster secret (and by extension all cryptovariables) to be recovered for the SSL handshake, the generator may also be vulnerable to a related-key attack as explained in Section 6.3.1. This flaw is found in the code surrounding several other generators as well, with further details given in the text that covers the individual generators.

- It should attempt to estimate whether it actually contains enough entropy to produce reliable output, and alert the caller in some manner if it is incapable of guaranteeing that the output that it will provide is suitably unpredictable. A number of generators don't do this and will quite happily run on empty, producing output by hashing all-zero buffers or basic values such as the current time and process ID.

- It should periodically or even continuously sample its own output and perform any viable tests on it to ensure that it isn't producing bad output (at least as far as the test is able to determine) or is stuck in a cycle and repeatedly producing the same output. This type of testing is a requirement of FIPS 140 [36], although it appears geared more towards hardware rather than software implementations since most software implementations are based on hash functions that will always pass the FIPS 140 tests. Apparently, hardware random number generators that sample physical sources are viewed with some mistrust in certain circles, although whether this arises from INFOSEC paranoia or COMINT experience is unknown.

Given the wide range of environments in which the generator would typically be employed, it is not possible within the confines of this work to present a detailed breakdown of the nature of, and capabilities of, an attacker. Because of this limitation we take all possible prudent precautions that might foil an attacker, but leave it to end users to decide whether this provides sufficient security for their particular application.

In addition to these initial considerations, there are a number of further design considerations whose significance will become obvious during the course of the discussion of other generators and potential weaknesses. The final, full set of generator design principles is presented in the conclusion. A paper that complements this work and focuses primarily on the cryptographic transformations used by generators was published by Counterpane in 1998 [37].

6.3 Existing Generator Designs and Problems

The model employed here to analyse generator designs divides the overall generator into three sections:

1. An entropy accumulator, which is used to gather random data (for example, by polling various entropy sources) and feed it into the second generator stage.

2. The generator proper, consisting of a randomness pool, which is used to contain the generator's internal state, and an associated mixing function, which is used to mix the data in the pool (in other words to update the internal state).

3.   A pseudo-random number generator (PRNG) or similar post-processing function, which is used to "stretch" the limited amount of generator internal state and to hide the details of the state from an outside observer.

The resulting abstract generator model is shown in Figure 6.7.

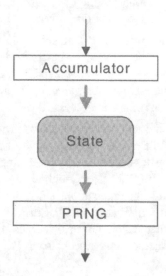

Figure 6.7. Generalised entropy accumulator and PRNG model.

When designing a generator, it is important to ensure that the three stages remain distinct, both to make analysis of the design simpler and to prevent any (potentially dangerous) interaction between the stages. For example, several generators combine the state update and PRNG functionality and as a consequence make the generator's internal state available as generator output since the separate PRNG no longer exists to isolate the internal state from the output. Other generators omit one of the stages altogether, significantly weakening the overall design. In the analysis of generators that follows, it is instructive to consider each design in terms of how effectively each of the three parts of the design is realised.

This is not to say that a generator that doesn't contain all three stages is fatally flawed, however. For example, the final stage of PRNG functionality is only needed in some cases. Consider a typical case in which the generator is required to produce a single quantum of random data (for example, to encrypt a piece of outgoing email or to establish an SSL shared secret). Even if the transformation function being used in the generator is a completely reversible one such as a (hypothetical) perfect compressor, there is no loss of security because everything nonrandom and predictable is discarded and only the unpredictable material remains as the generator output. Only when large amounts of data are drawn from the system does the "accumulator" functionality give way to the "generator" functionality, at which point a transformation with certain special cryptographic qualities is required (although, in the absence of a perfect compressor, it doesn't hurt to have these present anyway). Similarly, it is possible to design a generator with no entropy accumulator functionality if it can maintain some form of secret internal state, an (imperfect) example of this type of design being the X9.17 generator in Section 6.3.2.

Because of the special properties required when the accumulator and state update (rather than PRNG) functionality are dominant, the randomness pool and mixing function have to be carefully designed to meet the requirements given in the previous section. The following sections analyse a number of generators in current use. The descriptions omit some minor implementation details for simplicity, such as the fact that most generators mix in low-value data such as the time and process ID on the assumption that every little bit helps, will opportunistically use sources such as /dev/random where available (typically this is restricted to Linux and some x86 BSDs), and may store some state on disk for later reuse, a feature first popularised in PGP 2.x. In addition, most of the generators have changed slightly over time, most commonly by moving from MD5 to SHA-1 or sometimes to an even more conservative function such as RIPEMD-160. The following descriptions use the most generic form of the generator in order to avoid having to devote several pages to each generator's nuances.

6.3.1 The *Applied Cryptography* Generator

One of the simplest generators, shown in Figure 6.8, is presented in *Applied Cryptography* [10], and consists of a hash function such as MD5 combined with a counter value to create a pseudorandom byte stream generator running in counter mode with a 16-byte output. This generator has no entropy accumulator, a very simplistic state update function (the counter), and MD5 as the PRNG. The generator is very similar to the one used by Netscape and the RSAREF generator [38], and there may have been cross-pollination between the designs (the Netscape generator is practically identical to the RSAREF one, so it may have been inspired by that).

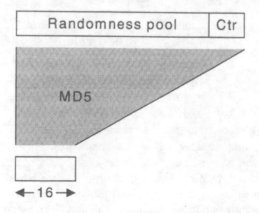

Figure 6.8. The *Applied Cryptography* generator.

This generator relies on the strength of the underlying hash function for security, and would be susceptible to a related-key attack since only one or two bits of input are changed for every block of output produced. A successful attack on this generator would also compromise the Netscape generator, which uses a similar technique and reveals the generator's previous output to an attacker. In contrast, the generator used in newer versions of BSAFE avoids this problem by adding a value of the same size as the generator state to ensure that a large portion of the state changes on each iteration. Specifically, the update process sets $state_{n+1} = state_n +$ (constant $\times n$), where the constant value is a fixed bit string initialised at startup [39].

6.3.2 The ANSI X9.17 Generator

The X9.17 generator [40] employs a combined state update function and PRNG, with no entropy accumulator. It relies on the triple DES encryption operation for its strength, as shown in Figure 6.9. The encryption step Enc_1 ensures that the timestamp that is employed as a seed value is spread over 64 bits and avoids the threat of a chosen-timestamp attack (for example, setting it to all-zero or all-one bits). The Enc_2 step acts as a one-way function for the generated encryption key, and the Enc_3 step acts as a one-way function for the encrypted seed value/internal state.

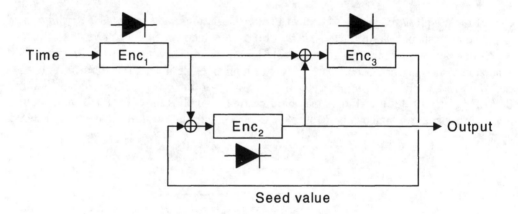

Figure 6.9. The ANSI X9.17 PRNG.

This generator has a problem in that the combined state update and PRNG steps make the internal state available to an attacker. This can occur, for example, when it is being used to generate a nonce that will be communicated in the clear. As a result, all of its security relies on the ability of the user to protect the value used to key the triple DES operation, and the hope that they will remember to change it from the factory-default all-zero key the first time that they use the device in which it is contained. This is a risky assumption to make. A better design would separate the two steps to prevent this problem from occurring.

6.3.3 The PGP 2.x Generator

PGP 2.x uses a slightly different method than that of X9.17 that involves "encrypting" the internal state with the MD5 compression function used as a CFB-mode stream cipher in a so-called message digest cipher (MDC) configuration [41]. The MDC construction turns a standard hash function into a block cipher by viewing the digest state (16 bytes or 128 bits for MD5) as the data block to be encrypted and the data to be hashed (64 bytes for MD5) as the encryption key. As with the X9.17 generator, this constitutes a combined state update function and PRNG.

The 64 bytes at the start of the randomness pool that constitutes the generator's internal state are used as the encryption key to transform successive 16-byte blocks of the pool by encrypting them with MDC. The initialisation vector (IV) that is used as the input to the first round of encryption is taken from the end of the pool, and the encryption proceeds down the pool until the entire pool has been processed. This process carries 128 bits of state (the IV) from one block to another, and is shown in Figure 6.10.

Once the pool contents have been mixed, the first 64 bytes are extracted to form the key for the next round of mixing, and the remainder of the pool is available for use by PGP. The pool itself is 384 bytes long, although other programs such as CryptDisk and Curve Encrypt for the Macintosh, which also use the PGP random pool management code, extend this to 512 bytes. PGP also preserves some randomness state between invocations of the program by storing a nonce on disk that is en/decrypted with a user-supplied key and injected into the randomness pool. This is a variation of the method used by the ANSI X9.17 generator, which utilises a user-supplied key and a timestamp as opposed to PGP's preserved state.

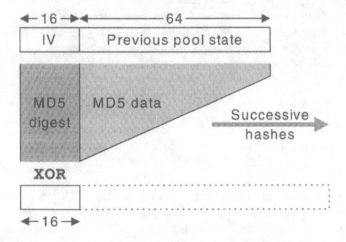

Figure 6.10. The PGP 2.x generator.

This generator exhibits something that will be termed the startup problem, in which processed data at the start of the pool (in other words the generator output) depends only on the initial data mixed in (the initial IV taken from the end of the pool will be all zeroes to start with). This means that data generated from or at the start of the pool is based on less entropy than data arising from further back in the pool, which will be affected by chaining of data from the start of the pool. This problem also affects a number of other generators, particularly those such as SSLeay/OpenSSL, covered in Section 6.3.8, that mix their data in very small, discrete blocks rather than trying to apply as much pool state as possible to each mixed data quantum. Because of this problem, newer versions of PGP and software that borrowed the PGP generator design, such as ssh, described in Section 6.3.7, perform a second pass over the pool for extra security and to ensure that data from the end of the pool has a chance to affect the start of the pool.

The pool management code allows random data to be read directly out of the pool with no protective PRNG stage for post-processing, and relies for its security on the fact that the previous pool contents, which are being used as the key for the MDC cipher, cannot be recovered. This problem is further exacerbated by the generator's startup problem. Direct access to the pool in this manner is rather dangerous since the slightest coding error could lead to a catastrophic failure in which the pool data is leaked to outsiders. A later version of the generator design, used in PGP 5.x and covered in Section 6.3.4, was changed to address this problem.

A problem with the implementation itself, which has been mentioned previously, is that the correct functioning of the PGP 2.x random number management code is not immediately obvious, making it difficult to spot design or implementation errors (at one point, the generator was redesigned and the code simplified because the developers could no longer understand the code with which they had been working). This led to problems such as the notorious xorbytes bug [42], in which a two-line function isolated from the rest of the code accidentally used a straight assignment operator in place of an xor-and-assign operator as shown in Figure 6.11. As a result, new data that was added overwrote existing data rather than being mixed into it through the XOR operation shown in Figure 6.10, resulting in no real increase in entropy over time, and possibly even a decrease if low-entropy data was added after high-entropy data had been added.

```
    while (len--)                    while (len--)
        *dest++ = *src++;                *dest++ ^= *src++;
```

Figure 6.11. The xorbytes bug (left) and corrected version (right).

Amazingly, the exact same bug occurred 8 years later in GPG, the logical successor to PGP [43]. Of interest to those who claim that the availability of source code guarantees security, this bug was present in the widely distributed source code of both PGP and GPG for a number of years before being discovered, and in the case of GPG was only discovered when someone happened to read through the code out of curiosity, rather than as the result of any conscious code review or audit.

6.3.4 The PGP 5.x Generator

PGP 5.x uses a slightly different update/mixing function that adds an extra layer of complexity to the basic PGP 2.x system. This retains the basic model used in PGP 2.x (with a key external to the randomness pool that constitutes the generator's internal state being used to mix the pool itself), but changes the hash function used for the MDC cipher from the compression function of MD5 to the compression function of SHA-1, the encryption mode from CFB to CBC, and adds feedback between the pool and the SHA-1 key data. The major innovation in this generator is that the added data is mixed in at a much earlier stage than in the PGP 2.x generator, being added directly to the key (where it immediately affects any further SHA-1-based mixing) rather than to the pool. The feedback of data from the pool to the key ensures that any sensitive material (such as a user passphrase) that is added isn't left lying in the key buffer in plaintext form.

In the generator pseudocode shown in Figure 6.12, the arrays are assumed to be arrays of bytes. Where a '32' suffix is added to the name, it indicates that the array is treated as an array of 32-bit words with index values appropriately scaled. In addition, the index values wrap back to the start of the arrays when they reach the end. Because of the complexity of the update process, it is not possible to represent it diagrammatically as with the other generators, so Figure 6.12 illustrates it as pseudocode.

```
pool[ 640 ], poolPos = 0;
key[ 64 ], keyPos = 0;

addByte( byte )
  {
  /* Update the key */
  key[ keyPos++ ] ^= byte;
  if( another 32-bit word accumulated )
    key32[ keyPos ] ^= pool32[ poolPos ];

  /* Update the pool */
  if( about 16 bits added to key )
    {
    /* Encrypt and perform IV-style block chaining */
    hash( pool[ poolPos ], key );
    pool[ next 16 bytes ] ^= pool[ current 16 bytes ];
    }
  }
```

Figure 6.12. The PGP 5.x Generator.

Once enough new data has been added to the key, the resulting key is used to MDC-encrypt the pool, ensuring that the pool data that was fed back to mask the newly added keying material is destroyed. The mechanism that is actually employed here is a digital differential analyser (DDA) that determines when enough new data has been added to make a (partial) state update necessary. This is analogous in function to the original DDA, which was used to determine when to perform an X or Y pixel increment when drawing a line on a graphics device. In this way, the entire pool is encrypted with a key that changes slightly for each block rather than a constant key, and the encryption takes place incrementally instead of using the monolithic state update technique preferred by other generators.

A second feature added by PGP 5.x is that the pool contents are not fed directly to the output but are first folded in half (a 20-byte SHA-1 output block has the high and low halves XORed together to produce a 10-byte result) and is then post-processed by a PRNG stage consisting of an X9.17 generator that uses Cast-128, PGP 5.x's default cipher, instead of triple DES. This ensures that an attacker can never obtain information about the internal generator state even if they can recover its output data. Since the X9.17 generator provides a 1:1 mapping of input to output, it can never reduce the entropy of its input. In addition, a separate X9.17 generator is used to generate non-cryptographically-strong random data for operations such as generating the public values used in discrete-logarithm-problem public keys such as Diffie–Hellman, DSA, and Elgamal, again helping to ensure that state information from the real generator is not leaked to an attacker. In terms of good, conservative designs, this generator is probably at the same level as the Capstone generator covered in Section 6.3.10.

6.3.5 The /dev/random Generator

Another generator inspired by the PGP 2.x design is the Unix /dev/random driver [44], of which a variant also exists for DOS. The driver was inspired by PGPfone (which seeded its generator from sampled audio data) and works by accumulating information such as keyboard and mouse timings and data, and hardware interrupt and block device timing information, which is supplied to it either by the Unix kernel or by hooking DOS interrupts. Since the sampling occurs during interrupt processing, it is essential that the mixing of the sample data into the pool be as efficient as possible (this was even more critical when it was used in PGPfone). For this reason the driver uses a CRC-like mixing function in place of the traditional hash function to mix the entropy data into the pool, with hashing only being done when data is extracted from the pool, as shown in Figure 6.13. Because the driver is in the kernel and is fed directly by data from system events, there is little chance of an attacker being able to feed it chosen input so there is far less need for a strong input mixing function than there is for other generators that have to be able to process user-supplied input.

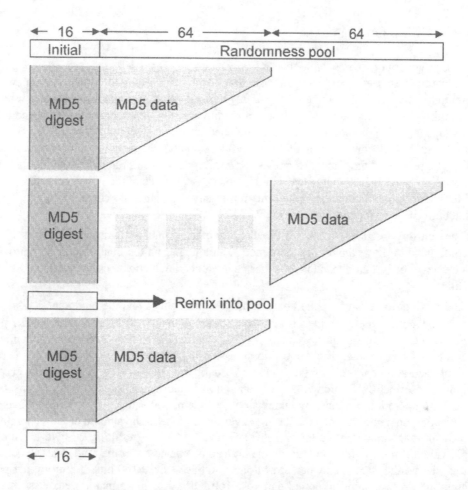

Figure 6.13. The /dev/random generator.

On extracting data, the driver hashes successive 64-byte blocks of the pool using the compression function of MD5 or SHA-1, mixes the resulting 16- or 20-byte hash back into the pool in the same way that standard input data is mixed in, hashes the first 64 bytes of the pool one more time to obscure the data which was fed back to the pool, and returns the final 16 or 20-byte hash to the caller. If more data is required, this process is iterated until the pool read request is satisfied. The driver makes two devices available, /dev/random which estimates the amount of entropy in the pool and only returns that many bits, and /dev/urandom which uses the PRNG described above to return as many bytes as the caller requests. This is another generator that combines the state update and PRNG functionality, although the final stage of hashing provides a reasonable amount of isolation when compared to designs such as those of X9.17 and PGP 2.x.

6.3.6 The Skip Generator

The Skip generator shares with the PGP generators a complex and convoluted update mechanism whose code takes some analysis to unravel. This generator consists of an entropy accumulator that reads the output of iostat, last, netstat, pstat, or vmstat (the target system is one running SunOS 4.x), and mixes it into a randomness pool that constitutes the generator's internal state. The use of such a small number of sources seems rather inadequate, for example last (which comes first in the code) produces output that is both relatively predictable and can be recovered days, months, or even years after the poll has run by examining the wtmp file, which is used as the input to last. In the worst case, if none of the polls succeed, the code will drop through and continue without mixing in any data, since no check on the amount of polled entropy is performed.

The entropy accumulator is followed by another combined state update and PRNG function, which follows the /dev/random model, although again the final hashing step provides a higher level of isolation than that of other generators, which combine the update and PRNG functions.

The mixing operation for polled data hashes the polled data and the randomness pool with SHA-1 and copies the resulting 20-byte hash back to the 20×20-byte randomness pool, cyclically overwriting one of the existing blocks. Unlike the earlier generators, this one uses the full SHA-1 hash rather than the raw compression function at its core, although this is done for implementation convenience rather than as a deliberate design feature as with the cryptlib generator described in Section 6.4. This operation is the initial one shown in Figure 6.14. The mixing operation continues by taking a copy of the previous hash state before the hashing was wrapped up and continuing the hashing over the 20-byte hash value, in effect generating a hash of the data shown in the lower half of Figure 6.14. The resulting 20-byte hash is the output value; if more output is required, the process is repeated over the randomness pool only (that is, the polling step is only performed once, adding at most 160 bits of entropy per poll). Although the reduction of all polled data to a 160-bit hash is not a major weakness (there is probably much less than 160 bits of entropy available from the polled sources), it would be desirable to take advantage of the full range of input entropy rather than restricting it to a maximum of 160 bits. In addition, only 20 bytes of the pool change each time the PRNG is stepped. Again, this isn't a major weakness, but it would be desirable to perturb the entire pool rather than just one small portion of it.

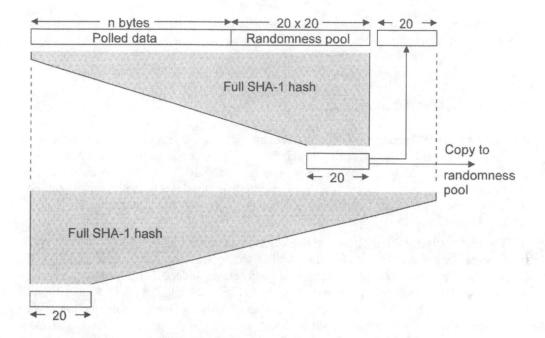

Figure 6.14. The Skip generator.

6.3.7 The ssh Generator

The ssh generator uses an entropy accumulator polling strategy similar to that of the Skip generator, employing the output of the ps, ls, w, and netstat commands [45]. These sources are even more predictable than those used by Skip, and the integrity of the polling process is threatened by a 30-second timeout on polling of all sources, a feature that was intended as a safety measure to prevent a slow-running source from halting ssh. This means that if a source blocks for any amount of time (in particular, if an attacker can cause ps, the first source, to block for at least 30 seconds), the code will continue without collecting any entropy.

The combined state update and PRNG is identical to the one used in newer versions of PGP 2.x, performing two passes of MDC mixing over a 1 kB pool and copying the internal pool contents directly to the output (although the first 64 bytes of pool data, which acts as the MDC key, is never copied out, and the two rounds of mixing avoid PGP 2.x's startup problem to some extent). In addition, the code makes no attempt to track the amount of entropy in the pool, so that it is possible that it could be running with minimal or even no entropy.

As with the Netscape generator, output from the ssh generator (in this case, 64 bits of its internal state) is sent out over the network when the server sends its anti-spoofing cookie as part of the SSH_SMSG_PUBLIC_KEY packet sent at the start of the ssh handshake process. It is thus possible to obtain arbitrary amounts of generator internal state information simply by repeatedly connecting to an ssh server. Less seriously, raw generator output is also used to pad messages, although recovering this would require compromising the encryption used to protect the session.

6.3.8 The SSLeay/OpenSSL Generator

The SSLeay/OpenSSL generator is the first one that uses more or less distinct state update and PRNG functions, although technically speaking it actually performs mixing both on data entry and egress, and doesn't truly separate the mixing on egress and PRNG functionality. Unlike most of the other generators, it contains no real entropy accumulator but relies almost entirely on data supplied by the user, a dangerous assumption whose problems are examined in Section 6.5.1.

The first portion of the generator is the randomness pool mixing function shown in Figure 6.15, which hashes a 20-byte hash value (initially set to all zeroes) and successive 20-byte blocks of a 1 kB randomness pool and user-supplied data to produce 20 bytes of output, which both become the next 20-byte hash value and are XORed back into the pool. Although each block of pool data is only affected by an equivalent-sized block of input data, the use of the hash state value means that some state information is carried across from previous blocks, although it would probably be preferable to hash more than a single 20-byte block to ensure that as much of the input as possible affects each output block. In particular, the generator suffers from an extreme case of the startup problem since the initial pool blocks are only affected by the initial input data blocks. When the generator is first initialised and the pool contains all zero bytes, the first 20 bytes of output are simply an SHA-1 hash of the first 20 bytes of user-supplied data.

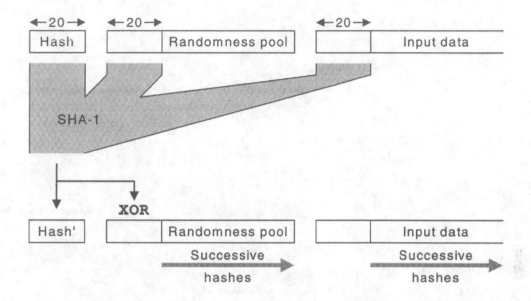

Figure 6.15. The SSLeay/OpenSSL generator's mixing function.

The second portion of the generator is the combined state update and PRNG function shown in Figure 6.16, which both mixes the pool and produces the generator's output. This works by hashing the second 10 bytes of the hash state value (the first 10 bytes remain constant and aren't used) and successive 1...10-byte blocks of the pool (the amount hashed depends on the number of output bytes requested). The first 10 bytes of the hash result are XORed back into the pool, and the remaining 10 bytes are provided as the generator's output and also reused as the new hash state. Again, apart from the 10-byte chaining value, all data blocks are completely independent.

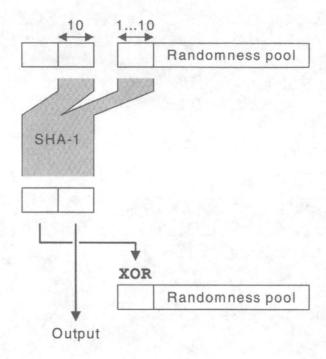

Figure 6.16. The SSLeay/OpenSSL generator's state update and PRNG function.

As used in SSLeay/OpenSSL, this generator shares with the ssh generator the flaw that it is possible for an attacker to suck infinite amounts of state information out of it by repeatedly connecting to the server, since it's used to create the 28-byte nonce (the SSL cookie/session ID) that is sent in the SSL server hello. In addition to this problem, the output also reveals the hash state (but not the pool state). The use on the client side is even more unsound, since it's used to first generate the client cookie that is sent in the SSL client hello and then immediately afterwards to generate the premaster secret from which all other cryptovariables are derived. What makes this practice even more dangerous is that, unlike the server, which has probably been running for some time so that the pool has been mixed repeatedly, clients are typically shut down and restarted as required. Combined with the generator's startup problem and (in older versions) the lack of entropy checking and possible lack of seeding described in Section 6.5.1, the first client hello sent by the client will reveal the generator seed data (or lack thereof) and hash state, and the premaster secret follows from this information.

This problem of revealing generator state information also occurs in the Netscape code, the SSLRef code which served as a reference implementation for SSL 3.0 (the cookie/session ID random data is actually initialised twice, the second initialisation overwriting the first one), and no doubt in any number of other SSL implementations. Part of the blame for this problem lies in the fact that both the original SSL specification [46] and later the TLS specification [47] specify that the cookies should be "generated by a secure random number generator" even though there is no need for this, and it can in fact be dangerously misleading for implementers. One book on SSL even goes to great lengths to emphasise that this (publicly-accessible) data should contain the output of a cryptographically strong generator and not simply a non-repeating nonce as is actually required [48].

Another problem, shared with the PGP generator, is the almost incomprehensible nature of the code that implements it, making it very difficult to analyse. For example, the generator contained a design flaw that resulted in it only feeding a small amount of random pool data (one to ten bytes) into the state update/PRNG function, but this wasn't discovered and corrected until July 2001 [49]. This problem, combined with the fact that the hash state from the PRNG stage is made available as the generator output as described above, would allow an attacker to recover the generator's internal state by making repeated 1-byte requests to the generator, which would respond with a hash of the (known) hash state and successive bytes of the randomness pool.

6.3.9 The CryptoAPI Generator

The CryptoAPI generator is the first one that completely separates the state update and PRNG functionality. The original design describes a state update stage, which hashes polled data using SHA-1, and a PRNG stage, which uses the SHA-1 output to key an RC4 stream cipher, as shown in Figure 6.17. The polled data consists of the traditional time and process ID and a few relatively poor additional sources such as the system's current memory and disk usage. The static data consists of the previous hash output recycled for further use [50]. The exact nature of this recycling isn't known, although it is saved to disk (in the Windows registry under HKEY_LOCAL_MACHINE\System\CurrentControlSet\Control\SecurityProviders\-SCHANNEL\RNGSeed and HKEY_CURRENT_USER\Software\Microsoft\Cryptography\-UserKeys*container_name*) and never updated once created. Unlike PGP, the preserved state doesn't appear to be protected by a user password.

A later description mentions the use of somewhat more entropy sources than in the earlier one, but erroneously states that the generator uses MD4 instead of SHA-1 [51]. A correction to this description mentions a significantly larger list of entropy sources, and the use of SHA-1 in a FIPS 186-2 configuration. There is some uncertainty as to the true nature of this generator, since it appears to have changed somewhat over time, although later versions have been considerably improved.

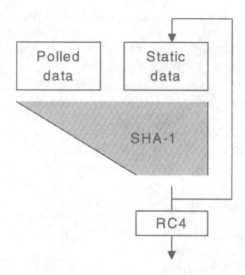

Figure 6.17. The CryptoAPI generator.

This generator in its original form is, at best, adequate. The static data saved to disk isn't password-protected like the PGP seed and in any case is never updated once created, and the polled data doesn't provide much entropy, particularly if the generator is seeded at system startup, which is typically the case as some Windows system components make use of CryptoAPI during the boot phase. Later versions of the generator appear to correct the problem with polled entropy. However, no steps are taken to mitigate problems such as the fact that RC4 exhibits correlations between its key and the initial bytes of its output [52][53][54][55] as well as having statistical weaknesses [56][57][58][59][60], resulting in the generator leaking part of its internal state in the first few bytes of PRNG output or producing slightly predictable output during its operation.

6.3.10 The Capstone/Fortezza Generator

The generator used with the Capstone chip (which presumably is the same as the one used in the Fortezza card) is shown in Figure 6.18. This is a nice conservative design that employs all three of the recommended accumulator, state update, and output processing stages. In addition, the generator utilises a variety of sources and mechanisms so that even if one mechanism fails, an adequate safety margin will be provided by the remaining mechanisms. The main feature of this generator is the incorporation of an X9.17-like generator that utilises Skipjack in place of triple DES and is fed from some form of (currently unknown) physical randomness source in place of X9.17's time value [61]. Since the randomness source provides a full 64 bits of entropy, there is no need for the input encryption operation that is required in the X9.17 generator to spread the time value over the entire 64 bits of data (the 224 bits of output correspond to 3½ Skipjack blocks).

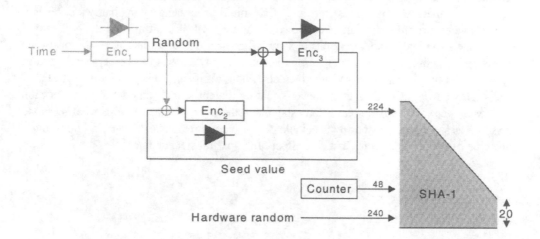

Figure 6.18. The Capstone/Fortezza generator.

In addition to the X9.17-like generator, this generator takes 240 bits of entropy directly from the physical source and also mixes in the output of a 48-bit counter, which guarantees that some input to the following hashing step will still change even if the physical source somehow gets stuck at a single output value.

Finally, the entire collection of inputs is fed through SHA-1. This constitutes the post-processing stage which is required to mix the bits and ensure that an attacker can never see any internal state information. Alternatively, if an attacker could (somehow) compromise the SHA-1 step, a means of attacking the X9.17 generator which feeds it they would still have to be found. As has been mentioned above, this is a good, conservative design that uses redundant sources to protect against the failure of any single input source, uses multiple dissimilar sources so that an attack that is effective against one particular source has less chance of compromising the others, and protects its internal state against observation by attackers[1]. A design that is very similar to the one used in the Capstone generator is employed in a generator presented in the open literature that dates from roughly the same time period [12].

Because further details of its usage are not available, it is not known whether the generator as used in the Fortezza card is used in a safe manner or not; for example, the card provides the function CI_GenerateRandom() which appears to provide direct access to the SHA-1 output and would therefore allow an attacker to obtain arbitrary amounts of generator output for analysis.

---

[1] As with literature analysis, it is possible that some of the meaning being read into this would surprise the original authors of the work. Unfortunately, the rationale for the Capstone/Fortezza generator design has never been made public.

6.3.11 The Intel Generator

The generator that is available with some chipsets used with the Intel Pentium III (and newer) CPUs samples thermal noise in resistors and, after initial processing by the hardware, feeds it to the software portion of the generator shown in Figure 6.19. Each time that the generator's internal state is updated, another 32 bits of sampled noise are injected into it, ready for use on the next update, ensuring that further entropy is continuously added to the generator as it runs. Details of the physical noise source are given elsewhere [62][63]. This generator uses SHA-1 as a complex partial mixing function, never updating the entire state and discarding a portion of it at each step. There is no real PRNG stage, and the overall design is somewhat messy to analyse — a single-source entropy accumulator, an incomplete state update function, and a vague type of PRNG that occurs as a side effect of the partial state update.

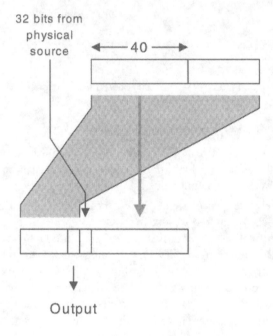

Figure 6.19. The Intel Pentium III generator.

The use of a single source for the entropy accumulator makes this generator slightly less conservative than the Capstone/Fortezza one, since a failure of the physical source at some point after it has passed the FIPS 140 tests applied at power-up would result in the generator eternally recycling its internal state, or at least a truncated portion thereof. This might occur if the generator functions correctly when cold (immediately after power-up, when the FIPS 140 tests are applied) but fails in some way once the system warms up.

The existing Pentium III unique serial number capability could be extended to provide a backup source of input for the entropy accumulator by storing with each processor a unique value (which, unlike the processor ID, cannot be read externally) that is used to drive some form of generator equivalent to the X9.17-like generator used in the Capstone/Fortezza generator, supplementing the existing physical randomness source. In the simplest case, one or more linear feedback shift registers (LFSRs) driven from the secret value would serve to supplement the physical source while consuming an absolute minimum of die real estate. Although the use of SHA-1 in the output protects the relatively insecure LFSRs, an extra safety margin could be provided through the addition of a small amount of extra circuitry to implement an enhanced LFSR-based generator such as a stop-and-go generator [64], which, like the basic LFSR generator, can be implemented with a fairly minimal transistor count.

In addition, like various other generators, this generator reveals a portion of its internal state every time that it is used because of the lack of a real PRNG post-processing stage. Since a portion of the generator state is already being discarded each time it is stepped, it would have been better to avoid recycling the output data into the internal state. Currently, two 32-bit blocks of previous output data are present in each set of internal state data.

6.4 The cryptlib Generator

Now that we have examined several generator designs and the various problems that they can run into, we can look at the cryptlib generator. This section mostly covers the random pool management and PRNG post-processing functionality, the entropy accumulation process is covered in Section 6.5.

6.4.1 The Mixing Function

The function used in this generator improves on the generally used style of mixing function by incorporating far more state than the 128 or 160 bits used by other code. The mixing function is again based on a one-way hash function (in which role MD5 or SHA-1 are normally employed) and works by treating the randomness pool as a circular buffer and using the hash function to process the data in the pool. Unlike many other generators that use the randomness-pool style of design, this generator explicitly uses the full hash (rather than just the core compression function) since the raw compression function is somewhat more vulnerable to attack than the full hash [65][66][67][68].

Assuming the use of a hash with a 20-byte output such as SHA-1 or RIPEMD-160, we hash the $20 + 64$ bytes at locations $n - 20 \ldots n + 63$ and then write the resulting 20-byte hash to locations $n \ldots n + 19$. The chaining that is performed explicitly by mixing functions such as those of PGP/ssh and SSLeay/OpenSSL is performed implicitly here by including the previously processed 20 bytes in the input to the hash function, as shown in Figure 6.20. We then move forward 20 bytes and repeat the process, wrapping the input around to the start of the pool when the end of the pool is reached. The overlapping of the data input to each hash means that each 20-byte block that is processed is influenced by all of the surrounding bytes.

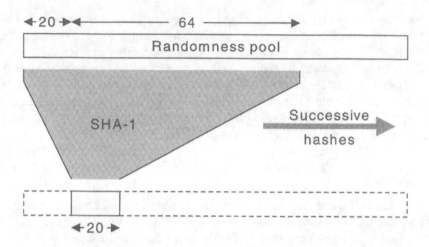

Figure 6.20. The cryptlib generator.

This process carries 672 bits of state information with it, and means that every byte in the pool is directly influenced by the 20 + 64 bytes surrounding it and indirectly influenced by every other byte in the pool, although it may take several iterations of mixing before this indirect influence is fully felt. This is preferable to alternative schemes that involve encrypting the data with a block cipher using block chaining, since most block ciphers carry only 64 bits of state along with them, and even the MDC construction only carries 128 or 160 bits of state.

The pool management code keeps track of the current write position in the pool. When a new data byte arrives from the entropy accumulator, it is added to the byte at the current write position in the pool, the write position is advanced by one, and, when the end of the pool is reached, the entire pool is remixed using the state update function described above. Since the amount of data that is gathered by the entropy accumulator's randomness polling process is quite considerable, we don't have to perform the input masking that is used in the PGP 5.x generator because a single randomness poll will result in many iterations of pool mixing as all of the polled data is added.

6.4.2 Protection of Pool Output

Data removed from the pool is not read out in the byte-by-byte manner in which it is added. Instead, the entire data amount is extracted in a single block, which leads to a security problem: If an attacker can recover one of these data blocks, comprising m bytes of an n-byte pool, the amount of entropy left in the pool is only $n - m$ bytes, which violates the design requirement that an attacker be unable to recover any of the generator's state by observing its output. This is particularly problematic in cases such as some discrete-log-based PKCs in which the pool provides data for first public and then private key values, because an attacker will have access to the output used to generate the public parameters and can then use this output to try to derive the private value(s).

One solution to this problem is to use a second generator such as an X9.17 generator to protect the contents of the pool as done by PGP 5.x. In this way the key is derived from the pool contents via a one-way function. The solution that we use is a slight variation on this theme. What we do is mix the original pool to create the new pool and invert every bit in a copy of the original pool and mix that to create the output data. It may be desirable to tune the operation used to transform the pool to match the hash function, depending on the particular function being used; for example, SHA-1 performs a complex XOR-based "key schedule" on the input data, which could potentially lead to problems if the transformation consists of XOR-ing each input word with 0xFFFFFFFF. In this case, it might be preferable to use some other form of operation such as a rotate and XOR, or the CRC-type function used by the /dev/random driver. If the pool were being used as the key for a DES-based mixing function, it would be necessary to adjust for weak keys; other mixing methods might require the use of similar precautions.

This method should be secure provided that the hash function that we use meets its design goal of preimage resistance and is a random function (that is, no polynomial-time algorithm exists to distinguish the output of the function from random strings). The resulting generator is very similar to the triple-DES-based ANSI X9.17 generator, but replaces the keyed triple-DES operations with an unkeyed one-way hash function, producing the same effect as the X9.17 generator, as shown in Figure 6.21 (compare this with Figure 6.9).

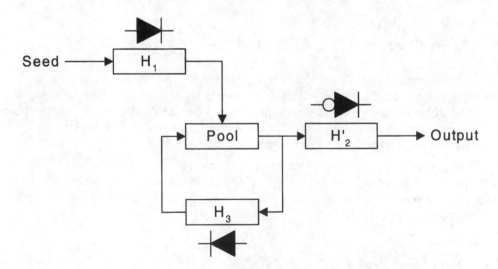

Figure 6.21. cryptlib generator equivalence to the X9.17 PRNG.

In this generator model, H_1 mixes the input and prevents chosen-input attacks, H'_2 acts as a one-way function for the output to ensure that an attacker never has access to the raw pool contents, and H_3 acts as a one-way function for the internal state. This design is therefore functionally similar to that of X9.17, but contains significantly more internal state and doesn't require the use of a rather slow triple-DES implementation and the secure storage of an encryption key.

6.4.3 Output Post-processing

The post-processed pool output is not sent directly to the caller but is first passed through an X9.17 PRNG that is rekeyed every time a certain number of output blocks have been produced with it, with the currently active key being destroyed. Since the X9.17 generator produces a 1:1 mapping, it can never make the output any worse, and it provides an extra level of protection for the generator output (as well as making it easier to obtain FIPS 140 certification). Using the generator in this manner is valid since X9.17 requires the use of DT, "a date/time vector which is updated on each key generation", and cryptlib chooses to represent this value as a complex hash of assorted incidental data and the date and time. The fact that 99.9999% of the value of the X9.17 generator is coming from the "timestamp" is as coincidental as the side effect of the engine-cooling fan in the Brabham ground-effect cars [69].

As an additional precaution to protect the X9.17 generator output, we use the technique which is also used in PGP 5.x of folding the output in half so that we don't reveal even the triple-DES encrypted one-way hash of a no longer existing version of the pool contents to an attacker.

6.4.4 Other Precautions

To avoid the startup problem, the generator will not produce any output unless the entire pool has been mixed at least ten times, although the large amount of internal state data applied to each hashed block during the state update process and the fact that the entropy accumulation process contributes tens of kilobytes of data, resulting in many update operations being run, ameliorates the startup problem to some extent anyway.

If the generator is asked to produce output and less than ten update operations have been performed, it mixes the pool (while adding further entropy at each iteration) until the minimum update count has been reached. As with a Feistel cipher, each round of mixing adds to the diffusion of entropy data across the entire pool.

6.4.5 Nonce Generation

Alongside the CSPRNG, cryptlib also provides a mechanism for generating nonces when random, but not necessarily cryptographically strong random, data is required. This mechanism is used to generate initialisation vectors (IVs), nonces and cookies used in protocols such as ssh and SSL/TLS, random padding data, and data for other at-risk situations in which secure random data isn't required and shouldn't be used.

Some thought needs to go into the exact requirements for each nonce. Should it be simply fresh (for which a monotonically increasing sequence will do), random (for which a hash of the sequence is adequate), or entirely unpredictable? Depending upon the manner in which it is employed, any of the above options may be sufficient [70]. In order to avoid potential problems arising from inadvertent use of a nonce with the wrong properties, cryptlib uses unpredictable nonces in all cases, even where it isn't strictly necessary.

The implementation of the nonce generator is fairly straightforward, and consists of 20 bytes of public state and 64 bits of private state data. The first time that the nonce generator is used, the private state data is seeded with 64 bits of output from the CSPRNG. Each time that the nonce PRNG is stepped, the overall state data is hashed and the result copied back to the public state and also produced as output. The private state data affects the hashing, but is never copied to the output. The use of this very simple alternative generator where such use is appropriate guarantees that an application is never put in a situation where it acts as an oracle for an opponent attacking the real PRNG. A similar precaution is used in PGP 5.x.

6.4.6 Generator Continuous Tests

Another safety feature that, although it is more of a necessity for a hardware-based generator, is also a useful precaution when used with a software-based generator, is to continuously run the generator output through whatever statistical tests are feasible under the circumstances to at least try to detect a catastrophic failure of the generator. To this end, NIST has designed a series of statistical tests that are tuned for catching certain types of errors that can crop up in random number generators, ranging from the relatively simple frequency and runs tests to detect the presence of too many zeroes or ones and too small or too large a number of runs of bits, through to more obscure problems such as spectral tests to determine the presence of periodic features in the bit stream and random excursion tests to detect deviations from the distribution of the number of random walk visits to a certain state [71]. Heavy-duty tests of this nature and those mentioned in Section 6.6.1, and even the FIPS 140 tests, assume the availability of a huge (relative to, say, a 128-bit key) amount of generator output and consume a considerable amount of CPU time, making them impractical in this situation. However, by changing slightly how the tests are applied, we can still use them as a failsafe test on the generator output without either requiring a large amount of output or consuming a large amount of CPU time.

The main problem with performing a test on a small quantity of data is that we are likely to encounter an artificially high rejection rate for otherwise valid data due to the small size of the sample. However, since we can draw arbitrary quantities of output from the generator, all we have to do is repeat the tests until the output passes. If the output repeatedly fails the testing process, we report a failure in the generator and halt. The testing consists of a cut-down version of the FIPS 140 statistical tests, as well as a modified form of the FIPS 140 continuous test that compares the first 32 bits of output against the first 32 bits of output from the last few samples taken, which detects stuck-at faults (it would have caught the JDK 1.1 flaw mentioned in Section 6.1) and short cycles in the generator.

Given that most of the generators in use today use MD5 or SHA-1 in their PRNG, applying FIPS 140 and similar tests to their output falls squarely into the warm fuzzy (some might say wishful thinking) category, but it will catch catastrophic failure cases that would otherwise go undetected. Without this form of safety-net, problems such as stuck-at faults may be detected only by chance, or not at all. For example, the author is aware of one security product where the fact that the PRNG wasn't RNG-ing was only detected by the fact that a DES key load later failed because the key parity bits for an all-zero key weren't being adjusted correctly, and a US crypto hardware product that always produced the same "random" number that was apparently never detected by the vendor.

6.4.7 Generator Verification

Cryptovariables such as keys lie at the heart of any cryptographic system and must be generated by a random number generator of guaranteed quality and security. If the generation process is insecure, then even the most sophisticated protection mechanisms in the architecture will do no good. More precisely, the cryptovariable generation process must be subject to the same high level of assurance as the kernel itself if the architecture is to meet its overall design goals.

Because of this requirement, the cryptlib generator is built using the same design and verification principles that are applied to the kernel. Every line of code that is involved in cryptovariable generation is subject to the verification process used for the kernel, to the extent that there is more verification code present in the generator than implementation code.

The work carried out by the generator is slightly more complex than the kernel's application of filter rules, so that in addition to verifying the flow-of-control processing as is done in the kernel, the generator code also needs to be checked to ensure that it correctly processes the data flowing through it. Consider for example the pool-processing mechanism described in Section 6.4.2, which inverts every bit in the pool and remixes it to create the intermediate output (which is then fed to the X9.17 post-processor before being folded in half and passed on to the user), while remixing the original pool contents to create the new pool. There are several steps involved here, each of which needs to be verified. First, after the bit-flipping, we need to check that the new pool isn't the same as the old pool (which would indicate that the bit-flipping process had failed) and that the difference between the old and new pools is that the bits in the new pool are flipped (which indicates that the transformation being applied is a bit-flip and not some other type of operation).

Once this check has been performed, the old and new pools are mixed. This is a separate function that is itself subject to the verification process, but which won't be described here for space reasons. After the mixing has been completed, the old and new pools are again compared to ensure that they differ, and that the difference is more than just the fact that one consists of a bit-flipped version of the other (which would indicate that the mixing process had failed). The verification checks for just this portion of code are shown in Figure 6.22.

This operation is then followed by the others described earlier, namely continuous sampling of generator output to detect stuck-at faults, post-processing using the X9.17

generator, and folding of the output fed to the user to mask the generator output. These steps are subject to the usual verification process.

```
/* Make the output pool the inverse of the original pool */
for( i = 0; i < RANDOMPOOL_SIZE; i++ )
  outputPool[ i ] = randomPool[ i ] ^ 0xFF;

/* Verify that the two pools differ, and the difference is in the flipped
   bits */
PRE( forall( i, 0, RANDOMPOOL_SIZE ),
     randomPool[ i ] != outputPool[ i ] );
PRE( forall( i, 0, RANDOMPOOL_SIZE ),
     randomPool[ i ] == ( outputPool[ i ] ^ 0xFF ) );

/* Mix the two pools so that neither can be recovered from the other */
mixRandomPool( randomPool );
mixRandomPool( outputPool );

/* Verify that the two pools differ, and that the difference is more than
   just the bit flipping (1/2^128 chance of false positive) */
POST( memcmp( randomPool, outputPool, RANDOMPOOL_SIZE ) );
POST( exists( i, 0, 16 ),
      randomPool[ i ] != ( outputPool[ i ] ^ 0xFF ) );
```

Figure 6.22. Verification of the pool processing mechanism.

As the description above indicates, the generator is implemented in a very careful (more precisely, paranoid) manner. In addition to the verification, every mechanism in the generator is covered by one (or more) redundant backup mechanisms, so that a failure in one area won't lead to a catastrophic loss in security (an unwritten design principle was that any part of the generator should be able to fail completely without affecting its overall security). Although the effects of this high level of paranoia would be prohibitive if carried through to the entire security architecture, it is justified in this case because of the high value of the data being processed and because the amount of data processed and the frequency with which it is processed is quite low, so that the effects of multiple layers of processing and checking aren't felt by the user.

6.4.8 System-specific Pitfalls

The discussion of generators has so far focused on generic issues such as the choice of pool mixing function and the need to protect the pool state. In addition to these issues, there are also system-specific problems that can beset the generator. The most serious of these arises from the use of fork() under Unix. The effect of calling fork() in an application that uses the generator is to create two identical copies of the pool in the parent and child processes, resulting in the generation of identical cryptovariables in both processes, as shown in Figure 6.23. A fork can occur at any time while the generator is active and can be repeated arbitrarily, resulting in potentially dozens of copies of identical pool information being active.

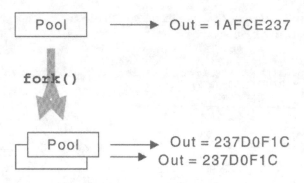

Figure 6.23. Random number generation after a fork.

Fixing this problem is a lot harder than it would first appear. One approach is to implement the generator as a stealth dæmon inside the application. This would fork off another process that maintains the pool and communicates with the parent via some form of IPC mechanism safe from any further interference by the parent. This is a less than ideal solution both because the code the user is calling probably shouldn't be forking off dæmons in the background and because the complex nature of the resulting code increases the chance of something going wrong somewhere in the process.

An alternative is to add the current process ID to the pool contents before mixing it, however this suffers both from the minor problem that the resulting pools before mixing will be identical in most of their contents and if a poor mixing function is used will still be mostly identical afterwards, and from the far more serious problem that it still doesn't reliably solve the forking problem because if the fork is performed from another thread after the pool has been mixed but before randomness is drawn from the pool, the parent and child will still be working with identical pools. This situation is shown in Figure 6.24. The exact nature of the problem changes slightly depending on which threading model is used. The Posix threading semantics stipulate that only the thread that invoked the fork is copied into the forked process so that an existing thread that is working with the pool won't suddenly find itself duplicated into a child process, however other threading models copy all of the threads into the child so that an existing thread could indeed end up cloned and drawing identical data from both pool copies.

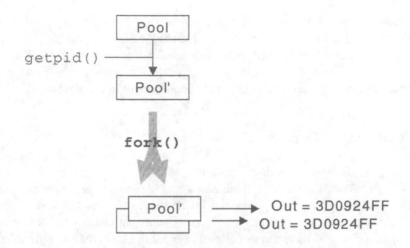

Figure 6.24. Random number generator with attempted compensation for forking.

The only way to reliably solve this problem is to borrow a technique from the field of transaction processing and use a two-phase commit (2PC) to extract data from the pool. In a 2PC, an application prepares the data and announces that it is ready to perform the transaction. If all is OK, the transaction is then committed; otherwise, it is rolled back and its effects are undone [72][73][74].

To apply 2PC to the problem at hand, we mix the pool as normal, producing the required generator output as the first phase of the 2PC protocol. Once this phase is complete, we check the process ID, and if it differs from the value obtained previously, we know that the process has forked, that we are the child, and that we need to update the pool contents to ensure that they differ from the copy still held by the parent process, which is equivalent to aborting the transaction and retrying it. If the process ID hasn't changed, then the transaction is committed and the generator output is returned to the caller.

These gyrations to protect the integrity of the pool's precious bodily fluids are further complicated by the fact that it isn't possible to reliably determine the process ID (or at least whether a process has forked) on many systems. For example, under Linux, the concept of processes and threads is rather blurred (with the degree of blurring changing with different kernel versions) so that each thread in a process may have its own process ID, resulting in continuous false triggering of the 2PC's abort mechanism in multithreaded applications. The exact behaviour of processes versus threads varies across systems and kernel versions so that it's not possible to extrapolate a general solution based on a technique that happens to work with one system and kernel version.

Luckily the most widely used Unix threading implementation, Posix pthreads, provides the `pthread_atfork()` function, which acts as a trigger that fires before and after a process forks. Strictly speaking, this precaution isn't necessary for fully compliant Posix threads implementations for the reason noted earlier; however, this assumes that all implementations are fully compliant with the Posix specification, which may not be the case for some almost-

Posix implementations (there exists, for example, one implementation which in effect maps `pthread_atfork()` to `coredump`). Other threading models require the use of functions specific to the particular threading API. By using this function on multithreaded systems and `getpid()` on non-multithreaded systems we can reliably determine when a process has forked so that we can then take steps to adjust the pool contents in the child.

6.4.9 A Taxonomy of Generators

We can now rank the generators discussed above in terms of unpredictability of output, as shown in Figure 6.25. At the top are those based on sampling physical sources, which have the disadvantage that they require dedicated hardware in order to function. Immediately following them are the best that can be done without employing specialised hardware, generators that poll as many sources as possible in order to obtain data to add to the internal state and from there to a PRNG or other postprocessor. Following this are simpler polling-based generators that rely on a single entropy source, and behind this are more and more inadequate generators that use, in turn, secret nonces and a postprocessor, secret constants and a postprocessor, known values and a postprocessor, and eventually known values and a simple randomiser. Finally, generators that rely on user-supplied values for entropy input can cover a range of possibilities. In theory, they could be using multi-source polling, but in practice they tend to end up down with the known value + postprocessor generators.

Combined physical source, generator and secret nonce + postprocessor	Capstone/Fortezza
Physical source + postprocessor	Intel Pentium III RNG
	Various other hardware generators
Multi-source entropy accumulator + generator + postprocessor	Cryptlib
Single-source entropy accumulator + generator + postprocessor	PGP 5.x
	PGP 2.x
	Skip
	CryptoAPI
	/dev/random
Secret nonce + postprocessor	Applied Cryptography
Secret fixed value + postprocessor	ANSI X9.17
Known value + postprocessor	Netscape
	Kerberos V4
	Sesame
	NFS file handles
	… and many more

Figure 6.25. A taxonomy of generators.

6.5 The Entropy Accumulator

Once we have taken care of the basic pool management code, we need to fill the pool with random data. There are two ways to do this; either to rely on the user to supply appropriate data or to collect the data ourselves. The former approach is particularly popular in crypto and security toolkits since it conveniently unloads the really hard part of the process of random number generation (obtaining entropy for the generator) on the user. Unfortunately, relying on user-supplied data generally doesn't work, as the following section shows.

6.5.1 Problems with User-Supplied Entropy

Experience with users of crypto and security toolkits and tools has shown that they will typically go to any lengths to avoid having to provide useful entropy to a random number generator that relies on user seeding. The first widely known case where this occurred was with the Netscape generator, whose functioning with inadequate input required the disabling of safety checks that were designed to prevent this problem from occurring [75]. A more recent example of this phenomenon was provided by an update to the SSLeay/OpenSSL generator, which in version 0.9.5 had a simple check added to the code to test whether any entropy had been added to the generator (earlier versions would run the PRNG with little or no real entropy). This change led to a flood of error reports to OpenSSL developers, as well as helpful suggestions on how to solve the problem, including seeding the generator with a constant text string [76][77][78], seeding it with DSA public-key components (whose components look random enough to fool entropy checks) before using it to generate the corresponding private key [79], seeding it with consecutive output byes from rand() [80], using the executable image [81], using /etc/passwd [82], using /var/log/syslog [83], using a hash of the files in the current directory [84], creating a dummy random data file and using it to fool the generator [85], downgrading to an older version such as 0.9.4 that doesn't check for correct seeding [86], using the output of the unseeded generator to seed the generator (by the same person who had originally solved the problem by downgrading to 0.9.4, after it was pointed out that this was a bad idea) [87], and using the string "0123456789ABCDEF0" [78]. Another alternative, suggested in a Usenet news posting, was to patch the code to disable the entropy check and allow the generator to run on empty (this magical fix has since been independently rediscovered by others [88]). In later versions of the code that used /dev/-random if it was present on the system, another possible fix was to open a random disk file and let the code read from that, thinking that it was reading the randomness device [89]. It is likely that considerably more effort and ingenuity has been expended towards seeding the generator incorrectly than ever went into doing it right.

The problem of inadequate seeding of the generator became so common that a special entry was added to the OpenSSL frequently asked questions (FAQ) list telling users what to do when their previously-fine application stopped working when they upgraded to version 0.9.5 [90]. Since this still didn't appear to be enough, later versions of the code were changed to display the FAQ's URL in the error message that was printed when the PRNG wasn't seeded. Based on comments on the OpenSSL developers list, quite a number of third-party applications that used the code were experiencing problems with the improved random number handling code in the new release, indicating that they were working with low-security cryptovariables and probably had been doing so for years. Because of this problem, a good basis for an attack on an application based on a version of SSLeay/OpenSSL before 0.9.5 is to assume that the PRNG was never seeded, and for versions after 0.9.5 to assume that it was seeded with the string "string to make the random number generator think it has entropy", a value that appeared in one of the test programs included with the code and which appears to be a favourite of users trying to make the generator "work".

The fact that this section has concentrated on SSLeay/OpenSSL seeding is not meant as a criticism of the software, the change in 0.9.5 merely served to provide a useful indication of how widespread the problem of inadequate initialisation really is. Helpful advice on bypassing the seeding of other generators (for example the one in the Java JCE) has appeared on other mailing lists. The practical experience provided by cases such as those given above shows how dangerous it is to rely on users to correctly initialise a generator — not only will they not perform it correctly, but they will go out of their way to do it wrong. Although there is nothing much wrong with the SSLeay/OpenSSL generator itself, the fact that its design assumes that users will initialise it correctly means that it (and many other user-seeded generators) will in many cases not function as required. It is therefore imperative that a generator handle not only the state update and PRNG steps but also the entropy accumulation step itself (while still providing a means of accepting user entropy data for those users who bother to initialise the generator correctly).

6.5.2 Entropy Polling Strategy

The polling process uses two methods: a fast randomness poll, which executes very quickly and gathers as much random (or apparently random) information as quickly as possible, and a slow poll, which can take a lot longer than the fast poll but performs a more in-depth search for sources of random data. The data sources that we use for the generator are chosen to be reasonably safe from external manipulation, since an attacker who tries to modify them to provide predictable input to the generator will either require superuser privileges (which would allow them to bypass any security anyway) or would crash the system when they change operating system data structures.

The sources used by the fast poll are fairly consistent across systems and typically involve obtaining constantly changing information covering mouse, keyboard, and window states, system timers, thread, process, memory, disk, and network usage details, and assorted other paraphernalia maintained and updated by most operating systems. A fast poll completes very quickly, and gathers a reasonable amount of random information. Scattering these polls throughout the application that will eventually use the random data (in the form of keys or other security-related objects) is a good move, or alternatively they can be embedded inside other functions in a security module so that even careless programmers will (unknowingly) perform fast polls at some point. No-one will ever notice that an SSL connection takes a few extra microseconds to establish due to the embedded fast poll, and although the presence of the more thorough slow polls may make it slightly superfluous, performing a number of effectively free fast polls can never hurt.

There are two general variants of the slower randomness-polling mechanism, with individual operating-system-specific implementations falling into one of the two groups. The first variant is used with operating systems that provide a rather limited amount of useful information, which tends to coincide with less sophisticated systems that have little or no memory protection and have difficulty performing the polling as a background task or thread. These systems include Win16 (Windows 3.x), the Macintosh, and (to some extent) OS/2, in which the slow randomness poll involves walking through global and system data structures recording information such as handles, virtual addresses, data item sizes, and the large amount of other information typically found in these data structures.

The second variant of the slow polling process is used with operating systems that protect their system and global data structures from general access, but which provide a large amount of other information in the form of system, network, and general usage statistics, and also allow background polling, which means that we can take as long as we like (within reasonable limits) to obtain the information that we require. These systems include Win32 (Windows 95/98/ME and Windows NT/2000/XP), BeOS, and Unix.

In addition some systems may be able to take advantage of special hardware capabilities as a source of random data. An example of this situation is the Tandem hardware, which includes a large number of hardware performance counters that continually monitor CPU, network, disk, and general message passing and other I/O activity. Simply reading some of these counters will change their values, since one of the things that they are measuring is the amount of CPU time consumed in reading them. When running on Tandem hardware, these heisencounters provide an ideal source of entropy for the generator.

6.5.3 Win16 Polling

Win16 provides a fair amount of information since it makes all system and process data structures visible to the user through the ToolHelp library, which means that we can walk down the list of global heap entries, system modules and tasks, and other data structures. Since even a moderately loaded system can contain over 500 heap objects and 50 modules, we need to limit the duration of the poll to a second or two, which is enough to get information on several hundred objects without halting the calling program for an unacceptable amount of time (under Win16, the poll will indeed lock up the machine until it completes).

6.5.4 Macintosh and OS/2 Polling

Similarly, on the Macintosh we can walk through the list of graphics devices, processes, drivers, and filesystem queues to obtain our information. Since there are typically only a few dozen of these, there is no need to worry about time limits. Under OS/2, there is almost no information available, so even though the operating system provides the capability to do so, there is little to be gained by performing the poll in the background. Unfortunately, this lack of random data also provides us with even less information than that provided by Win16.

6.5.5 BeOS Polling

The polling process under BeOS again follows the model established by the Win16 poll in which we walk the lists of threads, memory areas, OS primitives such as message ports and semaphores, and so on to obtain our entropy. BeOS provides a standard API for enumerating each of these sources, so the polling process is very straightforward. In addition to these sources, BeOS also provides other information such as a status flag indicating whether the system is powered on and whether the CPU is on fire or not; however, these sources suffer from being relatively predictable to an attacker since BeOS is rarely run on original 5V Pentium CPUs, and aren't useful for our purposes.

6.5.6 Win32 Polling

The Win32 polling process has two special cases, a Windows 95/98/ME version that uses the ToolHelp32 functions, which don't exist under earlier versions of Windows NT, and a Windows NT/2000/XP version, which uses the NetAPI32 functions and performance data information, which don't exist under Windows 95/98/ME. In order for the same code to run under both systems, we need to dynamically link in the appropriate routines at runtime using GetModuleHandle() or LoadLibrary() or the program won't load under one or both of the environments.

Once we have the necessary functions linked in, we can obtain the data that we require from the system. Under Windows 95/98/ME the ToolHelp32 functions provide more or less the same functionality as those for Win16 (with a few extras added for Win32), which means that we can walk through the local heap, all processes and threads in the system, and all loaded modules. A typical poll on a moderately loaded machine nets 5–15 kB of data (not all of which is random or useful, of course).

Under Windows NT the process is slightly different because it currently lacks ToolHelp functionality. This was added in Windows 2000/XP for Windows 95/98/ME compatibility, but we'll continue to use the more appropriate NT-specific sources rather than an NT → Windows 95 compatibility feature for a Windows 95 → Win16 compatibility feature. Instead of using ToolHelp, Windows NT/2000/XP keeps track of network statistics using the NetAPI32 library, and system performance statistics by mapping them onto keys in the Windows registry. The network information is obtained by checking whether the machine is a workstation or server and then reading network statistics from the appropriate network service. This typically yields around 200 bytes of information covering all kinds of network traffic statistics.

The system information is obtained by reading the system performance data, which is maintained internally by NT and copied to locations in the registry when a special registry key is opened. This creates a snapshot of the system performance statistics at the time that the key was opened and covers a large amount of system information such as process and thread statistics, memory information, disk access and paging statistics, and a large amount of other similar information. Unfortunately, querying the NT performance counters in this manner is rather risky since reading the key triggers a number of in-kernel memory overruns and can deadlock in the kernel or cause protection violations under some circumstances. In addition, having two processes reading the key at the same time can cause one of them to hang, and there are various other problems that make using this key somewhat dangerous. An additional problem arises from the fact that for a default NT installation the performance counters (along with significant portions of the rest of the registry) have permissions set to Everyone:Read, where "Everyone" means "Everyone on the local network", not just the local machine.

In order to sidestep these problems, cryptlib uses an NT native API function, as shown in Figure 6.26, that bypasses the awkward registry data-mapping process and thus avoids the various problems associated with it, as well as taking significantly less time to execute. Although Windows 2000 and XP provide a performance data helper (PDH) library which provides a ToolHelp interface to the registry performance data, this inherits all of the problems of the registry interface and adds a few more of its own, so we avoid using it.

```
for( type = 0; type < 64; type++ )
    {
    NtQuerySystemInfo( type, buffer, bufferSize, &length );
    add buffer to pool;
    }
```

Figure 6.26. Windows NT/2000/XP system performance data polling.

A typical poll on a moderately loaded machine nets around 30–40 kB of data (again, not all of it random or useful).

6.5.7 Unix Polling

The Unix randomness polling is the most complicated of all. Unix systems don't maintain any easily accessible collections of system information or statistics, and even sources that are accessible with some difficulty (for example, kernel data structures) are accessible only to the superuser. However, there is a way to access this information that works for any user on the system. Unfortunately, it isn't very simple.

Unix systems provide a large collection of utilities that can be used to obtain statistics and information on the system. By taking the output from each of these utilities and adding them to the randomness pool, we can obtain the same effect as using ToolHelp under Windows 95/98/ME or reading performance information under Windows NT/2000/XP. The general idea is to identify each of these randomness sources (for example, netstat -in) and somehow obtain their output data. A suitable source should have the following three properties:

1.   The output should (obviously) be reasonably random.

2.   The output should be produced in a reasonable time frame and in a format that makes it suitable for our purposes (an example of an unsuitable source is top, which displays its output interactively). There are often program arguments that can be used to expedite the arrival of data in a timely manner; for example, we can tell netstat not to try to resolve host names but instead to produce its output with IP addresses to identify machines.

3.   The source should produce a reasonable quantity of output (an example of a source that can produce far too much output is pstat -f, which weighed in with 600 kB of output on a large Oracle server. The only useful effect this had was to change the output of vmstat, another useful randomness source).

Now that we know where to get the information, we need to figure out how to get it into the randomness pool. This is done by opening a pipe to the requested source and reading from it until the source has finished producing output. To obtain input from multiple sources, we walk through the list of sources calling popen() for each one, add the descriptors to an fd_set, make the input from each source non-blocking, and then use select() to wait for output to become available on one of the descriptors (this adds further randomness because the fragments of output from the different sources are mixed up in a somewhat arbitrary order that depends on the order and manner in which the sources produce output). Once the source has finished producing output, we close the pipe. Pseudocode that implements this is shown in Figure 6.27.

```
for( all potential data sources )
    {
    if( access( source.path, X_OK ) )
        {
        /* Source exists, open a pipe to it */
        source.pipe = popen( source );
        fcntl( source.pipeFD, F_SETFL, O_NONBLOCK );
        FD_SET( source.pipeFD, &fds );

        skip all alternative forms of this source (eg /bin/pstat vs
            /etc/pstat);
        }
    }

while( sources are present and buffer != full )
    {
    /* Wait for data to become available */
    if( select( ..., &fds, ... ) == -1 )
        break;
```

```
foreach source
  {
  if( FD_ISSET( source.pipeFD, &fds ) )
    {
    count = fread( buffer, source.pipe );
    if( count )
      add buffer to pool;
    else
      pclose( source );
    }
  }
}
```

Figure 6.27. Unix randomness polling code.

Because many of the sources produce output that is formatted for human readability, the code to read the output includes a simple run-length compressor that reduces formatting data such as repeated spaces to the count of the number of repeated characters, conserving space in the data buffer.

Since this information is supposed to be used for security-related applications, we should take a few security precautions when we do our polling. Firstly, we use popen() with hard-coded absolute paths instead of simply exec()-ing the programs that are used to provide the information. In addition, we set our uid to "nobody" to ensure that we can't accidentally read any privileged information if the polling process is running with superuser privileges, and to generally reduce the potential for damage. To protect against very slow (or blocked) sources holding up the polling process, we include a timer that kills a source if it takes too long to provide output. The polling mechanism also includes a number of other safety features to protect against various potential problems, which have been omitted from the pseudocode for clarity.

Because the paths are hard-coded, we may need to look in different locations to find the programs that we require. We do this by maintaining a list of possible locations for the programs and walking down it using access() to check the availability of the source. Once we locate the program, we run it and move on to the next source. This also allows us to take into account system-specific variations of the arguments required by some programs by placing the system-specific version of the command to invoke the program first on the affected system. For example, IRIX uses a slightly nonstandard argument for the last command, so on SGI systems we try to execute this in preference to the more usual invocation of last.

Due to the fact that popen() is broken on some systems (SunOS doesn't record the pid of the child process, so it can reap the wrong child, resulting in pclose() hanging when it is called on that child), we also need to write our own version of popen() and pclose(), which conveniently allows us to create a custom popen() that is tuned for use by the randomness-gathering process.

Finally, we need to take into account the fact that some of the sources can produce a lot of relatively nonrandom output, the 600 kB of pstat output mentioned earlier being an extreme example. Since the output is read into a buffer with a fixed maximum size (a block of shared memory, as explained in Section 6.7), we want to avoid flooding the buffer with useless output. By ordering the sources in order of usefulness, we can ensure that information from the most useful sources is added preferentially. For example vmstat -s would go before df which would in turn precede arp -a. This ordering also means that late-starting sources like uptime will produce better output when the processor load suddenly shoots up into double digits due to all of the other polling processes being forked by the popen().

A typical poll on a moderately loaded machine nets around 20–40 kB of data (with the usual caveat about usefulness).

6.5.8 Other Entropy Sources

The slow poll can also check for and use various other sources that might only be available on certain systems. For example some systems have /dev/random drivers that accumulate random event data from the kernel or the equivalent user-space entropy gathering dæmons egd and PRNGD. Other systems may provide sources such as the kstat kernel stats available under Solaris and procfs available on many Unix systems. Still further systems may provide the luxury of attached crypto hardware that will provide input from physical sources, or may use a Pentium III-type chipset that contains the Intel RNG. The slow poll can check for the presence of these sources and use them in addition to the usual sources.

Finally, we provide a means to inject externally obtained randomness into the pool in case other sources are available. A typical external source of randomness would be the user password, which, although not random, represents a value that should be unknown to outsiders. Other sources include keystroke timings (if the system allows this), the hash of the message being encrypted (another constant quantity, but hopefully unknown to outsiders), and any other randomness source that might be available. Because of the presence of the mixing function, it is not possible to use this facility to cause any problems with the randomness pool — at worst, it won't add any extra randomness, but it's not possible to use it to negatively affect the data in the pool by (say) injecting a large quantity of constant data.

6.6 Randomness-Polling Results

Designing an automated process that is suited to estimating the amount of entropy gathered is a difficult task. Many of the sources are time-varying (so that successive polls will always produce different results), some produce variable-length output (causing output from other sources to change position in the polled data), and some take variable amounts of time to produce data (so that their output may appear before or after the output from faster or slower sources in successive polls). In addition many analysis techniques can be prohibitively expensive in terms of the CPU time and memory required, so we perform the analysis offline using data gathered from a number of randomness sampling runs rather than trying to analyse the data as it is collected.

6.6.1 Data Compression as an Entropy Estimation Tool

The field of data compression provides us with a number of analysis tools that can be used to provide reasonable estimates of the change in entropy from one poll to another (in fact the entire field of Ziv–Lempel data compression arose from two techniques for estimating the information content/entropy of data [91][92]). The tools that we apply to this task are an LZ77 dictionary compressor (which looks for portions of the current data which match previously seen data) and a powerful statistical compressor (which estimates the probability of occurrence of a symbol based on previously seen symbols) [93].

The LZ77 compressor uses a 32 kB window, which means that any blocks of data already encountered within the last 32 kB will be recognised as duplicates and discarded. Since the polls don't generally produce more than 32 kB of output, this is adequate for solving the problem of sources that produce variable-length output and sources that take a variable amount of time to produce any output — no matter where the data is located, repeated occurrences will be identified and removed.

The statistical compressor used is an order-1 arithmetic coder that tries to estimate the probability of occurrence of a symbol based on previous occurrences of that symbol and the symbol preceding it. For example although the probability of occurrence of the letter 'u' in English text is around 2%, the probability of occurrence if the previous letter was a 'q' is almost unity (the exception being words such as 'Iraq', 'Compaq', and 'Qantas'). The order-1 model therefore provides a tool for identifying any further redundancy that isn't removed by the LZ77 compressor.

By running the compressor over repeated samples, it is possible to obtain a reasonable estimate of how much new entropy is added by successive polls. The use of a compressor to estimate the amount of randomness present in a string leads back to the field of Kolmogorov–Chaitin complexity, which defines a random string as one that has no shorter description than itself, so that it is incompressible. The compression process therefore provides an estimate of the amount of non-randomness present in the string [94][95]. A similar principle is used in Maurer's universal statistical test for random-bit generators, which employs a bitwise LZ77 algorithm to estimate the amount of randomness present in a bit string [96][97], and in the NIST [98] and Crypt-XS [99] random number generator test suites.

The test results were taken from a number of systems and cover Windows 3.x, Windows 95/98/ME, Windows NT/2000/XP, and Unix systems running under both light and moderate-to-heavy loads. In addition, a reference data set, which consisted of a set of text files derived from a single file, with a few lines swapped and a few characters altered in each file, was used to test the entropy estimation process.

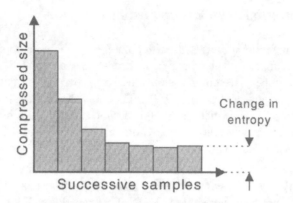

Figure 6.28. Changes in compressibility over a series of runs.

In every case, a number of samples were gathered, and the change in compressibility relative to previous samples taken under both identical and different conditions was checked. As more samples were processed by the compressor, it adapted itself to the characteristics of each sample and so produced better and better compression (that is, smaller and smaller changes in compression) for successive samples, settling down after the second or third sample. An indication of the change in compressibility over a series of runs is shown in Figure 6.28. The exception was the test file, where the compression jumped from 55% on the first sample to 97% for all successive samples due to the similarity of the data. The reason it did not go to over 99% was because of how the compressor encodes the lengths of repeated data blocks. For virtually all normal data, there are many matches for short to medium-length blocks and almost no matches for long blocks, so the compressor's encoding is tuned to be efficient in this range and it emits a series of short to medium-length matches instead of a single very long match of the type present in the test file. This means that the absolute compressibility is less than it is for the other data, but since our interest is the change in compressibility from one sample to another, this doesn't matter much.

The behaviour for the test file indicates that the compressor provides a good tool for estimating the change in entropy — after the first test sample has been processed, the compressed size changes by only a few bytes in successive samples, so the compressor is doing a good job of identifying data that remains unchanged from one sample to the next.

The fast polls, which gather very small amounts of constantly changing data such as high-speed system counters and timers and rapidly changing system information, aren't open to automated analysis using the compressor, both because they produce different results on each poll (even if the results are relatively predictable), and because the small amount of data gathered leaves little scope for effective compression. Because of this, only the more thorough slow polls that gather large amounts of information were analysed. The fast polls can be analysed if necessary, but vary greatly from system to system and require manual scrutiny of the sources used rather than automated analysis.

6.6.2 Win16/Windows 95/98/ME Polling Results

The Win16/Win32 systems were tested both in the unloaded state with no applications running, and in the moderately/heavily loaded states with MS Word, Netscape, and MS Access running. It is interesting to note that even the (supposedly unloaded) Win32 systems had around 20 processes and 100 threads running, and adding the three "heavy load" applications added (apart from the three processes) only 10–15 threads (depending on the system). This indicates that even on a supposedly unloaded Win32 system, there is a fair amount of background activity going on. For example, both Netscape and MS Access can sometimes consume 100% of the free CPU time on a system, in effect taking over the task of the idle process, which grinds to a halt while they are loaded but apparently inactive.

The first set of samples that we discuss are those that came from the Windows 3.x and Windows 95/98/ME systems, and were obtained using the ToolHelp/ToolHelp32 functions, which provide a record of the current system state. Since the results for the two systems were relatively similar, only those of Windows 95/98/ME will be discussed here. In most cases the results were rather disappointing, with the input being compressible by more than 99% once a few samples had been taken (since the data being compressed wasn't pathological test data, the compression match-length limit described above for the test data didn't occur). The tests run on a minimally configured machine (one floppy drive, hard drive, and CDROM drive) produced only about half as much output as tests run on a maximally configured machine (one floppy drive, two hard drives, network card, CDROM drive, SCSI hard drive and CDROM writer, scanner, and printer), but in both cases the compressibility had reached a constant level by the third sample (in the case of the minimal system it reached this level by the second sample). Furthermore, results from polls run one after the other showed little change to polls that were spaced at 1-minute intervals to allow a little more time for the system state to change.

The one very surprising result was the behaviour after the machine was rebooted, with samples taken in the unloaded state as soon as all disk activity had finished. In theory, the results should have been very poor because the machine should be in a pristine, relatively fixed state after each reboot, but instead the compressed data was 2½ times larger than it had been when the machine had been running for some time. This is because of the plethora of drivers, devices, support modules, and other paraphernalia that the system loads and runs at boot time. All of these vary in their behaviour and performance and in some cases are loaded and run in non-deterministic order so that they perturb the characteristics sufficiently to provide a relatively high degree of entropy after a reboot. This means that the system state after a reboot is relatively unpredictable, so that although multiple samples taken during one session provide relatively little variation in data, samples taken between reboots do provide a fair degree of variation.

This hypothesis was tested by priming the compressor using samples taken over a number of reboots and then checking the compressibility of a sample taken after the system had been running for some time relative to the samples taken after the reboot. In all cases, the compressed data was 4 times larger than when the compressor was primed with samples taken during the same session, which confirmed the fact that a reboot creates a considerable change in system state. This is an almost ideal situation when the data being sampled is used for cryptographic random number generation, since an attacker who later obtains access to the machine used to generate the numbers has less chance of being able to determine the system state at the time that the numbers were generated (provided the machine has been rebooted since then, which will be fairly likely for a Windows 95 machine).

6.6.3 Windows NT/2000/XP Polling Results

The next set of samples came from Windows NT/2000/XP systems and records the current network statistics and system performance information. Because of its very nature, it provides far more variation than the data collected on the Windows 3.x/Windows 95/98/ME systems, with the data coming from a dual-processor P6 server in turn providing more variation than the data from a single-processor P5 workstation. In all cases the network statistics provide a disappointing amount of information, with the 200-odd bytes collected compressing down to a mere 9 bytes by the time the third sample was taken. Even rebooting the machine didn't help much. Looking at the data collected revealed that the only things that changed much were one or two packet counters, so that virtually all of the entropy provided in the samples comes from these sources.

The system statistics were more interesting. Whereas the Windows 3.x/Windows 95/98/-ME polling process samples the absolute system state, the NT/2000/XP polling samples the change in system state over time, and it would be expected that this time-varying data would be less compressible. This was indeed the case, with the data from the server only compressible by about 80% even after multiple samples were taken (compared to 99+% for the non-NT machines). Unlike the non-NT machines though, the current system loading did affect the results, with a completely unloaded machine producing compressed output that was around one tenth the size of that produced on the same machine with a heavy load, even though the original, uncompressed data quantity was almost the same in both cases. This is because, with no software running, there is little to affect the statistics kept by the system (no disk or network access, no screen activity, and virtually nothing except the idle process active). Attempting to further influence the statistics (for example, by having several copies of Netscape trying to load data in the background) produced almost no change over the canonical "heavy load" behaviour.

The behaviour of the NT/2000/XP machines after being rebooted was tested in a manner identical to the tests that had been applied to the non-NT machines. Since NT/2000/XP exhibits differences in behaviour between loaded and unloaded machines, the state after reboot was compared to the state with applications running rather than the completely unloaded state (corresponding to the situation where the user has rebooted their machine and immediately starts a browser or mailer or other program that requires random numbers). Unlike the non-NT systems, the data was slightly more compressible relative to the samples taken immediately after the reboot (which means that it compressed by about 83% instead of 80%). This is possibly because the relative change from an initial state to the heavy-load state is less than the change from one heavy-load state to another heavy-load state.

6.6.4 Unix Polling Results

The final set of samples came from a variety of Unix systems ranging from a relatively lightly loaded Solaris machine to a heavily-loaded multiprocessor student Alpha. The randomness output varied greatly between machines and depended not only on the current system load and user activity but also on how many of the required randomness sources were available. Many of the sources are BSD-derived, so systems that lean more towards SYSV, such as the SGI machines which were tested, had less randomness sources available than BSD-ish systems such as the Alpha.

The results were fairly mixed and difficult to generalise. Like the NT/2000/XP systems, the Unix sources mostly provide information on the change in system state over time rather than absolute system state, so the output is inherently less compressible than it would be for sources that provide absolute system state information. The use of the run-length coder to optimise use of the shared memory buffer further reduces compressibility, with the overall compressibility between samples varying from 70% to 90% depending on the system.

Self-preservation considerations prevented the author from exploring the effects of rebooting the multi-user Unix machines.

6.7 Extensions to the Basic Polling Model

On a number of systems we can hide the lengthy slow poll by running it in the background while the main program continues execution. As long as the slow poll is started a reasonable amount of time before the random data is needed, the slow polling will be invisible to the user. In practice, by starting the poll as soon as the program is run, and having it run in the background while the user is connecting to a server, typing in a password or whatever else the program requires, the random data is available when required.

The background polling is run as a thread under Win32 and as a child process under Unix. Under Unix, the polling information is communicated back to the parent process using a block of shared memory. Under Win32, the thread shares access to the randomness pool with the other threads in the process, which makes the use of explicitly shared memory unnecessary. To prevent problems with simultaneous access to the pool, we wait for any currently active background poll to run to completion before we try to use the pool contents (cryptlib's internal locking is sufficiently fine-grained that it would be possible to interleave read and write accesses, but it's probably better to let a poll run to completion once it has started). The code to handle pool access locking (with other features such as entropy testing omitted for clarity) is shown in Figure 6.29.

```
extractData()
    {
    if( no random data available and no background poll in progress )
       /* Caller forgot to perform a slow poll */
       start a slow poll;

    wait for any background poll to run to completion;
    if( still no random data available )
       error;

    extract/mix data from the pool;
    }
```

Figure 6.29. Entropy pool access locking for background polling.

On systems that support threading, we can provide a much finer level of control than this somewhat crude "don't allow any access if a poll is in progress" method. By using mutexes, we can control access to the pool so that the fact that a background poll is active doesn't stop us from using the pool at the same time. This is done by wrapping up access to the random pool in a mutex to allow a background poll to independently update the pool in between reading data from it. The previous pseudocode can be changed to make it thread-safe by changing the last few lines as shown in Figure 6.30.

```
lockResource( ... );
extract/mix data from the pool;
unlockResource ( ... );
```

Figure 6.30. Pool locking on a system with threads.

The background-polling thread also contains these calls, which ensures that only one thread will try to access the pool at a time. If another thread tries to access the pool, it is suspended until the thread that is currently accessing the pool has released the mutex, which happens extremely quickly since the only operation being performed is either a mixing operation or a copying of data. As mentioned above, this process isn't currently used in the cryptlib implementation since it's probably better to let the poll run to completion than to interleave read and write accesses, since the slightest coding error could lead to a catastrophic failure in which either non-initialised/mixed data is read from the pool or previous mixed data is reread.

Now that we have a nice, thread-safe means of performing more or less transparent updates on the pool, we can extend the basic manually controlled polling model even further for extra user convenience. The first two lines of the extractData() pseudocode contain code to force a slow poll if the calling application has forgotten to do this (the fact that the application grinds to a halt for several seconds will hopefully make this mistake obvious to the programmer the first time the application is tested). We can make the polling process even more foolproof by performing it automatically ourselves without programmer intervention. As soon as the security or randomness subsystem is started, we begin performing a background slow poll, which means that the random data becomes available as soon as possible after the application is started. This also requires a small modification to the function that manually starts a slow poll so that it won't start a redundant background poll if the automatic poll is already taking place.

In general, an application will fall into one of two categories, either a client-type application such as a mail reader or browser that a user will start up, perform one or more transactions or operations with, and then close down again, and a server-type application that will run over an extended period of time. In order to take both of these cases into account, we can perform one poll every few minutes on startup to quickly obtain random data for active client-type applications, and then drop back to occasional polls for longer-running server-type applications. This is also useful for client applications that are left to run in the background, mail readers being a good example.

6.8 Protecting the Randomness Pool

The randomness pool presents an extremely valuable resource, since any attacker who gains access to it can use it to predict any private keys, encryption session keys, and other valuable data generated on the system. Using the design philosophy of "Put all your eggs in one basket and watch that basket very carefully", we go to some lengths to protect the contents of the randomness pool from outsiders. Some of the more obvious ways to get at the pool are to recover it from the page file if it gets swapped to disk, and to walk down the chain of allocated memory blocks looking for one that matches the characteristics of the pool. Less obvious ways are to use sophisticated methods to recover the contents of the memory that contained the pool after power is removed from the system.

The first problem to address is that of the pool being paged to disk. Fortunately several operating systems provide facilities to lock pages into memory, although there are often restrictions on what can be achieved. For example, many Unix versions provide the `mlock()` call, Win32 has `VirtualLock()` (which, however, is implemented as `{ return TRUE; }` under Windows 95/98/ME and doesn't function as documented under Windows NT/2000/XP), and the Macintosh has `HoldMemory()`. A discussion of various issues related to locking memory pages (and the difficulty of erasing data once it has been paged to disk) is given in Gutmann [100].

If no facility for locking pages exists, then the contents can still be kept out of the common swap file through the use of memory-mapped files. A newly created memory-mapped file can be used as a private swap file that can be erased when the memory is freed (although there are some limitations on how well the data can be erased — again, see Gutmann [100]). Further precautions can be taken to make the private swap file more secure, for example, the file should be opened for exclusive use and/or have the strictest possible access permissions, and file buffering should be disabled if possible to avoid the buffers being swapped (under Win32 this can be done by using the `FILE_FLAG_NO_BUFFERING` flag when calling `Create-File()`; some Unix versions have obscure ioctls that achieve the same effect).

The second problem is that of another process scanning through the allocated memory blocks looking for the randomness pool. This is aggravated by the fact that, if the randomness polling is built into an encryption subsystem, the pool will often be allocated and initialised as soon as the security subsystem is started, especially if automatic background polling is used.

Because of this, the memory containing the pool is often allocated at the head of the list of allocated blocks, making it relatively easy to locate. For example, under Win32, the `VirtualQueryEx()` function can be used to query the status of memory regions owned by other processes, `VirtualUnprotectEx()` can be used to remove any protection, and `ReadProcessMemory()` can be used to recover the contents of the pool or, for an active attack, set its contents to zero. Generating encryption keys from a buffer filled with zeroes (or the hash of a buffer full of zeroes) can be hazardous to security.

Although there is no magic solution to this problem, the task of an attacker can be made considerably more difficult by taking special precautions to obscure the identity of the memory being used to implement the pool. This can be done both by obscuring the characteristics of the pool (by embedding it in a larger allocated block of memory containing other data) and by changing its location periodically (by allocating a new memory block and moving the contents of the pool to the new block). The relocation of the data in the pool also means that it is never stored in one place long enough to be retained by the memory in which it is being stored, making it harder for an attacker to recover the pool contents from memory after power is removed [101].

This obfuscation process is a simple extension of the background-polling process and is shown in Figure 6.31. Every time a poll is performed, the pool is moved to a new, random-sized memory block and the old memory block is wiped and freed. In addition, the surrounding memory is filled with non-random data to make a search based on match criteria of a single small block filled with high-entropy data more difficult to perform (that is, for a pool of size n bytes, a block of m bytes is allocated and the n bytes of pool data are located somewhere within the larger block, surrounded by $m - n$ bytes of camouflage data). This means that as the program runs, the pool becomes buried in the mass of memory blocks allocated and freed by typical GUI-based applications. This is especially apparent when used with frameworks such as MFC, whose large (and leaky) collection of more or less arbitrary allocated blocks provides a perfect cover for a small pool of randomness.

```
allocate new pool;
write nonrandom data to surrounding memory;
lock randomness state;
copy data from old pool to new pool;
unlock randomness state;
zeroize old pool;
```

Figure 6.31. Random pool obfuscation.

Since the obfuscation is performed as a background task, the cost of moving the data around is almost zero. The only time when the randomness state is locked (and therefore inaccessible to the program) is when the data is being copied from the old pool to the new one.

This assumes that operations that access the randomness pool are atomic and that no portion of the code will try to retain a pointer to the pool between pool accesses.

We can also use this background thread or process to try to prevent the randomness pool from being swapped to disk. This is necessary because the techniques suggested previously for locking memory are not completely reliable. mlock() can only be called by the superuser, and VirtualLock() doesn't do anything under Windows 95/98/ME and even under Windows NT/2000/XP, where it is actually implemented, it doesn't do what the documentation says. Instead of making the memory non-swappable, it is only kept resident as long as at least one thread in the process that owns the memory is active (that is, it locks the page in the working set rather than in memory). Once all threads are pre-empted, the memory can be swapped to disk just like non-"locked" memory [102]. The more memory that is locked into the working set, the less is available for the other pages touched by the program. As a result, paging is increased, so that using VirtualLock() increases, rather than eliminates, the chances of sensitive data being swapped to disk (as well as slowing application performance, increasing disk I/O due to consumption of memory normally used by the file cache, and other deleterious effects) [103]. The Windows 95/98/ME implementation, which does nothing, is actually better than the Windows NT/2000/XP implementation, which tries to do something but does it wrong. In fact, there doesn't seem to be any sensible use for this function as implemented rather than as documented by Microsoft. Windows 2000 finally added a function AllocateUserPhysicalPages() which appears to allow the allocation of non-swappable memory, although whether this is another VirtualLock() remains to be seen.

Since the correct functioning of the memory-locking facilities provided by the system cannot be relied on, we need to provide an alternative method to try to retain the pages in memory. The easiest way to do this is to use the background thread that is being used to relocate the pool to continually touch the pages, thus ensuring that they are kept at the top of the swapper's LRU queue. We do this by decreasing the sleep time of the thread so that it runs more often, and keeping track of how many times we have run it so that we only relocate the pool as often as the previous, less frequently active thread did as shown in Figure 6.32.

```
touch randomness pool;
if( time to move the pool )
  {
  move the pool;
  reset timer;
  }
sleep;
```

Figure 6.32. Combined pool obfuscation and memory-retention code.

This is especially important when the process using the pool is idle over extended periods of time, since pages owned by other processes will be given preference over those of the process owning the pool. Although the pages can still be swapped when the system is under heavy load, the constant touching of the pages makes it less likely that this swapping will occur under normal conditions.

6.9 Conclusion

This work has revealed a number of pitfalls and problems present in current random number generators and the way that they are employed. In order to avoid potential security compromises, the following requirements for good generator design and use should be followed when implementing a random number generator for cryptographic purposes:

- All data fed into the generator should be pre-processed in some way to prevent chosen-input attacks (this processing can be performed indirectly; for example, as part of the state update process).

- The input pre-processing should function in a manner that prevents known-input attacks; for example, by adding unknown (to an attacker) data into the input mixing process rather than simply hashing the data and copying it to the internal state.

- All output data should be post-processed through a preimage-resistant random function (typically a hash function such as SHA-1) in order to avoid revealing information about the internal state to an attacker.

- Output data should never be recycled back into the internal state, since this violates the previous design principle.

- The generator should not depend on user-supplied input to provide entropy information, but should be capable of collecting this information for itself without requiring any explicit help from the user.

- As an extension of the previous principle, the generator should estimate the amount of entropy present in its internal state and refuse to provide output that does not provide an adequate level of security. In addition, the generator should continuously check its own output to try to detect catastrophic failures.

- The generator should use as many dissimilar input sources as possible in order to avoid susceptibility to a single point of failure.

- The state update operation should use as much state data as possible to try and ensure that every bit of state affects every other bit during the mixing. The hash functions typically used for this purpose can accept arbitrarily large amounts of input. Full advantage should be taken of this capability rather than artificially constraining it to 64 (a block cipher in CBC mode) or 128/160 (the hash function's normal chaining size) bits.

- The generator should avoid the startup problem by ensuring that the internal state is sufficiently mixed (that is, that accumulated entropy is sufficiently spread throughout the state) before any output is generated from it.

- The generator should continuously sample its own output and perform any viable tests on it to ensure that it isn't producing bad output or is stuck in a cycle and producing the same output repeatedly.

- Applications that utilise the generator should carefully distinguish between cases where secure random numbers are required and ones where nonces are required, and never use the generator to produce at-risk data. Standards for crypto protocols should explicitly specify whether the random data being used at a given point needs to be secure random data or whether a nonce is adequate.

- The generator needs to take into account OS-specific booby traps such as the use of `fork()` under Unix, which could result in two processes having the same generator internal state. Working around this type of problem is trickier than it would first appear since the duplication of generator state could occur at any moment from another thread.

- Generator output should always be treated as sensitive, not only by the producer but also by the consumer. For example the PKCS #1 padding that an application that is processing may contain the internal state of the sender's (badly implemented) generator. Any memory that contains output that may have come from a generator should therefore be zeroized after use as a matter of common courtesy to the other party. This principle holds for cryptovariables in general, since other attacks on carelessly discarded crypto material are also possible [104].

6.10 References

[1] "Cryptographic Randomness from Air Turbulence in Disk Drives", Don Davis, Ross Ihaka, and Philip Fenstermacher, *Proceedings of Crypto '94*, Springer-Verlag Lecture Notes in Computer Science, No.839, 1994.

[2] "Truly Random Numbers", Colin Plumb, *Dr.Dobbs Journal*, November 1994, p.113.

[3] "PGP Source Code and Internals", Philip Zimmermann, MIT Press, 1995.

[4] "Random noise from disk drives", Rich Salz, posting to cypherpunks mailing list, message-ID `9601230431.AA06742@sulphur.osf.org`, 22 January 1996.

[5] "A Practical Secure Physical Random Bit Generator", Markus Jacobsson, Elizabeth Shriver, Bruce Hillyer, and Ari Juels, *Proceedings of the 5th ACM Conference on Computer and Communications Security*, 1998, p.103.

[6] "IBM-PC flawless true random number generator", Nico de Vries, posting to sci.crypt newsgroup, message-ID `2670@accucx.cc.ruu.nl`, 18 June 1992.

[7] "My favourite random-numbers-in-software package (unix)", Matt Blaze, posting to cypherpunks mailing list, message-ID `199509301946.PAA15565@crypto.com`, 30 September 1995.

[8] "Using and Creating Cryptographic-Quality Random Numbers", John Callas, `http://www.merrymeet.com/jon/usingrandom.html`, 3 June 1996.

[9] "Suggestions for random number generation in software", Tim Matthews, RSA Data Security Engineering Report, 15 December 1995 (reprinted in RSA Laboratories' Bulletin No.1, 22 January 1996).

[10] "Applied Cryptography (Second Edition)", Bruce Schneier, John Wiley and Sons, 1996.

[11] "Cryptographic Random Numbers", IEEE P1363 Working Draft, Appendix G, 6 February 1997.

[12] "Zufallstreffer", Klaus Schmeh and Dr.Hubert Uebelacker, *c't*, **No.14**, 1997, p.220.

[13] "Randomness Recommendations for Security", Donald Eastlake, Stephen Crocker, and Jeffrey Schiller, RFC 1750, December 1994.

[14] "The Art of Computer Programming: Volume 2, Seminumerical Algorithms", Donald Knuth, Addison-Wesley, 1981.

[15] "Handbook of Applied Cryptography", Alfred Menezes, Paul van Oorschot, and Scott Vanstone, CRC Press, 1996.

[16] "Exploring Randomness", Gregory Chaitin, Springer-Verlag, December 2000.

[17] "Foundations of Cryptography: Basic Tools", Oded Goldreich, Cambridge University Press, August 2001.

[18] "Netscape's Internet Software Contains Flaw That Jeopardizes Security of Data", Jared Sandberg, *The Wall Street Journal*, 18 September 1995.

[19] "Randomness and the Netscape Browser", Ian Goldberg and David Wagner, *Dr.Dobbs Journal*, January 1996.

[20] "Breakable session keys in Kerberos v4", Nelson Minar, posting to the cypherpunks mailing list, message-ID 199602200828.BAA21074@nelson.santafe.edu, 20 February 1996.

[21] "X Authentication Vulnerability", CERT Vendor-Initiated Bulletin VB-95:08, 2 November 1995.

[22] "glibc resolver weakness", antirez, posting to the bugtraq mailing list, message-ID 20000503034046.A9579@nagash.marmoc.net, 3 May 2000.

[23] "A Stateful Inspection of FireWall-1", Thomas Lopatic, John McDonald, and Dug Song, posting to the bugtraq mailing list, message-ID 20000816140955.-5CD7E10865E@naughty.monkey.org, 16 August 2000.

[24] "FWTK, Gauntlet 'random seed' security problem", 'kadokev', posting to the bugtraq mailing list, message-ID 19990416203627.15201.qmail@msg.net, 16 April 1999.

[25] "'Pseudo-random' Number Generation Within Cryptographic Algorithms: The DDS [sic] Case", Mihir Bellare, Shafi Goldwasser, and Daniele Micciancio, *Proceedings of Crypto'97*, Springer-Verlag Lecture Notes in Computer Science No.1294, August 1997, p.276.

[26] "Crypto Blunders", Steve Burnett, *Proceedings of the 2nd Systems Administration and Networking Conference (SANE 2000)*, Netherlands Unix Users Group, May 2000, p.239 (also available on the CD accompanying "RSA Security's Official Guide To Cryptography", Steve Burnett and Stephen Paine, McGraw-Hill, 2001).

[27] "RE: Signature certification", Ross Anderson, posting to the ukcrypto mailing list, message-ID E14jz1F-00041d-00@wisbech.cl.cam.ac.uk, 2 April 2001.

[28] "Murphy's law and computer security", Wietse Venema, *Proceedings of the 6th Usenix Security Symposium*, July 1996, p.187.

[29] "Internet Gambling Software Flaw Discovered by Reliable Software Technologies Software Security Group", Reliable Software Technologies, `http://www.-rstcorp.com/news/gambling.html`, 1 September 1999.

[30] "A sure bet: Internet gambling is loaded with risks", Ann Kellan, CNN news story, 3 September 1999.

[31] "Re: New standart for encryption software", Albert P.Belle Isle, posting to the sci.crypt newsgroup, message-ID `v8e3asks612a3iu8pmr5677uhfes7gupun@4ax.com`, 9 February 2000.

[32] "Key Generation Security Flaw in PGP 5.0", Germano Caronni, posting to the coderpunks mailing list, message-ID `20000523141323.A28431@olymp.org`, 23 May 2000.

[33] Bodo Möller, private communications, 31 May 2000.

[34] "Yarrow-160: Notes on the Design and Analysis of the Yarrow Cryptographic Pseudorandom Number Generator", John Kelsey, Bruce Schneier, and Niels Ferguson, *Proceedings of the 6th Annual Workshop on Selected Areas in Cryptography (SAC'99)*, Springer-Verlag Lecture Notes in Computer Science, No.1758, August 1999, p.13.

[35] "Proper Initialisation for the BSAFE Random Number Generator", Robert Baldwin, *RSA Laboratories' Bulletin*, **No.3**, 25 January 1996.

[36] "Security Requirements for Cryptographic Modules", FIPS PUB 140-2, National Institute of Standards and Technology, July 2001.

[37] "Cryptanalytic Attacks on Pseudorandom Number Generators", John Kelsey, Bruce Schneier, David Wagner, and Chris Hall, *Proceedings of the 5th Fast Software Encryption Workshop (FSE'98)*, Springer-Verlag Lecture Notes in Computer Science, No.1372, March 1998, p.168.

[38] "RSAREF Cryptographic Library, Version 1.0", RSA Laboratories, February 1992.

[39] "Preliminary Analysis of the BSAFE 3.x Pseudorandom Number Generators", Robert Baldwin, *RSA Laboratories' Bulletin* **No.8**, 3 September 1998.

[40] "American National Standard for Financial Institution Key Management (Wholesale)", American Bankers Association, 1985.

[41] "SFS — Secure FileSystem", Peter Gutmann, `http://www.cs.auckland.-ac.nz/~pgut001/sfs.html`.

[42] Changes.doc, PGP 2.6.1 documentation, 1994.

[43] "GnuPG PRNG insecure?", Stefan Keller, posting to the gnupg-devel mailing list, message-ID `20020207200603.A28608@harry.cs.tu-berlin.de`,   7 February 2002.

[44] `/dev/random` driver source code (random.c), Theodore T'so, 24 April 1996.

[45] "SSH — Secure Login Connections over the Internet", Tatu Ylönen, *Proceedings of the 6th Usenix Security Symposium*, July 1996, p.37.

[46] "The SSL Protocol", Alan Freier, Philip Karlton, and Paul Kocher, Netscape Communications Corporation, March 1996.

[47] "RFC 2246, The TLS Protocol, Version 1.0", Tim Dierks and Christopher Allen, January 1999.

[48] "SSL and TLS Essentials", Stephen Thomas, John Wiley and Sons, 2000.

[49] "OpenSSL Security Advisory: PRNG weakness in versions up to 0.9.6a", Bodo Moeller, posting to the bugtraq mailing list, 10 July 2001, message-ID 20010710130317.A1949@openssl.org.

[50] "Non-biased pseudo random number generator", Matthew Thomlinson, Daniel Simon, and Bennet Yee, US Patent No.5,778,069, 7 July 1998.

[51] "Writing Secure Code", Michael Howard and David LeBlanc, Microsoft Press, 2002.

[52] "A Class of Weak Keys in the RC4 Stream Cipher", Andrew Roos, posting to sci.crypt.research newsgroup, message-ID 43vf2e$sr8@net.auckland.ac.nz, 22 September 1995.

[53] "Re: is RC4 weak for the first few K?", Paul Kocher, posting to sci.crypt newsgroup, message-ID pckE035up.4y1@netcom.com, 30 October 1996.

[54] "Disclosures of Weaknesses in RC4 (Re: RC4 Weaknesses?)", Ian Farquhar, posting to sci.crypt newsgroup, message-ID 329A242A.41C6@sydney.sgi.com, 26 November 1996.

[55] "Iterative Probabilistic Cryptanalysis of RC4 Keystream Generator", Jovan Golić, *Proceedings of the 5ʰ Australasian Conference on Information Security and Privacy (ACISP'00)*, Springer-Verlag Lecture Notes in Computer Science No.1841, July 2000, p.220.

[56] "Linear Statistical Weakness of Alleged RC4 Keystream Generator", Jovan Golić, *Proceedings of Eurocrypt '97*, Springer-Verlag Lecture Notes in Computer Science, No.1233, May 1997, p.226.

[57] "Cryptanalysis of RC4-like Ciphers", Serge Mister and Stafford Tavares, *Proceedings of the 5ʰ Annual Workshop on Selected Areas in Cryptography (SAC'98)*, Springer-Verlag Lecture Notes in Computer Science, No.1556, August 1998, p.131.

[58] "Statistical Analysis of the Alleged RC4 Keystream Generator", Scott Fluhrer and David McGrew, *Proceedings of the 7ʰ Fast Software Encryption Workshop (FSE 2000)*, Springer-Verlag Lecture Notes in Computer Science, No.1978, April 2000, p.19.

[59] "A Practical Attack on Broadcast RC4", Itsik Mantin and Adi Shamir, *Proceedings of the 8ʰ Fast Software Encryption Workshop (FSE 2001)*, Springer-Verlag Lecture Notes in Computer Science, No.2355, April 2001, p.152.

[60] "(Not So) Random Shuffles of RC4", Ilya Mironov, *Proceedings of Crypto 2002*, Springer-Verlag Lecture Notes in Computer Science, to appear.

[61] "CAPSTONE (MYK-80) Specifications", R21 Informal Technical Report R21-TECH-30-95, National Security Agency, 14 August 1995.

[62] "Intel 82802 Firmware Hub: Random Number Generator Programmer's Reference Manual", Intel Corporation, December 1999.

[63] "The Intel Random Number Generator", Benjamin Jun and Paul Kocher, Cryptography Research Inc white paper, 22 April 1999.

[64] "Alternating Step Generators Controlled by de Bruijn Sequences", Christoph Günther, *Proceedings of Eurocrypt'97*, Springer-Verlag Lecture Notes in Computer Science, No.304, April 1987, p.5.

[65] "An attack on the last two rounds of MD4", Bert den Boer and Antoon Bosselaers, *Proceedings of Crypto'91*, Springer-Verlag Lecture Notes in Computer Science, No.576, December 1991, p.194.

[66] "The First Two Rounds of MD4 are Not One-Way", Hans Dobbertin, *Proceedings of Fast Software Encryption'98 (FSE'98)*, Springer-Verlag Lecture Notes in Computer Science, No.1372, March 1998, p.284.

[67] "The Status of MD5 After a Recent Attack", Hans Dobbertin, *CryptoBytes*, **Vol.2**, **No.2** (Summer 1996), p.1.

[68] "On Recent Results for MD2, MD4 and MD5", Matt Robshaw, *RSA Laboratories Bulletin*, **No.4**, November 1996.

[69] "Formula 1 Technology", Nigel McKnight, Hazelton Publishing, 1998.

[70] "Prudent engineering practice for cryptographic protocols", Martin Abadi and Roger Needham, *IEEE Transactions on Software Engineering*, **Vol.22**, **No.1** (January 1996), p. 2. Also in *Proceedings of the 1994 IEEE Symposium on Security and Privacy*, May 1994, p.122.

[71] "Statistical Testing of Random Number Generators", Juan Soto, *Proceedings of the 22nd National Information Systems Security Conference* (formerly the National Computer Security Conference), October 1999, CDROM distribution.

[72] "Transaction Processing: Concepts and Techniques" Jim Gray and Andreas Reuter, Morgan Kaufmann, 1993.

[73] "Atomic Transactions", Nancy Lynch, Michael Merritt, William Weihl, and Alan Fekete, Morgan Kaufmann, 1994.

[74] "Principles of Transaction Processing", Philip Bernstein and Eric Newcomer, Morgan Kaufman Series in Data Management Systems, January 1997.

[75] "Re: A history of Netscape/MSIE problems", Phillip Hallam-Baker, posting to the cypherpunks mailing list, message-ID `3238962F.1372@ai.mit.edu`, 12 September 1996.

[76] "Re: Problem Compiling OpenSSL for RSA Support", David Hesprich, posting to the openssl-dev mailing list, 5 March 2000.

[77] "Re: "PRNG not seeded" in Window NT", Pablo Royo, posting to the openssl-dev mailing list, 4 April 2000.

[78] "Re: PRNG not seeded ERROR", Carl Douglas, posting to the openssl-users mailing list, 6 April 2001.

[79] "Bug in 0.9.5 + fix", Elias Papavassilopoulos, posting to the openssl-dev mailing list, 10 March 2000.

[80] "Re: setting random seed generator under Windows NT", Amit Chopra, posting to the openssl-users mailing list, 10 May 2000.

[81] "1 RAND question, and 1 crypto question", Brian Snyder, posting to the openssl-users mailing list, 21 April 2000.

[82] "Re: unable to load 'random state' (OpenSSL 0.9.5 on Solaris)", Theodore Hope, posting to the openssl-users mailing list, 9 March 2000.

[83] "RE: having trouble with RAND_egd()", Miha Wang, posting to the openssl-users mailing list, 22 August 2000.

[84] "Re: How to seed before generating key?", 'jas', posting to the openssl-users mailing list, 19 April 2000.

[85] "Re: "PRNG not seeded" in Windows NT", Ng Pheng Siong, posting to the openssl-dev mailing list, 6 April 2000.

[86] "Re: Bug relating to /dev/urandom and RAND_egd in libcrypto.a", Louis LeBlanc, posting to the openssl-dev mailing list, 30 June 2000.

[87] "Re: Bug relating to /dev/urandom and RAND_egd in libcrypto.a", Louis LeBlanc, posting to the openssl-dev mailing list, 30 June 2000.

[88] "Error message: random number generator:SSLEAY_RAND_BYTES / possible solution", Michael Hynds, posting to the openssl-dev mailing list, 7 May 2000.

[89] "Re: Unable to load 'random state' when running CA.pl", Corrado Derenale, posting to the openssl-users mailing list, 2 November 2000.

[90] "OpenSSL Frequently Asked Questions", `http://www.openssl.org/-support/faq.html`.

[91] "A Universal Algorithm for Sequential Data-Compression", Jacob Ziv and Abraham Lempel, *IEEE Transactions on Information Theory*, **Vol. 23**, **No.3** (May 1977), p.337,

[92] "Compression of Individual Sequences via Variable-Rate Coding", Jacob Ziv and Abraham Lempel, *IEEE Transactions on Information Theory*, **Vol.24**, **No.5** (September 1978), p.530.

[93] "Practical Dictionary/Arithmetic Data Compression Synthesis", Peter Gutmann, MSc thesis, University of Auckland, 1992.

[94] "Compression, Tests for Randomness and Estimation of the Statistical Model of an Individual Sequence", Jacob Ziv, in "Sequences", Springer-Verlag, 1988, p.366.

[95] "Ziv-Lempel Complexity for Periodic Sequences and its Cryptographic Application", Sibylle Mund, *Proceedings of Eurocrypt'91*, Springer-Verlag Lecture Notes in Computer Science, No.547, April 1991, p.114.

[96] "A Universal Statistical Test for Random Bit Generators", Ueli Maurer, *Proceedings of Crypto '90*, Springer-Verlag Lecture Notes in Computer Science, No.537, 1991, p.409.

[97] "An accurate evaluation of Maurer's universal test", Jean-Sébastian Coron and David Naccache, *Proceedings of the 5th Annual Workshop on Selected Areas in Cryptography (SAC'98)*, Springer-Verlag Lecture Notes in Computer Science, No.1556, August 1998, p.57.

[98] "Random Number Testing and Generation", `http://csrc.nist.gov/rng/`.

[99] "Crypt-X'98", `http://www.isrc.qut.edu.au/cryptx/`.

[100] "Secure deletion of data from magnetic and solid-state memory", Peter Gutmann, *Proceedings of the 6th Usenix Security Symposium*, July 1996, p.7.

[101] "Data Remanence in Semiconductor Devices", Peter Gutmann, *Proceedings of the 10th Usenix Security Symposium*, August 2001, p.39.

[102] "Advanced Windows (third edition)", Jeffrey Richter, Microsoft Press, 1997.

[103] "Developing Windows NT Device Drivers: A Programmer's Handbook", Edward Dekker and Joseph Newcomer, Addison-Wesley, April 1999.

[104] "On the importance of securing your bins: The garbage-man-in-the-middle attack", Marc Joye and Jean-Jacques Quisquater, *Proceedings of the 4th ACM Conference on Computer and Communications Security (CCS'97)*, April 1997, p.135.

7 Hardware Encryption Modules

7.1 Problems with Crypto on End-User Systems

The majority of current crypto implementations run under general-purpose operating systems with a relatively low level of security, alongside which exist a limited number of smart-card assisted implementations that store a private key in, and perform private-key operations with, a smart card. Complementing these are an even smaller number of implementations that perform further operations in dedicated (and generally very expensive) hardware.

The advantage of software-only implementations is that they are inexpensive and easy to deploy. The disadvantage of these implementations is that they provide a very low level of protection for cryptovariables, and that this low level of security is unlikely to change in the future. For example Windows NT provides a function `ReadProcessMemory()` that allows a process to read the memory of (almost) any other process in the system. This was originally intended to allow debuggers to establish breakpoints and maintain instance data for other processes [1], but in practice it allows both passive attacks such as scanning memory for high-entropy areas that constitute keys [2] and active attacks in which a target process' code or data is modified to provide supplemental functionality of benefit to a hostile process.

This type of modification would typically be performed by obtaining the target process' handle, using `SuspendThread()` to halt it, `VirtualProtectEx()` to make the code pages writeable, `WriteProcessMemory()` to modify the code, and `ResumeThread()` to restart the process' execution (these are all standard Windows functions and don't require security holes or coding bugs in order to work). By subclassing an application such as the Windows shell, the hostile process can receive notification of any application (a.k.a. "target") starting up or shutting down, after which it can apply the mechanisms mentioned previously. A very convenient way to do this is to subclass a child window of the system tray window, yielding a system-wide hook for intercepting shell messages [3]. Another way to obtain access to other process' data is to patch the user-to-kernel-mode jump table in a process' Thread Environment Block (TEB), which is shared by all processes in the system rather than being local to each one, so that changing it in one process affects every other running process [4]. Sometimes it isn't even necessary to perform heuristic scans for likely keying information, for example by opening a handle to **WINLOGON.EXE** (the Windows logon process), using `ReadProcessMemory()` to read the page at 0x10000, and scanning for the text string `lMprNotifyPassword=`, it's possible to obtain the current user's password, which isn't cleared from memory by the logon process [5].

Although the use of functions such as `ReadProcessMemory()` requires Administrator privileges, most users tend to either run their system as Administrator or give themselves equivalent privileges since it's extremely difficult to make use of the machine without these privileges. In the unusual case where the user isn't running with these privileges, it's possible to use a variety of tricks to bypass any OS security measures that might be present in order to perform the desired operations. For example, by installing a Windows message hook, it's possible to capture messages intended for another process and have them dispatched to your own message handler. Windows then loads the hook handler into the address space of the process that owns the thread for which the message was intended, in effect yanking your code across into the address space of the victim [6]. Even simpler are mechanisms such as using the HKEY_LOCAL_MACHINE\Software\Microsoft\Windows NT\CurrentVersion\Windows\-AppInit_DLLs key, which specifies a list of DLLs that are automatically loaded and called whenever an application uses the USER32 system library (which is automatically used by all GUI applications and many command-line ones). Every DLL specified in this registry key is loaded into the processes' address space by USER32, which then calls the DLL's DllMain() function to initialise the DLL (and, by extension, trigger whatever other actions the DLL is designed for).

A more sophisticated attack involves persuading the system to run your code in ring 0 (the most privileged security level usually reserved for the OS kernel) or, alternatively, convincing the OS to allow you to load a selector that provides access to all physical memory (under Windows NT, selectors 8 and 10 provide this capability). Running user code in ring 0 is possible due to the peculiar way in which the NT kernel loads. The kernel is accessed via the int 2Eh call gate, which initially provides about 200 functions via NTOSKRNL.EXE but is then extended to provide more and more functions as successive parts of the OS are loaded. Instead of merely adding new functions to the existing table, each new portion of the OS that is loaded takes a copy of the existing table, adds its own functions to it, and then replaces the old one with the new one. To add supplemental functionality at the kernel level, all that's necessary is to do the same thing [7]. Once your code is running at ring 0, an NT system starts looking a lot like a machine running DOS.

Although the problems mentioned thus far have concentrated on Windows NT, many Unix systems aren't much better. For example, the use of ptrace with the PTRACE_ATTACH option followed by the use of other ptrace capabilities provides headaches similar to those arising from ReadProcessMemory(). The reason why these issues are more problematic under NT is that users are practically forced to run with Administrator privileges in order to perform any useful work on the system, since a standard NT system has no equivalent to Unix's su functionality and, to complicate things further, frequently assumes that the user always has Administrator privileges (that is, it assumes that it's a single-user system with the user being Administrator). Although it is possible to provide some measure of protection on a Unix system by running crypto code as a dæmon in its own memory space under a different account, under NT all services run under the single System Account so that any service can use ReadProcessMemory() to interfere with any other service [8]. Since an Administrator can dynamically load NT services at any time and since a non-administrator can create processes running under the System Account by overwriting the handle of the parent process with that of the System Account [9], even implementing the crypto code as an NT service provides no escape.

7.1.1 The Root of the Problem

The reason why problems such as those described above persist, and why we're unlikely to ever see a really secure consumer OS, is because it's not something that most consumers care about. One survey of Fortune 1000 security managers showed that although 92% of them were concerned about the security of Java and ActiveX, nearly three quarters allowed them onto their internal networks, and more than half didn't even bother scanning for them [10]. Users are used to programs malfunctioning and computers crashing (every Windows user can tell you what the abbreviation BSOD means even though it's never actually mentioned in the documentation), and see it as normal for software to contain bugs. Since program correctness is difficult and expensive to achieve, and as long as flashiness and features are the major selling point for products, buggy and insecure systems will be the normal state of affairs [11]. Unlike other Major Problems such as Y2K (which contained their own built-in deadline), security generally isn't regarded as a pressing issue unless the user has just been successfully attacked or the corporate auditors are about to pay a visit, which means that it's much easier to defer addressing it to some other time [12]. Even in cases where the system designers originally intended to implement a rigorous security system employing a proper TCB, the requirement to add features to the system inevitably results in all manner of additions being crammed into the TCB as application-specific functionality starts migrating into the OS kernel. The result of this creep is that the TCB is neither small, nor verified, nor secure.

An NSA study [13] lists a number of features that are regarded as "crucial to information security" but that are absent from all mainstream operating systems. Features such as mandatory access controls that are mentioned in the study correspond to Orange Book B-level security features that can't be bolted onto an existing design but generally need to be designed in from the start, necessitating a complete overhaul of an existing system in order to provide the required functionality. This is often prohibitively resource-intensive; for example, the task of reengineering the Multics kernel (which contained a "mere" 54,000 lines of code) to provide a minimised TCB was estimated to cost $40M (in 1977 dollars) and was never completed [14]. The work involved in performing the same kernel upgrade or redesign from scratch with an operating system containing millions or tens of millions of lines of code would make it beyond prohibitive.

At the moment security and ease of use are at opposite ends of the scale, and most users will opt for ease of use over security. JavaScript, ActiveX, and embedded active content may be a security nightmare, but they do make life a lot easier for most users, leading to comments from security analysts like "You want to write up a report with the latest version of Microsoft Word on your insecure computer or on some piece of junk with a secure computer?" [15], "Which sells more products: really secure software or really easy-to-use software?" [16], "It's possible to make money from a lousy product [...] Corporate cultures are focused on money, not product" [17], and "The marketplace doesn't reward *real* security. Real security is harder, slower and more expensive, both to design and to implement. Since the buying public has no way to differentiate real security from bad security, the way to win in this marketplace is to design software that is as insecure as you can possibly get away with [...] users prefer cool features to security" [18]. Even the director of the National Computer Security Centre refused to use any C2 or higher-evaluated products on his system, reporting that they were "not user friendly, too hard to learn, too slow, not supported by good maintenance, and too costly" [19].

One study that examined the relationship between faults (more commonly referred to as bugs) and software failures found that one third of all faults resulted in a mean time to failure (MTTF) of more than 5,000 years, with somewhat less than another third having an MTTF of more than 1,500 years. Conversely, around 2% of all faults had an MTTF of less than five years [20]. The reason for this is that even the most general-purpose programs are only ever used in stereotyped ways that exercise only a tiny portion of the total number of code paths, so that removing (visible) problems from these areas will be enough to keep the majority of users happy. This conclusion is backed up by other studies such as one that examined the behaviour of 30 Windows applications in the presence of random (non-stereotypical) keyboard and mouse input. The applications were chosen to cover a range of vendors, commercial and non-commercial software, and a wide variety of functionality, including word processors, web browsers, presentation graphics editors, network utilities, spreadsheets, software development environments, and assorted random applications such as Notepad, Solitaire, the Windows CD player, and similar common programs. The study found that 21% of the applications tested crashed and 24% hung when sent random keyboard/mouse input, and when sent random Win32 messages (corresponding to events other than direct keyboard- and mouse-related actions), *all* of the applications tested either crashed or hung [21].

Even when an anomaly is detected, it's often easier to avoid it by adapting the code or user behaviour that invokes it ("don't do that, then") because this is less effort than trying to get the error fixed[1]. In this manner problems are avoided by a kind of symbiosis through which the reliability of the system as a whole is greater than the reliability of any of its parts [22]. Since most of the faults that will be encountered are benign (in the sense that they don't lead to failures for most users), all that's necessary in order for the vendor to provide the perception of reliability is to remove the few percent of faults that cause noticeable problems. Although it may be required for security purposes to remove every single fault (as far as is practical), for marketing purposes it's only necessary to remove the few percent that are likely to cause problems.

In many cases users don't even have a choice as to which software they can use. If they can't process data from Word, Excel, PowerPoint, and Outlook and view web pages loaded with JavaScript and ActiveX, their business doesn't run, and some companies go so far as to publish explicit instructions telling users how to disable security measures in order to maximise their web-browsing experience [23]. Going beyond basic OS security, most current security products still don't effectively address the problems posed by hostile code such as trojan horses (which the Bell–LaPadula model was designed to combat), and the systems that the code runs on increase both the power of the code to do harm and the ease of distributing the code to other systems.

Financial considerations also need to be taken into account. As has already been mentioned, vendors are rarely given any incentive to produce products secure beyond a basic level which suffices to avoid embarrassing headlines in the trade press. In a market in which network economics apply, Nathan Bedford Forrest's axiom of getting there first with the most takes precedence over getting it right — there'll always be time for bugfixes and upgrades later on. Perversely, the practice of buying known-unreliable software is then rewarded by

---

[1] This document, prepared with MS Word, illustrates this principle quite well, having been produced in a manner that avoided a number of bugs that would crash the program.

labelling it "best practice" rather than the more obvious "fraud". This, and other (often surprising) economic disincentives towards building secure and reliable software, are covered elsewhere [24].

This presents a rather gloomy outlook for someone wanting to provide secure crypto services to a user of these systems. In order to solve this problem, we adopt a reversed form of the Mohammed-and-the-mountain approach: Instead of trying to move the insecurity away from the crypto through various operating system security measures, we move the crypto away from the insecurity. In other words although the user may be running a system crawling with rogue ActiveX controls, macro viruses, trojan horses, and other security nightmares, none of these can come near the crypto.

7.1.2 Solving the Problem

The FIPS 140 standard provides us with a number of guidelines for the development of cryptographic security modules [25]. NIST originally allowed only hardware implementations of cryptographic algorithms (for example, the original NIST DES document allowed for hardware implementation only [26][27]); however, this requirement was relaxed somewhat in the mid-1990s to allow software implementations as well [28][29]. FIPS 140 defines four security levels ranging from level 1 (the cryptographic algorithms are implemented correctly) through to level 4 (the module or device has a high degree of tamper-resistance, including an active tamper response mechanism that causes it to zeroise itself when tampering is detected). To date, only one general-purpose product family has been certified at level 4 [30][31].

Since FIPS 140 also allows for software implementations, an attempt has been made to provide an equivalent measure of security for the software platform on which the cryptographic module is to run. This is done by requiring the underlying operating system to be evaluated at progressively higher Orange Book levels for each FIPS 140 level, so that security level 2 would require the software module to be implemented on a C2-rated operating system. Unfortunately, this provides something of an impedance mismatch between the actual security of hardware and software implementations, since it implies that products such as a Fortezza card [32] or Dallas iButton (a relatively high-security device) [33] provide the same level of security as a program running under Windows NT. As Chapter 4 already mentioned, it's quite likely that the OS security levels were set so low out of concern that setting them any higher would make it impossible to implement the higher FIPS 140 levels in software due to a lack of systems evaluated at that level.

Even with sights set this low, it doesn't appear to be possible to implement secure software-only crypto on a general-purpose PC. Trying to protect cryptovariables (or more generically critical security parameters, CSPs in FIPS 140-speak) on a system which provides functions like ReadProcessMemory seems pointless, even if the system does claim a C2/E2 evaluation. On the other hand, trying to source a B2 or, more realistically, B3 system to provide an adequate level of security for the crypto software is almost impossible (the practicality of employing an OS in this class, whose members include Trusted Xenix, XTS 300, and Multos, speaks for itself). A simpler solution would be to implement a crypto coprocessor using a dedicated machine running at system high, and indeed FIPS 140 explicitly recognises this by stating that the OS security requirements only apply in cases where the system is running programs other than the crypto module (to compensate for this, FIPS 140 imposes its own software evaluation requirements which in some cases are even more arduous than those of the Orange Book).

An alternative to a pure-hardware approach might be to try to provide some form of software-only protection that attempts to compensate for the lack of protection present in the OS. Some work has been done in this area involving obfuscation of the code to be protected, either mechanically [34][35] or manually [36]. The use of mechanical obfuscation (for example, reordering of code and the insertion of dummy instructions) is also present in a number of polymorphic viruses, and can be quite effectively countered [37][38]. Manual obfuscation techniques are somewhat more difficult to counter automatically; however, computer game vendors have trained several generations of crackers in the art of bypassing the most sophisticated software protection and security features they could come up with [39][40][41], indicating that this type of protection won't provide any relief either, and this doesn't even go into the portability and maintenance nightmare that this type of code presents (it is for these reasons that the obfuscation provisions were removed from a later version of the CDSA specification where they were first proposed [42]). There also exists a small amount of experimental work involving trying to create a form of software self-defence mechanism that tries to detect and compensate for program or data corruption [43][44][45][46]; however, this type of self-defence technology will probably stay restricted to Core Wars Redcode programs for some time to come. As the final nail in the coffin, a general proof exists that shows that real code obfuscation is impossible [47].

7.1.3 Coprocessor Design Issues

The main consideration when designing a coprocessor to manage crypto operations is how much functionality we should move from the host into the coprocessor unit. The baseline, which we'll call a tier[2] 0 coprocessor, has all of the functionality in the host, which is what we're trying to avoid. The levels above tier 0 provide varying levels of protection for cryptovariables and coprocessor operations, as shown in Figure 7.1. The minimal level of coprocessor functionality, a tier 1 coprocessor, moves the private key and its operations out of the host. This type of functionality is found in smart cards, and is only a small step above having no protection at all, since although the key itself is held in the card, all operations performed by the card are controlled by the host, leaving the card at the mercy of any malicious software on the host system. In addition to these shortcomings, smart cards are very slow, offer no protection for cryptovariables other than the private key, and often can't even fully protect the private key (for example, a card with an RSA private key intended for signing can be misused to decrypt a session key or message since RSA signing and decryption are equivalent).

---

[2] The reason for the use of this somewhat unusual term is because almost every other noun used to denote hierarchies is already in use; "tier" is unusual enough that no-one else has gotten around to using it in their security terminology.

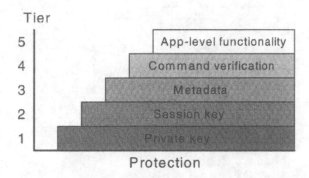

Figure 7.1. Levels of protection offered by crypto hardware.

The next level of functionality, tier 2, moves both public/private-key operations and conventional encryption operations, along with hybrid mechanisms such as public-key wrapping of content-encryption keys, into the coprocessor. This type of functionality is found in devices such as Fortezza cards and a number of devices sold as crypto accelerators, and provides rather more protection than that found in smart cards since no cryptovariables are ever exposed on the host. Like smart cards however, all control over the device's operation resides in the host, so that even if a malicious application can't get at the keys directly, it can still apply them in a manner other than the intended one.

The next level of functionality, tier 3, moves all crypto-related processing (for example certificate generation and message signing and encryption) into the coprocessor. The only control that the host has over processing is at the level of "sign this message" or "encrypt this message". All other operations (message formatting, the addition of additional information such as the signing time and signer's identity, and so on) are performed by the coprocessor. In contrast, if the coprocessor has tier 1 functionality, the host software can format the message any way that it wants, set the date to an arbitrary time (in fact, it can never really know the true time since it's coming from the system clock, which another process could have altered), and generally do whatever it wants with other message parameters. Even with a tier 2 coprocessor such as a Fortezza card, which has a built-in real-time clock (RTC), the host is free to ignore the RTC and give a signed message any timestamp it wants. Similarly, even though protocols such as CSP, which is used with Fortezza, incorporate complex mechanisms to handle authorisation and access control issues [48], the enforcement of these mechanisms is left to the untrusted host system rather than the card (!!). Other potential problem areas involve handling of intermediate results and composite call sequences that shouldn't be interrupted, such as loading a key and then using it in a cryptographic operation [49]. In contrast, with a tier 3 coprocessor that performs all crypto-related processing independent of the host, the coprocessor controls the message formatting and the addition of information such as a timestamp taken from its own internal clock, moving them out of reach of any software running on the host. The various levels of protection when the coprocessor is used for message decryption are shown in Figure 7.2.

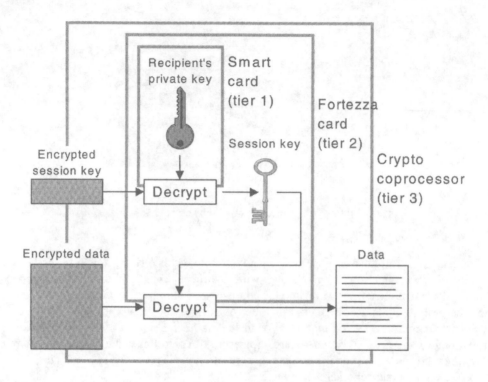

Figure 7.2. Protection levels for the decrypt operation.

Going beyond tier 3, a tier 4 coprocessor provides facilities such as command verification that prevent the coprocessor from acting on commands sent from the host system without the approval of the user. The features of this level of functionality are explained in more detail in Section 7.4, which covers extended security functionality.

Can we move the functionality to an even higher level, tier 5, giving the coprocessor even more control over message handling? Although it's possible to do this, it isn't a good idea since at this level the coprocessor will potentially need to run message viewers (to display messages), editors (to create/modify messages), mail software (to send and receive them), and a whole host of other applications, and of course these programs will need to be able to handle MIME attachments, HTML, JavaScript, ActiveX, and so on in order to function as required. In addition, the coprocessor will now require its own input mechanism (a keyboard), output mechanism (a monitor), mass storage, and other extras. At this point, the coprocessor has evolved into a second computer attached to the original one, and since it's running a range of untrusted and potentially dangerous code, we need to think about moving the crypto functionality into a coprocessor for safety. Lather, rinse, repeat.

The best level of functionality therefore is to move all crypto and security-related processing into the coprocessor, but to leave everything else on the host.

7.2 The Coprocessor

The traditional way to build a crypto coprocessor has been to create a complete custom implementation, originally with ASICs and more recently with a mixture of ASICs and general-purpose CPUs, all controlled by custom software. This approach leads to long design cycles, difficulties in making changes at a later point, high costs (with an accompanying strong incentive to keep all design details proprietary due to the investment involved), and reliance on a single vendor for the product. In contrast an open-source coprocessor by definition doesn't need to be proprietary, so it can use existing commercial off-the-shelf (COTS) hardware and software as part of its design, which greatly reduces the cost (the coprocessor described here is one to two orders of magnitude cheaper than proprietary designs while offering generally equivalent performance and superior functionality). This type of coprocessor can be sourced from multiple vendors and easily migrated to newer hardware as the current hardware base becomes obsolete.

The coprocessor requires three layers

1. The processor hardware.
2. The firmware that manages the hardware, for example, initialisation, communications with the host, persistent storage, and so on.
3. The software that handles the crypto functionality.

The following sections describe the coprocessor hardware and resource management firmware on which the crypto control software runs.

7.2.1 Coprocessor Hardware

Embedded systems have traditionally been based on the VME bus, a 32-bit data/32-bit address bus incorporated onto cards in the 3U (10×16 cm) and 6U (23×16 cm) Eurocard form factor [50]. The VME bus is CPU-independent and supports all popular microprocessors including Sparc, Alpha, 68K, and x86. An x86-specific bus called PC/104, based on the 104-pin ISA bus, has become popular in recent years due to the ready availability of low-cost components from the PC industry. PC/104 cards are much more compact at 9×9.5 cm than VME cards, and unlike a VME passive backplane-based system can provide a complete system on a single card [51]. PC/104-Plus, an extension to PC/104, adds a 120-pin PCI connector alongside the existing ISA one, but is otherwise mostly identical to PC/104 [52].

In addition to PC/104 there are a number of functionally identical systems with slightly different form factors, of which the most common is the biscuit PC shown in Figure 7.3, a card the same size as a 3½" or occasionally 5¼" drive, with a somewhat less common one being the credit card or SIMM PC, roughly the size of a credit card. A biscuit PC provides most of the functionality and I/O connectors of a standard PC motherboard. As the form factor shrinks, the I/O connectors do as well so that a SIMM PC typically uses a single enormous edge connector for all of its I/O. In addition to these form factors, there also exist card PCs (sometimes called slot PCs), which are biscuit PCs built as ISA or (more rarely) PCI-like cards. A typical configuration for an entry-level system is a 5x86/133 CPU (roughly equivalent in performance to a 133 MHz Pentium), 8-16 MB of DRAM, 2-8 MB of flash memory emulating a disk drive, and every imaginable kind of I/O (serial ports, parallel ports, floppy disk, IDE hard drive, IR and USB ports, keyboard and mouse, and others). High-end embedded systems built from components designed for laptop use provide about the same level of performance as a current laptop PC, although their price makes them rather impractical for use as crypto hardware. To compare this with other well-known types of crypto hardware, a typical smart card has a 5 MHz 8-bit CPU, a few hundred bytes of RAM, and a few kB of EEPROM, and a Fortezza card has a 10- or 20 MHz ARM CPU, 64 kB of RAM and 128 kB of flash memory/EEPROM.

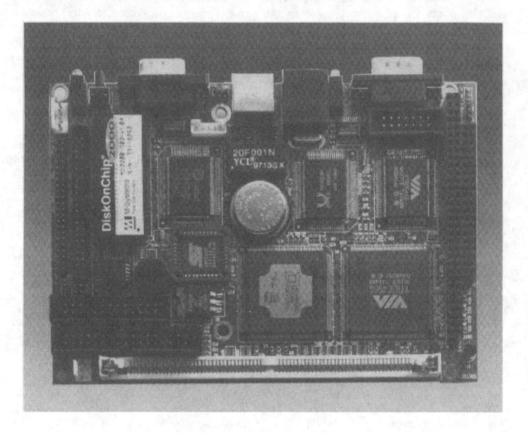

Figure 7.3. Biscuit PC (life size).

All of the embedded systems described above represent COTS components available from a large range of vendors in many different countries, with a corresponding range of performance and price figures. Alongside the x86-based systems there also exist systems based on other CPUs, typically ARM, Dragonball (embedded Motorola 68K), and to a lesser extent PowerPC; however, these are available from a limited number of vendors and can be quite expensive. Besides the obvious factor of system performance affecting the overall price, the smaller form factors and use of exotic hardware such as non-generic PC components can also drive up the price. In general, the best price/performance balance is obtained with a very generic PC/104 or biscuit PC system.

7.2.2 Coprocessor Firmware

Once the hardware has been selected, the next step is to determine what software to run on it to control it. The coprocessor is in this case acting as a special-purpose computer system running only the crypto control software, so that what would normally be thought of as the operating system is acting as the system firmware, and the real operating system for the device is the crypto control software. The control software therefore represents an application-specific operating system, with crypto objects such as encryption contexts, certificates, and envelopes replacing the user applications that are managed by conventional OSes. The differences between a conventional system and the crypto coprocessor running one typical type of firmware-equivalent OS are shown in Figure 7.4.

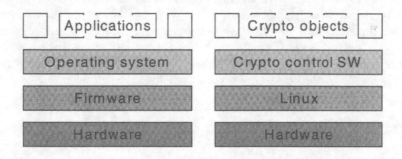

Figure 7.4. Conventional system versus coprocessor system layers.

Since the hardware is in effect a general-purpose PC, there is no need to use a specialised, expensive embedded or real-time kernel or OS since a general-purpose OS will function just as well. The OS choice is then something simple like one of the free or nearly-free embeddable forms of MSDOS [53][54][55] or an open source operating system such as one of the x86 BSDs or Linux that can be adapted for use in embedded hardware. Although embedded DOS is the simplest to get going and has the smallest resource requirements, it's really only a bootstrap loader for real-mode applications and provides very little access to most of the resources provided by the hardware. For this reason it's not worth considering except on extremely low-end, resource-starved hardware (it's still possible to find PC/104 cards with 386/40s on them, although having to drive them with DOS is probably its own punishment). In fact cryptlib is currently actively deployed on various embedded systems running DOS-based network stacks with processors as lowly as 80186es, but this is an unnecessarily painful approach used only because of requirements to be compatible with existing hardware.

A better choice than DOS is a proper operating system that can fully utilise the capabilities of the hardware. The only functionality that is absolutely required of the OS is a memory manager and some form of communication with the outside world (again, cryptlib is currently running on embedded systems with no memory management, filesystem, or real communications channels, it is because of experience with these that something better is preferred). Also useful (although not absolutely essential) is the ability to store data such as private keys in some form of persistent storage. Finally, the ability to handle multiple threads may be useful where the device is expected to perform multiple crypto tasks at once. Apart from the multithreading, the OS is just acting as a basic resource manager, which is why DOS could be pressed into use if necessary.

Both FreeBSD and Linux have been stripped down in various ways for use with embedded hardware [56][57]. There's not really a lot to say about the two; both meet the requirements given above, both are open-source systems, and both can use a standard full-scale system as the development environment — whichever one is the most convenient can be used. At the moment, Linux is a better choice because its popularity means that there is better support for devices such as flash memory mass storage, so the coprocessor described here uses Linux as its resource management firmware. A convenient feature that gives the free Unixen an extra advantage over alternatives such as embedded DOS is that they'll automatically switch to using the serial port for their consoles if no video drivers and/or hardware are present, which enables them to be used with cheaper embedded hardware that doesn't require additional video circuitry just for the one-off setup process. A particular advantage of Linux is that it'll halt the CPU when nothing is going on (which is most of the time), greatly reducing coprocessor power consumption and heat problems.

7.2.3 Firmware Setup

Setting up the coprocessor firmware involves creating a stripped-down Linux setup capable of running on the coprocessor hardware. The services required of the firmware are:

- Memory management
- Persistent storage services
- Communication with the host
- Process and thread management (optional)

All newer embedded systems support the M-Systems DiskOnChip (DOC) flash disk, which emulates a standard IDE hard drive by identifying itself as a BIOS extension during the system initialisation phase (allowing it to install a DOC filesystem driver to provide BIOS support for the drive) and later switching to a native driver for OSes that don't use the BIOS for hardware access [58]. More recently, systems have begun moving to the use of compact flash cards that emulate IDE hard drives, due to their popularity in digital cameras and somewhat lower costs than DOCs.

The first step in installing the firmware involves formatting the DOC or compact flash card as a standard hard drive and partitioning it prior to installing Linux. The flash disk is configured to contain two partitions, one mounted read-only, which contains the firmware and crypto control software, and one mounted read/write with additional safety precautions such as `noexec` and `nosuid`, for storage of configuration information and encrypted keys.

The firmware consists of a basic Linux kernel with every unnecessary service and option stripped out. This means removing support for video devices, mass storage (apart from the flash disk and a floppy drive), multimedia devices, and other unnecessary bagatelles. Apart from the TCP/IP (or similar protocol) stack needed by the crypto control software to communicate with the host, there are no networking components running (or even present) on the system, and even the TCP/IP stack may be absent if alternative, more low-level means of communicating with the host (explained in more detail further on) are employed. All configuration tasks are performed through console access via the serial port, and software is installed by connecting a floppy drive and copying across pre-built binaries.

These security measures both minimise the size of the code base that needs to be installed on the coprocessor, and eliminate any unnecessary processes and services that might constitute a security risk. Although it would be easier if we provided a means of FTPing binaries across, the fact that a user must explicitly connect a floppy drive and mount it in order to change the firmware or control software makes it much harder to accidentally (or maliciously) move problematic code across to the coprocessor, provides a workaround for the fact that FTP over alternative coprocessor communications channels such as a parallel port is tricky without resorting to the use of even more potential problem software, and makes it easier to comply with the FIPS 140 requirements that (where a non-Orange Book OS is used) it not be possible for extraneous software to be loaded and run on the system. Direct console access is also used for other operations such as setting the onboard real-time clock, which is used to add timestamps to signatures. Finally, all paging is disabled, both because it isn't needed or safe to perform with the limited-write-cycle flash disk, and because it avoids any risk of sensitive data being written to backing store, eliminating a major headache that occurs with all virtual-memory operating systems [59].

At this point we have a basic system consisting of the underlying hardware and enough firmware to control it and provide the services that we require. Running on top of this will be a dæmon that implements the crypto control software that does the actual work.

7.3 Crypto Functionality Implementation

Once the hardware base and functionality level of the coprocessor have been established, we need to design an appropriate programming interface for it. An interface that employs complex data structures, pointers to memory locations, callback functions, and other such elements won't work with the coprocessor unless a sophisticated RPC mechanism is employed. Once we get to this level of complexity, we run into problems both with lowered performance due to data marshalling and copying requirements, and potential security problems arising from inevitable implementation bugs. A better way to handle this is to apply the forwarder-receiver model shown in Figure 7.5, which takes cryptlib function calls on the local machine and forwards them to the coprocessor, returning the results to the local machine in a similar manner.

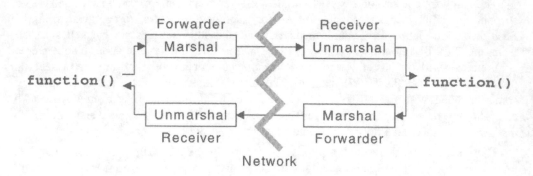

Figure 7.5. Coprocessor communication using the forwarder-receiver model.

The interface used by cryptlib is ideally suited for use in a coprocessor since only the object handle (a small integer value) and one or two arguments (either an integer value or a byte string and length) are needed to perform most operations. This use of only basic parameter types leads to a very simple and lightweight interface, with only the integer values needing any canonicalisation (to network byte order) before being passed to the coprocessor. A coprocessor call of this type, illustrated in Figure 7.6, requires only a few lines of code more than what is required for a direct call to the same code on the host system. In practice, the interface is further simplified by using a pre-encoded template containing all fixed parameters (for example, the type of function call being performed and a parameter count), copying in any variable parameters (for example, the object handle) with appropriate canonicalistion, and dispatching the result to the coprocessor. The coprocessor returns results in the same manner.

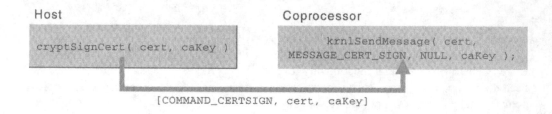

Figure 7.6. Command forwarding to the coprocessor.

The coprocessor interface is further simplified by the fact that even the local cryptlib interface constitutes a basic implementation of the forwarder-receiver model in which both ends of the connection happen to be on the same machine and in the same address space, reducing the use of special-case code that is only required for the coprocessor.

7.3.1 Communicating with the Coprocessor

The next step after designing the programming interface is to determine which type of communications channel is best suited to controlling the coprocessor. Since the embedded controller hardware is intended for interfacing to almost anything, there are a wide range of I/O capabilities available for communicating with the host. Many embedded controllers provide an Ethernet interface either standard or as an option, so the most universal interface uses TCP/IP for communications. For card PCs that plug into the host's backplane, we should be able to use the system bus for communications, and if that isn't possible we can take advantage of the fact that the parallel ports on all recent PCs provide sophisticated (for what was intended as a printer port) bidirectional I/O capabilities and run a link from the parallel port on the host motherboard to the parallel port on the coprocessor. Finally, we can use more exotic I/O capabilities such as USB and similar high-speed serial links to communicate with the coprocessor. By using (or at least emulating via a sockets interface) TCP/IP over each of these physical links, we can provide easy portability across a wide range of interface types.

7.3.2 Communications Hardware

The most universal coprocessor consists of a biscuit PC that communicates with the host over Ethernet (or, less universally, a parallel or USB port). One advantage that an external, removable coprocessor of this type has over one that plugs directly into the host PC is that it's very easy to unplug the entire crypto subsystem and store it separately from the host, moving it out of reach of any covert access by outsiders [60] while the owner of the system is away. In addition to the card itself, this type of standalone setup requires a case and a power supply, either internal to the case or an external wall-wart type (these are available for about $10 with a universal input voltage range that allows them to work in any country). The same arrangement is used in a number of commercially available products, and has the advantage that it interfaces to virtually any type of system, with the commensurate disadvantage that it requires a dedicated Ethernet connection to the host (which typically means adding an extra network card), as well as adding to the clutter surrounding the machine.

The alternative option for an external coprocessor is to use the parallel port, which doesn't require a network card but does tie up a port that may be required for one of a range of other devices such as external disk drives, CD writers, and scanners that have been kludged onto this interface alongside the more obvious printers. Apart from its more obvious use, the printer port can be used either as an Enhanced Parallel Port (EPP) or as an Extended Capability Port (ECP) [61]. Both modes provide about 1–2 MB/s data throughput (depending on which vendor's claims are to be believed) which compares favourably with a parallel port's standard software-intensive maximum rate of around 150 kB/s and even with the throughput of a 10Mbps Ethernet interface.

EPP was designed for general-purpose bidirectional communication with peripherals and handles intermixed read and write operations and block transfers without too much trouble, whereas ECP (which requires a DMA channel, which can complicate the host system's configuration process) requires complex data-direction negotiation and handling of DMA transfers in progress, adding a fair amount of overhead when used with peripherals that employ mixed reading and writing of small data quantities. Another disadvantage of DMA is that its use paralyses the CPU by seizing control of the bus, halting all threads that may be executing while data is being transferred. Because of this the optimal interface mechanism is EPP. From a programming point of view, this communications mechanism looks like a permanent virtual circuit that is functionally equivalent to the dumb wire for which we're using the Ethernet link, so the two can be interchanged with a minimum of coding effort.

To the user, the most transparent coprocessor would consist of some form of card PC that plugs directly into their system's backplane. Currently, virtually all card PCs have ISA bus interfaces (the few which support PCI use a PCI/ISA hybrid which won't fit a standard PCI slot [62]), which unfortunately doesn't provide much flexibility in terms of communications capabilities since the only viable means of moving data to and from the coprocessor is via DMA, which requires a custom kernel-mode driver on both sides. The alternative, using the parallel port, is much simpler since most operating systems already support EPP and/or ECP data transfers, but comes at the expense of a reduced data-transfer rate and the loss of use of the parallel port on the host. Currently, the use of either of these options is rendered moot since the ISA card PCs assume that they have full control over a passive backplane bus system, which means that they can't be plugged into a standard PC, which contains its own CPU that is also assuming that it solely controls the bus. It's possible that in the future card PCs that function as PCI bus devices will appear, but until they do it's not possible to implement the coprocessor as a plug-in card without using a custom extender card containing an ISA or PCI connector for the host side, a PC104 connector for a PC104-based CPU card, and buffer circuitry in between to isolate the two buses. This destroys the COTS nature of the hardware, limiting availability and raising costs.

The final communications option uses more exotic I/O capabilities such as USB (and occasionally other high-speed serial links such as FireWire) that are present on newer embedded systems. These are much like Ethernet but have the disadvantage that they are currently rather poorly supported by operating systems targeted at embedded systems.

7.3.3 Communications Software

The discussion so far has looked at the communications mechanism either as an interface-specific one or an emulated TCP/IP sockets interface, with the latter being built on top of the former. Although the generic sockets interface provides a high level of flexibility and works well with existing code, it requires that each device and/or device interface be allocated its own IP address and creates extra code overhead for providing the TCP/IP-style interface. Instead of using the standard AF_INET family, the sockets interface could implement a new AF_COPROCESSOR family with the address passed to the connect() function being a device or interface number or some similar identifier, which avoids the need to allocate an IP address. This has the disadvantage that it loses some of the universality of the TCP/IP interface, which by extension makes it more difficult to perform operations such as direct device-to-device communications for purposes such as load balancing. Another advantage of the TCP/IP interface, covered in more detail in Section 7.4.3, is that it frees the coprocessor from having to be located in the same physical location as the host or coprocessor that it is communicating with it.

Since we are using Linux as the resource manager for the coprocessor hardware, we can use a multithreaded implementation of the coprocessor software to handle multiple simultaneous requests from the host. After initialising the various cryptlib subsystems, the control software creates a pool of threads that wait on a mutex for commands from the host. When a command arrives, one of the threads is woken up, processes the command, and returns the result to the host. In this manner, the coprocessor can have multiple requests outstanding at once, and a process running on the host won't block whenever another process has an outstanding request present on the coprocessor.

7.3.4 Coprocessor Session Control

When cryptlib is being run on the host system, the concept of a user session doesn't exist since the user has whatever control over system resources is allowed by their account privileges. When cryptlib is being used in a coprocessor that operates independently from the host, the concept of a session with the coprocessor applies. This works much like a session with a more general-purpose computer except that the capabilities available to the user are usually divided into two classes, those of a security officer or SO (the super-user- or administrator-equivalent for the coprocessor) and those of a standard user. The SO can perform functions such as initialising the device and (in some cases) perform key loading and generation actions but can't actually make use of the keys, whereas the user can make use of the keys but can't generally perform administrative actions. In addition to these two standard roles, cryptlib provides an additional role, that of a certification authority (CA) which acts as a type of SO for certificate management operations. The principles behind this role are similar to those of the SO role, so it won't be discussed further.

The exact details of the two roles are somewhat application-specific; for example, the Fortezza card allows itself to be initialised and initial keys and certificates to be loaded by the SO (in the circles in which Fortezza is used, the term is site security officer or SSO), after which the initial user PIN is set, which automatically logs the SO out. At this point the card initialisation functions are disabled, and the SO can log in again to perform maintenance operations or the user can log in to use the card to sign or encrypt data. When logged in as SO it's not possible to use the card for standard operations, and when logged in as user it's not possible to perform maintenance operations [63]. The reason for enforcing this sequence of operations is that it provides a clear chain of control and responsibility for the device, since the card is moved into its initial state by the SO, who started with a pristine (at least as far as the FIPS 140 tamper-evident case is able to indicate) card into which they loaded initial values and handed the device on to the user. The SO knows (with a good degree of certainty) that the card was untampered, and initialises it as required, after which the user knows that the card is initialised and was configured for them by the SO. This simplified version of the Fortezza life cycle (the full version has a more fine-grained number of states) is shown in Figure 7.7.

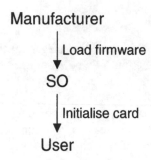

Figure 7.7. Fortezza card life cycle.

A similar function is played by the SO in the Dallas iButton (in iButton terms, the crypto officer), who is responsible for initialising the device and setting various fixed parameters, after which they set the initial user PIN and hand the device over to the user. At the point of manufacture the iButton is initialised with the Dallas Primary Feature Set, which includes a private key generated in the device when the feature set was initialised. The fixed Primary Feature Set allows the SO to initialise the device and allows the user to check whether the SO has altered various pre-set options. Since the Dallas Primary key is tied to an individual device and can only sign data under control of the iButton internal code, it can be used to guarantee that certain settings are in effect for the device and to guarantee that a given user key was generated in and is controlled by the device. Again, this provides a trusted bootstrap path that allows the user and any relying parties to determine with a good degree of confidence that everything is as it should be.

An even more complex secure bootstrap process is used in the IBM 4758. This is a multi-stage process that begins with the layer 0 miniboot code in ROM. This code allows (under carefully controlled conditions) layer 1 miniboot code to be loaded into flash memory, which in turn allows layer 2 system software to be loaded into flash, which in turn loads and runs layer 3 user applications [30][64]. The device contains various hardware-based interlocks that are used to protect the integrity of each layer. During the boot process, each boot phase advances a ratchet that ensures that once execution has passed through layer n to a lower-privileged layer $n + 1$, it can never move back to layer n. As execution moves into higher and higher layers, the capabilities that are available become less and less, so that code at layer $n + 1$ can no longer access or modify resources available at layer n. An attempt to reload code at a given layer can only occur under carefully controlled conditions either hardcoded into or configured by the installer of the layer beneath it. A normal reload of a layer (that is, a software update with appropriate authorisation) will leave the other data in that layer intact; an emergency reload (used to initially load code and for emergencies such as code being damaged or non-functional) erases all data such as encryption keys for every layer from the one being reloaded on up. This has the same effect as the Fortezza multi-stage bootstrap where the only way to change initial parameters is to wipe the card and start again from scratch. Going beyond this, the 4758 also has an extensive range of authorisation and authentication controls that allow a trusted execution environment within the device to be preserved.

As discussed in a Chapter 3, cryptlib's flexible security policy can be adapted to enforce at least the simpler Fortezza/iButton-type controls without too much trouble. At present, this area has seen little work since virtually all users are working with either a software-only implementation or a dedicated coprocessor under the control of a single user; however, in future work the implications of multiuser access to coprocessor resources will be explored. Since cryptlib provides native SSL/TLS and ssh capabilities, it's likely that multiuser access will be protected with one of these mechanisms, with per-user configuration information being stored using the PKCS #15 format [65], which was designed to store information in crypto tokens and which is ideally suited for this purpose.

7.3.5 Open versus Closed-Source Coprocessors

There are a number of vendors who sell various forms of tier 2 coprocessors, all of which run proprietary control software and generally go to some lengths to ensure that no outsiders can ever examine it. The usual way in which vendors of proprietary implementations try to build the same user confidence in their product as would be provided by having the source code and design information available for public scrutiny is to have it evaluated by independent labs and testing facilities, typically to the FIPS 140 standard when the product constitutes crypto hardware (the security implications of open source versus proprietary implementations have been covered exhaustively in various fora and won't be repeated here). Unfortunately, this process leads to prohibitively expensive products (thousands to tens of thousands of dollars per unit) and still requires users to trust the vendor not to insert a backdoor or to accidentally void the security via a later code update or enhancement added after the evaluation is complete (strictly speaking, such post-evaluation changes would void the evaluation, but vendors sometimes forget to mention this in their marketing literature). There have been numerous allegations of the former occurring [66][67][68], and occasional reports of the latter.

In contrast, an open source implementation of the crypto control software can be seen to be secure by the end user with no degree of blind trust required. The user can (if so inclined) obtain the raw coprocessor hardware from the vendor of their choice in the country of their choice, compile the firmware and control software from the openly available source code, and install it knowing that no supplemental functionality known only to a few insiders exists. For this reason, the entire suite of coprocessor control software is made available in source code form for anyone to examine, build, and install as they see fit.

A second, far less theoretical advantage of an open-source coprocessor is that until the crypto control code is loaded into it, it isn't a controlled cryptographic item, as crypto source code and software aren't controlled in most of the world. This means that it's possible to ship the hardware and software separately to almost any destination (or source it locally) without any restrictions and then combine the two to create a controlled item once they arrive at their destination. Like a two-component glue, things don't get sticky until you mix the parts.

7.4 Extended Security Functionality

The basic coprocessor design presented thus far serves to move all security-related processing and cryptovariables out of reach of hostile software, but by taking advantage of the capabilities of the hardware and firmware used to implement it, it's possible to do much more. By tying some of the controls enforced by the cryptlib security kernel to features of the coprocessor, it's possible to obtain an extended level of control over its operation as well as avoiding some of the problems that have traditionally plagued this type of security device. Although this isn't a panacea (there are too many ways to get at sensitive information that don't require any type of attack on the underlying cryptosystem or its implementation [69]), these measures help close some of the more glaring holes.

7.4.1 Controlling Coprocessor Actions

The most important type of extra functionality that can be added to the coprocessor is extended failsafe control over any actions that it performs. This means that instead of blindly performing any action requested by the host (purportedly on behalf of the user), it first seeks confirmation from the user that they have indeed requested the action to be taken. The most obvious application of this mechanism is for signing documents where the owner has to indicate their consent through a trusted I/O path rather than allowing a rogue application to request arbitrary numbers of signatures on arbitrary documents. This contrasts with other tier 1 and 2 processors, which are typically enabled through user entry of a PIN or password, after which they are at the mercy of any commands coming from the host. Apart from the security concerns, the ability to individually control signing actions and require conscious consent from the user means that the coprocessor provides a mechanism that is required by a number of digital signature laws that recognise the dangers inherent in systems that provide an automated (that is, with little control from the user) signing capability.

The means of providing this service is to hook into the security kernel's sign action and decrypt action processing mechanisms. In normal processing, the kernel receives the incoming message, applies various security policy-related checks to it, and then forwards the message to the intended target, as shown in Figure 7.8.

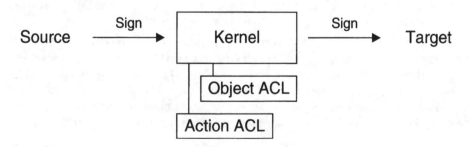

Figure 7.8. Normal message processing.

In order to obtain additional confirmation that the action is to be taken, the coprocessor can indicate the requested action to the user and request additional confirmation before passing on the message. If the user chooses to deny the request or doesn't respond within a certain time, the request is blocked by the kernel in the same manner as if the object's ACL didn't allow it, as shown in Figure 7.9. This mechanism is similar to the command confirmation mechanism in the VAX A1 security kernel, which takes a command from the untrusted VMS or Ultrix-32 OSes running on top of it, requests that the user press the (non-overridable) secure attention key to communicate directly with the kernel and confirm the operation ("Something claiming to be you has requested X. Is this OK?"), and then returns the user back to the OS after performing the operation [70].

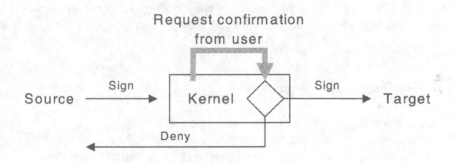

Figure 7.9. Processing with user confirmation.

The simplest form of user interface involves two LEDs and two pushbutton switches connected to a suitable port on the coprocessor (for example, the parallel port or serial port status lines). An LED is activated to indicate that confirmation of a signing or decryption action is required by the coprocessor. If the user pushes the confirmation button, the request is allowed through, if they push the cancel button or don't respond within a certain time, the request is denied.

7.4.2 Trusted I/O Path

The basic user-confirmation mechanism presented above can be generalised by taking advantage of the potential for a trusted I/O path that is provided by the coprocessor. The main use for a trusted I/O path is to allow for secure entry of a password or PIN that is used to enable access to keys stored in the coprocessor. Unlike typical tier 1 devices that assume that the entire device is secure and therefore can afford to use a short PIN in combination with a retry counter to protect cryptovariables, the coprocessor makes no assumptions about its security and instead relies on a user-supplied password to encrypt all cryptovariables held in persistent storage (the only time that keys exist in plaintext form is when they're decrypted to volatile memory prior to use). Because of this, a simple numeric keypad used to enter a PIN is not sufficient (unless the user enjoys memorising long strings of digits for use as passwords). Instead, the coprocessor can optionally make use of devices such as PalmPilots for password entry, perhaps in combination with novel password entry techniques such as graphical passwords [71]. Note though that, unlike a tier 0 crypto implementation, obtaining the user password via a keyboard sniffer on the host doesn't give access to private keys since they're held on the coprocessor and can never leave it, so that even if the password is compromised by software on the host, it won't provide access to the keys.

In a slightly more extreme form, the ability to access the coprocessor via multiple I/O channels allows us to enforce strict red/black separation, with plaintext being accessed through one I/O channel, ciphertext through another, and keys through a third. Although cryptlib doesn't normally load plaintext keys (they are generated and managed internally and can never pass outside the security perimeter), when the ability to load external keys is required, FIPS 140 mandates that they be loaded via a separate channel rather than the one used for general data, a provision that can be made by loading them over a channel such as a serial port (a number of commercial crypto coprocessors come with a serial port for this reason).

7.4.3 Physically Isolated Crypto

It has been said that the only truly tamperproof computer hardware is Voyager 2, since it has a considerable air gap (strictly speaking a non-air gap) that makes access to the hardware somewhat challenging (space aliens notwithstanding). We can take advantage of air-gap security in combination with cryptlib's remote-execution capability by siting the hardware performing the crypto in a safe location well away from any possible tampering. For example, by running the crypto on a server in a physically secure location and tunnelling data and control information to it via its built-in ssh or SSL/TLS capabilities, we can obtain the benefits of physical security for the crypto without the awkwardness of having to use it from a secure location or the expense of having to use a physically secure crypto module. The implications of remote execution of crypto from countries such as China or the UK (with the RIPA act in force) with keys and crypto being held in Europe or the US are left as an exercise for the reader.

Physical isolation at the macroscopic level is also possible due to the fact that the cryptlib separation kernel has the potential to allow different object types (and, at the most extreme level, individual objects) to be implemented in physically separate hardware. For those requiring an extreme level of isolation and security, it should be possible to implement the different object types in their own hardware; for example, keyset objects (which don't require any real security since certificates contain their own tamper protection) could be implemented on the host PC, the kernel (which requires a minimum of resources) could be implemented on a cheap ARM-based plug-in card, envelope objects (which can require a fair bit of memory but very little processing power) could be implemented on a 486 card with a good quantity of memory, and encryption contexts (which can require a fair amount of CPU power but little else) could be implemented using a faster Pentium-class CPU. In practice though it is unlikely that anyone would consider this level of isolation worth the expense and effort.

7.4.4 Coprocessors in Hostile Environments

Sometimes, the coprocessor will need to function in a somewhat hostile environment, not so much in the sense of it being exposed to extreme environmental conditions but more that it will need to be able to withstand a larger than usual amount of general curiosity by third parties. The standard approach to this problem is to embed the circuitry in some form of tamper-resistant envelope which in its most sophisticated form has active tamper-response circuitry that will zeroise cryptovariables if it detects any form of attack.

Such an environmental enclosure is difficult and expensive to construct for the average user; however, there exist a variety of specialised enclosures that are designed for use with embedded systems that are expected to be used under extreme environmental conditions. A typical enclosure of this form, the HiDAN system[3], is shown in Figure 7.10. This contains a PC104 system mounted on a heavy-duty aluminium-alloy chassis that acts as a heatsink for the PC and provides a substantial amount of physical and environmental protection for the circuitry contained within it.

Figure 7.10. HiDAN embedded PC internals (image courtesy RTD).

This type of enclosure provides a high degree of shielding and isolation for the internal circuitry, with a minimum of 85 dB of EMI shielding from 10–100MHz and 80 dB of shielding to 1 GHz, sufficient to meet a number of TEMPEST emission standards. All I/O is

---

[3] HiDAN images copyright Real Time Devices USA, all rights reserved.

via heavily shielded milspec connectors, and the assembly contains a built-in power supply module (present in the lower compartment) to isolate the internal circuitry from any direct connection to an external power source. As Figure 7.11 indicates, the unit is constructed in a manner capable of withstanding medium-calibre artillery fire.

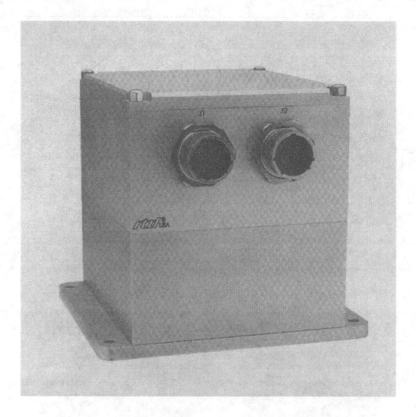

Figure 7.11. HiDAN embedded PC system (image courtesy RTD).

This type of enclosure can be easily adapted to meet the FIPS 140 level 2 and 3 physical security requirements. For level 2, "the cryptographic module shall provide evidence of tampering (e.g., cover, enclosure, and seal)" (Section 4.5.1) and "the cryptographic module shall be entirely contained within a metal or hard plastic production-grade enclosure" (Section 4.5.4), requirements that the unit more than meets (the EMI shielding includes a self-sealing gasket compound that provides a permanent environmental seal to a tongue-and-groove arrangement once the case is closed).

For level 3, "the cryptographic module shall be encapsulated within a hard potting material (e.g., a hard opaque epoxy)" (Section 4.5.3), which can be arranged by pouring a standard potting mix into the case before it is sealed shut.

7.5 Conclusion

This chapter has presented a design for an inexpensive, general-purpose cryptlib-based cryptographic coprocessor that is capable of keeping crypto keys and crypto processing operations safe even in the presence of malicious software on the host from which it is controlled. Extended security functionality is provided by taking advantage of the presence of trusted I/O channels to the coprocessor. Finally, the open-source nature of the design and use of COTS components means that anyone can easily reassure themselves of the security of the implementation and can obtain a coprocessor in any required location by refraining from combining the hardware and software components until they are at their final destination.

7.6 References

[1] "Inside Windows NT", Helen Custer, Microsoft Press, 1993.

[2] "Playing Hide and Seek with Stored Keys", Nicko van Someren and Adi Shamir, 22 September 1998, presented at Financial Cryptography 1999.

[3] "Monitoring System Events by Subclassing the Shell", Eric Heimburg, *Windows Developers Journal*, **Vol.9**, **No.2** (February 1998), p.35.

[4] "Windows NT System-Call Hooking", Mark Russinovich and Bryce Cogswell, *Dr.Dobbs Journal*, January 1997, p.42.

[5] "Win NT 4.0 UserId and Password available in memory", Russ Osterlund, posting to the ntbugtraq mailing list, message-ID `C12566CD.00485E7F.00@ZurichNotes.-com`, 1 December 1998.

[6] "In Memory Patching", Stone / UCF & F4CG, 1998

[7] "A *REAL* NT Rootkit, Patching the NT Kernel", Greg Hoglund, *Phrack*, **Vol.9**, **Issue 55**.

[8] "Design a Windows NT Service to Exploit Special Operating System Features", Jeffrey Richter, *Microsoft Systems Journal*, **Vol.12**, **No.10** (October 1997), p.19.

[9] "A Programming Fusion Technique for Windows NT", Greg Hoglund, SecurityFocus.com forum, guest feature `http://www.securityfocus.com/-templates/forum_message.html?forum=2&head=2137&id=557`, 14 December 1999.

[10] "Securing Java and ActiveX", Ted Julian, Forrester Report, *Network Strategies*, **Vol.12**, **No.7** (June 1998).

[11] "Death, Taxes, and Imperfect Software: Surviving the Inevitable", Crispin Cowan and Castor Fu, *Proceedings of the ACM New Security Paradigms Workshop'98*, September 1998.

[12] "User Friendly, 6 March 1998", Illiad, 6 March 1998, `http://www.-userfriendly.org/cartoons/archives/98mar/19980306.html`.

[13] "The Inevitability of Failure: The Flawed Assumption of Security in Modern Computing Environments", Peter Loscocco, Stephen Smalley, Patrick Muckelbauer, Ruth Taylor, S.Jeff Turner, and John Farrell, *Proceedings of the 21st National Information Systems Security Conference*, (formerly the National Computer Security Conference), October 1998, CDROM distribution.

[14] "The Importance of High Assurance Computers for Command, Control, Communications, and Intelligence Systems", W. Shockley, R. Schell, and M.Thompson, *Proceedings of the 4th Aerospace Computer Security Applications Conference*, December 1988, p.331.

[15] Jeff Schiller, quoted in *Communications of the ACM*, **Vol.42, No.9** (September 1999), p.10.

[16] "Software Security in an Internet World: An Executive Summary", Timothy Shimeall and John McDermott, *IEEE Software*, **Vol.16, No.4** (July/August 1999), p.58.

[17] "Formal Methods and Testing: Why the State-of-the-Art is Not the State-of-the-Practice", David Rosenblum, *ACM SIGSOFT Software Engineering Notes*, **Vol21, No.4** (July 1996), p.64.

[18] "The Process of Security", Bruce Schneier, *Information Security*, **Vol.3, No.4** (April 2000), p.32.

[19] "The New Security Paradigms Workshop — Boom or Bust?", Marv Schaefer, *Proceedings of the 2001 New Security Paradigms Workshop*, September 2001, p.119.

[20] "Optimizing Preventive Service of Software Products", Edward Adams, *IBM Journal of Research and Development*, **Vol.28, No.1** (January 1984), p.2.

[21] "An Empirical Study of the Robustness of Windows NT Applications Using Random Testing", Justin Forrester and Barton Miller, *Proceedings of the 4th USENIX Windows Systems Symposium*, August 2000.

[22] "How Did Software Get So Reliable Without Proof?", C.A.R.Hoare, *Proceedings of the 3rd International Symposium of Formal Methods Europe (FME'96)*, Springer-Verlag Lecture Notes in Computer Science No.1051, 1996, p.1

[23] "How to bypass those pesky firewalls", Mark Jackson, in *Risks Digest*, **Vol.20, No.1**, 1 October 1998.

[24] "Why Information Security is Hard — An Economic Perspective", Ross Anderson, *Proceedings of the 17th Annual Computer Security Applications Conference (ACSAC'01)*, December 2001, p.358.

[25] "Security Requirements for Cryptographic Modules", FIPS PUB 140-2, National Institute of Standards and Technology, July 2001.

[26] "Data Encryption Standard", FIPS PUB 46, National Institute of Standards and Technology, 22 January 1988.

[27] "General Security Requirements for Equipment Using the Data Encryption Standard", Federal Standard 1027, National Bureau of Standards, 14 April 1982.

[28] "Data Encryption Standard", FIPS PUB 46-2, National Institute of Standards and Technology, 30 December 1993.

[29] "Security Requirements for Cryptographic Modules", FIPS PUB 140, National Institute of Standards and Technology, 11 January 1994.

[30] "Building a High-Performance Programmable, Secure Coprocessor", Sean Smith and Steve Weingart, *Computer Networks and ISDN Systems*, **Issue 31** (April 1999), p.831.

[31] "Building the IBM 4758 Secure Coprocessor", Joan Dyer, Mark Lindemann, Ronald Perez, Reiner Sailer, Leendert van Doorn, Sean Smith, and Steve Weingart, *IEEE Computer*, **Vol.34**, **No.10** (October 2001), p.57.

[32] "Fortezza Program Overview, Version 4.0a", National Security Agency, February 1996.

[33] "iButton Home Page", http://www.ibutton.com.

[34] "A Tentative Approach to Constructing Tamper-Resistant Software", Masahiro Mambo, Takanori Murayama, and Eiji Okamoto, *Proceedings of the ACM New Security Paradigms Workshop'97*, September 1997.

[35] "Evaluation of Tamper-Resistant Software Deviating from Structured Programming Rules", Hideaki Goto, Masahiro Mambo, Hiroki Shizuya, and Yasuyoshi Watanabe, *Proceedings of the 6th Australian Conference on Information Security and Privacy (ACISP'01)*, Springer-Verlag Lecture Notes in Computer Science No.2119, 2001, p.145.

[36] "Common Data Security Architecture", Intel Corporation, 2 May 1996.

[37] "The Giant Black Book of Computer Viruses (2nd ed)", Mark Ludwig, American Eagle Publications, 1998.

[38] "Understanding and Managing Polymorphic Viruses", Symantec Corporation, 1996.

[39] "Fravia's Page of Reverse Engineering", http://www.fravia.org.

[40] "Phrozen Crew Official Site", http://www.phrozencrew.com/index2.htm.

[41] "Stone's Webnote", http://www.users.one.se/~stone/.

[42] "Common Security: CDSA and CSSM, Version 2", CAE specification, The Open Group, November 1999.

[43] "The Human Immune System as an Information Systems Security Reference Model", Charles Cresson Wood, *Computers and Security*, **Vol.6**, **No.6** (December 1987), p.511.

[44] "A model for detecting the existence of software corruption in real time", Jeffrey Voas, Jeffery Payne, and Frederick Cohen, *Computers and Security*, **Vol.12**, **No.3** (May 1993), p.275.

[45] "A Biologically Inspired Immune System for Computers", Jeffrey Kephart, *Proceedings of the Fourth International Workshop on the Synthesis and Simulation of Living Systems*, MIT Press, 1994, p.130.

[46] "Principles of a Computer Immune System", Anil Somayaji, Steven Hofmeyr, and Stephanie Forrest, *Proceedings of the 1997 New Security Paradigms Workshop*, ACM, 1997, p.75.

[47] "On the (Im)possibility of Obfuscating Programs (Extended Abstract)", Boaz Barak, Oded Goldreich, Rusell Impagliazzo, Steven Rudich, Amit Sahai, Salil Vadhan, and Ke Yung, *Proceedings of Crypto 2001*, Springer-Verlag Lecture Notes in Computer Science No.2139, 2001, p.1.

[48] "Common Security Protocol (CSP)", ACP 120, 8 July 1998.

[49] "Cryptographic API's", Dieter Gollman, *Cryptography: Policy and Algorithms*, Springer-Verlag Lecture Notes in Computer Science No.1029, July 1995, p.290.

[50] "The VMEbus Handbook", VMEbus International Trade Association, 1989.

[51] "PC/104 Specification, Version 2.3", PC/104 Consortium, June 1996.

[52] "PC/104-Plus Specification, Version 1.1", PC/104 Consortium, June 1997.

[53] "EZ Dos Web Site", http://members.aol.com/RedHtLinux/.

[54] "The FreeDOS Project", http://www.freedos.org.

[55] "OpenDOS Unofficial Home Page", http://www.deltasoft.com/opendos.-htm.

[56] "PicoBSD, the Small BSD", http://www.freebsd.org/~picobsd/-picobsd.html.

[57] "Embedded Linux", http://www.linuxembedded.com/.

[58] "DiskOnChip 2000: MD2200, MD2201 Data Sheet, Rev.2.3", M-Systems Inc, May 1999.

[59] "Secure Deletion of Data from Magnetic and Solid-State Memory", Peter Gutmann, *Proceedings of the 6th Usenix Security Symposium*, July 1996.

[60] "Physical access to computers: can your computer be trusted?", Walter Fabian, *Proceedings of the 29th Annual International Carnahan Conference on Security Technology*, October 1995, p.244.

[61] "IEEE Std.1284-1994: Standard Signaling Method for a Bi-Directional Parallel Peripheral Interface for Personal Computers", IEEE, March 1994.

[62] "PCI-ISA Passive Backplace: PICMG 1.0 R2.0", PCI Industrial Computer Manufacturers Group, 10 October 1994.

[63] "Interface Control Document for the Fortezza Crypto Card, Revision P1.5", National Security Agency, 22 December 1994.

[64] "Application Support Architecture for a High-Performance, Programmable Secure Coprocessor", Joan Dyer, Ron Perez, Sean Smith, and Mark Lindemann, *Proceedings of the 22nd National Information Systems Security Conference* (formerly the National Computer Security Conference), October 1999, CDROM distribution.

[65] "PKCS #15 v1.1: Cryptographic Token Information Syntax Standard", RSA Laboratories, 6 June 2000.

[66] "Verschlüsselt: Der Fall Hans Buehler", Res Strehle, Werd Verlag, Zurich, 1994.

[67] "No Such Agency, Part 4: Rigging the Game", Scott Shane and Tom Bowman, *The Baltimore Sun*, 4 December 1995, p.9.

[68] "Wer ist der befugte Vierte? Geheimdienste unterwandern den Schutz von Verschlüsselungsgeräten", *Der Spiegel*, No.36, 1996, p.206.

[69] "Beyond Cryptography: Threats Before and After", Walter Fabian, *Proceedings of the 32nd Annual International Carnahan Conference on Security Technology*, October 1998, p.97.

[70] "A Retrospective on the VAX VMM Security Kernel", Paul Karger, Mary Ellen Zurko, Douglas Bonin, Andrew Mason, and Clifford Kahn, *IEEE Transactions on Software Engineering*, **Vol.17**, **No.11** (November 1991), p.1147.

[71] "The Design and Analysis of Graphical Passwords", Ian Jermyn, Alain Mayer, Fabian Monrose, Michael Reiter, and Aviel Rubin, *Proceedings of the 8th Usenix Security Symposium*, August 1999.

8 Conclusion

8.1 Conclusion

The goal of this book was to examine new techniques for designing and verifying a high-security kernel for use in cryptographic security applications. The vehicle for this was an implementation of a security kernel employed as the basis for an object-based cryptographic architecture. This was combined with an analysis of existing methods of verifying security kernels, followed by a proposed new design and verification strategy. The remainder of this section summarises each individual contribution.

8.1.1 Separation Kernel Enforcing Filter Rules

The cryptlib security kernel is a separation kernel that acts as a mediator for all interactions within the architecture. Communication from subject to object is carried out through message passing, with the kernel acting as a reference monitor for all accesses by subjects to objects. The kernel is a standard separation kernel on top of which more specific security policies can be implemented.

Accompanying the kernel security mechanism is a policy portion that consists of a collection of filter rules that are applied to all messages processed by the kernel, which means all messages sent to objects, which in turn means all interactions with objects.

The use of this kind of kernel is unique in (non-classified) encryption technology. The kernelised design has proven to be both flexible and powerful, since the filter rules provide a powerful and user-configurable means of expressing an arbitrary security policy that doesn't usually conform to more traditional policy models such as Bell–LaPadula or Clark–Wilson. This policy will typically also include features such as the ability to require that operations on objects be performed in certain sequences, or under certain conditions, or with restrictions on how and when they may be performed. Similar constraints are either impossible to implement, or at best very difficult to provide in conventional designs, which consist of a collection of functions with no centralised controlling element. An additional benefit of the rule-based design is that it forces a rigorous implementation, since the kernel prohibits the use of common tricks such as using the value −1 to represent a don't-care value, requiring the implementer to actually think about why having a don't-care value is necessary and fixing the design to avoid it.

Since the filter rules are user-configurable, they can be easily adapted to meet the requirements of a particular situation. For example, a single change to one of the rules is sufficient to meet FIPS 140 requirements for key handling, with the resulting new policy being immediately reflected throughout the entire architecture. Again, such a change can only be made with some difficulty in a conventional, decentralised design.

A final benefit of the kernelised design is that the whole acts as a rule-based expert system that is able to detect inconsistencies and security problems that weren't noticed by humans. There currently exist several examples of faulty cryptographic items such as certificates and smart cards that are being deployed for widespread use because conventional implementations couldn't detect any problem with them.

8.1.2 Kernel and Verification Co-design

Rather than take the conventional approach of either designing the implementation using a collection-of-functions approach and ignoring verification issues or choosing a verification methodology and force-fitting the design and implementation to it, the approach presented in this book constitutes a meet-in-the-middle attack on the problem. By using closely matched techniques for the kernel design and verification, it significantly reduces the amount of effort required to perform the verification.

Obviously, this approach does not constitute a silver bullet. The kernel design is rather specialised and works only for situations that require a reference monitor to enforce security and functionality. This design couldn't be used, for example, in a reactor control system since this is best modelled as a state-based system using one of the methodologies that were found to be so unsuitable for analysing the separation kernel.

This restriction is by no means a shortcoming. The intent of the kernel/verification co-design process was to do what you can with what you've got, not to find a universal security elixir. The result is something that is both practical and functional without requiring an unreasonable amount of effort to realise.

8.1.3 Use of Specification-based Testing

Once the kernel design has been implemented, it needs to be verified to ensure that it performs as designed and/or intended. The traditional approach to this problem has been the application (or in some cases attempted application) of formal methods-based approaches, but this is not necessarily the best or most cost-effective way of building a secure system. In order to analyse and verify the implementation of the architecture presented here, an approach using established software engineering principles and tools is developed. In combination with a design-by-contract methodology coupled with a matching specification technique, this allows for verification all the way down to the running code. This level of verification, put in the "beyond A1" class in the Orange Book, is a goal which to date has not been achieved using more traditional means.

In parallel with the external verification code, the design of the kernel with its filter-rule-based approach makes it amenable to the (relatively crude) checking available through the use of assertions compiled into the code, so that significant portions of the kernel's functionality can be verified using no more than a standard compiler and a coverage analysis tool. The fact that the code is auto-verifying when it runs has helped catch several implementation errors both in kernel and non-kernel code. Problems with the kernel code were relatively few since it had been subjected to, and is still subject to, continuous scrutiny, and were mostly located in recently-changed areas that had not yet been subject to detailed analysis. Assertions were also occasionally triggered because it was convenient to use the kernel in expert-system mode, testing a proposed change to see how the kernel would react to it rather than spending hours thinking through the design to try and determine the effects of a change.

The ability to instantly draw attention to problems in non-kernel code (for example, an incorrect parameter passed in a message) proved to be of considerable benefit. The use of assertion-based verification can point out the precise problem with a parameter, for example that its length should be exactly 16 bytes, no more, no less. A more general error status value as returned by the kernel could report only that the parameter is in error, but would then require the user to determine the exact source of the problem. An additional benefit is that it can point out the problem immediately rather than once it has been subject to arbitrary amounts of other processing to be returned as a general error status value by higher-level code.

8.1.4 Use of Cognitive Psychology Principles for Verification

Although existing verification attempts have lamented the incomprehensibility of the verification process to outsiders, no-one appears to have seriously looked at how this problem can be fixed. The fact that almost no-one can understand the verification process or its results is simply accepted as the price of doing business in this field. This book has taken an entirely new approach based on concepts from cognitive psychology, examining how the real world works and then attempting to apply those same concepts towards building a system in a manner that facilitates its analysis. This approach can be contrasted with the formal-methods-based approach, which takes an abstract mathematical model and then attempts to constrain the real world to fit within the model.

Although relatively few users have needed to understand the kernel at the implementation level, those who have worked with it appear to have had few problems. This can be contrasted with an equivalent implementation specified using a system such as Z, which would be incomprehensible to the same users and therefore impossible to work with. The benefits are clear: This is a system that ordinary, untrained users can handle.

8.1.5 Practical Design

Although this should go without saying, the work presented in this book is not just a research model or prototype but a practical, real-world implementation that has been in extensive world-wide use for several years in implementations ranging from 16-bit microcontrollers through to supercomputers, as well as various unusual areas such as security modules for ATMs and cryptographic coprocessors.

8.2 Future Research

Although the specification process using the Assertion Definition Language is fairly straightforward, it is also rather tedious and mechanical, so that a full specification of the kernel (or more precisely of the behaviour of each filter rule) has not yet been performed. This task awaits a time when the author has attained tenure and a suitable supply of graduate students.

The cryptlib architecture is ideally suited for use in cryptographic hardware modules, with the security kernel being used to control all access to crypto data and operations provided by the hardware. Work to produce cryptlib-based cryptographic hardware is currently in progress. One area of future research interest is that the interaction with the cryptographic hardware becomes somewhat unclear once it's taken beyond the basic crypto-accelerator level of functionality employed by almost all existing crypto hardware devices. For example, through the use of cryptlib, it now becomes possible to establish simultaneous access to multiple remote coprocessors. This type of capability isn't normally an issue with standard cryptographic hardware, which is at most concerned with whether the commands coming to it from the controlling host system are to be interpreted in the role of a user or security officer. The extra flexibility offered by cryptlib carries with it the requirement for a corresponding amount of further research into appropriate access control mechanisms to ensure that this flexibility can only be applied in an appropriate manner.

Another future area of research is the secure bootstrap process required for a cryptographic coprocessor, of which an outline is provided in Chapter 7. Currently, only two (non-classified) devices, the Fortezza card and the IBM 4758 (and to a lesser extent the Dallas iButton) appear to have had much thought devoted to ensuring that users can safely zeroise a device and bootstrap it up through various security levels, locking down security further and further as more of the device features are initialised. Both the Fortezza card and 4758 feature a one-way ratchet that ensures that once the initial parameters have been set, they cannot be changed or reset without starting again from scratch. cryptlib currently includes basic functionality along these lines, but it will require use in production cryptographic coprocessors to gain experience in this area.

Another possible area of research would be to use the kernel's ability to monitor all cryptographic operations carried out by the architecture to try and create a form of crypto intrusion detection system (IDS) that checks operation traces for anomalous patterns. If analysis of real-world data revealed that crypto operations always followed fixed patterns, the kernel filter rules could be extended to check for deviations from these patterns and either sound an alarm or disallow the abnormal operation.

9 Glossary

This glossary is intended to explain uncommon technical terms and acronyms in the context in which they are used in this book. It is not intended to serve as a general-purpose glossary, or as a complete glossary of security terms. Readers in search of a general-purpose glossary of security terminology are referred to RFC 2828 "Internet Security Glossary" by Robert Shirey.

*-property

"No write down", an axiom of the Bell–LaPadula security model which states that a subject may only write to an object of an equal or higher security level. This prevents the inadvertent (or deliberate) release of sensitive data.

ACL

Access Control List, an access control enforcement mechanism that lists permitted access types for subjects to an object.

ADF

Access Decision Facility, the portion of a GFAC access control mechanism that decides whether access is allowed or not.

ADL

Assertion Definition Language, a C-like specification language.

AEF

Access Enforcement Facility, the portion of a GFAC access control mechanism that enforces the decisions made by the ADF.

APKI

Architecture for Public-Key Infrastructure, a proposed PKI architecture design from the Open Group.

ASIC

Application-Specific Integrated Circuit, a custom IC created to a user's specifications.

BAN logic

Burrows–Abadi–Needham logic, a logic for describing and analysing authentication protocols.

CA

Certification Authority, an entity that issues certificates (and sometimes performs various checks before doing so).

CBC

Cipher Block Chaining, a mode of operation for a block cipher that chains encrypted blocks together, thus breaking up patterns in the plaintext.

CC

Common Criteria, successor to ITSEC and the Orange Book. ISO 9000 for security.

CDI

Constrained Data Item, the equivalent of objects in the Clark–Wilson security model.

CDSA

Cryptographic Data Security Architecture, a cryptographic API and architecture created by Intel and now managed by the Open Group. The emacs of crypto APIs.

CFB

Ciphertext Feedback, a mode of operation for a block cipher that allows it to function as a stream cipher. This has properties similar to CBC, but operates at the byte or bit level rather than the block level.

CISS

Comprehensive Integrated Security System, a cryptographic and security service API.

CMS

Cryptographic Message Syntax, the new name for PKCS #7, a data format for signed, encrypted, or otherwise cryptographically processed data.

COE SS

Common Operating Environment Security Services API, a GSS-API-like wrapper for SSL used by the US government.

CRL

Certificate Revocation List, a blacklist of no-longer-valid certificates.

DACL

Discretionary Access Control List, an ACL that may be changed by an object's owner.

DES

Data Encryption Standard, formerly the de facto standard encryption algorithm but now deprecated because of its short 56-bit key.

DSA

Digital Signature Algorithm, an alternative to RSA proposed by the US government.

DTLS

Descriptive Top-Level Specification, the specification for a security system that is created when it's discovered that no-one can understand the FTLS.

DTOS

Distributed Trusted Operating System, Mach with extra security features added.

ECB

Electronic Codebook, a mode of operation for a block cipher with the drawback that it reveals patterns in the plaintext.

FDM

Formal Development Methodology (one of many).

FDR

Failures-Divergence Refinement, a model checker.

FIPS 140

A US government security standard for cryptographic modules. The standard covers both software and hardware modules, but leans more towards hardware.

FPGA

Field-Programmable Gate Array, a customisable IC that can be reprogrammed by the user.

FTLS

Formal Top-Level Specification, the specification for a security system expressed in a formal notation that no-one can understand, resulting in the creation of a DTLS.

GFAC

Generalised Framework for Access Control, a general-purpose model of access control mechanisms that is comprised of an ADF for making access control decisions and an AEF for enforcing them.

GSS-API

Generic Security Service API, a standardised API for security services.

GTCB

Generalised TCB, a generalisation of the TCB concept to include things such as a security system composed from untrusted components via TNIUs or similar hardware.

GVE

Gypsy Verification Environment, a formal development methodology

IDUP-GSS

Independent Data Unit Protection API, a generalisation of GSS-API for protecting data such as files and email.

ITSEC

Information Technology Security Evaluation Criteria, successor to the Orange Book and in turn superseded by the Common Criteria.

IV

Initialisation Vector, a random value used when encrypting data in CBC or CFB mode to hide patterns in the plaintext.

IVP

Integrity Verification Procedure, a check performed on a CDI before and after it has been processed by a TP in the Clark–Wilson security model.

HDM

Hierarchical Development Methodology, a formal development methodology.

KEK

Key Encryption Key, a key used to encrypt other keys (as opposed to encrypting general data).

LCRNG

Linear Congruential Random Number Generator, a random number generator that produces predictable output.

LFSR

Linear Feedback Shift Register, a random number generator that produces predictable output.

LTM

Long-term (human) memory.

MAC

Mandatory Access Control, an ACL that is enforced by the system and cannot be changed.

MD5

A cryptographic hash function. Formerly the de facto standard for cryptographic hash functions but now superseded by SHA-1.

MLS

Multilevel Secure, a system with subjects and objects at more than one security level. The Orange Book and Bell–LaPadula security model cover MLS systems.

MSP

Message Security Protocol, the US DOD equivalent of S/MIME and PGP.

NIST

National Institute of Standards and Technology, formerly the National Bureau of Standards. The US government organisation that manages government security standards.

NKSR

Non-Kernel Security Related function, a means of bypassing the restrictions imposed by a security kernel.

NOFORN

No Foreign (that is, "no access by foreigners"), a paper-document security classification that may be realised in computers via PAC and ORAC controls.

NRL protocol analyser

Navy Research Labs protocol analyser, initially a proof checker which then switches to using model checking for the final stage.

O-function

Observation-function, a (mathematical) function that changes the state of a state machine.

ORAC

Owner-Retained Access Controls, a security mechanism in which the originator controls all further dissemination.

Orange Book

Term commonly used for the Trusted Computer System Evaluation Criteria or TCSEC, a standard for evaluating the security of operating systems. Later expanded to cover other areas and include an entire rainbow of books, this was superseded by the Common Criteria.

ORCON

Originator-Controlled, a paper-document security classification that may be realised in computers via PAC and ORAC controls.

PAC

Propagated Access Controls, a security mechanism in which the originator controls all further dissemination.

PGP

Pretty Good Privacy, an email encryption program incorporating decentralised key management techniques originally written by Phil Zimmerman in 1991, later amended and updated into a variety of other, occasionally compatible implementations.

PKCS #7

Public Key Cryptography Standard #7, a.k.a. Cryptographic Message Syntax, a data format for signed, encrypted, or otherwise cryptographically processed data.

PKCS #11

Public Key Cryptography Standard #11, a standard programming interface for cryptographic tokens such as smart cards and crypto accelerators.

PKCS #12

Public Key Cryptography Standard #12, a data format for private key and certificate storage. Superseded by PKCS #15.

PKCS #15

Public Key Cryptography Standard #15, a data format for private key and certificate storage without the problems of PKCS #12.

PRNG

Pseudo-Random Number Generator, a means of generating random data that, although not truly random (such as, for example, one which functions by sampling a physical noise source), is nonetheless sufficient for most purposes. PRNGs are usually used to "stretch" the output from true random sources.

RAMP

Ratings Maintenance Program, a means of maintaining a product's security rating while allowing minor updates to be made.

RC4

A fast stream cipher, formerly proprietary to RSA Data Security Inc.

RSA

Rivest–Shamir–Adelman, the de facto standard public-key algorithm.

SESAME

A European Kerberos clone, later extended with other functionality.

SET

Secure Electronic Transaction, a protocol jointly developed by MasterCard and VISA to reduce the risk in card-not-present transactions.

SHA-1

A cryptographic hash function, defined in FIPS 180-1. The de facto standard cryptographic hash function.

Simple security property

"No read up", an axiom of the Bell–LaPadula security model which states that a subject may only from read an object of equal or lower security level. This prevents unauthorised access to sensitive data.

S/MIME

Secure MIME, PKCS #7 (later renamed CMS) wrapped in MIME encoding to make it usable with email.

SMO

Security Meta-Object, a special-purpose object attached to an existing standard object that enforces access controls.

SO

Security Officer, the person responsible for administering security on a system, which for cryptographic items typically involves secure initialisation and key management. In practice, the user and SO are usually the same person, although it's useful for security purposes to maintain the fiction that they're not.

SRL

Subject Restriction List, an access control mechanism that functions like an ACL but which is tied to the subject rather than the object.

ssh

Secure Shell, initially an encrypted and authenticated replacement for the rsh and rcp utilities, later a protocol similar to SSL but with a different data format.

SSL

Secure Sockets Layer, an application-level protocol providing integrity, confidentiality, and authentication services.

SSO

System Security Officer, the person responsible for administering security on a system, which for cryptographic items typically involves secure initialisation and key management. The US government and military have SSOs; civilians have SOs.

STM

Short-term (human) memory.

TCB

Trusted Computing Base, the collection of protection mechanisms responsible for enforcing a security policy.

TCSEC

Trusted Computer System Evaluation Criteria, usually referred to as the Orange Book.

TEMPEST

A term used to describe specifications and standards for restricting electromagnetic emanations from information processing equipment, making it less vulnerable to eavesdropping.

TLS

Transport Layer Security, the new name for SSL.

TNIU

Trusted Network Interface Unit, a means of creating a security exokernel by regulating the communications between untrusted systems.

TP

Transformation Procedure, a means of transforming the state of a CDI in the Clark–Wilson security model.

ULM

Universal Lattice Machine, a Turing machine for security models.

Verilog

A hardware description language used to specify the design of an ASIC.

V-function

Value-returning function, a (mathematical) function that returns the state of a state machine.

VHDL

A hardware description language used to specify the design of an ASIC.

VMM

Virtual Machine Monitor, a hardware virtualisation mechanism useful (among other things) for enforcing security controls on otherwise insecure operating systems.

X.509

A public-key-certificate format and minor religion.

X9.17

An ANSI key management standard famous mostly because of a one-page appendix that describes a triple-DES-based PRNG.

Z

A formal methods notation.

Zeroize

Erasure of sensitive data such as cryptovariables (this term has a specific meaning that goes further than, say, "clear the memory").

Index

Printed by Publishers' Graphics LLC